The Killing Fields of Scotland

For Ella and Louie, in the hope that they will never experience the terrible tragedy of war

The Killing Fields of Scotland

of Scotland

AD 83 to 1746

Roy Pugh

Pen & Sword
MILITARY

First published in Great Britain in 2013 by
Pen & Sword Military
an Imprint of
Pen & Sword Books Ltd
47 Church Street
Barnsley
South Yorkshire
S70 2AS

ISBN: 978 1 78159 019 5

Typeset in 11pt Ehrhardt by
Mac Style, Driffield, E. Yorkshire

Printed and bound in the UK by CPI Group (UK) Ltd, Croydon, CRO 4YY

Pen & Sword Books Ltd incorporates the Imprints of Pen & Sword Aviation,
Pen & Sword Family History, Pen & Sword Maritime, Pen & Sword Military,
Pen & Sword Discovery, Wharncliffe Local History, Wharncliffe True Crime,
Wharncliffe Transport, Pen & Sword Select, Pen & Sword Military Classics,
Leo Cooper, The Praetorian Press, Remember When, Seaforth Publishing
and Frontline Publishing.

For a complete list of Pen & Sword titles please contact
PEN & SWORD BOOKS LIMITED
47 Church Street, Barnsley, South Yorkshire, S70 2AS, England
E-mail: enquiries@pen-and-sword.co.uk
Website: www.pen-and-sword.co.uk

Contents

List of Maps

Battle maps courtesy of Moira Dempster, Dunbar. © Moira Dempster 2013.
The map of the battle of Dunbar 1650 featured in *The Life of General George
Monck: For King & Cromwell* by Peter Reese is reproduced by kind permission
of Peter Reese and Paul H. Vickers. © Paul H. Vickers, 2008

List of Illustrations

List of Abbreviations

APS	= Acts of the Parliaments of Scotland
CDS	= Calendar of Documents relating to Scotland
CPS	= Calendar of State Papers relating to Scotland
ERs	= Exchequer Rolls of Scotland

Acknowledgements

My first thanks go to the Historic Scotland team who kindly offered advice and information about their initiative in preserving Scotland's battlefields. Special thanks are due to Kevin Munro, Senior Designations Officer (Battlefields and Conflict Heritage), for taking the time to read the manuscript, offer advice, support, correcting several errors of fact and for providing the Introduction. Andrew Burnet, Publications and Information Manager, Historic Scotland, gave general advice on various matters, for which I am grateful. I also wish to thank Michelle Andersson, Image Librarian, Historic Scotland, who directed me to sources where some of the illustrations I have used were available.

For documents and State papers quoted in the Notes to each chapter, my thanks are due to the staffs of the National Library of Scotland and Edinburgh Central Library (Scottish Room).

I wish to thank Christina Watson, Search Room, Royal Commission on Historical and Ancient Monuments of Scotland, who kindly directed me to sources which assisted in the production of this book Thanks are also due to George Wilson and Ian Riches, National Trust for Scotland, who provided me with information on the battlefields of Bannockburn, Glenshiel and Culloden.

I am indebted to Moira Dempster, illustrator, Dunbar, for producing all but one of the maps of some of the battle sites featured; her professionalism as an illustrator speaks for itself. Thanks are also due to Peter Reese, author of *Cromwell's Masterstroke Dunbar 1650* and *The Life of General George Monck For King and Cromwell* published by Pen & Sword Books Ltd and his colleague Paul H. Vickers, who gave me their permission to reproduce Mr Vickers's excellent map of the battle of Dunbar 1650 which appears in *Monck*.

I also wish to pay tribute to my dear friend Kate Covey, who kindly agreed to read the manuscript and in the process, correct my many typing errors and offer sound advice, especially on those occasions when I over-egged the pudding! Thanks are also due to Simon Lee, Operator and Guide, Spirit of

Scotland Tours, and my good friend John Harris, who both provided some of the illustrations. Double thanks to John who compiled the Index and, in the process, made me think again about certain aspects of the text.

Finally, last but by no means least, I would like to thank Jamie Wilson and Richard Doherty, my editors at Pen & Sword Books Ltd, who gave me support, encouragement and sound advice in the process of producing this book

R. J. M. Pugh,
Dunbar,
East Lothian
2012

Foreword

In terms of warfare, the history of Scotland is hardly comparable to that of ancient Rome, Greece, Persia, nor the great dynastic nations of Europe – France, Spain, Germany, Austria, Spain, Russia and England. However, in many ways, Scotland's history was not dissimilar to these nations except in scale. It is the nature of human society to wage wars in order to obtain self-government, independence, internal security, political stability, all of which are vital to economic, social and cultural development. Scotland was no different.

The modern, mainland and island territorial boundaries of Scotland date only from 1266, in which year Magnus, King of Norway, ceded the Hebrides (the Western Isles) to King Alexander III of Scotland. The Orkney and Shetland Islands remained Danish territory until 1468, when they were pledged to Scotland as part of the dowry of Margaret, King Christian of Denmark's daughter who married King James III of Scotland. The islands were not fully annexed by Scotland until 1472.

The boundaries of Scotland were drawn over several centuries of conflict, with various tribes, then factions vying with each other for supremacy. During its long and colourful history, Scotland has known many bloody battles, the killing fields which took place along the road to unification, especially during the bitter Wars of Independence from 1296 to 1560. These wars were foisted on Scotland by her aggressive neighbour, England; ultimately successful, the kingdom of Scotland would survive as an independent, sovereign nation until her union with England in 1707. Even then, the killing did not cease until a further four decades passed.

This account begins with the Roman occupation of Scotland, a period of which we know very little. There are scant references to or dependable evidence written about this period of over three centuries; we know virtually nothing about the fierce and bloody conflicts which took place in Scotland's early history. When primitive man first inhabited the northern part of Britain, he was preoccupied with survival; struggling against Nature – herself red in tooth and claw – early man learnt to fashion tools and weapons, not just to obtain food but to defend and protect his territory. Tribal man's life was one of constant fear and danger; his rudimentary existence gave him a taste for blood, not just that of the animals he hunted for food but also neighbours who threatened his survival. These early, nameless tribes have left little to mark their presence save for the occasional finds of implements, weapons and fragments of settlements which at least offer the archaeologist a glimpse into the past. The conflicts which occurred during Scotland's primitive period are not unexpectedly lost in the mists of time. Scotland's landscape is, however, liberally sprinkled with hill-forts and settlements both great and small, usually circular with outer and inner walls built of earth, turf and even stone. These offer few clues about their builders, although the purpose of these structures is clear. Primitive man built on high ground to enable him to observe the land he occupied and warn satellite settlements on lower ground of approaching danger. Thus he prepared himself for defence as well as protecting the flocks and herds on which his survival depended.

The history of Scotland does not come alive – in the written, recorded sense – until the Roman occupation of Britain. However, we know from the writings of the Greek poet Homer that the island was visited by Phoenician traders; the commerce of the Phoenician seaport of Tyre (now in the Lebanon) spread over the known world. The Phoenician traders came to Britain with the express purpose of obtaining tin from the mines of Devon and Cornwall. Julius Caesar's two expeditions in 55 BC and 54 BC made Britain's existence known to Rome but it was not until the reign of Emperor Claudius (10 BC–AD 54) that the Romans made a serious attempt to incorporate Britain into the Roman Empire. The first invasion of north Britain by trained, disciplined soldiers did not occur until AD 80, when Agricola, the governor of Britain, crossed the river Tweed into Caledonia (the ancient name for Scotland) to conquer the disparate tribes in the north. What persuaded him to do so is not entirely clear. Not only was the country barbaric, with large tracts of uninhabitable, unproductive land, it also offered little of material value. Furthermore, the country suffered from harsh winters that seemed to – and did – last longer than those in the sunnier, drier climate in Roman England. It was in part these factors but more so the threat to Rome herself in AD 410 by the Visigoths of northern Europe which brought about the evacuation of Britain. However, in AD 81, Agricola was determined to subdue the tribes of northern Britain. To do so, he built a line of forts from the Firth of Clyde to the Firth of Forth (these were subsequently consolidated into a turf wall by Antoninius, a later governor).

Little is known about the Roman occupation of northern Britain apart from an account of the battle of Mons Graupius in AD 83. Although a defeat for the

Caledonians, Mons Graupius taught the native tribes a valuable lesson – that strength lay in unity, which would ultimately bring about the unification of Scotland.

After the departure of the Romans, northern Britain descended into chaos, with the Caledonians (now known as the Picts) constantly at odds with the Scots of Dalriada, the Britons of Strathclyde and the Angles of Bernicia (modern Northumberland). During the so-called Dark Ages, the main external aggressors were the Angles, then Danes and Norsemen (the terms are often confused but I have tried to resist using the term Vikings wherever possible). When Duke William of Normandy – the Normans were descendants of the Vikings – invaded England in 1066 and defeated the Anglo-Saxon King Harold, William drew the boundary of England at the river Tweed. Thus it was a Normanized England which would pose the greatest threat to Scotland in her entire history. This struggle, known as the Wars of Independence, would last for nearly three centuries until Scotland regained her former independence, finally recognized by England as a free and sovereign nation.

This account examines the battles which took place between AD 83 and 1746. Each chapter roughly relates to the period, political events and cultural developments which took place and which led to these conflicts. Beginning with the Roman occupation, then the Dark Ages – a period of a thousand years when little was recorded; what *was* written down is both fragmentary and obscure. Scotland's history becomes better documented around the late thirteenth century, the beginning of the Wars of Independence. However, from the early fifteenth to the mid-eighteenth centuries, detailed descriptions were written down about the conflicts during the Stewart dynasty, the Civil Wars, the Covenanter uprisings and the Jacobite rebellions. Apart from two Border battles fought on the English bank of the river Tweed, this account does not investigate those such as Flodden; nor does it cover the clan battles, of which there were hundreds, probably even thousands, of scraps and skirmishes.

As this account hopefully makes clear, many of the battles fought after the Wars of Independence were in fact civil wars; northern Scotland fought against southern Scotland, Protestant fought Catholic and Protestant fought Protestant. In the Highlands, a long and bitter rivalry between the over-powerful Clan Campbell of Argyle and the MacDonalds of Skye, Clanranald, Glengarry and Glencoe often resolved their traditional feuds by finding a safety valve in major conflicts such as the Jacobite rebellions, justifying their grudges by supporting pretenders to the Scottish throne. That bitterness and squabbling survived until Culloden and continues in a milder vein to the present day; in certain districts of the Highlands, mention of the name Campbell still raises eyebrows ...

This book owes its existence to what is documented and stored in the National Archives of Scotland, Historic Scotland and contemporary accounts of battles in the Second Millenium, including those of modern historians. Looking at the overall Scottish historical canvas, we will find that in the first ten centuries of the Christian Era, battles are briefly mentioned by the early chroniclers, their accounts often suspect, having more to do with the stuff of legend and romance rather than historical fact. Some of these follow the romantic traditions in which Scotland is steeped; it is possible that there were battles which went unrecorded because they did not kindle the imagination of the chroniclers of the time. It is equally likely that accounts of other battles have not survived. The hard-nosed historian, labouring in the sticky clay of historical fact, demands factual proof and evidence of these battles – and rightly so. History is about what was, what happened; fiction is about what did not. However, this rule cannot be written in tablets of stone, since fiction does not combust spontaneously out of thin air. It is based on human experience, the human condition and is often rooted in fact. If we ignore folk-memory, we do so at our peril, inflicting an injustice upon the people of Scotland who for many centuries could not write, let alone read. They could, however, converse with each other and handed down history from generation to generation in tales told by the fireside. Few, if any, of these folk had the opportunity, let alone the power or the knowledge to influence events other than to stand in the battle lines and await their fate, which lay in the hands of others.

It was not just in the domestic battles that Scotsmen proved themselves tenacious, brave – if undisciplined – warriors and soldiers on the killing fields. Scottish mercenaries fought in the armies of the kings of France, Spain, Sweden, the Low Countries and Russia, often facing their own countrymen. Was this a particular trait in the Scottish psyche? Did these men reach instinctively for the sword rather than the pen to resolve their problems? Only the professional psychologist can answer the question. One is reminded of the comment made during the American Civil War (1861–65) by the Confederate General Robert E. Lee at the battle of Fredericksburg in December, 1862: 'It is well that war is so terrible. We should grow too fond of it.'

A final word on this book. It has been said that history may not always repeat itself but historians invariably do. This is inevitable, given that history happened; what is important are the arguments and the theories postulated by historians and the conclusions they draw from these. I trust that, in writing this book, I have not simply revisited other works – both ancient and modern – but hopefully produced a fresh, concise and useful account of Scotland's killing fields.

R. J. M. Pugh,
July 2012

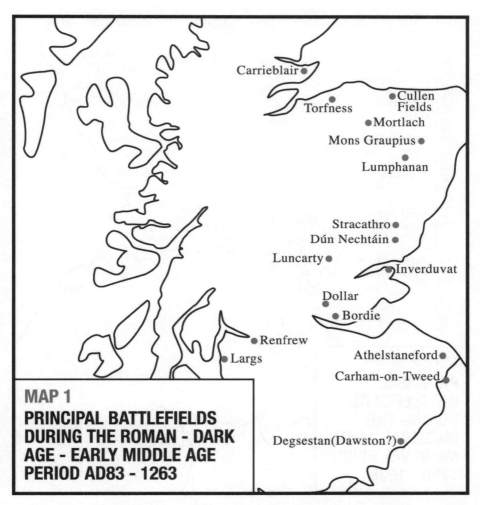

MAP 1
PRINCIPAL BATTLEFIELDS
DURING THE ROMAN - DARK
AGE - EARLY MIDDLE AGE
PERIOD AD83 - 1263

Map 1. Principal battlefields during the Roman–Dark Age–Early Middle Age period AD 83–1263.

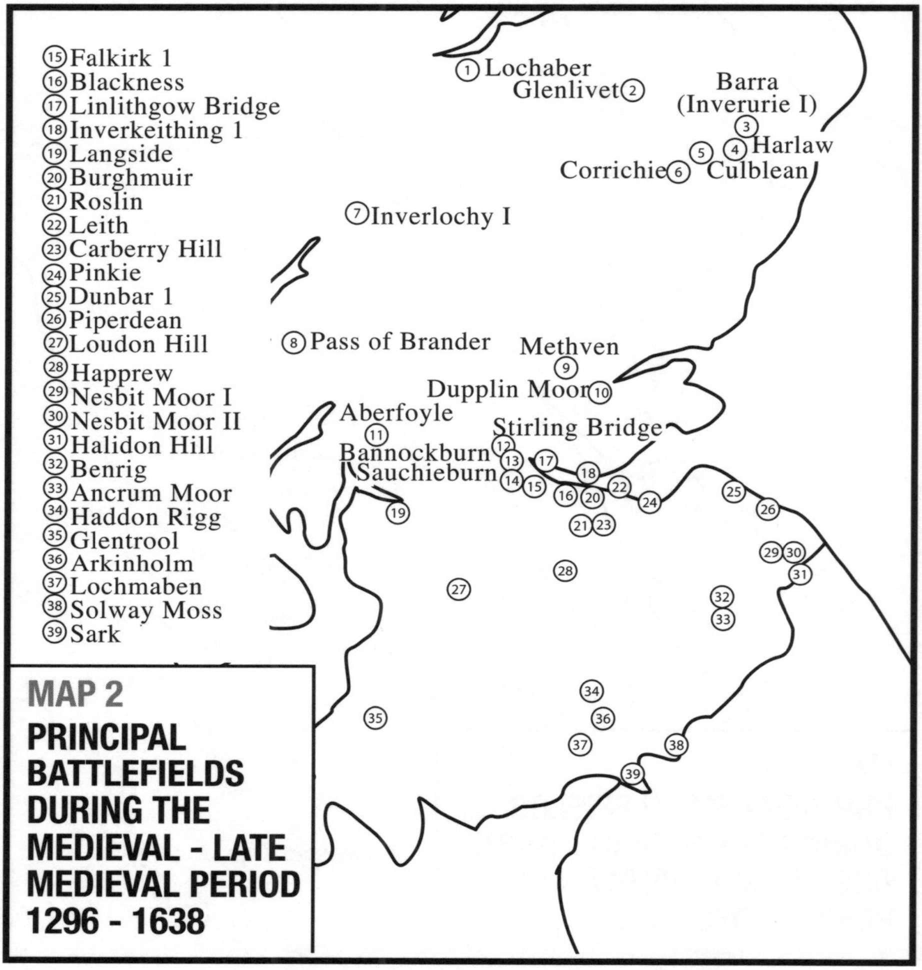
15 Falkirk 1
16 Blackness
17 Linlithgow Bridge
18 Inverkeithing 1
19 Langside
20 Burghmuir
21 Roslin
22 Leith
23 Carberry Hill
24 Pinkie
25 Dunbar 1
26 Piperdean
27 Loudon Hill
28 Happrew
29 Nesbit Moor I
30 Nesbit Moor II
31 Halidon Hill
32 Benrig
33 Ancrum Moor
34 Haddon Rigg
35 Glentrool
36 Arkinholm
37 Lochmaben
38 Solway Moss
39 Sark
1 Lochaber
Glenlivet 2
Barra (Inverurie I) 3
4 Harlaw
5 Culblean
Corrichie 6
7 Inverlochy I
8 Pass of Brander
Methven 9
Dupplin Moor 10
Aberfoyle 11
Stirling Bridge 12
Bannockburn 13
Sauchieburn 14
MAP 2
PRINCIPAL BATTLEFIELDS DURING THE MEDIEVAL - LATE MEDIEVAL PERIOD 1296 - 1638

Map 2. Principal battlefields during the Medieval–Late Medieval period 1296-1638.

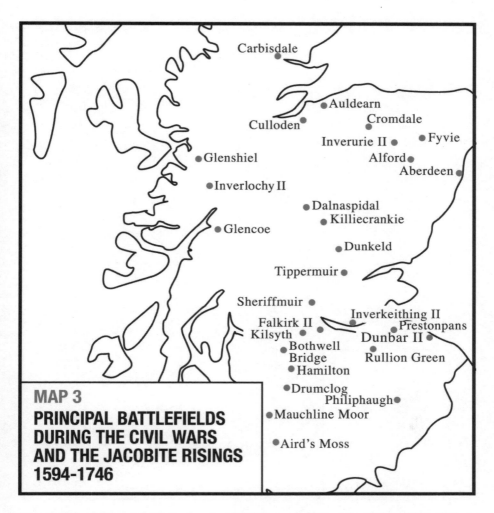

Map 3. Principal battlefields during the Civil Wars and the Jacobite Risings 1594–1746.

Introduction

For the fortunate majority of people living in Scotland today, war is a far-off thing, whether in distance, through images and reports of modern conflicts in the media, or in time, held in the memories of those who lived through the dark days of the First and Second World Wars. However, for much of Scotland's history, warfare was far more familiar to her people. Indeed, Scotland's history as a whole is inextricably connected to the martial history of the country. The long centuries of internal struggle and external strife affected every layer of society, from peasants and serfs displaced by the actions of war, to kings of the nation slain on the field of battle.

Today, evidence of this violent history is all around us in Scotland. The national flag, the Saltire, is visible across the country and is said to come from the legend of a cross appearing in the sky before the battle of Athelstaneford. Many stories and songs have been passed down through the centuries as part of Scotland's oral tradition and then been written down, telling tales of mighty warriors and great battles of old, some true, others mythical. These range from Aneirin's *Y Gododdin*, an ancient poem telling the tale of 300 warriors, who marched south from Edinburgh to their deaths in battle at Catterick, through to the work of men such as Robert Burns, a great collector of old stories and songs, and are part of Scottish culture today through music, literature and even Hollywood movies, such as *Braveheart*, *Rob Roy* and *Brave*. Scottish art also displays this influence, with examples like the Romantic portraits of legendary figures like Robert Bruce, Mary, Queen of Scots and Bonnie Prince Charlie, and the stunning carving of the Aberlemno churchyard stone's battle scene, through to vast canvases depicting battles like Culloden and even the recently created Prestonpans Tapestry, a 104-metre-long embroidery telling the story of the Jacobite victory of 1745.

With such a notable presence in the nation's history and culture, it can often seem strange how little attention and care has traditionally been given to the places where many of these stories began: the battlefields of Scotland. At many of the sites, the sole testament to their bloody history is a battlefield memorial, sometimes a simple cairn, other times an elaborate obelisk or column. At others, there is nothing at all to mark the momentous events that the landscape bore witness to. In addition, over the centuries since armies clashed on the battlefields, many of the sites have changed considerably, sometimes drastically, by the ongoing life of the landscape. The sites of the battles of Langside (1568) in Glasgow and Aberdeen II (1644) were slowly subsumed by the growth of their respective cities. Other changes over time, such as new farming techniques, development of transport and communication routes, quarrying and forestry, have all had an impact on some of the fields of conflict of Scotland's past. While some sites, such as Culloden, with its excellent new visitor centre, may appear to be unchanged since the day of the battle, even here there has been impact, with much of the area afforested until relatively recently, and a road formerly running directly through the site.

It was in recognition of the risks faced by many of the battlefields in the modern age that the Scottish Government took steps to introduce new legislation, in order to manage and maintain this fragile and finite resource for future generations. And so, with the publication of Scottish Historic Environment Policy in 2009 and the Historic Environment (Amendment) (Scotland) Act in 2011, Historic Scotland, on behalf of Scottish Ministers, was given an additional statutory duty to 'compile and maintain (in such form as they think fit) an inventory of such battlefields as appear to them to be of national importance', which would provide specific protection through the planning system for the battlefields included on the Inventory. Following a period of extensive research work in association with the Centre for Battlefield Archaeology at the University of Glasgow, the 'Inventory of Historic Battlefields' was formally launched on 21 March 2011. Initially containing seventeen sites, another eleven battlefields were added in November 2011, with work continuing on a further group for inclusion in summer 2012.

The basis of the Inventory, to protect Scotland's nationally important battlefields, is laid out in the revised Scottish Historic Environment Policy (2011). For a battlefield to be included it must meet certain criteria. The battle must be considered to be of national importance, either for its association with key historical events or figures; or for the physical remains and/or archaeological potential it contains; or for its landscape context. In addition, it must be possible to define the site on a modern map with a reasonable degree of accuracy. This is vital in order for the Inventory to be a useful tool which can help inform the decisions of planning authorities.

Over time the Inventory is intended to grow as a resource. It will take into account new research and new discoveries, with records being updated where new information has come to light. In addition, evidence may lead to further sites being added to the Inventory in future, for example, where the location of a battlefield is currently uncertain.

Even though it is still in its relative infancy, since its launch the Inventory and its associated guidance has proved to be a valuable and popular resource, aiding planning authorities in making informed decisions which safeguard the valuable heritage of the sites, while at the same time not obstructing the modern life of the landscape. It has also become a valued resource for both education and tourism, and has attracted interest from around the world and from a wide range of people – from academics and researchers to members of the public and serving and retired members of the military. However, despite its success, the Inventory is only one of many ways in which Scotland's battlefields are being preserved for future generations.

Across Scotland there is a vibrant network of local societies and battlefield groups, actively campaigning for and working on numerous battlefield sites, bringing them to the attention of both the local community and people farther afield, and turning them into a resource for the area. Each year more sites are commemorated with new memorials, and anniversaries, both small and large, are marked on some of the sites. Battlefield tours become more popular and publications such as this book continue to inform and educate the public about the battlefields and martial history of Scotland. Interpretation panels are appearing at a growing number of sites and, with the rise in new forms of media, there are exciting opportunities to provide interpretation and information in new ways, such as through smartphones, apps and the internet. The new 'high-tech' visitor centre that opened at Culloden in 2007 has been a great success and, as I write, work is underway at Bannockburn to create another new centre in advance of the 700th anniversary of the Battle of Bannockburn in 2014.

Around the world, battlefields have long been a source of fascination to those interested in history – whether that of their family, their local area, their nation or even the world. This interest is clearly seen on the sites themselves, where visitors from across the globe can be found returning to the spot where history was made, where stories started and ended, and where ancestors fought and died. Some visitors to battlefields treat them as an educational resource, some simply as a leisure trip and some as an almost spiritual pilgrimage to remember the fallen at the place where they died. Yet, regardless of their motives, all their experiences are connected by the very location where the battle took place. An individual may read books about battles, or see them depicted in paintings, films and on television, but it is only at a battlefield site that someone can experience the battlefield. By placing themselves physically in the landscape, people can understand better what happened, where and why, and can also place themselves mentally and emotionally 'in' the battle. Without the battlefield itself that connection is lost, and if the battlefield itself is lost, the connection is gone forever. The survival of Scotland's battlefields depends not just on the Inventory of Historic Battlefields, but also on the dedication of the many staff and volunteers striving to protect and promote battlefield sites across the nation. By working together to share expertise, understanding and resources, there is every reason to think that the future of the killing fields of Scotland may be happier than their history.

Kevin Munro,
May 2012

Chapter 1

The Roman Occupation

The Roman occupation of Britain lasted from AD 43, when the Emperor Claudius, or, to give him his full name, Tiberius Claudius Drusus Nero Germanicus (10 BC–AD 54) sent his legions to conquer the southern part of the island. The legions remained in Britain until AD 410, when they abandoned Hadrian's Wall, recalled to Rome to defend the Eternal City against the Visigoths. Thirty-four years after the Claudian invasion, the Emperor Titus Flavius Vespasianus, or Vespasian (AD 9–79) appointed Julius Agricola (AD 37–93) as governor of Brittania, as Britain was then known. In the third year of his governorship, Agricola was said to have 'discovered new nations'[1] – meaning peoples – in the northern part of Britain known to the Romans as Caledonia, named after the tribe which lived there.

Between AD 80 and 83, Agricola, the ablest of the Roman generals, first subdued the Lowlands of Scotland, extending the limits of the *Provincia Romana* as far as a line from the Firth of Clyde to the Firth of Forth. In AD 81 Agricola constructed a network of twenty forts from Clyde to Forth covering a distance of eighty miles to protect the southern part of Caledonia. (This chain of forts would form the route of the wall built in AD 123 by a later governor, Titus Aurelius Fulvus Pius Antoninus; the Antonine wall, built on a sandstone base and topped with turf only ran for thirty miles but it was strengthened by many more forts per mile than Agricola's wall.)

After establishing his defensive line, Agricola returned to southern Britain, content for the moment with the progress he had made. He consolidated his partial conquest of the north by creating 1,300 miles of roads from the river Tyne in Northumberland into Caledonia. However, in AD 83, the Caledonians began to resist the Roman invaders; that year, the warrior tribes wiped out the Ninth Legion in Galloway, which brought Agricola north with a large army. On this occasion, he began his campaign in the west, subduing Galloway, then marched north at the head of 17,000 legionaries and 3,000 cavalry, intent on subjugating the entire region.

Agricola's army was supplied by Roman galleys hugging the eastern seaboard. During his progress, he met with little resistance and was able to build an impressive fort at Ardoch, Perthshire. Ardoch is a classic example of Roman military and engineering skills in planned entrenchments adapted to suit the geographical conditions and the terrain.

However, despite his unopposed advance, the Caledonian tribes were gathering in strength, united in their determination to be rid of the invaders. The subsequent battle of Mons Graupius, fought in the autumn of AD 83, was neither the first nor the last confrontation between the Romans and the Caledonians. However, it is unique in that we are fortunate in having a well-written account of the battle. For this historians are indebted to the Roman historian and writer Gaius Cornelius Tacitus, Agricola's son-in-law. Tacitus was present on the field of Mons Graupius and provided posterity with a detailed, eyewitness account of the action – albeit embellished – but not written until AD 98. Tacitus's *De Vita et Moribus Julii Agricolae* (*The Life and Death of Julius Agricola*) is a pious tribute to his father-in- law, extolling his virtues and achievements, written five years after Agricola's death. More of this follows.

Our knowledge of the main tribes of Scotland – the Caledonians and the Maetae – at the time of Agricola's campaign is sketchy and obscure. Tacitus described the Caledonians as large-limbed and red-haired. According to an account by Cassius Dio (AD 155–post 229) a Roman consul in AD 211,[2] a contemporary of and *praetor* (chief magistrate) in the reign of Emperor Lucius Septimus Severus (AD 146–211), the Caledonians and the Maetae ruled various sub-tribes; the Maetae occupied the region close to Hadrian's Wall in Northumberland, the Caledonians occupying the rest of north Britain. Neither tribe built walled towns or settlements; they lived in tents, wattled structures and *crannogs* – the name given in both Ireland and Scotland to artificially-constructed platforms supported by piles driven into the beds of rivers and lochs which served as domestic habitations as well as places of refuge in time of war. The native tribes depended on hunting, agriculture and pillage for their survival. Cassius Dio tells us that, on their foraging expeditions, the Caledonians subsisted on a special kind of compressed food which apparently satisfied both hunger and thirst[3] – rather like their descendants, the Highland clansmen who could survive on a bag of oatmeal mixed with water. The Caledonians possessed chariots drawn by small but sturdy ponies – possibly the breed known as *garrons* – and the tribesmen carried dirks and short spears with a bronze knob on the un-business end of the haft which they beat against their small shields to intimidate the foes upon whom they advanced – rather in the manner of the *impis* of King Cetewayo during the Zulu war with Britain in 1879. The Caledonians also bore long swords with a cutting edge but lacking a point, somewhat unwieldy and not suited to close-quarter combat. Caledonian warriors were fleet of foot and extraordinarily brave; Tacitus admired their courage and skill in war. They went into battle practically naked so that the animal images tattooed on their bodies could be seen, thus intimidating their enemies. (The Roman soldiers called the Caledonians *Picti*, or the Painted People.) Such were the men against whom Agricola led his legions in the autumn of AD 83.

Mons Graupius

Precisely why the Caledonians chose to attack the Roman legions at this point may well be explained by the time of year. The Romans may have burnt the harvest or appropriated the grain needed to feed the native population during the coming winter. The force which confronted Agricola was a confederacy of disparate tribes united under a local tribal leader, whom Tacitus identifies as Calgacus. Of this man, we know nothing apart from the speech attributed to him by Tacitus before the battle of Mons Graupius – the Grampian Mountain.[4]

Calgacus's Latinized name may derive from the Celtic *Calg-ac-os* 'The Swordsman', or perhaps the Irish *Calgach*, meaning 'Possesser of a Blade'. (In the tenth century, the area around Morayshire was known to Scottish kings as 'The Swordlands.') Whatever the truth of it, Tacitus describes Calgacus as 'the most distinguished for [sic] birth and valour among the [Caledonian] chieftains'.

There were, of course, many chieftains in the Caledonian host facing Agricola, but Calgacus alone is named. On that autumn day 30,000 Celtic warriors were positioned on the upper slopes of an unidentified mountain or moor, looking down on 20,000 Roman infantry and horse. Agricola ordered his cohorts forward. As they advanced uphill, the intimidating host of half-naked warriors greeted them with hoarse war cries and imprecations until one man stepped from the throng, calling for silence so that he might address them. Tacitus records Calgacus's words as follows:

> battles have been lost and won before, but never without hope. We were always there in reserve. We, the choicest flower of Britain's manhood, we the last men on earth, the last of the free, have been shielded before today by the very remoteness and seclusion for which we are famed ... [to] robbery, slaughter, plunder, they [the Romans] give the lyric name of Empire ... the Romans have created a desolation[5] and they call it peace ...

Fine words worthy of William Wallace and Winston Churchill, designed to stir a people's blood in the coming fight – if indeed Calgacus ever spoke them.

Setting aside the fact that, in all probability, neither Calgacus nor Tacitus were conversant in each other's tongue, it is also extremely unlikely that Tacitus could have been within earshot of Calgacus and the Caledonian host. The words Tacitus put into a barbaric warrior's mouth owe more to fiction than historical fact. Calgacus's speech is couched in the manner of perfect, measured Latin prose and we cannot accept it as genuine. Tacitus had an altogether different motive for attributing this speech to Calgacus, as we shall presently learn.

At the commencement of the battle of Mons Graupius, Tacitus tells us that both sides hurled missiles at each other – Roman *pilum* (javelin), Caledonian javelin and rocks and stones. After these preliminaries, Agricola ordered forward 8,000 of his soldiers, six cohorts of Batavian and Tungrian auxiliaries, men who would bear the brunt of the battle. No doubt the auxiliaries advanced in the famous Roman *testudo* (tortoise) formation of three sides, the heads of the soldiers protected by their long shields held aloft. When they neared the Caledonian front line, the veteran auxiliaries shook out into battle formation to prepare for close-quarter combat with their *gladii* (short swords).

Tacitus describes how the Caledonian chariots raced across the slopes of the battlefield, driving aggressively against the 3,000 Roman cavalry and momentarily throwing them into confusion. However, it was a different matter attacking the disciplined lines of Roman infantry, marching forward in faultless step. Confounded by the solid mass of Roman troops and the broken ground, the Caledonian charioteers lost their initial impetus, becoming intermingled with each other, which further reduced their effectiveness.

The Batavian and Tungrian auxiliaries were gripped by a bloodlust; veterans well trained in the use of the *gladius*, they smashed into the mass of Caledonian warriors, striking their faces with the bosses of their long shields and stabbing with their short swords, ideally suited to hand-to-hand combat. This frontal attack wrong- footed the Caledonians; then the arrival of the re-organized 3,000 Roman cavalry on their flanks spread panic in the brawling mob. The Caledonian host shivered, then crumbled in the onslaught on their front and flanks. The host quickly disintegrated, the warriors fleeing in panic. In what must have lasted only a few minutes, Agricola had won the day, committing only slightly more than half his entire force. This may have been deliberate; Agricola probably husbanded the rest in reserve for mopping-up or reinforcing the Batavian and Tungrian cohorts if they had come to grief.

The carnage was great. When night fell, 10,000 Caledonian warriors lay stark and stiff in the heather. Twelve centuries would pass until a defeat of similar magnitude would befall Scotland.[6] According to Tacitus, Agricola suffered only 400 casualties. Even so, he allowed 20,000 tribesmen to escape into the surrounding mountains – hardly a desirable result, given the nature of the type of warfare practised by the Caledonians. Agricola's force was now equal in number to his enemy and half of his men were as yet untried. Why did he fail to follow up his spectacular victory? We shall never know.

Tacitus's account briefly described the scene on the day following the battle:

> The next day revealed the effects of the victory more fully. An awful silence reigned on every hand; the hills were deserted, houses [sic] smoking in the distance, and our scouts did not meet a soul.

Viewing the devastation of burning, smoking settlements, Tacitus may have reflected on the nature of the politics, if not the morality, of the *Pax Romana*.

The precise location of the battle of Mons Graupius has never been accurately or satisfactorily identified. Some accounts[7] favour the Perthshire moor or muir of Ardoch whose topographical and physical features seem to fit the description in Tacitus's narrative. Also, General William Roy's *Military Survey of Scotland*[8] includes a detailed report on the Roman camp at Ardoch; Roy estimated that the camp was capable of accommodating an army of 30,000, a figure suspiciously close to the strength of Agricola's army.

However, on balance, most accounts[9] consider the battle took place near Bennachie, in Aberdeenshire. In this author's view Bennachie seems more likely for two reasons; it is only eighteen miles inland from the Aberdeenshire coast and we know that Agricola's army was provisioned by the Roman navy. Also, Tacitus calls the battle *Mons Graupius* – the Grampian Mountain. After his victory, Agricola probed further north into Morayshire, beyond the Grampians, creating a further ten stations or marching camps, remains of which can still be seen today.

Despite the victory at Mons Graupius and the creation of mighty fortifications at Ardoch, Inchtuthil and Strageth in Perthshire, Camelon in Stirlingshire, the various stations on the Antonine Wall, the naval base at Cramond, Edinburgh, Inveresk near Musselburgh, Newstead, Melrose, Cappuck, near Jedburgh, Birrens, Dumfriesshire, Lynne in Peebleshire and Hadrian's Wall – all built between AD 80 and 128 – the Roman hold on Scotland was far from secure. Roman occupation between AD 80 and 380 was at best fragmentary; ultimately, for strategic and economic reasons, the legions abandoned Scotland, confining their activities behind Hadrian's Wall from AD 380 until their departure from Britain in 410. During these three centuries, other battles were fought between the Romans and the Caledonians, although none of these is described in anything approaching the detail of Tacitus's account of Mons Graupius.

In AD 86 Agricola was recalled to Rome by the Emperor Titus Flavius Domitianus Augustus because, as a general, Agricola was entitled to a 'triumph' or public celebration in the streets of Rome bestowed on Roman leaders successful in war. However, Agricola's triumph was mere window-dressing as Emperor Domitian was jealous of his achievements which dwarfed his own; this was the real reason for his recall from Britain. Domitian's subsequent ill-treatment of Agricola spurred Tacitus on to write his father-in-law's biography – one of the finest ever written – five years after Agricola's death in AD 93. As for Domitian, he was universally hated by his people; his cruel and corrupt reign (AD 81–96) came to an end with his murder by a freedman.

As for Gaius Cornelius Tacitus, all we know of him derives from his fragmentary writings[10] and the *Letters* of his friend Pliny the Younger. A successful barrister, then Consul of Rome in AD 97, Tacitus was closely associated with Pliny in the prosecution in AD 99 of Marius Priscus, the extortionate and rascally governor of Africa. Despite his scant works, Tacitus's reputation is unsurpassed by most other Roman prose writers of his time.

Tacitus's best known work in Britain is, of course, his *De Vita et Moribus Julii Agricolae* (*The Agricola*) for its description of conditions in Roman Britain. To understand *The Agricola* fully, we have to examine its author's mindset. On the surface, the account was a tribute to a famous father-in-law and remarkable for its attention to a historical event which, had Tacitus not set it down in words, would have been lost to posterity. On the one hand, *The Agricola* is the seamless dovetailing of Agricola's achievements; on the other, it is Tacitus' propaganda vehicle criticizing the Emperor Domitian – as opposed to a sweeping condemnation of the Roman Empire – and his unjust treatment of a famous son of Rome of whom Domitian was obsessively jealous.

Tacitus's account reflects both its author's bitterness and that of his late father-in-law. The main thrust of his criticism of Domitian was expressed through Calgacus, a man he believed to be a valiant – if barbarous – Caledonian leader who addressed his embattled people before Mons Graupius. His speech was pure Tacitus, words he put into the Caledonian hero's mouth to criticize a corrupt and inefficient emperor whose misrule had created a 'desolation' or a desert in his own empire, masquerading as peace. Tacitus believed Domitian had betrayed the lofty principles enshrined in the *Pax Romana*, which had promised a better life for the peoples Rome had conquered. Tacitus is a master of the biting phrase, innuendo, force and conciseness, all these being the hallmarks of a successful lawyer, which he was.

As for Calgacus, had he been slain at Mons Graupius, Tacitus would undoubtedly have written of his death and the manner of it. Calgacus was never taken prisoner; if he had been, he would have been dragged in chains behind Agricola's chariot through the streets of Rome to serve as a warning to other tribes and peoples who dared to oppose Roman rule.

After Mons Graupius, Calgacus disappears from the pages of history – if he ever in fact existed and was not simply a figment of Tacitus's imagination, an invention he put to use in his propagandist account. Today, there is no memorial to Calgacus in Scotland, no stone or even cairn to commemorate his heroic stand against the Roman invaders. It is not too late for Scotland to honour him in some small way.

Although Mons Graupius is unique in being the sole battle recorded – albeit by a Roman eyewitness – we know from contemporary Roman sources that the war between the Caledonians (Picts) and the Romans raged on for the next three centuries. On account of the increasing unrest caused by the Picts and the Maetae, Emperor Severus (AD 197–211) came to Britain and marched north in AD 208. Carried on a litter on account of old age and infirmity, Severus was determined to lead a punitive expedition into Caledonia and subdue the rebellious tribes once and for all. Ambition does not always guarantee success however, as we know from countless examples in history. The legions of Severus were attacked time and time again by an elusive foe, although Severus was able to exact terms from the Picts who conceded a considerable part of their territory. Details of Severus are scant and very little is recorded about his conquests, not even his line of march into north Britain. He is said to have constructed a new defence between the river Tyne and the Solway; it may be that he simply repaired an existing earth or turf wall built by Agricola. The treaty Severus imposed on the Picts was hardly inscribed before the Picts and the Maetae were again menacing Roman territory south of the Tyne–Solway line. Only Severus's death at York in AD 211 prevented further action against the rebellious tribes.

For the next century and a half, we know nothing of events in north Britain until AD 368, when the Emperor Valentinian despatched Theodosius (father of the emperor of the same name) to Britain to subdue the Picts. In two campaigns, Theodosius is said to have broken the power of the Picts and their allies; he also recovered territories whose precise location is unknown to us but which were called Valentia in honour of Emperor Valentinian. However, Theodosius's campaigns only postponed the inevitable – the evacuation of Britain when Alaric, King of the Visigoths, sacked Rome in AD 410.

After the Romans departed, the peoples of Britain were left to shift for themselves. As in southern Britain, the northern territories would confront new and challenging invaders in the coming six centuries, as we shall see.

Notes

1. Tacitus, *De Vita et Moribus Julii Agricolae* (*The Agricola*).
2. Cassius Dio, *A History of Rome.*
3. Ibid.
4. Tacitus, *De Vita etc.*
5. Other translations of Tacitus give 'desert' and 'desolation'.
6. The battle of Dunbar, 1296.
7. Brotchie, *The Battlefields of Scotland*, pp.16–17.
8. Roy, *Military Survey of Scotland* 1747–55.
9. Notably Oliver, *A History of Scotland*, p.33.
10. In addition to *De Vita et Moribus Julii Agricolae*, Tacitus (AD 55–120) wrote *Dialogus de Oratoribus* (AD 76), a treatise on the Roman educational system; *De Germania*, a propaganda pamphlet exploiting the fallacy of the concept of 'the noble savage' in order to attack the degeneracy and servility of contemporary Rome; the *Histories* (AD 69–97) and the *Annals*, a record of the reigns of the Emperors Tiberius to Nero, excluding the reign of Caligula and most of Claudius's and Nero's reigns.

Chapter 2

The Dark Ages

After the departure of the Romans, north Britain enjoyed a period of development, although progress was hampered by unrest. In western Europe, various races and peoples freed from the restraining power of the Roman Empire migrated to Britain. The newcomers, Angles and Saxons, came into conflict with the indigenous tribes although, at first, northern Britain was spared. The main trouble in the north was caused by internecine warfare. This struggle went on for nearly six centuries, those known as the Dark Ages – not in the sense of the absence of light but because we know very little about post-Roman Britain. However, Pictish art blossomed, particularly after north Britain experienced the unifying influence of Christianity. The link with the educated western world had been broken with the departure of the Romans; it would be re-established by the evangelical saints who converted the north in the coming centuries. What was 'dark' during the fifth to the eleventh centuries was the absence of recorded history; even what has survived is fragmentary and obscure. We are obliged to rely on the early chronicles, many of which were written several years after the events they describe. These chronicles offer a window – albeit opaque – through which we catch glimpses of the main drift and character of the several forces which would ultimately transform northern Britain into Scotland.

Christianity was the key. The missionary Saint Ninian (AD ?–550) began the task of converting the Picts in the lower, or southern part of the Pictish kingdom; he was ordained bishop of the southern Picts by Pope Siricius in AD 394. Ninian made his chief seat at *Candida Casa*, or Whithorn, Wigtownshire, although his mission was centred on the south, it extended to the Grampians; his death in AD 550 prevented conversion of the northern Picts. This was completed by Saint Columba (AD 521–597). Columba originated in Donegal, coming to north Britain in AD 563 and making Iona his chief seat. Around AD 565 he went on a mission to convert the whole of northern Pictland, preaching the Christian faith and founding monasteries.

About the same time Saint Kentigern, or Mungo, (AD 518–612), who was born in what is now East Lothian, carried the Word to the west, becoming Bishop of Glasgow. The process was completed by Saint Cuthbert (AD 633–687) who evangelized parts of the modern counties of the Borders and Northumberland, where he established himself at Lindisfarne. These evangelical preachers united the pagan tribes of north Britain by preaching peace, just as the Romans had united them through war.

By the fourth century AD, the Caledonians and their sub-tribes were known as Picts, the name first given to the tribes by the Romans. Afterwards, the tribal name *Caledoni* dropped out of use; the territory called Caledonia became known as Pictland, or Pictavia. The Picts became the predominant tribe, although other tribes such as the Goidelic Celts, or Gaels, later known as the Scots, established their kingdom of Dalriada in Argyleshire. For two centuries after the Roman withdrawal, a twilight descended on north Britain and we know nothing whatsoever about the history of this period. We must assume that it was an age dominated by the use of axe, spear and sword, as the Picts and the Scots struggled for mastery of the country.

The ethnological divisions in north Britain at this time are complex; in the interests of clarity however, we need only concern ourselves with the four main peoples – the Picts, the Scots, the Britons of Strathclyde and, in the seventh century AD, the Angles of Bernicia, or modern Northumberland. Of these four peoples, the Picts and the Britons had established themselves over an indeterminable period prior to AD 500. The Dalriadic Scots originated in Antrim, Ireland, and arrived in north Britain around AD 500. The Angles settled in Northumberland in AD 547 and would invade Strathclyde in AD 603, then Lothian in AD 638. These four powerful and disparate peoples vied with each other for supremacy over what would become the kingdom of Scotland.

The Picts were the predominant race. As mentioned in the previous chapter, of the Picts we know little apart from the haunting images they carved in stone – obscure symbols, animals and occasionally warriors. The Pictish language is completely unknown to us. The kingdom of Pictland stretched from Caithness in the north to the Firth of Forth in the south, although until the ninth century AD, it was constantly under threat from the Dalriadic Scots and, to a lesser extent, the Britons of Strathclyde. The greatest threat would come from the Angles of Bernicia, in the seventh century, as we shall see.

However, let us examine the Picts' main adversaries in the sixth century, the Scots of Dalriada. The Scots made their capital at Dunadd, near the modern Crinan Canal. Dunadd began its existence as an Iron Age hill-fort. It is situated near Kilmartin, Argyle, rising out of the barren flatness of the Crinan Moss. Today, Dunadd is enveloped in an eerie silence broken only by the random cawing of rooks, or the wind. The natural fortress has several entrances, some blocked artificially with loose stones for defence. It is renowned for its unique stone carvings below the uppermost enclosure; these include a human footprint and a basin hollowed from the stone, symbols thought to be linked to the coronation rituals of Dalriadic kings. On the same flat outcrop is the image of a boar in the Pictish style, with an example of *ogham* script – a form of writing consisting of straight lines and dots which appears in ancient British inscriptions and named for the Gaulish Ogmios, the god of language – a language unknown to us. Dunadd is surrounded by vitrified hill-forts, prehistoric structures found in Scotland, Ireland and Europe. (Their peculiarity is that the stones of which they are constructed are wholly or partly vitrified, transformed into a kind of glass by the action of heat effected deliberately by means of piled-up fuel set alight.)

Occupied from about AD 500, Dunadd was evacuated around AD 850 because it was vulnerable to Viking raids. It was relocated in Scone, Perthshire, the centre of the Picto-Scottish kingdom of Alba, as ancient Scotland was named. The graveyard in the nearby village of Kilmartin, Argyle, contains many intricately carved stones dating from the early Christian period to the Middle Ages. It is possible some originated in Dunadd.

The Strathclyde Britons were descended from a Celtic-British tribe known as the Damnoni. Their kingdom was centred on Dumbarton, which they made their capital. The kingdom of Strathclyde stretched from the modern shires of Dumbarton, Renfrew, Lanark, Ayr, Peebles, Dumfries and across the Border to Cumberland and Westmorland. The kingdom survived intact until the Norman Conquest, when Cumberland and Westmorland were annexed by William Rufus, William II (1056–1100) into Norman England.[1] Before that, the Strathclyde Britons were probably joined by the remnants of the Votadini (or Gododdin) whose kingdom in the Lothians was annexed by the Angles of Bernicia who occupied Din Eidyn or modern Edinburgh in AD 638.

This rich and colourful broth of Picto-Scottish cultures would survive until Kenneth mac Alpin, King of the Dalriadic Scots – his mother was a Pict – united the Picts and Scots in AD 844. Before that, the chief threat to the area north of the modern Border came from the Bernician Angles.

Degsastan

We first learn of the Angles in AD 547, when they established a kingdom based at Bamburgh, in Northumberland under their ruler, Ida. Ida's kingdom was known as Bernicia and Deira, the neighbouring province of modern Yorkshire which the Bernician Angles annexed in AD 588. The northern part of Bernicia would extend over the river Tweed into the kingdom of the Votadini, as we shall presently see.

In AD 603 Ida's grandson, King Aethelfrith began to menace the area occupied by the Britons of Strathclyde. Aethelfrith drove the Strathclyde governors from their provinces, planting his own sub-kings in their place. These events were closely monitored by the Dalriadic Scots who knew that if Strathclyde fell they would be next. So with a great army King Aidan mac Gabrian of Dalriada met Aethelfrith at Degsastan, close to the boundary of Bernicia (modern Northumberland). So great was the slaughter of Aidan's army that no Scottish sub-king dared challenge the Bernicians for the next eight decades.

Little is known of the battle of Degsastan, nor its precise location. The modern historian Professor Michael Lynch believes the battle took place in Northumberland.[2] Other accounts[3] argue that Degsastan was fought in southern Scotland, either at Jedburgh in the Borders or Dawston in Liddesdale, Roxburghshire. The jury remains undecided on this, although this author believes that Dawston is the likeliest location.

Despite the failed attempt by Dalriada to protect itself from Anglian expansionism and, in the process, safeguard its near neighbours, the Strathclyde Britons, the Dalriadic Scots cast envious eyes on Strathclyde. If they could annex that kingdom the Scots would be better placed against their main rivals for supremacy – the Picts. Matters came to a head in AD 642 when King Domnall Brec of Dalriada attempted to seize territory in Strathclyde. Domnall was confronted by King Owain of Strathclyde who defeated him at the battle of Strathcarron, a battle of which we know practically nothing. However, the battle reinforced the position of Strathclyde as a powerful kingdom, a power which neither the Scots of Dalriada nor the Picts could ignore.

By the seventh century Pictish power south of the Grampians was centred at Fortriu, west Perthshire, Angus and Fife. In AD 685 the main threat to Pictish supremacy did not come from the Dalriadic Scots or the Britons of Strathclyde. It was the growing power of the Angles of Bernicia which challenged the Picts. The Angles, a Germanic people who originated in Schleswig came to Britain, settled in Mercia (south England), Deira (Yorkshire) and Bernicia (Northumberland). It was not long before the Bernician Angles began to plan the expansion of their kingdom across the river Tweed, where there were fertile lands. In this, the seventh century Angles were following their rapacious King Ida – more robber than monarch who founded the Eadwulfing dynasty [4] which would rule Bernicia and south-east Scotland from the seventh to the early eleventh centuries.

At first, the Bernician Angles confined their expansionist policy to *Laudonia*, as the counties of Berwickshire and East Lothian were then known. This was an area occupied by the warrior tribe known as the Votadini or

Gododdin. The Votadini established their capital at Din Eidyn (modern Edinburgh) where their King Mynnydog 'the Wealthy' built his power base at Maiden's Castle (now Edinburgh Castle) on the summit of a volcanic rock which dominated Din Eidyn. The Votadini-Gododdin held out against the Bernician Angles for about sixty years; at one point, in AD 603, they invaded Bernicia-Deira, believing that the Bernicians and Deirans were at odds with each other, which was not the case. At the battle of Catreath (Catterick), the Gododdin faced a united army of Bernician and Deiran Angles. The flower of the Gododdin nobility were slaughtered. There were only two survivors of that conflict – Cynon the Stubborn and Aneirin, the latter a poet who later wrote an epic poem *Y Gododdin* as a tribute to the fallen heroes.[5]

By AD 638, the Bernician Angles had conquered the entire south-east as far as Edinburgh, controlling the entire *Merse* (Berwickshire) and *Laudonia* (the Lothians, also known as *Saxonia*). Not content with these gains, the Angles crossed the Firth of Forth, entering southern Pictland. Now it was the turn of the Picts.

As the Anglian army advanced the Picts were discomfited, retreating into the mountain fastnesses until AD 671 when they rallied and drove out one of the Anglian puppet sub-kings appointed by King Ecgfrith or Ecgfrid. An enraged Ecgfrid came north, intent on bringing the southern Picts into submission. In an unidentified encounter in AD 672 many Pictish settlements were burnt and men, women and children slaughtered. Again, the Picts retreated to lick their wounds until Pictish hopes of victory were re-kindled by a new king, Bredei mac Bili who encouraged his embattled people to resist the Anglian yoke. In AD 685 Ecgfrid was angered by news of Pictish resurgence; he was not a man who would allow any challenge to his authority, especially by a race he considered no better than savages. To restore Anglian hegemony and salve his injured pride, King Ecgfrid crossed the Forth at the head of a large army.

Dún Nechtáin or Dunnichen Moss

Once again faced by a formidable force, the Picts appeared to retreat. However, this was part of Bredei mac Bili's strategy; he lured Ecgfrid ever north into terrain which suited his purpose. It is thought traditionally that Dún Nechtáin took place in Forfar, Angus,[6] where on 20 May 685, Bredei turned to face Ecgfrid. The massed, disciplined ranks of Pictish spearmen fell on the Angles, driving them into a loch, butchering them without quarter in the cold waters.[7] During the slaughter, Ecgfrid was slain.

Dunnichen, or Dún Nechtáin, is known to the English as Nechtansmere (literally, the mere or loch of Nechtan). However, the site of the battle is disputed, as some historians consider it took place farther north, in the

Cairngorm Mountains. The Venerable Bede does not identify the site; he simply wrote that the battle was fought 'in tight places amid inaccessible mountains'. Recent research[8] suggests that while traditionally, Dún Nechtáin took place in Forfar, an alternative site is Dunachton in Badenoch, Inverness-shire, lying on the shores of Loch Insh in terrain which fits Bede's description. Wherever the battle occurred, it ranks alongside Bannockburn as a major milestone on the long road to Scotland's independence. By his determination and, it must be said, his ruthlessness, Bredei not only won a spectacular victory but also united the Picts. (For many years, he had waged war on his own people, attacking strongholds like Dunottar, Aberdeen and the hill-fort of Dundurn, Perthshire.)[9] Bredei was a man determined to become king; he forged the Picts into a nation, something which had not been achieved since Calgacus at the battle of Mons Graupius, although that unity had lasted briefly. After Dunnichen Moss, the united nation of Pictland ensured the security of northern Britain. Never again would the Angles of Bernicia cross the Firth of Forth.

There is no contemporary written record of Dunnichen Moss, although it is generally believed[10] that a pictorial representation of the battle survives on one of a series of five intricately carved Pictish stones, known as the Aberlemno Stones I–V. Aberlemno II (see illustrations) is one of the most beautiful of these, depicting what some historians believe to be a representation of the battle of Dunnnichen Moss. Surmounted on one side by a Celtic Cross, one of its decorated surfaces shows two horsemen, one Pictish chasing a helmeted Anglian who has cast away his shield in flight. (The helmet, with its distinctively long nose-guard is typically Anglian, similar to several found during excavations in Coppersgate, York.) The undocked tail of the horse and its large saddle-blanket suggest that the fleeing warrior is a person of importance – possibly Ecgfrid himself. Other Pictish and Anglian figures are depicted; in one corner, a raven is seen pecking at a dead Anglian soldier.

Carrieblair

In the coming years, the Picts gained the upper hand over their neighbours, the Dalriadic Scots and the Strathclyde Britons, so that by the ninth century, the kingdom of Pictland was the dominant power in north Britain. The Picts' war with the Bernician Angles, still firmly established south of the Firth of Forth, would continue. The Picts also suffered attacks from Vikings, probably in the north. We know of one possible battle, that at Carrieblair, near Tain, Easter Ross. The date of the battle is uncertain but it probably took place at some point after Dunnichen Moss and before the unification of the Scots and Picts by Kenneth macAlpin (Kenneth I, 844– 860). Before and after these dates, Picto-Scottish tribes repeatedly raided Anglian settlements in *Saxonia*.

Athelstaneford

One of the most memorable of these raids occurred in East Lothian or the Merse in the autumn of AD 832. By that year, the Picts and Scots were drawing closer together; in the previous half-century, for brief periods, a Pictish or Scottish king had occasionally ruled both peoples. The raid of AD 832 was unquestionably for plunder as, being harvest-time and given the rich agricultural yields in the area, the Picto-Scots were seeking grain to tide them over the coming winter. The Picts were led by their King Oengus (Angus), the Scots by their King Eochaid. We do not know how deeply the Picto-Scottish army penetrated *Saxonia* but their incursion brought an Anglian army led by Athelstan, possibly a Bernician under-king. Athelstan pursued the raiders to Markle, a village near East Linton, East Lothian, where the Picto- Scottish army found their escape route barred by the river Peffer, which, given the time of year, may have been in spate. The Anglian army surrounded the Picts and Scots as darkness descended, expecting to engage and defeat them the following morning. That night, King Angus, a Christianized Pict, prayed for a miracle to save his people. According to legend, Saint Andrew appeared to Angus in a dream, promising him that not only would he be saved but that he would be victorious in battle. Angus swore that if these things came to pass, he would adopt Saint Andrew as the patron saint of Pictland.

The next morning, it is said that a white cloud formation appeared in the sky as a saltire, or x-shaped *decussate* cross on which Saint Andrew had been martyred by the Romans in c. AD 70. The morale of the Picto-Scots thus boosted, the ensuing battle of Athelstaneford brought them a complete victory, with Athelstan being slain. From that day on, the saltire was adopted as the flag of Scotland, Andrew becoming the nation's patron saint.

After Athelstaneford, events moved quickly towards the unification of the Picts and Scots. In AD 844, Kenneth, son of Alpin, King of Dalriada, became ruler of the Picts and Scots. Kenneth's accession was achieved by his father's marriage to a Pictish woman; in Pictland, it was the sons of the mother who inherited the crown. Of kindred blood and common language, the Christian faith brought the two races together; in addition, increasing attacks by Viking pirates forced them into united counsel and action. In the following two centuries, the Picto-Scottish kingdom would annex Strathclyde and that part of Bernicia north of the river Tweed.

Kenneth set himself the task of reclaiming *Saxonia*; he invaded it no fewer than six times, burning the *urbs regis* (royal town) of Dunbar in AD 856.[11] Kenneth was never strong enough to expel the Angles, despite the anarchy within Bernicia which led to its political collapse. The Angles were also being challenged from the sea by Danish pirates who plundered Northumberland after they took York in AD 867. The threat to Kenneth's kingdom did not come from the Angles or English but the Norwegians and Danes, known to us as Vikings. At first these Scandinavian peoples were freebooters, raiding the coastlines of Britain for plunder; those that settled in England in the ninth, tenth and eleventh centuries and against whom Alfred the Great and his descendants waged war were Danes, not Norwegians (Norsemen). The Norsemen who settled in Orkney and Shetland included Danes; from these islands, they migrated into Caithness, spreading along the coast as far south as the Moray Firth. Other bands formed colonies in Dumfriesshire, Kirkcudbright and Peebles, part of the kingdom of Strathclyde; Norsemen also populated the Western Isles which for several centuries belonged to the kingdom of Norway.

Dollar and Inverduvat

Kenneth's son Constantin II (AD 863–877) struggled to withstand the repeated raids in the north and south of his kingdom. In AD 867 Olaf the White, the Norwegian King of Dublin, landed on the west coast, invading Constantin's kingdom, raiding for plunder only for a few months. Olaf returned four years later but, on that occasion, Constantin's kingdom was spared, the Norwegians being preoccupied with capturing Dumbarton, the capital of Strathclyde. However, this respite did not last; in AD 877 a fresh army of Norwegians from Ireland invaded Constantin's kingdom, inflicting a serious defeat on him at Dollar, near Stirling. Constantin made a final stand against the invaders at Inverduvat, in the parish of Forgan, Fife, where he was slain along with the greater part of his army. Constantin was succeeded by his nephew Eochaid, one of a succession of four kings between 877 and 900 of whom little is known. The Danish-Norwegian presence in the outlying islands would continue for the next four centuries.

When Constantin III (AD 900–942) ascended the throne, he rigorously attacked the Norsemen, inflicting a severe defeat on them in an unidentified battle in AD 904, driving them from the mainland of Alba, as the new kingdom became known in AD 900. For the moment Alba was secure, although Constantin's victory did not prevent further Norse invasions. The Norsemen came back in AD 918; Regnwald, the leader of the Irish Norsemen crossed the Irish sea to assist his kinsmen occupying the southern half of Bernicia-Northumberland who were being menaced by Edward the Elder, the West Saxon king. The united Danish-Norse force entered *Saxonia*, then ruled by Eldred of Northumberland, whose base was at Bamborough. The conquest of *Saxonia* by the Norsemen would have threatened Constantin's kingdom, so he joined Eldred to make war on the common enemy. There are obscure and conflicting accounts of the battle which ensued; Constantin and Eldred were beaten, although the Norsemen were unable to follow up their advantage. This was the last Norse attempt to extend a hold on Britain although they continued to raid Alba in the north. Mainland Alba was also threatened by Norwegians from the Hebrides or Western Isles.

It was in the reign of King Indulph (AD 954–962) that Edinburgh was finally abandoned by the Bernician Angles. By AD 966, the kingdom of Bernicia had come to an end, its southern half ruled by Oslac, an English earl who was subject to the overlordship of Edgar, King of England (AD 959–975). However, the reign of Kenneth II (AD 971–995) was troubled by unrest as much as had been that of his namesake, Kenneth I.

Luncarty

In about AD 986 a Danish force of rover-pirates invaded middle Alba. The Danish fleet lay off the coast of Angus for several days, then it sailed up the river Esk, capturing Montrose and putting the civilian population to the sword. The Danes then marched inland along the river Tay estuary to invest the ancient town of Perth. Kenneth II was holding court in Stirling; when he learnt of the Danish invasion, he hastily gathered together an army which he drew up in order of battle near the small village of Luncarty, a few miles north of Perth. The Danes marched from Perth to engage the Scots. The battle began well for Kenneth; his army forced the Danes from their strong position on a hill. Then the Danes regrouped and counter-attacked Kenneth, putting to flight the right and left wings of his army, leaving him isolated in the centre. Then, if we can believe Boece's *History of Scotland*,[12] a dramatic turnabout occurred. According to Boece, a ploughman and his two sons were working in a nearby field and saw Kenneth's men fleeing from the Danes. These three men decided to stop the rout. Armed with nothing else but their ox-plough yokes, they rallied Kenneth's men, exhorting them to return and destroy their enemy, which they did, decisively defeating the enemy. (There is a feature near Luncarty known as Turnabout Hill.) Again, in Boece's account, the ploughman is given the surname Hay, which is highly improbable. The de Haya or Hay family did not arrive in Scotland until the twelfth century; they originated in Cotentin, Normandy and joined the army of William the Conqueror who invaded Britain in 1066.

Whatever the ploughman's name, Kenneth granted him as much of the fruitful soil of the Carse of Gowrie as a falcon could encompass in a single flight without touching land. (This story has a certain quaint ring of truth about it, given similar tales recorded in the chronicles of the Middle Ages.) From this acreage of land in Errol, the Hay family took its name. According to *Burke's Landed Gentry of Scotland* (19th Edition), William de la Haye, butler to Kings Malcolm IV and William I (The Lion) married Eva, the Celtic heiress of Pitmily (which included the Errol estate) and received her lands as dowry, according to custom and law in thirteenth-century Scotland. The rising Hay family became hereditary constables of Scotland; they adopted a coat-of-arms depicting two 'savages' bearing ox-plough yokes, with the motto *Serua Jugem* (Keep the Yoke).

Cullen Fields

Scotland and England continued to be raided by the Danes for the next two decades after the battle of Luncarty. Northumberland was subjected to repeated raids, as well as its satellite in south-east Scotland. Save what is recorded by Buchanan,[13] little is known about the battle of Cullen Fields, in Banffshire. Fought in AD 961 during the reign of King Indulfus (AD 954–962), the battle was a victory for the Scots. One of Indulfus's captains was Patrick de Dunbar, also known as Thane (earl) of Lothian, which suggests that Patrick was an Englishman in the service of the Scots.[14] At Cullen the Danes were thrown off balance by the timely arrival on the field of a noble known only by the name Graeme (Graham?) who, with Patrick Dunbar, led the Scots to victory.

Mortlach or Mortlake

Of the next four kings, we know most about Malcolm II (1005–1034). He began his reign with the usual invasion of *Saxonia*. Invading northern England as far as Durham in 1005 or 1006, Malcolm was soundly beaten by Earl Uhtred of Northumberland, a reversal so severe that he made no further attempts to annex *Saxonia* until 1018.

However, further attempts by the Danes to colonize the northern part of his kingdom took Malcolm north in 1005 to Banff to expel the intruders. Again, we learn that one of Malcolm's captains was a Thane Patrick Dunbar, probably not the same Dunbar who had fought at Cullen Fields in AD 961. There are scant references to the battle of Mortlach, the historic name of Dufftown in the Spey Valley; one account[15] states that due to their impetuosity, Thanes Dunbar and Strathearn along with Kenneth of the Isles were slain. Mortlach was perhaps not quite the victory Malcolm had anticipated but he was able to expel the Danes from Morayshire that year.

In the next chapter, we shall examine Malcolm's reign which was chiefly noted for his annexation of *Saxonia*, thus completing the unification of mainland Scotland in 1018.[16]

Notes

1. The part of Strathclyde in Cumberland and Westmorland remained independent for some years after the Norman Conquest; a principality of Scotland as was Wales of England, the Scottish rump of Strathclyde was the appanage of the heir-apparent to the Scottish throne.

2. Lynch, *Scotland: A New History*, p.17.
3. Hume Brown, *History of Scotland*, vol i, p.18; Matthews, *England Versus Scotland: Great British Battles*; Pugh, *Swords, Loaves and Fishes: A History of Dunbar*, p.66.
4. Successive occupants of the Bernician throne were named Eadwulf or Eadulf.
5. For centuries, it was thought *Y Gododdin* was a Welsh poem, cymric being akin to the Votadini tongue. *The Gododdin* is in fact the earliest surviving Scottish poem (see Jackson, *The Gododdin: The Oldest Scottish Poem*).
6. Oliver, *A History of Scotland*, p.45 gives Aviemore; Brotchie, *The Battlefields of Scotland*, p.22 identifies a site in Forfarshire, in Angus, as does Lynch op. cit., p.19.
7. Brotchie, op. cit., p.22.
8. Woolf, Alex, *Dún Nechtáin, Fortriu and the Geography of the Picts* (Scottish Historical Review, vol. LXXXV, 2: No 22, October 2006).
9. Oliver, op. cit., p.45.
10. For example, Oliver, op. cit., p.45.
11. *Encyclopedia Britannica*; Hume Brown op. cit., vol. i, p.32. The burning was probably the Anglian wooden stockade and settlements near the modern Victoria Harbour.
12. Boece, *History of Scotland*, is a mixture of romantic fiction and fact; Buchanan, *History of Scotland* contains an account of Luncarty but omits the story of the falcon. Other accounts are found in Abercromby, *Martial Achievements in Scotland* and Pratt, *Buchan*. Hume Brown states that the 'Danes were worsted in so singular a manner at Luncarty' op. cit., vol. i, p.41.
13. Buchanan, op. cit; Crammond, *Annals of Cullen*.
14. Pugh, RJM, op cit., pp.38–39.
15. Shaw, *History of the Province of Moray*. Miller, *The History of Dunbar* gives Mar, Aberdeenshire.
16. The Danes maintained their hold on Orkney and Shetland until the fifteenth century; the Norwegians occupied the Western Isles, Bute and Arran until 1266, three years after the battle of Largs.

Chapter 3

The Early Middle Ages

During the early years of the eleventh century, the reign of Malcolm II proved that he was more than equal to the task of introducing new policies in his realm, bringing these to a satisfactory conclusion. Under Malcolm, Alba attained a degree of unprecedented cohesion through the sheer, ruthless force of his personality which brought the warring factions of Celts, Scots, Britons and Norwegians to an understanding of each other even if they remained unreconciled. In Caithness and Sutherland, Malcolm enjoyed cordial relations with the Norwegian *jarl* (earl) Sigurd the Stout, even giving his daughter in marriage to Sigurd. When Sigurd was slain at the battle of Clontarf in Ireland in 1014, Malcolm conferred Caithness and Sutherland on Sigurd's son Thorfinn, a mere boy; this suggests that Malcolm was grooming the child as an ally in any future conflicts with the native Celtic *mormaers* (great stewards) in the north. Although the frontier in the north remained fluid, the establishment of a southern boundary at the river Tweed was uppermost in Malcolm's mind; in the year 1018 Malcolm was resolved to achieve that border line.

As we saw in the previous chapter, in the first year of his reign, Malcolm had attempted to annex Lothian but had over-reached himself by invading northern England as far as Durham, where he was rebuffed by Earl Uhtred of Northumberland. However, by 1018, Uhtred was dead and Northumberland was split in two. A powerful leader ruled the southern half but the northern part was held lightly by a weaker man, Eadwulf (also known as Eadulf Cudel). Malcolm raised an army and was joined by Owen the Bald, the last king of the kingdom of Strathclyde. For thirty nights before Malcolm reached the river Tweed, a comet (possibly Haley's Comet) appeared in the night sky, striking fear into the Northumbrians who saw it as a portent of coming disaster.

Carham-on-Tweed

The battle of Carham, sometimes known as the battle of Coldstream, as the site lies three miles to the south-west of that town, actually took place just south of the river Tweed. Malcolm won a spectacular victory over Eadulf Cudel which gave him control of the Merse (Berwickshire) and East Lothian. Although fought on English soil, Carham is included in this account because, not only did it secure Lothian and the Merse for the kingdom of Alba, it also established the Scottish border at the Tweed. It could be argued that Carham itself was included in Malcolm's annexation although contemporary and modern historians agree that the Scottish border ends on the north bank of the river Tweed.

Carham has been the subject of dispute among modern historians, who doubt its importance in the securing of Lothian (the Merse, or Berwickshire and East Lothian) as an integral part of Scotland. Some insist that Lothian was granted to Kenneth II (971–995) by King Edgar of England on condition that Kenneth recognized him as his superior. Professor Hume Brown states that the authority for this is doubtful.[1] One has to ask the question; if Edgar had in fact ceded Lothian to Kenneth, why did Malcolm II 'invade' northern England in 1018 and fight a battle to annex it? A possible answer is that Malcolm knew of this arrangement and decided to rid himself of the need to pay homage to England for the territory. The modern historian Professor M. Lynch disputes the importance of Carham, a view not shared by this author; Lynch contends that 'Carham could not have seemed so decisive at the time' and that 'Carham solved nothing'.[2] Hume Brown ventures to say that the annexation of Lothian, on account of Carham, was the most important event in Scotland's history.[3] Malcolm had achieved what his forebears had failed to do in the past century and a half; even if the benefits were not immediately apparent, Malcolm II was described as 'King of Alba' in the Irish *Annals of Tigernach*.

A postscript to Carham illustrates Malcolm's generosity to a defeated opponent, Eadulf Cudel, who knew that by signing Lothian away his co-ruler in southern Northumberland would punish him for his profligacy. Malcolm was magnanimous; he offered Eadulf sanctuary in Berwickshire where he lived out his remaining years in what was once known as Eadulf's Ton (*ton* being Anglo-Saxon for village). In time Eadulf's Ton became known as Eddleston.

What, then, was the effect of Carham? The answer is perhaps obvious. Had Lothian remained in English possession, the history of Scotland might have been vastly different. For example, the battles of Dunbar of 1296 and 1650 might have been fought elsewhere. These are but two crude examples. The earldom of Dunbar, a vital area and important cockpit during the Wars of

Independence, would have been occupied by the English and supported by the dynasty of Dunbar earls until the fifteenth century and possibly beyond that, a thorn in the side of Scottish kings from Robert the Bruce and the Stewart or Stuart dynasty of kings until the union with England in 1707.

As for the remainder of Malcolm II's reign, his failure to produce a male heir to succeed him would cause constitutional problems and give rise to further battles. Malcolm had three daughters. One married Sigurd the Stout; their son Thorfinn became ruler of Caithness and Sutherland. Another, known as Bethoc became the wife of Thane Crinan, lay Abbot of Dunkeld, whose son Duncan became king in 1034. The third, Doada married Findlaech, *mormaer* of Moray; their son Macbeth would challenge and kill King Duncan with the help of Thorfinn, his cousin. Like Duncan, Macbeth had a legitimate claim to the throne through the female line. These three marriages led to events which were turning points in Scotland's history.

Malcolm's reign achieved the annexation of the sprawling kingdom of Strathclyde, although this gain and that of Lothian must be set against his failure to check the expansionist policies of the Norwegian earls of Orkney to colonize mainland Scotland. However, under Malcolm, Scotland became the country we know today, apart from the continuing presence of Norsemen in Orkney, Shetland and the Western Isles. After his acquisition of Lothian, Malcolm became virtual ruler of the country from the river Tweed to the Pentland Firth. Even the troublesome kingdom of Strathclyde was subdued, not by martial means but through diplomacy, after its last independent king, Owen, Malcolm's ally at Carham died in 1018. Malcolm attempted to install his grandson Duncan (the product of his daughter Bethoc's marriage to Crinan the Thane) as prince of Strathclyde. The Strathclyde Britons were unhappy about this but reluctantly accepted Duncan as their leader. When Malcolm died in 1034, the unpopular Duncan ascended the throne.

Duncan I (1034–40) was troubled by the Norwegians in Caithness and Sutherland as well as by his cousin Macbeth in Morayshire. Duncan's reign was as brief as it was unfortunate. Possibly because of his weakness or youth, or both, his kingdom was threatened by Aldred, Earl of Northumberland, who invaded Strathclyde and embarked on a brief but bloody campaign. Either before or after this invasion – contemporary accounts are obscure – Duncan invaded Northumberland and laid siege to Durham where, despite having a large army of foot and horse, he was badly beaten; so great was the defeat his heavy casualties forced him to retreat.[4] At least the Northumbrians did not pursue him.

Duncan's main worries were in the north, however. Thorfinn, his cousin, proved more troublesome, refusing to acknowledge Duncan as rightful King of Scotland. Duncan attempted to install another cousin, Moddan, in

Caithness and Sutherland; Moddan's army was soundly beaten by Thorfinn, which allowed the latter to add Rosshire to his dominions. Duncan responded by raising another army and a fleet which entered the Pentland Firth to attack Thorfinn from the sea, while Moddan engaged him by land. Duncan's fleet was scattered by Thorfinn's ships; Thorfinn then attacked Moddan at Thurso, where he personally slew Moddan, after setting fire to the house Moddan was using as his headquarters.

Torfness

In c.1034 a dispirited Duncan raised yet another army and met Thorfinn at Torfness, thought to be Burghead on the Moray Firth, where again, the Norwegian defeated him.

Bordie

Bordie, or the battle of Culross Moor, Fife, is considered to be the site of a battle in 1038 between the Scots and the Vikings, possibly Norwegians. The outcome was yet another defeat for Duncan. According to folklore, great slaughter occurred; little is known of the protagonists or the precise number of fatal casualties. The Scottish standard was reputedly placed in a flat outcrop of rock which (with difficulty) can still be seen today. Duncan's lacklustre reign was nearing its end. Enter Macbeth, *mormaer* of Moray whose wife Gruoch was the granddaughter of Kenneth III. In addition, Macbeth's mother Doada was the daughter of Malcolm II and these links to the throne encouraged him to make a bid for it. Taking advantage of Duncan's parlous situation, Macbeth allied himself with Thorfinn, killing Duncan in an unidentified battle near Elgin in 1040. Macbeth then drove both of Duncan's sons Malcolm and Donald into exile.[5] In 1045 Crinan the Thane attempted to unseat Macbeth in favour of his son Duncan I's son Malcolm (the future Malcolm III) but was slain along with ' nine times twenty heroes'.[6] In 1046 we witness the beginnings of interference in Scotland's constitution by Earl Siward of Northumberland; according to the historian Fordun, Siward was related to the House of Crinan through the marriage of his relative Suthen – possibly a sister – to Duncan.[7] A second attempt against Macbeth at Dunsinnan by Siward in 1054 was more successful; Duncan's son Malcolm – later Malcolm III – was appointed king, but only in Strathclyde and Lothian.[8] Macbeth retreated northwards to Moray to await his expected confrontation with Malcolm.

Macbeth was as we know unfairly demonized in Shakespeare's eponymous play written five centuries later. How historically accurate was Shakespeare? While his play is a masterpiece, it is bad history. The playwright drew his story from Raphael Holinshed's *Chronicles* (1577) and, in turn, Holinshed based his account on John of Fordun's *Scotichronicon* or *Chronica Gentis Scotorum* (The Chronicle of the People of Scotland, c.1380) and Andrew Wyntoun's *Oryginale Cronykil* (Original Chronicle, 1420). Fordun was the better historian; Wyntoun's account is steeped in romance and folklore. Both these chronicles were incorporated in Hector Boece's *Scotorum Historiae* (The History of Scotland, 1574); it was his history which was bowdlerised by Holinshed and dramatized by Shakespeare. There were no witches, no Banquo (let alone his ghost!), no midnight murder of Duncan. Macbeth was never tempted by three witches but by plain, old-fashioned ambition.

Shakespeare's *Macbeth* (1606) is steeped in the preoccupations of James VI and I – the rights of succession, the relationship between Scotland and England, witchcraft and – horror of horrors – the Gunpowder Plot of 1605, an attempt on the king's life. James believed in the divine right of kings, that monarchs were God's representatives and regents. Killing a king was the ultimate crime against Nature. Macbeth's disaffection with Duncan may have originated with the killing of his wife Gruoch's nephew by Malcolm II 'the aggressor', one of the most ruthless kings in the mac Alpin dynasty.[9] What, then was the reason for demonizing Macbeth? That question is fairly simple to answer. Macbeth and his line were men of Morayshire, the last of the old Celtic rearguard; Moray remained the main obstacle to the Normanization and Anglicization of Scotland by the House of Alpin, spearheaded by Malcolm III and his descendants.

Lumphanan

In point of fact, Macbeth ruled wisely and justly until 1057. His reputation as a strong but generous ruler is accepted by modern historians.[10] Shakespeare's play and certain hostile chronicles present Macbeth as a usurper and murderer, Lady Macbeth as a monster encouraging her husband; the myth refuses to go away.

Macbeth was respected by his people; he was also generous to the Church. For example, in 1050, he is said to have distributed money to the poor in Rome[11] which confirms that he had gone on pilgrimage to the Eternal City, where he 'scattered money like seed'.[12] Macbeth's wife Gruoch gave lands to the Culdee (from the Celtic *Cele De*, meaning an associate or attendant of God) community of St Serfs, Lochleven, a religious order associated with the Celtic branch of the Catholic Church in Scotland.*

Finally, at Lumphanan, near The Mounth in Aberdeenshire, Malcolm attacked and slew Macbeth in 1057. There are scant details of the battle.

---

* *Liber Cartorum Prioratus St. Andrew in Scotland* (Bannotyne Club, 1841). The Culdees also had lands in St. Andrew, Glasgow, Iona, Dunkeld and Monymusk (Aberdeenshire).

Malcolm was crowned king at Scone but the death of Macbeth did not guarantee peace. Macbeth's stepson Lulach 'the Simple' challenged Malcolm until 1058 when he slew Lulach at Strathbogie, Aberdeenshire. Malcolm III (1058–93) became the undisputed ruler of Scotland. To strengthen his hold on the north, Malcolm married Ingibiorg, the widow of Thorfinn who had challenged Malcolm's father, Duncan I. Malcolm's position was stronger than any of his predecessors, which explains why he invaded Northumberland no fewer than five times during his reign, seeking to extend his southern border. By 1070 Malcolm's wife Ingibiorg had died as that year he married Margaret, sister of Edgar Atheling, the Saxon heir to the English throne whom William the Conqueror had driven from England in 1068. In his last attempt take Northumberland in 1093, Malcolm was slain – some say treacherously – by a a friend.[13] His queen, Margaret, died of grief a few days later.

There was, however, a continuing division in the country now known as Scotia; no single ruler, no matter how resolute and determined was likely to be acceptable to the northern Celts and the southern peoples. However, be that as it may, the reigns of Malcolm III's sons Edgar (1097–1107), Alexander I (1107–24) and David I (1124–53) were fortunate in that they were free from any significant battles. When David I inherited the throne in 1124, his reign saw the second period of consolidation of Scotland as a nation. It has to be said that the most potent support which sustained him in all his undertakings came from the Norman knights and barons he had invited to Scotland to settle and marry into the noble families. The Norman parvenues readily offered David support when the landowners of Moray revolted against his rule. Angus and Malcolm MacHeth, grandsons of Lulach, raised an army to challenge David's right to the throne of Scotland. This came about in 1130 during David's absence in England attending to his affairs and estates there, gained through his marriage to Matilda, granddaughter of Earl Siward of Northumberland.

Stracathro
Fortunately for David, he had a strong Constable of Scotland, Edward fitz Siward of Mercia (no relation to Earl Siward of Northumberland) to govern the country during his visit south. At the subsequent battle of Stracathro near Brechin, Forfarshire (modern Angus), on 16 April 1130 Edward of Mercia defeated Angus MacHeth, slaying 4,000 of his followers; Edward's casualties were 1,000. Despite this crushing defeat, for the next five years Angus MacHeth's elder brother Malcolm would hold out against David. Eventually an exasperated David appealed to the barons in the north of England to assist him in subduing his troublesome Celtic subjects. Learning of this, Malcolm's supporters handed him over without a fight to David who imprisoned the

troublesome Celt in Roxburgh Castle for the next twenty-three years. Thus Moray became an integral part of the kingdom. By way of reward, David divided Morayshire between those northern England barons and the native nobles he felt he could trust.

When David died in 1153, his younger brother Malcolm IV (1153–65), known to history as 'The Maiden' succeeded him. Despite his less than manly soubriquet, Malcolm was courageous and was never slow to bring to account those who opposed his rule. In 1153 Donald MacHeth, son of that Malcolm MacHeth still held prisoner in Roxburgh, was titular head of the House of Moray and was determined to challenge Malcolm IV. On his own it is doubtful if Donald could have achieved very much but he formed an alliance with a much more powerful man in the person of Somerled, Lord of Argyle and Kintyre who established a 'Kingdom' of the Isles and refused to acknowledge Malcom IV as his superior. Having given his daughter in marriage to Donald MacHeth, Somerled had hopes that his son-in-law would ascend the throne. For three years Somerled and Donald carried out raids in various parts of the kingdom until finally, in 1156, Donald was taken prisoner at Whithorn and joined his father in Roxburgh Castle. As for Somerled, his attention was drawn elsewhere until, in 1164, he again challenged Malcolm IV.

Renfrew
Somerled's bile had been quietly simmering away for the past eight years despite the release of Malcolm and Donald MacHeth from imprisonment in Roxburgh. More powerful than ever, Somerled, styling himself King of the Western Isles and Lord of Argyle, gathered an army of Western Islesmen reinforced by troops from Ireland and landed at Renfrew. Supported by a fleet of 100 galleys, Somerled threw down a gauntlet which Malcolm IV accepted. However, the young king was spared a battle. Sailing up the Clyde to Renfrew, Somerled had hardly disembarked when he and his son Gillecolm were slain in an act of treachery at the 'Bloody mire of Renfrew'.[14] Hardly a bloody battle, the men of Glasgow who opposed Somerled offered thanks for their victory to their patron saint, Kentigern.

So what was the significance of Renfrew? The historian T. C. F. Brotchie contends that the Highland Celts and the Galloway Irish – meaning the Gallgaels or descendants of the old Dalriadic Scots – never fully recovered from Renfrew.[15] The event does not support Brotchie's claim that it was a major battle. More of a raid, Renfrew's importance lay in the fact that it would be a century before the reign of a Scottish monarch was threatened again.

The reign of Alexander III (1249–86) was unmarked by any major battle save one action, more running fight than battle. Known as 'the peaceful king', like his father, Alexander II (1214–49), Alexander III attempted to purchase the Western Isles[16] from Haakon IV of Norway. He sent a diplomatic mission to Norway in 1262, hoping that Haakon would respond favourably to his offer. The Norwegian king had not changed in his resolve since the death of Alexander II thirteen years earlier, nor was he in the mood to submit to the overtures of a mere stripling whose offer he regarded as derisory as his father's had been. Besides, around 1260, Haakon's subject peoples on Skye had been attacked by the Earl of Ross, no doubt with the knowledge and agreement of Alexander. The Earl of Ross had indiscriminately slaughtered men, women and children; accounts of this lurid episode appear in the Norwegian sagas.[17]

Haakon detained the Scottish royal envoys under house arrest until he was pressurized by Henry III of England – Alexander's father-in-law – to release the hostages. Haakon complied, informing Henry that he had no hostile intentions towards Scotland, but this was simply a delaying tactic. In the spring of 1263 Haakon commanded all his peoples to meet him at Bergen where he assembled a fleet of 120-160 war galleys – the precise figure is disputed – and set sail for Orkney in the summer of that year. While anchored in Ronaldsvoe, Orkney, a strange sight was seen in the heavens – that of a lunar eclipse of the sun.[18] Despite this unfavourable portent, Haakon was undeterred; his fleet proceeded down the west coast of Scotland, sweeping round the Mull of Kintyre and anchored off Arran and in the bay of Ayr.

Largs

News of Haakon's 'invasion' reached Alexander who immediately gathered an army which he assembled near the coast at Kilbirnie, Ayrshire. Word reached him that sixty of the war-galleys had detached from the main fleet, making their way up the Firth of Clyde to disappear into Loch Long. At Kilbirnie, Alexander watched Haakon's main fleet closely.

On his route along the west coast, Haakon had proceeded to Arran, visiting several islands and receiving homage from their chieftains. Lying off Arran, Haakon invited Alexander to the negotiating table. The Scottish king then played a waiting game; he sent his negotiators to Haakon to ascertain the Norwegian's intentions. Haakon informed the royal envoys that his minimum demand was the unconditional surrender of the Western Isles to Norway in perpetuity. He sailed to the Cumbrae Islands and prepared to invade mainland Scotland near Ayr. Meanwhile, the Scottish army decamped from Kilbirnie during the continuing negotiations, encamping on the heights of the bay of Largs. It was late in the season. The notoriously fierce gales of autumn were due. Save for the severity of the weather, the events which followed on 2 October 1263 are far from clear and there are contradictory accounts of the action in the Norwegian sagas and the Scottish chronicles.[19]

That day the long-awaited gales arrived. The tempest of hail and rain created havoc in the Norwegian fleet. After the storm abated the Scots looked down on the grey beaches between Largs and Fairlie. They saw five galleys beached while, in the bay of Ayr, many others were dismasted, labouring at their anchor cables. Haakon ordered his dispirited warriors ashore. Drawn up in battle order, his men were determined to rescue the beached galleys. Sensing victory, the Scots charged down from the heights, scattering the Norsemen. In the ensuing skirmish the Norsemen lost heart. Accounts of the battle of Largs – if it may be called that – differ greatly, depending on which side the protagonists fought. The Norwegian accounts glorify the brave stand of their countrymen, defiant and heroic in the face of defeat. The Scottish annals tell a different story, proving that accepted history is written by the victorious. Largs conforms to this rule. We must concede that the victory was not won by Alexander III; it was achieved by Nature. Haakon's mighty fleet was neutralized by Scottish weather. The few Norsemen engaged in battle with the Scottish army had little choice but to return to their longships and make their escape. In the stormy seas, many of the disabled vessels foundered, their crews drowned.

A dispirited Haakon withdrew to Orkney where he took ill at the end of October, dying at Kirkwall in December. In itself Largs achieved nothing for Scotland. However, in 1264, Haakon's successor Magnus 'The Law-Maker' came to the negotiating table. But it would be a further two years before the Western Isles question would be resolved for once and for all. Under the Treaty of Perth in 1266 Norway sold the Western Isles to the Scottish Crown. The settled price was 4,000 merks (about £2,666) with an annuity of 1,000 merks (£66) paid indefinitely; the annuity was paid until the fourteenth century on condition that Norway would continue to occupy Orkney and Shetland. In 1281, in a gesture of friendship, Alexander III gave his daughter Margaret in marriage to King Eric of Norway, the successor to Magnus, the wedding taking place at Roxburgh.

Largs was the highwater mark of Norwegian aspirations in offshore Scotland.[20] The Scandivanian presence was limited to Orkney and Shetland and even that would soon disappear. All that is left today to mark the Viking occupation are place names such as Brodick (Norwegian *brodvick*, meaning a broad bay) on the island of Arran. After Largs, Scotland would enjoy over two decades of peace. Alexander's untimely and tragic death in 1286 without an heir to his throne would plunge Scotland into chaos for years, as we shall presently see.

Notes

1. Hume Brown, *History of Scotland*, vol. i, p.40.
2. Lynch, *Scotland: A New History*, p.47.
3. Hume Brown, op. cit., p.43.
4. Hume Brown, op. cit., p.52.
5. Oliver, *A History of Scotland*, p.60.
6. Hume Brown, op. cit., p.54.
7. Marshall, R. K., *Scottish Queens*, p.3; also, Duncan's brother Maldred married Algatha, daughter of Uchtred, Earl of Northumberland before Siward (Pugh, *Swords, Loaves and Fishes: A History of Dunbar*, p.58)
8. Lynch, op. cit., p.50.
9. Lynch, op. cit., p.49.
10. Hume Brown, op. cit., pp.54–55.
11. Hume Brown, op. cit., p54.
12. Lynch, op, cit., p.50.
13. Notably Hume Brown, op. cit., p.61.
14. Brotchie, *The Battlefields of Scotland*, p.27. Brotchie states there is reason to believe that Somerled and his son were slain in an act of treachery.
15. Brotchie, op. cit., p.28.
16. The Hebrides (Western Isles) consist of Lewis, Harris, Benbecula, North and South Uist, Barra, Skye, Mull, Islay, Jura, Coll, Rum, Tiree and Colonsay. (Arran, Bute and the Great and Little Cumbrae islands are not considered part of the Hebrides.)
17. *The Surlunga Saga* (1260) and the *Flateyan* and *Frisian* MSS (quoted in Brotchie, op. cit., p.38.)
18. Brotchie, op. cit., p.40.
19. The Scottish version of events are to be found in the *Chronicle of Melrose* and Andrew Wyntoun's *Orygynale Cronikyl of Scotland*.
20. However, although after Largs, Alexander effectively annexed the Western Isles, in 1346, a chief of the Clan MacDonald descended from Somerled assumed the title 'Lord of the Isles'. This MacDonald may have been Angus Mor MacDonald, great-grandson of Somerled. Angus MacDonald's successors affected to be semi-independent from Scotland until King James V annexed the Western Isles into Scotland in 1540.

Chapter 4

The Wars of Independence: 1296–1313

The Wars of Independence justifiably occupy a defining place in the history of Scotland. Before embarking on a record of the events which took place during the long, dour Wars of Independence, let us first examine the condition of the country in the remaining years of the reign of Alexander III (1249–86). In the latter half of the thirteenth century Scotland's population was about 500,000. The majority of the people lived and worked in the countryside, earning their daily bread from the land. However, the royal burghs which David I established in the twelfth century in the interests of trade – both domestic and overseas – had increased in number, attracting a significant percentage of the working population to settle in towns on the east coast like Berwick-upon-Tweed. Others such as Edinburgh, Dundee, Aberdeen, Elgin, Inverness and Perth were not only trading with their less privileged neighbours but Europe as well; we know that by the thirteenth century, Scottish royal burghs were engaged in commerce with towns such as Lübeck and Hamburg, two of the Hanseatic League of trading ports. In the west, Ayr, Dumfries, Glasgow, Irvine and Renfrew exchanged trade with Ireland and even western England.

The country's wealth lay chiefly in wool; the great Abbeys of Melrose, Dryburgh, Jedburgh and others grew rich on the wool-clip from the vast flocks of sheep pastured not only in their own immediate vicinity of the Merse but through the Lammermuir Hills and into East Lothian. (The name Lammermuir derives from the old Celtic *lamber-mohr* meaning great sheep hills.) Trade in fish, timber and animal hides was also profitable and, like wool, these were exported to the Continent.

As we have seen, Alexander III had made a good marriage to Margaret, daughter of Henry III. Among the honoured guests at their wedding was a prince who would earn the epithet 'Hammer of the Scots' when he became Edward I (1272–1307). Alexander was determined to present his kingdom as a free, independent nation to the English crown, an equal partner as well as an equally important realm.

Alexander III's marriage to Margaret of England had produced three children, two sons, Alexander and David and a daughter, Margaret, before she died in 1275. The succession seemed secure. As we saw in the previous chapter, Alexander gave his daughter Margaret in marriage to King Eric II of Norway to cement the new-found friendship between the two countries following the Norwegian debacle at the battle of Largs. However, before the wedding took place, the young Prince David died. A year later, Margaret and Eric produced their only child, a daughter named after her mother; sadly Queen Margaret died giving birth to her daughter. At least Alexander's remaining son, Prince Alexander, was healthy; he married in 1283 and there seemed every likelihood that his marriage would produce a son and heir. However, Prince Alexander fell ill and died in January 1284.

Immediately after the death of his last male heir, Alexander convened a council at Scone to settle the succession on his granddaughter, known to Scottish history as 'The Fair Maid of Norway'. His nobles agreed to this, albeit reluctantly, as many held the view that only a male heir should succeed to the throne. However, aged forty-three, Alexander could still produce heirs and to this end he married Yolande, the young and fertile daughter of Robert IV, Comte de Dreux, Dreux being a town near Chartres in France. It was highly likely that Yolande would give Alexander the male heir he wanted. This was not to be.

On 19 March 1286 Alexander held a council in Edinburgh Castle. It was a wild, tempestuous day, with equinoctial gales that brought sleet and hail. It was nightfall before Alexander completed consultations with his nobles. Despite the atrocious weather and against the advice of his counsellors, Alexander insisted on taking horse to join Queen Yolande at Kinghorn. While, to modern eyes, his decision seems foolhardy, we must judge Alexander on the prevailing issue uppermost in his mind – his need for a male heir.

When he reached the Firth of Forth, even the ferryman who would row him to Inverkeithing argued against the journey. Alexander was adamant and disembarked with his small retinue. When the party reached Inverkeithing the night was so dark that his companions could distinguish each other only by their voices and even their words were carried away on the fierce winds. Alexander pressed on with only two guides, trusting on the instincts of their horses to make safe passage. Just before reaching Kinghorn, Alexander's horse stumbled in the dark and plunged over a steep cliff on to the sands below. The next morning, the King was found dead, his neck broken. When news of his death was broadcast the nation was plunged into despair.

Alexander left Scotland a prosperous and consolidated kingdom but his failure to produce a male heir to succeed him was as tragic as his untimely death. An assembly was convened at Scone on 11 April to discuss the late king's successor. The sole legitimate descendant of Alexander, his granddaughter Margaret, 'The Fair Maid of Norway', an infant in a foreign country, could hardly be expected to rule the country. A regency of six lords spiritual and temporal was appointed to govern Scotland. This unhappy council faced insurmountable problems. An infant female heir was bad enough; quarrels broke out among the nobility which formed into factions and there was a band of competitors eager to profit from the Fair Maid's death should that occur before she reached her majority, which was years away. Also, hovering in the wings was a ruthless English king who was hell-bent on annexing Scotland and making it his feudal fiefdom. Trouble came in the person of Robert the Bruce of Annandale. In 1238 Alexander II had designated him as his successor before Alexander III was born. Bruce, known in this account as Bruce the Competitor, was in advanced years but his claim to the throne would be supported by his son Robert, known as Bruce the Elder and his grandson, also Robert, known as Bruce the Younger until he became King Robert the Bruce in 1306.

It was in the year 1289 that events began to develop at an ever-increasing pace. In that year Eric II of Norway sent commissioners to England concerning the affairs of his daughter, the Fair Maid and lawful heir to the throne of Scotland. Eric was hardly in a position to act independently of the council of six guardians appointed to rule Scotland during his daughter's minority. That council was comprised of two clergymen, William Fraser, Bishop of St Andrews and Robert Wishart, Bishop of Glasgow, Alexander Comyn, 2nd Earl of Buchan, Duncan MacDuff, Earl of Fife and two barons, John Comyn, 2nd Lord of Badenoch and James the Steward. Together, the six represented the major political parties – the Bruce/Stewart and the Comyn/Balliol factions. (John Balliol, Lord of Galloway had family ties with the Comyns in the north as his sister had married into the Comyn family.)

At the request of Edward I and apparently with the unanimous agreement of the six guardians, four commissioners from Scotland were sent to England to support King Eric of Norway's claim on behalf of his daughter as rightful queen of Scotland. Three of the commissioners were guardians – Wishart, Fraser and Comyn, 2nd Lord of Badenoch; the fourth was Bruce the Competitor. These commissioners were charged with the task of assenting to whatever King Eric of Norway's representatives proposed. The resulting treaty did not mince matters; the Scots would receive their young queen only on condition that order would be established in the country and that the council of guardians were to be no more than in nominal command and appointed by Edward I. A further condition was that the young queen could not be married without the consent of her father, advised by Edward. One does not have to be a genius to understand the motives behind these conditions; Edward had his mind set on the subjugation of Scotland and expected her monarch – whoever that would be – to pay homage to him as Scotland's feudal superior.

Edward I had already decided that the Fair Maid of Norway should marry none other than his son Edward of Caernarfon. Edward submitted no formal overture to the Scottish Council of Guardians, nor to Eric of Norway but by 1290 his intentions became known to the Scots. In March 1290 the Scottish parliament met at Brigham-on-Tweed; it was attended by Scotland's nobles, clergy and the Community of the Realm. The parliament engrossed a charter signed by twelve earls giving their consent to the marriage of the Fair Maid of Norway to Edward's son, the future Edward II. This decision was relayed to Eric of Norway and Edward I, both of whom accepted it; a 'Solemn Treaty' between the Scottish parliament and Edward's commissioners was drawn up at Brigham-on-Tweed on 18 July 1290 ratifying the proposed marriage while preserving Scotland's sovereignty. The treaty also stipulated that no vassal of the Scottish crown would be required to pay homage for their Scottish lands to Edward I; further, Scotland's laws, rights and ancient liberties would continue entire and inviolate. Eric of Norway was also required to send the Fair Maid of Norway to England at the earliest possible moment.

The Treaty of Brigham was a compromise which Edward I exploited to his fullest advantage. On the surface, his initial reaction seemed favourable; he even took an oath to defend the laws of Scotland, appointing Anthony Bek, Bishop of Durham to reinforce his oath in Scotland and to protect the Fair Maid's interests – meaning his own. This was a cynical move on Edward's part; Bek's presence in the Scottish Council of Guardians can be interpreted in only one way; he was thus able to monitor the Council's activities. Emboldened by this, Edward next demanded that all the main strongholds in Scotland should be surrendered into his hands, a demand the Scots resolutely opposed. Edward apparently took the rebuff in good part – for the moment.

Then, as if the Scots had not suffered enough with the death of their King, a further calamity threw the realm into panic and despair. In the month of September 1290 the Fair Maid set sail from Norway for England and her wedding; tragically, she died at Orkney in October. The Maid's death denied Edward the special position he had engineered to interfere in Scotland's constitutional and domestic affairs; however, his hopes were boosted by assistance from an unexpected quarter. On 7 October 1290 William Fraser, Bishop of St Andrews wrote to him, describing the parlous state of the kingdom and claimed that it was poised on the brink of civil war, with factions of Scottish nobles quarrelling with each other. Matters concerning the succession to the throne had come to a head with the rival claims for kingship by Bruce the Competitor and John Balliol. Fraser urged Edward to intervene in the dispute to avoid bloodshed. Edward grasped this opportunity with unconcealed glee. He responded by inviting the Scottish nobles and clergy to meet him at Norham-on-Tweed on 10 May 1291. (Norham Castle was the fortified home of Bishop Bek.) At the outset of the proceedings, Edward described himself as Superior and Lord Paramount of Scotland and that he saw his role as settling the affairs of the country. The Scottish Guardians, nobility and clergy were stunned by his audacity but they had little choice other than to submit to Edward's demands in the interests of settling the succession question. This became known as 'The Great Cause' – the bid to decide the rightful heir to the Scottish throne, with Edward I as judge and jury. Thirteen claimants[1] submitted their petitions, Bruce the Competitor coming first, John Balliol last.

Events had reached a watershed in the spring of 1291. The Scottish Guardians agreed to meet Edward at Norham on 10 May. Edward demanded they acknowledge his rights as feudal superior over Scotland; he gave the Scots three weeks to prepare their reply. The Guardians responded in courteous and diplomatic terms but were unequivocal in one respect. The Guardians informed Edward they had no knowledge of any document confirming his right to claim superiority over Scotland:

> Nor did they [the Guardians] ever see it claimed by you and your ancestors, therefore they answer you as far as in them lies, that they have no power to reply to your statement in default of a Lord to whom that demand ought to be addressed and who will have power to answer to it.[2]

On 5 June Edward appointed 140 commissioners to examine the claims of the thirteen competitors – forty each for Bruce and Balliol and sixty for the other eleven. On 6 and 11 June nine competitors solemnly swore that *saisin* (ownership) of Scotland and its royal castles be surrendered to Edward who by then had promised to announce his decision on the succession by 2 August.[3]

Shabby though the events of June 1291 appear to modern eyes, they were necessary and inevitable. There was not a single direct or legitimate – in terms of birth – survivor from the last three generations of Scottish kings; many of the thirteen claimants were foreign, remote, their claims based on extremely shaky and tenuous grounds. Only four, all descended from Henry, son of David I, had anything approaching a legitimate claim. Of these, Edward himself acknowledged that only Bruce the Competitor and John Balliol had strong claims – hence the appointment of forty auditors each to investigate their merits. Bruce had the claim of nearness of degree, whereas Balliol enjoyed the prerogative of seniority of line.

So, as mentioned above, the demeaning 'negotiations' of June 1291 must be viewed in the context of their time. In Scotland, a system of government had collapsed; underlying this were the serious divisions between the nobility and the senior clergymen as to whom should rule the country. Without a king the feudal system could not operate effectively and decisively. Edward I, self-confessed champion of the code of chivalry and feudal law – when these suited his purpose – was a devious and cunning ruler who would brook no challenge to his authority and was devoid of any genuine compassion for a country he knew to be prostrated at his feet. All he had to do was to summon his scribes and dictate terms in the full knowledge that the Scottish magnates could hardly refuse his demands, even if they wanted to.

The way seemed clear for Edward's decision but he stalled, rubbing salt into already smarting wounds on 13 June 1291 at Uppsettlington[4], a small hamlet on the north bank of the Tweed (now known as Ladykirk, which has a certain ring of irony in its name). It was there that the Scottish Guardians and other nobles were required to swear fealty to Edward. Among the twenty-seven signatories were the Bruces of Annandale (Robert the Competitor and Bruce the Elder), Balliol, Atholl, Mar, Randolph, Comyn of Badenoch, two de Umfravilles and Stewart of Menteith.

Gradually the thirteen contenders were reduced to two – Bruce the Competitor and John Balliol. Under modern Scottish law, Bruce's claim was the stronger as he was closer to the throne through his mother Isabella, daughter of William I's brother, David of Huntingdon. However, under feudal law, John Balliol's claim took precedence; although he was the great-grandson of Isabella's sister Margaret, the latter was senior which gave him the edge on Bruce. Bruce argued against Balliol's claim, declaring it to be weaker than his own since it was based on Balliol's mother Dervorgilla's relationship to the royal line whereas Bruce's claim was based on his father's marriage to Isabella. He was also at pains to remind Edward's auditors that he had been named as Alexander II's heir in 1238. Bruce's appeals were dismissed out of hand. Edward chose Balliol for legal and political reasons; in Bruce the Competitor, Edward saw a man who would be less compliant than the weak John Balliol. To his credit Bruce the Competitor accepted Edward's judgement; on 7 November 1291 he quietly transferred his claim to the throne to his son, Bruce the Elder and his heirs. Two days later Bruce the Elder gave his earldom of Carrick to his son Bruce the Younger, then aged eighteen. It was clear that the two senior Bruces saw the younger Bruce as potential ruler of Scotland. By 1310 the propaganda of the Bruce cause would assert that the patriotic people of Scotland had always believed that Bruce the Competitor had had the rightful and legal claim to the throne of Scotland and that his grandson, Robert the Bruce, had inherited the right to be king.

Balliol, that unhappy king, was crowned at Scone on St Andrew's Day, 30 November 1292. He would be the last king of Scotland to be crowned on the Stone of Destiny which would be appropriated by Edward I in 1296.*

From the outset Balliol was nothing more than a vassal of the King of England, bending his knee to his feudal superior Edward I at every turn. At Newcastle, on 26 December 1292, Balliol swore fealty to Edward, addressing him as 'Lord Superior of the Realm of Scotland'. Bruce the Competitor withdrew from what he considered an ignominious and shameful ceremony; he died in 1295, never having sworn allegiance to Edward.

Edward's true intentions towards Scotland soon became apparent. In 1294 he summoned the English parliament to advise and provide funds for a contemplated expedition into his fiefdom of Gascony, English interests there being managed by Philip IV of France. Edward summoned Balliol to his side and on 29 June ordered the Scottish king and ten of his earls and fourteen barons who possessed lands in England to reinforce him in his expedition. Balliol returned to Scotland to raise money and troops for the forthcoming campaign; he found his nobles and subjects in no mood to defer to Edward's demands. A defiant council held at Scone agreed that all English subjects were to be expelled from the Scottish court, their Scottish estates being forfeited to the Crown. Edward had other problems to preoccupy him; in addition to his proposed French campaign, a rebellion in Wales had to be subdued and so the expedition to Gascony was postponed. Angered by Balliol's intransigence, Edward demanded reparation; Balliol protested his loyalty and, by way of appeasing the English King, offered the castles of Roxburgh, Berwick and Jedburgh to the Bishop of Carlisle. It was an empty gesture. By now the Scottish nobles were in despair of their weak King.

On 5 July 1295 the Scottish parliament effectively removed the reins of power from the lacklustre Balliol's hands. A council, or Standing Committee of twelve magnates – four earls, four barons and four bishops – was appointed to govern the country. Earlier that year Philip IV of France had appealed to the Scots to enter – or renew – an alliance with France against England. The Council of Twelve ratified this, the Treaty of Paris pledging mutual support against England; this formal treaty became known as the *Auld Alliance*.[5] The treaty was signed by Balliol and Philip IV, 'Le Bel', and kept secret from

---

* The stone of destiny was returned to Scotland in 1997, on the inauguration of the Scottish Parliament.

Edward; ratified by the Scottish parliament on 23 October 1295, the alliance would remain in place for over three centuries.

Meanwhile, events in Scotland were proceeding at a pace with a *wapinshaw* (a medieval muster of able-bodied men) being called in February 1296. Parliament issued a summons for war, an order which Bruce the Elder, de Umfraville of Angus and the Earl of Dunbar studiously ignored; Balliol's reaction was to declare their estates forfeit to the Crown. The three nobles were hardly troubled; they had sworn allegiance to Edward I and knew he would restore their lands. Edward retaliated to Scotland's declaration of war by issuing writs for the seizure of all English estates owned by those Scottish nobles who refused to join him against Balliol. Perhaps because Scottish morale was low, more than eighty Scottish nobles met Edward at Wark Castle, Northumberland, to pay homage to him. Among those present were Bruce the Elder, de Umfraville and Dunbar who swore they would serve him

> well and loyally against all mortal men, on every occasion we are so required or instructed by our lord the king of England and his heirs ...[6]

Even so, there was no mass exodus of the patriotic nobles to France; instead, the common army and the feudal host gathered at the traditional mustering-point at Caddonlee, near Selkirk, on 11 March 1296. An invasion force was organized and led by John 'the Black' Comyn, 2nd Lord of Badenoch, his son, John 'the Red' Comyn and Badenoch's cousin, John Comyn, 3rd Earl of Buchan. The expedition entered Cumberland; apart from an orgy of looting and plundering, the raid was inconclusive, although for a single day, the Scots besieged Carlisle Castle held by Bruce the Elder for Edward. Edward would wreak a terrible revenge for this insult. In the spring of 1296 the English army numbered 4,000 heavy cavalry and 25,000 infantry, many of whom were veterans of Edward's Welsh campaigns. By contrast, the Scottish host was inexperienced, having seen no action in the field since Largs in 1263; it contained few archers and only light cavalry which were scant in number. As for the 40,000 infantry, many were old men and boys, armed with mere farm tools for weapons.

While the Scottish host was attacking Carlisle, Edward's army had mustered at Newcastle and now confronted Berwick, one of the earliest of the Scottish royal burghs. Crossing the Tweed at Coldstream, Edward exacted a terrible price from the people of Berwick on 30 March 1296, offering no quarter. The siege of Berwick lasted three hours, the sack of the town three days. Between 7,000 and 8,000 were put to the sword; only thirty Flemish merchants occupying the town's Red Hall put up any resistance but they were slaughtered to a man. Comyn of Badenoch (the Black Comyn) had retreated over the Border after the unsuccessful siege of Carlisle, then he re-crossed the Tweed on 1 April, leading an inconclusive raid in Northumberland. Balliol's sole response to the sack of Berwick was to withdraw his *diffidato* (the feudal term for homage) to Edward; this was delivered by the Abbot of Arbroath to the English king in Berwick on 5 April.

War had broken out suddenly and brutally. The populations of the Merse (Berwickshire) and East Lothian were panic-stricken, even if their feudal superior, Patrick, 8th Earl of Dunbar had sworn allegiance to Edward. The knight-tenants who owed homage to Dunbar were obliged – and probably glad – to do so as their lands would hopefully escape the retribution Edward had wrought on Berwick. Then, on 23 April, news reached the English king at Berwick that the Scottish host had laid siege to Dunbar Castle. Edward lost no time in meeting the challenge.

Dunbar I

The spirit of revolt in 1296 was far-reaching; just as the untimely death of Alexander III in 1286 had deprived the nobles and the Community of the Realm of a figurehead on whom the functioning of the feudal system depended, the Scottish nobles had taken a dangerous step in dismissing John Balliol as their lawful king. Men such as Sir John de Graham, John Comyn, 2nd Lord of Badenoch, John Comyn, 3rd Earl of Buchan, Sir John de Soulis, Sir Andrew Murray of Bothwell, John de Strathbogie, Earl of Atholl, Alexander, Earl of Menteith, Bishop William Lamberton of St Andrews and Bishop William Wishart of Glasgow were determined to resist the invader even without a resolute king to lead them in battle.

In April 1296 Patrick, 8th Earl of Dunbar was in Berwick, attending the war council convened by Edward I when news arrived there that Dunbar's Countess Marjorie Comyn had handed over his castle to her brother, John Comyn of Buchan. Dunbar, who lived in perpetual fear and awe of Edward I, was devastated; not only had he lost face on account of his wife's insolent act, but his pledge to hand over Dunbar Castle to Edward as a base for operations in the south-east was broken. Nothing appears to have been recorded about Edward's views on the matter but, doubtless, he held Dunbar in contempt and would have shown it. No matter, he detached a portion of his large army under the command of John de Warenne, 7th Earl of Surrey, and William de Beauchamp, 9th Earl of Warwick, the latter a veteran of Edward's campaigns in Wales. Warenne and Warwick were given express orders to relieve Dunbar Castle; on 25 April, they marched out of Berwick with a force of 1,000 heavy cavalry and 10,000 infantry. It is not known if the Earl of Dunbar accompanied them.

Countess Marjorie Dunbar, daughter of the late Alexander Comyn, 2nd Earl of Buchan did not share her husband's enthusiasm for Edward I. Whether she acted on impulse or was persuaded by her Comyn kinsmen to give up Dunbar Castle is not recorded; it is more than likely that, appalled by the reports of the massacre at Berwick, she decided to support her kinsmen. (According to one source the Earl of Mar declared Patrick Dunbar a traitor and persuaded Marjorie to surrender his castle as a matter of honour.) Dunbar's brother Alexander, who was in command of the castle, knew he could not hold out against the Comyns with his pitifully small garrison; on 25 April he surrendered the castle to the patriots.

Dunbar Castle was placed in the charge of Sir Richard Siward, a man renowned and respected in feats of arms. Warenne and Warwick arrived at Dunbar Castle on 26 April and immediately laid siege to it from both land and sea. For a day the defenders did little more than glower at the besieging forces until Warenne learnt that the Scottish host commanded by the Comyns of Badenoch and Buchan was camped at the foot of Doon Hill, which overlooks Dunbar. Warenne left the siege of the castle to a few junior officers in command of a token force as he knew the garrison was hardly able to sally out; Siward and his defenders were going nowhere, expecting Warenne and Warwick to be defeated by the Comyns. Warenne led the bulk of his force, intent on engaging the Scottish host which he knew was camped about two miles south of Dunbar.

According to English chroniclers of the day the Scottish host numbered 40,000; the figure was probably closer to 4,000, with Warenne's 10,000 nearer 1,000. Contemporary accounts tended to exaggerate the strengths of armies to make the victors more victorious, the defeated ignominious; it is thought that each army at Dunbar and in other conflicts was a tenth of the figures given by the chroniclers, a fact which many modern historians support. Whatever the precise strengths of the Scottish and English armies, the Comyns outnumbered Warenne and Warwick by four to one at least.

It is not entirely certain where the battle was fought. Some historians consider it took place near a part of Spott Glen in the vicinity of a farm called *The Standards* for obvious reasons. One has to question whether the name dates as far back as 1296. However, more recent research suggests the battle took place near Wester Broomhouse which is within a bowshot or two of Spott Glen and its continuation, Oswald Dean. The valley, a deep defile formed by glacial activity, runs from the east of Spott village to Broxmouth on the coast. It is a picturesque glen, watered by a small, unimpressive burn or stream; its sides are steep, covered by straggles of gorse and stunted, windswept hawthorn bushes. In spring it is a bleak place which even a profusion of primroses fails to soften. It was in this obscure glen that cold steel would determine the fate of King John Balliol and the nation of Scotland.

The Scottish host was camped on or near Doon Hill. On the morning of 27 April, Comyn of Badenoch would have easily discerned the approach of Warenne's army, marching to Wester Broomhouse on the road to Spott Village. The dust raised by the men and horses would have pinpointed the English advance for more than a mile. The Scots waited, confident in the superiority of their numbers; however, apart from the fact that their largely untrained army was unaccustomed to warfare, it also lacked heavy cavalry and archers, crucial elements that day and in many to come in the Wars of Independence.

On that cold but bright spring day any flocks of sheep or cattle grazing in Spott Glen would have been driven away to safer fields. The English came on relentlessly, confident of victory and marching in good order. When Warenne reached Spott Glen or Oswald Dean the forward 'battles', as the medieval group formations – comparable to modern infantry battalions – were then known, descended into 'a valley' to form their line of battle. Changing from column to line was a delicate business; the most effective way of deploying an army into battle formation was to march it on to the field with units of the column wheeling right until the entire force was ordered to halt and then turn left to form a line facing the enemy. Although this sounds simple it would have been difficult to execute in the narrow confines of Oswald Dean. During this deploying movement the Scots thought Warenne was retreating.

Comyn of Badenoch appears to have planned no strategy or tactics other than to mount a frontal attack on the English; few if any troops were kept in reserve. For his part Warenne knew that his numerically inferior force would be hard-pressed to rebuff a frontal assault made by the superior number of Scots on the higher ground at the base of Doon Hill. He deployed his troops carefully, posting archers among the infantry in the front line; it was his intention to engage the Scottish left or right wing, then roll up the centre, a tactic Oliver Cromwell would use at Dunbar in 1650.

We can imagine the scene at Oswald Dean on that cold April day. Steel reflecting the weak sunshine, the only sound being that of neighing horses and the English pennons and banners snapping in the stiff wind that blew along the narrow valley. From his vantage point on Doon Hill Comyn of Badenoch had watched Warenne deploy his men; observing no further movement in the serried ranks of the English army, he ordered a full attack, launched from his strong position on the hill. (History would repeat itself in 1650). The Scottish van was packed with men and boys eager to engage the enemy; the undisciplined mass charged across the plain at the foot of Doon Hill, then down the slopes of Oswald Dean, blowing their horns to encourage those who followed. The precipitate charge was a disaster.

The unruly, screaming horde of peasants armed with inferior weapons – spades, scythes, axes and pitchforks – did not in the least confound the ranks of Warenne's disciplined professionals. Warenne protected his flanks with his 1,000 cavalry, with archers interspersed among the front-line infantry. That day the English fought under the banner of Edward I and their protecting saints – John of Beverley, Cuthbert of Durham and Wilfrid of York.

The English infantry stood fast, confident that their flanks were well protected by the horse which could quickly deploy and scatter any Scots who attempted to get behind them. The infantry and archers, observing the undisciplined mob that was the Scottish vanguard, let confusion do their work for them. Too many men in a confined space at Oswald Dean reduced the effect of Comyn's superiority in numbers, turning it to disadvantage. The order was given for the English archers to loose their deadly arrows that surely must have filled the sky. The shafts could scarcely fail to find a mark among the ragged mob leaping over Spott Burn in tightly packed, undisciplined bunches.

The foremost elements of the Scottish host were cut down in minutes, if not seconds; the fallen hindered the progress of those who followed. Dead and wounded began to pile up on the green sward. The tide of battle did not even remotely threaten the English foot, commanded by dismounted knights who no doubt stiffened their resolve by standing alongside their men, taunting the Scots. A welter of blood soon began to stain the turf at Oswald Dean.

The agony was over in less than half an hour. Hundreds – thousands, if the English chronicles of the day can be trusted – of dead eyes stared at the sky that dreadful April day. The English chroniclers numbered the Scottish dead in their thousands – 10,055, a suspiciously precise and high figure, even given the devastation wreaked by the English archers. We have little choice but to accept the contemporary English accounts, although it is often said that, in battle, the victors write the history. It made good propaganda for home consumption. Warenne's army had been out-numbered, yet he had prevailed. There does not appear to be any record of the English casualties.

The shattered bands of survivors ran from the field, seeking refuge in the Border forests, leaving their wounded at the mercy of Warenne's men. Among the undoubtedly numerous slain was Sir Patrick de Graham of Montrose who gave and expected no quarter; he alone was praised by the English for valiantly standing his ground. Another noble, Walter, Earl of Menteith, was taken prisoner and executed on Edward I's orders; other prisoners included the Earls of Atholl and Ross, members of the oldest Celtic noble families in Scotland. Dunbar Castle surrendered the same day as the battle; sheltering within its walls were Sir Richard Siward, John 'the Red' Comyn, son of Comyn of Badenoch and many other ransomable notables. More than 100 knights were taken into captivity in chains; they were sent to no fewer than twenty-five castles in England, the most prestigious including the Red Comyn – and valuable in terms of ransom money – being imprisoned in the Tower of London.

As for Countess Marjorie, doubtless she was rebuked by her husband, Patrick, Earl of Dunbar for her contumacy although the marriage survived. As far as is known, no such rebuke came from Edward I; in point of fact, Edward showed an unusual clemency towards the wives and daughters of those taken prisoner in Dunbar Castle, even to the extent of awarding them pensions. The English king could be chivalrous when it suited him.

After the battle of Dunbar, Edward I conquered Scotland with almost derogatory ease. Scottish resistance collapsed like a house of cards. In the subsequent weeks the castles of Roxburgh, Edinburgh, Perth and Stirling surrendered. As for his part, King John Balliol – ex-king in Edward's eyes – sent the English king a grovelling letter in which he confessed his fault, blaming his actions on false counsel. He apparently renounced the Treaty of Paris – the *Auld Alliance* – but this failed to pacify Edward; he was determined to humiliate Balliol to serve as a warning to any others attempting to gain the throne of Scotland and rise in rebellion. Balliol was attended by John Comyn, 3rd Earl of Buchan at Montrose Castle, where, on 5 July, Balliol surrendered to Edward. When the English king learnt of the alliance Balliol had made with France he was enraged. In an ignominious ceremony, Edward stripped the hapless king of his royal trappings; this involved the physical removal of Balliol's *tabard* – a knight's decorated outer garment worn over armour and blazoned with his coat of arms – his hood and knightly girdle, a punishment usually meted out to a knight found guilty of treason. Balliol became known in Scotland's history as *Toom Tabard* (Empty Coat); he was taken to the Tower of London along with his closest advisers, there to languish for a time before he was exiled to France, where he died in obscurity a few years later.

Edward was determined to strip Scotland herself of any symbols of her right to independence, along with every document held in the national archive supporting this claim. The Stone of Destiny at Scone, where many Scottish monarchs were crowned, the Holy Rood, the personal relic of Scotland's only saint, Margaret, wife of Malcolm III, and many documents were taken over the Border. The Great Seal of Scotland (*Magni Sigilli Regum Scotorum*) was broken up. This act tellingly revealed Edward's utter contempt for the country; on destroying the seal, Edward is supposed to have commented that 'a man does good business when he rids himself of a turd'.

Edward's sojourn in Scotland did not last long. The country was prostrated; Edward appointed John de Warenne, Earl of Surrey, as governor of Scotland and Hugh Cressingham as its treasurer. There is an interesting account of Edward's brief stay at Dunbar which goes thus:

On the day of St George, 24 [sic] April [1296] (St George's Day is actually 23 April), news came to the king that they of Scotland had besieged the Castle of Dunbar, which belonged to the earl [sic] Patrick, who held strongly with the king of England. It was upon a Monday that the king sent his troops to raise the siege. Before they came there, the castle had surrendered and they of Scotland were within when the troops of the king of England came there. They besieged the castle with three hosts on the Tuesday that they arrived before it. On the Wednesday, they who were within sent out privately [i.e. sent couriers to John Comyn, leader of the Scottish army] and on the Thursday and Friday came the host of Scotland all the afternoon to have raised the siege of the Englishmen. And when the Englishmen saw the Scotchmen [sic] they fell upon them and discomfited the Scotchmen, and the chase continued more than five leagues [about fifteen miles] of way, and until the hours of vespers [evening prayers] and there died sir [sic] Patrick de Graham, a great lord, and 10,055 by right reckoning. On the same Friday by night, the king came from Berwick to go to Dunbar, and lay that night at Coldingham [Priory] and on the Saturday [28 April] at Dunbar and on the same day they of the castle surrendered themselves to the king's pleasure. And there were the earl [sic] of Atholl, the earl of Ross, the earl of Menteith, sir [sic] John [the Red] Comyn of Badenoch, sir Richard Suart [Siward], sir William de Saintler [Sinclair] and as many as fourscore [sic] men-at-arms and sevenscore footmen. There tarried the king three days.[8]

The message that came loud and clear from the battle of Dunbar in 1296 was that patriotism alone was not enough. Edward had, however, forged a dangerous weapon. The rise of a strong and determined Nationalism would in time create a cohesive political and military force that would resist the kings of England for the next three centuries.

Edward I conquered Scotland in five months – April to August 1296, considerably less than the three wars over two decades he took to subdue Wales. In a parliament convened at Berwick on 28 August 1296, Edward made the final arrangements for the governing of Scotland. This time there would be no puppet king to interfere with whatever policy he might choose to adopt. In addition to Warenne and Cressingham, William Ormsby was appointed as Justiciar, or high judge. Edward also demanded the presence of every significant landowner in Scotland to pay him homage, accepting him as their liege lord. About 1,900 barons, knights and ecclesiastics answered his summons and attached their seals to what became known as the *Ragman's Roll*, so-named because it was festooned with waxen or lead endorsements. The names of Robert Bruce the Elder and Bruce the Younger appear which is of some significance; much more important were those signatures which are absent – notably that of William Wallace, knight of Elderslie, who in 1297, in the brief but stirring words of the historian John of Fordun, 'lifted up his head'.

Until 1296, Wallace was an obscure squire, living on the small estate of Elderslie, near Renfrew. His elder brother Malcolm held the land but the absence of their names from *Ragman's Roll* is surprising. Lesser men than the Wallaces saw fit to sign the roll and swear an oath of allegiance, so it cannot be said that the Wallaces were considered lowly.

It is probable that the family de Waleys was of Norman origin who came to England with William the Conqueror in 1066. William was the younger son of Sir Malcolm Wallace of Elderslie by marriage to Margaret, daughter of Sir Reynold Crawford, Sheriff of Ayr. William was born in c.1270; little of his life is known to us save through *The Actis and Deidis of the Illustere and Vailzeand Campioun Schir William Walleis, Knicht of Elderslie* (Acts and Deeds of the Illustrious and Valiant Champion, Sir William Wallace etc.) by Henry the Minstrel, better known as Blind Harry. Written two centuries after Wallace's death, Blind Harry's account owes more to romantic fiction than fact which obliges us to rely on the equally imperfect and heavily biased accounts of contemporary English chroniclers.

William Wallace's name comes to us first in 1297 when he appears to have been at odds with the by now occupying English administrators. Matters came to a head in May 1297, when the English murdered Wallace's common-law wife, Marion or Marron Braidfute; in revenge, Wallace slew William de Hazelrig, Sheriff of Lanark. In the same month Warenne and Cressingham were absent on business in England; Justiciar Ormsby was holding court at Scone when Wallace and his small following broke into the place, looted it and very nearly took Ormsby prisoner.[9] The idea persists that Wallace and his men were landless peasants, virtual outlaws, but this was not entirely the case. What mattered was that Wallace had shown the Scottish nobility it was possible to challenge England's authority and succeed. Contemporary English chroniclers certainly portray Wallace as an outlaw, a view echoed by Patrick, 8th Earl of Dunbar who, if we can believe Blind Harry, reputedly said this of him:

This king of Kyll I can nocht understand
Of him I held niver a fur [long] *of land.*[10]

It is thought that *Kyll* may derive from the Celtic *coille*, meaning a wood; Dunbar is therefore describing Wallace as a kind of Robin Hood, an outlaw of the forest.

While we rightly acknowledge Wallace as the dedicated, unflinching patriot that he undoubtedly remains in Scotland to this day, key leaders of the revolt against England were two of the former Guardians, Robert Wishart, Bishop of Glasgow and James the Steward, the latter being Wallace's feudal superior. They were joined by MacDuff, son of the Earl of Fife and Bruce the Younger, Earl of Carrick. After a farcical encounter with the English at Irvine in Ayrshire, Wishart and the Steward surrendered to the English commander. To his discredit, Bruce the Younger turned his coat for Edward I; he would continue in this fashion for nearly a decade, shifting his political position like a weather vane driven by the winds of change.

Only in the north was the revolt gaining momentum. Andrew Murray, son of a leading baron in Morayshire, was gaining a reputation for his bold and successful resistance to England's authority. Murray and his father had been prominent on the field of Dunbar in April 1296; both had been taken prisoner but the younger Murray escaped from his prison in Chester Castle intent on continuing the fight. By early autumn 1297 the series of isolated outbreaks against English authority had become co-ordinated.

During the summer of 1297 Wallace had engaged in a period of intensive training of his raw levies; he taught them discipline and how to fight in *schiltrons*, tightly packed circular formations of men with long spears, the only effective defence against the English heavy cavalry. Because of Murray's and Wallace's successes, they were made joint Guardians of Scotland, acknowledged as 'commanders of the army of the kingdom of Scotland and the Community of the Realm'.[11]

Stirling Bridge

Wallace was besieging Dundee Castle when word reached him that John de Warenne, Earl of Surrey, and Hugh Cressingham had crossed the Border with a large army intent on confronting the rebellious Scots at Stirling. Wallace broke off his siege of Dundee and hastened to meet up with Murray against Warenne and Cressingham at the bridge of Stirling. On 10 September Wallace took up position on the Abbey Craig, the precipitous height on the north bank of the river Forth, looking across to the town of Stirling and down upon a small, narrow wooden bridge which had been built by the monks of Cambuskenneth Abbey, near Stirling.

What followed is recorded by the English chroniclers of the day; the ensuing battle was as great a proof of the folly of the overconfidence of Warenne and Cressingham as much as Wallace's superior skill in strategy. An approach was made to Wallace, stationed on ground at one end of Stirling Brig, by the English high command, urging him to sue for peace. Wallace's reply was brief and resolute; he informed the English envoys he would fight for Scotland's freedom.

The only approach across the difficult and treacherous river Forth was by way of the wooden bridge. Despite being warned that the bridge would only allow passage of two horsemen riding abreast at one time, Warenne was adamant that his force would cross over. Cressingham was anxious to engage the Scots but argued that his colleague's tactics were unsound. Warenne was over-confident and irked by Cressingham's criticism; his 200 mounted knights and men-at-arms backed by several thousand well-armed foot soldiers were advised to cross the Forth at a ford about a mile upriver but Warenne was impatient. He ordered his men across Stirling Brig.

On the Abbey Craig Wallace and Murray could not believe their eyes. At the rate of passage across the bridge, it would have taken many hours before the entire English army could cross over and form up to engage the Scottish army. When the foremost units of the English cavalry reached the other side of the Forth they found themselves on ground too soft for an effective charge against the Scots. Also, at that point, the river Forth meandered in loops; the only passage which would allow the heavy English cavalry to advance was a narrow strip of dry and firm ground between two loops or curves of the Forth. Added to this, the English had their backs to the deep, fast-flowing river, their only exit being by way of the walkway they crossed – that crowded, narrow wooden bridge that would give its name to the defeat which followed. As one English chronicler put it, there was no better place to deliver the English into the hands of the Scots.[12]

Wallace and Murray stayed their hand until about half of Warenne's men were across the Forth, then they ordered the spearmen forward in *schiltron* formations. Neither English horsemen nor infantry were spared that day; riders were dragged from their terrified horses and slain. Cressingham himself was hauled from his horse and hacked to pieces. (It was said later that Wallace had the skin flayed from Cressingham's body to be made into a swordbelt.)[13]

Five thousand cavalry and infantrymen were killed at Stirling Brig. As for Warenne, he never ventured across the Bridge; he watched the slaughter from the south side of the Forth. After the

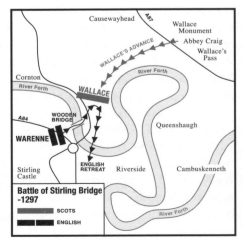

battle he ordered the bridge to be destroyed, then led the remainder of his shattered army to Stirling Castle, where he installed a Yorkshire knight who rejoiced in the faintly comical name of Sir Marmaduke Twenge as governor of the castle. Warenne then fled across the Border to report his defeat to Edward I.

The unthinkable had happened. A professional, well trained and well equipped English army had been virtually destroyed by a horde of amateurs, ill equipped and lacking proper arms. (It is likely that Wallace and Murray's men possessed little else by way of weapons other than the spades, axes and pitchforks the peasant army of John Comyn of Badenoch had fought with at Dunbar the year before.) The Scots had not only won a battle, they had gained a stunning, staggering victory, word of which spread not only in England but also on the Continent. Edward I's military machine, that had seemed invincible in Wales and had struck fear in the hearts of Frenchmen, had been beaten by a raggle-taggle army of peasants and minor clergy; true to his nature, James the High Steward of Scotland changed sides and reputedly joined in the looting of the English baggage train at Stirling.

However, Wallace's victory was bought at a price. Andrew Murray was mortally wounded at Stirling Brig, which left Wallace to continue the struggle as sole Guardian of Scotland. Wallace followed up his triumph by raiding East Lothian, then he carried the war into northern England, devastating parts of Northumberland as far as Hexham and looting Cumbria as far south as Cockermouth. For a month Wallace continued his raiding, sparing none – not even the clergy – then re-crossed the Border to be welcomed as the leader of Scotland's armies 'in the name of the illustrious King John [Balliol]'.[13] There is more than a hint of irony and even sarcasm in this although Wallace always maintained he was fighting in the name of Balliol, the lawful king of Scotland.

Edward, preoccupied with his French campaign, did not return to England until March 1298. He convened a parliament at York, summoning his barons and those of Scotland who had affixed their seals to the *Ragman's Roll*; most of these ignored his call to arms, perhaps not just because of Wallace's spectacular victory at Stirling but also because they feared reprisals from Wallace if they did.

Edward moved quickly. On 25 June 1298 he ordered the English army to muster at Roxburgh; it was a formidable force numbering 3,000 cavalry and 26,000 infantry. As he proceeded through the south-east, Edward devastated the land he marched over; only Dirleton Castle in East Lothian held out against him. Wallace withdrew before him, laying waste to stores of food to deny sustenance to the enemy. However, Edward had had the foresight to commission a fleet of provision ships to offload stores at Berwick; bad weather prevented this and soon the English army began to run low on food. By July, having reached Kirkliston in Midlothian, Edward's men were facing starvation when he received timely news. Wallace's army was a mere twenty miles away at Falkirk.

Falkirk I

On 21 July Edward confronted Wallace outside Falkirk. The English force which took the field numbered 1,500 cavalry and 10,000 infantry; although numerically inferior, Wallace's men were well positioned on rising ground. Formed up in four or five *schiltrons*, each containing 1,500 spearmen, with mounted spearmen in the centre, the Scots were determined to resist the invader at all costs. Apparently, the front rank in each *schiltron* knelt with their spear hafts fixed in the ground; the rear ranks levelled their twelve-foot long spears over the front rank's heads. In between each *schiltron* were positioned Selkirk bowmen, arguably the only accomplished archers ever to serve in the Scottish armies other than Highland clansmen. The flanks were protected by what little cavalry Wallace commanded.

Battle was joined on 22 July. The initial charges of the heavy English cavalry were repulsed by the unbreakable resolve of the Scottish spearmen, secure in their virtually impregnable formations. The English infantry were committed next but fared no better. It was deadlock. Tragically, it was the Scottish cavalry which broke that deadlock. Led by the few lords who had decided to throw in their lot with Wallace, they simply quitted the field; there is no evidence to prove the Scottish horse acted treacherously or out of cowardice but there were rumours of this at the time.

With the withdrawal of the Scottish horse, the Ettrick forest bowmen were left exposed to the English cavalry which cut them to pieces. Then Edward committed his archers who took their toll of the men in the *schiltrons* suffering the onslaught of the grey goose-shafted arrows; flight after flight of the deadly missiles must have almost blocked out the sun above Falkirk. Tormented to the limit of endurance, the Scottish formations broke and ran. A massacre ensued, Wallace being forced to flee the field. His brief and bloody success was over. The defeat at Falkirk brought his leadership of the Scottish cause to an end.

Wallace resigned his role as Guardian of Scotland and visited the court of Philip IV in the hope of renewing the *Auld Alliance* in Scotland's favour – meaning the despatch of a French army to Scotland to resist Edward. But Philip was too involved in fighting his own battles for survival against his Flemish opponents to trouble himself with a treaty he had signed in 1295 promising support for Scotland against England.

Wallace returned to Scotland, the fugitive outlaw the Scottish 'Establishment' of nobles had always believed him to be, the son of a lesser knight who had exceeded his place in the hierarchy of the day. In the years that remained to him, Wallace led a life of obscurity; these seven years are virtually unknown to us. Constantly on the run, his former friends and followers deserted him. In a parliament convened by Edward I at St Andrews in March 1303, Wallace was declared an outlaw; also, some 129 Scottish landowners accepted Edward as their liege lord. However, as late as 1304, Wallace was still carrying the fight to the English but only in what can be described as spoiling raids. His power was broken, his time was past.

Roslin

In 1303 Scotland's morale was at a low ebb, particularly after Wallace's defeat at Falkirk in 1298. However, in February 1303, an English expeditionary force, commanded by Sir John Seagrave, crossed the Border, ostensibly to restore his bruised ego. According to the annals of the St Clair (Sinclair) family of Roslin Castle, Midlothian, Seagrave had been promised the hand of Margaret Ramsay of Dalhousie; Margaret changed her mind and married Hugh St Clair. Accounts of the subsequent 'battle' have been greatly exaggerated, as well as the size of Seagrave's army of 30,000 which was engaged by a Scottish force of 8,000 led by John 'the Red' Comyn, 3rd Lord of Badenoch. (William Wallace was present on the day but refused to assume command on account of his disgrace at Falkirk – or so it is said.) The strengths of the respective armies quoted above have been questioned; it is now thought that they numbered hundreds rather than thousands, yet another example of the exaggerations of chroniclers. Even so, the skirmish at Roslin was a victory for the Red Comyn and Scotland. (The highly-coloured account of Roslin in Walter Bower's *Scotichronicon* is not supported by contemporary evidence, nor do modern historians accept Bower's version of the 'battle'. Prominent among the detractors is the eminent and highly respected medieval historian Dr Chris Brown.)[14] Nonetheless, the bloody nose suffered by the English at Roslin must have restored the morale of many in Scotland, coming at a time when the country's will to resist England was at a low ebb.

In May 1303 a peace treaty was signed between France and England, one which deliberately excluded Scotland. The former alliance between France and Scotland now being at an end allowed Edward to prosecute the war in Scotland to its final conclusion.

Happrew

Edward I invaded northern Scotland as far as Morayshire, spending the autumn and winter at Dunfermline Abbey. Then, early in 1304, an English force, commanded by Lord Robert Clifford and accompanied by Bruce the Younger, defeated Wallace and Simon Fraser at Happrew[15] in the vicinity of

Peebles. It was the last throw of the dice for Wallace even if he escaped capture. The Scots conceded defeat; in the first few months of 1304, John 'the Red' Comyn of Badenoch entered negotiations with Edward for a conditional surrender, which was accepted. The only unresolved issue was Wallace, an outlaw still at large.

Wallace was betrayed by his own countrymen and handed over to the English by Sir John Menteith, an uncle of Sir John Stewart who had bled and died for Wallace at Falkirk. On the night of 3 August 1305 Wallace was surprised by Menteith in a house at Robroyston, near Glasgow. Dragged to London at the tail of a horse, he was led before Edward's judges in Westminster Hall. In a bitterly ironic and cruel, mocking imitation of Christ's crown of thorns placed on his head before the Crucifixion, Wallace's head was adorned with a crown of laurel leaves.[16]

Wallace's trial was a travesty of justice. It was in point of fact not a trial in any sense of the word. To English eyes he was nothing more than an outlaw who had wrought havoc and death on England's people. When accused of being guilty of treason, Wallace did not hesitate in his reply. He informed his judges that at no time had he sought to obtain the crown of Scotland nor had he ever sworn allegiance to Edward I – his name was absent from the *Ragman's Roll*.[17] He enquired why he could be called a traitor to England, it being a foreign country in his eyes.

Sir William Wallace, the patriot par excellence, was cruelly tortured and despatched on 23 August 1305. He was sentenced as a traitor, throttled within an inch of his death, then his genitals were cut from his body. His abdomen was sliced open by the same knife, his internal organs drawn from within. Finally, his heart was cut out and held aloft for the appreciation of the English mob. His corpse was beheaded, his head put on a spike and displayed on London Bridge. His remains were quartered, the four parts being taken to Newcastle, Berwick, Stirling and Perth.[18]

Edward was content to rest on his laurels; he did not realize that he had woken a sleeping tiger, with hundreds if not thousands of hearts determined to oppose England at every turn. Wallace's death served to strengthen the resolve of the Scottish people. Patriotism and love of country were not the causes of the Wars of Independence – they were a product of them.

During Wallace's wilderness years between Falkirk and his brutal execution Edward I believed Scotland was prostrate. In 1304 Stirling Castle fell and, with it, the last of the hopes of many Scots. Edward took it upon himself to provide Scotland with a constitution; ten Scottish and twenty English commissioners were appointed to draw up an 'Ordinance for the Government of Scotland'. Edward's nephew, John of Brittany, was appointed Guardian of the country. The ink was scarcely dry on the parchment when the Scots rejected it out of hand. The Scots would no longer accept anything from England; eight years of Edward's harsh and imperious dealing had stiffened their resolve. Yet again, Edward was forced to invade Scotland.

Matters came to a head on 10 February 1306 when Bruce the Younger slew John 'the Red' Comyn, the former regent, in the chapel of the Franciscan Minorite Convent of the Grey Friars at Dumfries. The Red Comyn, nephew of former King John Balliol, had a certain, if tenuous, claim to the throne. There was no love lost between the Bruces and the Comyns; they had been at loggerheads even before the *Great Cause* had set the crown on Balliol's head. Bruce the Younger also had a claim to the throne after his father Bruce the Elder died in 1304. Comyn had been acting in Edward I's interests – at least on the surface like his rival Bruce the Younger. Whatever passed between these two men in the chapel at Dumfries that cold winter morning is not recorded. However, we know that an argument flared up; possibly Bruce learnt that Comyn had informed Edward that Bruce was not to be trusted and harsh words were exchanged by the two men. In a fit of temper, Bruce drew his dagger and plunged it into his rival's body. Comyn was taken to the kirk vestry to be tended by the friars and given the sacrament, although he was still alive; some accounts[19] credit Sir Roger Kirkpatrick of Closeburn with the *coup de grace* that despatched Comyn, fulfilling the promise he made to the Bruce that he would 'mak siccar' [make sure] of Comyn's demise. Having disposed of his strongest rival for the throne, Bruce, tainted with 'the dark stain of treachery'[20] had no recourse other than to proclaim himself King of Scotland. Six weeks after the murder of the Red Comyn, Bruce had himself crowned at Scone on 25 March 1306. It was hardly a significant event. Bruce was attended by earls – Atholl and Lennox – and possibly only one bishop, David Murray of Moray. The ceremony was performed by Isabella of Fife, Countess of Buchan, as the Earl of Fife, whose traditional and ancient privilege it was to inaugurate a new Scottish king, was a prisoner in England.

Methven

When he learnt of the Red Comyn's murder and Bruce's audacity in assuming the throne of Scotland, Edward I was beside himself with anger. For his part, Bruce informed the English king that he should recognize him as lawful king of Scotland or else he would 'defend himself with the longest stick' that he had.[21] This challenge added insult to injury in Edward's mind; he sent Aymer de Valence, Earl of Pembroke (brother-in-law of the murdered Comyn), to Scotland with orders to quell what he saw as yet another rebellion. In June 1306 Pembroke surprised Bruce's small force camped at Methven, near Perth, forcing Bruce with an entourage of about 200 followers to flee into the mountains. Undeterred by this setback, Bruce made a sortie on the borders of

Argyle and Perthshire, where he was attacked and beaten by John, Lord of Lorn, uncle of the slaughtered Comyn.[22] With no army, little money and few provisions, Bruce had no option but to quit the mainland. With a mere handful of followers he spent the winter months on Rathlin Island, off the north-east coast of Ireland. Contrary to popular belief Bruce did not spend his time there studying arachnidology, the science of spiders and the way they spin their webs. In point of fact he used the time to plan how best he might prosecute the civil war now raging in Scotland. For that is what it had become, a Bruce-Comyn/Balliol conflict to determine who was Scotland's king.

Edward I lost no time in punishing Bruce's supporters. Bruce's brother Neil was butchered in the same way as Wallace had been, John of Strathbogie, Earl of Atholl was taken prisoner while attempting to spirit away Bruce's twenty-four-year-old daughter Mary and Isabella, Countess of Buchan. Strathbogie was hanged and Mary and Isabella were placed in cages at Roxburgh and Berwick Castles; the cages were suspended from turrets so that all could see the women languishing within. (The two women would remain thus until 1310, when they were probably removed to convents.) The eleven-year-old Marjorie, Bruce's daughter by his first wife Isabella of Mar, was confined in a Yorkshire nunnery, as was Bruce's sister Christian; his queen, Elizabeth de Burgh, was placed under house arrest in Holderness, Yorkshire.

Meanwhile, Bruce was languishing in a cave somewhere off the Scottish coast, although some historians maintain that he took refuge in Ireland or Norway. Whatever the truth of it, in the spring of 1307, Bruce returned to mainland Scotland to resume the struggle. He planned a three-pronged attack; his two brothers, Alexander and Thomas, landed in Galloway with a small force. This came to grief at the very outset; the brothers were captured, their men either killed or taken prisoner. On Edward I's orders, Alexander and Thomas Bruce were taken to Carlisle Castle where they were executed. The second attack on the Isle of Arran, led by James Douglas and Robert Boyd achieved some success; they ambushed the garrison of Brodick Castle while the English troops were unloading stores, although they failed to take the castle. Laden with booty, Douglas and Boyd returned to their galleys and sailed off.

Bruce, commanding the largest of the three forces led the main attack. His group numbered about 300, mainly Irishmen led no doubt by a kinsman of his queen, Elizabeth de Burgh. He landed on the Ayrshire coast at night, entering his earldom of Carrick near Turnberry Castle, where he had been born in 1275. However, the support he expected there never materialized; also, Turnberry Castle was garrisoned with a strong force so numerous that the overspill had to camp in the village of Turnberry. Bruce, shaken by the lack of support from his own vassals, was nonetheless encouraged by his brother

Edward to attack the English camp. The small party fell on the sleeping English, killing as many as they could but Edward I's forces soon recovered and scoured the west coast to find Bruce. Once again, the unhappy king was forced to go into hiding.

Glen Trool

With few men under his command Bruce was obliged to resort to guerrilla tactics in which he particularly excelled. Unlike Wallace who whenever he gathered a sizeable force fought set-piece battles, Bruce husbanded his scarce resources, using them to maximum effect. Edward I charged Aymer de Valence, Earl of Pembroke, the victor of Methven, with the task of hunting down Bruce. In March 1307 Bruce surprised Pembroke's much larger force at Glen Trool, a steep-sided glen containing the cold waters of Loch Trool, in Galloway. Bruce's men were positioned just outside a wood through which the English were advancing, having received word that the Scots were in the vicinity. When the vanguard of the English emerged from the wood, they found Bruce's spearmen waiting for them. Bruce led his men forward and caught the English off balance, driving them back into the wood. However, it seems that the English were in even greater strength than Bruce supposed, so he withdrew in good order although his small force was pursued for several miles.

Two months after Glen Trool Pembroke threw down the gauntlet, intent on finally crushing Bruce in the field. Curiously, Bruce accepted the challenge which went against his usual guerrilla tactics; however, he had no intention of fighting the set-piece battle Pembroke envisaged, with knights charging in full armour against Bruce and the rabble he commanded. Bruce chose his ground carefully.

Loudon Hill

Pembroke expected Bruce to respect the rules of chivalry, a fatal error on his part; the king had endured much privation, grief and frustration, hunted like an animal over the past year, with the deaths of three brothers still to be avenged. Loudon Hill, near Darvel in Ayrshire, would be no set-piece affair. The English knights were animated by the prospect of a brisk gallop over the gentle, rolling fields of Ayrshire, winning honours and acclaim from their king.

Bruce chose the only high ground in the vicinity, the volcanic plug rock of Loudon Hill, with its boggy base. There, the road was narrow due to the encroaching slopes of the hill; the English would have to charge uphill to reach the Scottish spearmen. In addition, Bruce had his men dig trenches bristling with sharpened stakes, with gaps to allow egress only by limited numbers of the English heavy cavalry, drawing them piecemeal on to his foot soldiers. (Bruce would employ similar tactics at Bannockburn seven years later.) At Loudon Hill, Bruce's strategy was simple; what he lacked in strength – his army of 600 was outnumbered five to one by Pembroke's 3,000 – would be compensated for by his careful preparations.

On 10 May 1307 Pembroke ordered his heavy cavalry forward; he believed he had little to do other than charge the well disciplined but pitifully thin line of Scottish spearmen. His horsed knights and men-at-arms made straight for Bruce's camouflaged trenches, containing their murderous *chevaux de frises*. On came the thundering cavalry, the blood lust on them. They seemed unstoppable – until it was too late. Hundreds of Pembroke's men and their horses were skewered on Bruce's sharp stakes. The Scottish spearmen raced down the hill to put the wounded survivors out of their misery, then they drove through the tangled mass of horses and men milling in front of those bloody trenches, the confused English infantry to the rear uncertain of what they should do. The surviving cavalry were speared and Pembroke ordered a retreat. The battle of Loudon Hill was over in minutes. Although English losses were minimal – reckoned to be about 100 – Pembroke's army withdrew in utter confusion. Bruce had won his first battle, a resounding victory. Neither Glen Trool nor Loudon Hill can be considered major engagements but, for Robert Bruce, they were political dynamite. Bruce had emerged undefeated from both skirmishes, a major victory for a patriot who not only had to contend with England but also his own countrymen to prove his worth and his right to be Scotland's king.

Bruce's triumph at Loudon Hill was crowned by an even greater event which overshadowed it. On 7 July 1307 Edward I, the relentless opponent of Scottish freedom died a bitter old man – he was sixty-eight – at Burgh-on-Sands on the English side of the Solway Firth, leading yet another campaign into Scotland to crush its people. His son, Edward of Caernarfon, now Edward II, led his father's army into Scotland, bearing his father's bones as instructed in the late king's will. He achieved nothing, contenting himself with the homage he received from some minor nobles in the south-west of Scotland; in the south-east, Patrick, 8th Earl of Dunbar and his son and heir also called Patrick pledged their allegiance to the new king. Edward II returned to England and would not trouble Scotland again for the next three years.

Barra

As for Bruce, he made good use of his time, now being unhindered by English armies. In May 1308 he subdued Aberdeenshire – Comyn territory – at the battle of Barra, also known as the battle of Inverurie and the battle of Old

Meldrum. Bruce was confronted by John Comyn, 3rd Earl of Buchan, in one of the many episodes in Bruce's civil war with domestic enemies such as the Comyns. In the spring of 1308 Bruce's army of 3,000 had been reduced to 700; he was also ill, suffering from an unspecified complaint; he lay on his sick bed in camp at Inverurie, near Old Meldrum. When Comyn's force approached, Bruce's lieutenants carried him from his sick bed and put him on a horse. It is said that Comyn's men had been told that Bruce was ill and near death; when they saw the king apparently well and ready to do battle, Comyn's men broke and ran as far away as Fyvie, several miles north of Inverurie.

Pass of Brander

The next conflict occurred in late summer 1308 or early spring 1309 – the date is still in dispute – between John Macdougall of Lorn and Bruce at the Pass of Brander. Little is known of this battle but the defeat of Macdougall ended the opposition of the Comyn-Balliol faction against Bruce, who went on to subdue Galloway – Balliol country – which effectively ended Comyn resistance. (John Comyn fled to England, where he died in 1309. The Comyns were a spent force; they would never again challenge Bruce. Any hopes of the Comyn family returning to their former power would be finally extinguished at Bannockburn.)

Bruce's able lieutenant James 'the Black' Douglas gained further territory in Tweeddale, bringing to the Scottish camp Thomas Randolph, Bruce's nephew. Randolph, son of a Roxburghshire knight, had supported Bruce following the murder of the Red Comyn in 1306; he was taken prisoner at Methven and was promised the return of his Scottish lands if he swore allegiance to Edward I, which he did. Then, during James Douglas's campaign in Tweeddale, Randolph was captured and brought before his uncle. Bruce greeted him cordially, expecting Randolph to switch his allegiance, which Randolph refused to do. He even went as far as to criticize Bruce for the way he was conducting the war with England, reputedly saying that his tactics were unchivalrous, even cunning and cowardly.[22] Bruce was taken aback and ordered his nephew to be kept in close custody. In time, however, the two men were reconciled. Randolph was the father of three stout warrior sons and two daughters, one of whom would gain immortality in the defence of Dunbar Castle in 1338.

Bruce was on a roller coaster run of successes. One by one his Scottish opponents – including those who had sworn allegiance to England – withered before him. He took Inverary Castle, near Oban, Urquhart Castle on the shore of Loch Ness and Inverness Castle. Although these were minor successes, they did much to bolster Bruce's reputation. At a provincial council held at Dundee in February 1310, the leading Scottish clergy declared to England

and beyond that Robert Bruce was the lawful King of Scotland. Bruce had been excommunicated by Rome after the murder of the Red Comyn in Dumfries; now the Scottish church and the clergy were determined to re-instate Bruce, with or without the consent of Pope Clement V.

Bruce had no use for the castles he took; in his eyes, they were wasteful of his scant manpower, requiring garrisons to defend them. So he embarked on a policy of 'slighting' them – walls were torn down, roofs removed and wells filled in.

The cause of Bruce and his loyal supporters was growing in momentum. In the autumn of 1310 Edward II, anxious to test his standing as Scotland's overlord brought an army to Roxburgh; from there he marched to Biggar, then Renfrew, returning to Berwick via Linlithgow, where his father had built a stout castle. Having marched unopposed throughout his campaign, Edward was confident that Bruce's revolt was a spent force. This was far from being the case. To prove the point, Bruce invaded northern England, devastating the Bishopric of Durham. Then, in 1311, Bruce took Linlithgow Castle, possibly to irritate Edward's already bruised ego. In the same year Bruce again invaded northern England as far as Durham. In early 1314, in quick succession Bruce captured the castles of Roxburgh, Dumfries and Edinburgh – the Black Douglas took Roxburgh, Edward Bruce captured Dumfries and Thomas Randolph took Edinburgh. The one stronghold which still held out for England in 1314 was Stirling Castle. In November 1313 Bruce's brother Edward was besieging Stirling Castle. Here, we encounter yet another example of the code of chivalry in medieval Britain. Stirling's governor, Sir Philip de Mowbray, made a rash promise to Edward Bruce, one which was equally rashly accepted; if Stirling was not relieved by Edward II in midsummer – 24 June 1314 – de Mowbray agreed to hand it over to the Scots. Bruce was incensed when he learnt of Edward's bargain. He had no wish to fight a set-piece battle because he simply did not have a large enough army to withstand Edward, with his unlimited resources. In the following chapter we will learn that in this author's opinion one of Edward's staunchest allies, almost *the* only Scottish noble still supporting him, would bring an English army to Scotland.

Bruce was at least consoled by the welcome lifting of the Papal excommunication which had without doubt affected his ability to raise a sizeable army. Also, Bruce the waverer, Bruce the opportunist, seeking favour first in Scotland, then in England as the political scene shifted, had a great deal to live down before he would be universally accepted by both the nobles and the common people as Scotland's rightful king. On Midsummer's Day 1314 Bruce would face the ultimate and final test of his acceptance as King of Scotland in a battle that would elevate him above the rank of king to that of hero.

Notes

1. Many accounts give twelve Competitors but thirteen are named in the *Great Roll of Scotland* (*Calendar of Documents Relating to Scotland*, vol. ii, No.507.)
2. *Anglo-Scottish Relations* 1174–1328.
3. *CDS* vol.ii, Nos.492 and 496.
4. *Ibid*, No. 499 5.
5. *Anglo-Scottish Relations* 1174–1328.
6. *Anglo-Scottish Relations* 1174–1328.
7. *Scalacronica* (1356).
8. Extract from a journal of movements of king Edward in Scotland (from an MS of the fourteenth century held in the Imperial Library at Paris – Fonds Lat. 6049, fol. 30.b.; see also Stevenson, *Historical Documents of Scotland* 1286–1786.
9. Hume Brown, *History of Scotland* vol.ii, p.145.
10. Blind Harry; Pugh, *Swords, Loaves and Fishes: A History of Dunbar*, p.92.
11. They were styled thus in a famous and preserved letter of October 1297 sent to the prominent trading towns of Lübeck and Hamburg, members of the Hanseatic League with whom Scotland had traded for many years. The letter virtually makes it known that Scotland was 'open for business'.
12. *Chronicle of Walter Guisborough.*
13. Hume Brown, op.cit., p.147.
14. Hume Brown, op.cit., p.149: Brown, Chris, *William Wallace* (2005)
15. *CDS* vol. ii. No.1432.
16. Oliver, *A History of Scotland*, p.98.
17. Oliver, op. cit., p.87.
18. Hume Brown, op. cit., p.149.
19. Brotchie, op. cit., p.70.
20. *Vita*, p.12.
21. *Anglo-Scottish Relations* 1174–1328.
22. Hume Brown, op. cit., p.154; Barbour, *The Bruce*, pp.166–9.

Chapter 5

The Wars of Independence: Bannockburn, 1314

It is generally accepted by those interested in the history of Scotland that the battle of Bannockburn was a mistake, one which Robert the Bruce had not wished to fight, a commitment foisted upon him by his ebullient and chivalrous brother, Edward. In November 1313 Edward Bruce was besieging Stirling Castle, the most important Scottish stronghold in English hands. The Constable of Stirling Castle was a Scot, Sir Philip de Mowbray, in the pay of Edward II; he commanded a garrison of about 100 men. Mowbray had fought against Bruce at Methven in 1306 and was appointed governor of Stirling Castle in 1311.[1] At the outset of the siege, Bruce invited de Mowbray to surrender the castle. De Mowbray refused. When Edward Bruce assumed command of the siege, he entered negotiations with de Mowbray, after which the two men concluded an agreement for the conditional surrender of Stirling. De Mowbray had intelligence that Edward II was raising an army to invade Scotland in 1314, so he proposed that he would surrender to Edward Bruce if the English army failed to be within three leagues (nine miles) of Stirling Castle on Midsummer's Day, on the Feast of John the Baptist, 24 June 1314.

To understand Edward II's mindset in the autumn of 1313, we must briefly revisit the events which occurred between 1304 and 1313, the focus being on the largely English-held south-east of Scotland, with particular emphasis on the earldom of Dunbar. As we saw in the previous chapter, Patrick, 8th Earl of Dunbar was one of the few staunch supporters of Edward I – more, it has to be said out of fear than love of the ruthless Hammer of the Scots. When Edward I appointed Dunbar as governor of Ayr Castle in 1304 many questioned the king's judgement. Ayr Castle was a strategically important base. Dunbar had proved himself to be nothing short of incompetent, indecisive and something of a liability; for example, he was criticized by the pro-English garrison of Ayr who went to the trouble of sending Edward I a petition suggesting Dunbar be relieved of his command. The soldiers at Ayr complained of Dunbar's lack of military skills and that he was doing nothing to counter the threat from nearby Turnberry Castle, held by Scottish forces. The Ayr petition does not mince words:

[The men at Ayr] have heard nothing from Earl Patrick whom the king has given the keeping of the country, at which they wonder much.[2]

Despite Patrick Dunbar's lamentable performance, Edward seems to have developed a fondness for his son and heir, also called Patrick. He sent a cask of wine to the young man's wife Ermigarda and other gifts to the earl-in-waiting. When the 8th Earl died in 1308, his son Patrick, 9th Earl of Dunbar and 2nd of March, swore fealty to Edward II who ascended the throne of England when his father died at Burgh-on-Sands in 1307, leading yet another army against Scotland. By 1308 many of Dunbar's knight-tenants had loosened their ties with England, declaring for Bruce. Those who remained loyal to 'the King's peace' – meaning Edward II's – began to pay heavily as a result of Edward's ineffective 'immunity' which he declared would protect them from Bruce's men foraging for food in the rich agricultural earldom of Dunbar which covered a fair portion of East Lothian and the Merse (Berwickshire). By 1313 only Patrick, 9th Earl of Dunbar and Sir Adam de Gordon supported Edward and even by then Gordon was beginning to waver. The *Chronicle of Lanercost* accused those Scots who remained loyal to Edward of doing so 'insincerely' and only to safeguard the lands they held of Edward in England. Despite their continuing presence in the south-east, with its castles of Jedburgh, Selkirk, Berwick, Dunbar and Yester, the English were sorely tried in their attempts to maintain order and offer protection from Bruce's roving war-bands, which constantly plundered farms and carried off food and livestock. By autumn 1313 East Lothian and Berwickshire were close to exhaustion. The 9th Earl of Dunbar's lands were not only being plundered by Bruce but were also at the mercy of the Berwick and Roxburgh garrisons – Dunbar's supposed allies – whose rascally leaders demanded ransom money and food in return for their 'protection' from Bruce. By September 1313 Dunbar was a man at the end of his tether. In desperation he wrote an impassioned letter to Edward II, complaining bitterly about the blackmail and robbery suffered by his tenants. His letter is quoted in part:

Petition to the king by the people of Scotland [sic] by their envoys, Sir Patrick Dunbar, earl of March and Sir Adam de Gordon ... Matters are daily getting worse, as for the 'suffraunce' [protection from molestation] they [Dunbar and Gordon] have [been granted] till this Martinmas [11 November] they had to give 1,000 qrs. [quarters, or about thirteen tons] of corn yet their livestock is plundered, partly by the enemy [Bruce] and partly by the garrisons of Berwick and Roxburgh, especially by Gilbert de Medilton [Middleton] and Thomas de Pencaitlande and their company at Berwick ... when 'upplaunde' [people living in the hills] go to buy their vivers [provisions] in Berwick, the garrison spy out and seize them, Confining them in houses and carrying off others to Northumberland, holding them in concealment and 'duresce' [restraint] there till they get a ransom – and the Scots in Northumberland for resettling them ... some of them at the end of their 'suffraunce' at Midsummer purchase from Sir Robert de Bruys [Dunbar refuses to acknowledge Bruce as king of Scotland] at his late coming, a truce of fifteen days, and on his [Bruce's] retreat, after they had returned to their houses, the next morning the warden and the whole garrison of Berwick came and took the people in their beds, carrying them off dead and alive to Berwick, and held them to ransom viz. on their foray within the bounds of the earldom of Dunbar, both gentlemen and others, to the number of 30. Also 300 fat beasts, 4,000 sheep besides horses and dead stock [i.e. beef salted for the winter] ... some of the Berwick garrison, with Thomas de Pencaitlande as 'Guyde' [i.e. leader] carried of [sic] some of the poor people to Berwick. Those who had wherewithal were ransomed; those who had nothing were killed and thrown into the Water of the Tweed.[3]

A sorry tale indeed. But was it enough to bring Edward to Scotland with an army? Edward responded to Dunbar on 29 November 1313,[4] promising that an English army would come to Scotland in the summer of 1314. We know that Edward was determined to engage Bruce in open battle and thus rid himself of the troublesome Scot. What is perhaps astonishing about Edward's decision was that he had no intelligence of the deal struck between Sir Philip de Mowbray and Edward Bruce to relieve Stirling Castle by Midsummer's Day 1314. It is certain that Edward knew of the siege of the castle but Dunbar's letter surely played an important part in his decision and which, excepting two recent accounts,[5] most historians have chosen to ignore. Of course it is true that Edward's subsequent invasion was a matter of chivalry; he was only apprised of the de Mowbray-Edward Bruce arrangement less than four weeks before he took the field at Bannockburn. As to the troubles caused by his garrisons in southern Scotland, these were caused by Edward's failure to pay or provision them, so they resorted to preying on their own allies to feed themselves.

It seems incredible that Edward contemplated an invasion of Scotland in 1314, particularly after Bruce's capture of the castles of Roxburgh, Edinburgh and other lesser fortresses early in 1314. In February, Roxburgh fell to Sir James Douglas and Randolph, Earl of Moray, took Edinburgh the following month. With only the relatively strong castles of Berwick and Dunbar in English hands, why did Edward attempt a major invasion of Scotland, the first for several years? It was not solely to lift the siege of Stirling; he was determined to draw Bruce into a set-piece battle and settle the future of Scotland once and for all. But he was not the man his father had been ...

Many English knights and pro-English Scots in the south-east of Scotland were growing weary and disillusioned ('many say openly victory will go to Bruce')[6] defending a country where Bruce's guerrilla form of waging war brought sudden – and bloody – attacks. When the English parliament met that autumn of 1313 Edward was granted a subsidy to finance his campaign. On 23 December summons were issued to the English magnates, minor officials and clergy to organize forces and muster at Berwick on 10 June 1314.

When Bruce learnt of his brother's pact with Sir Philip de Mowbray, he was devastated. Bruce knew he had neither the manpower nor the weaponry to engage the might of England in a set-piece battle, particularly in defence of a castle he would have simply dismantled on its surrender. Bruce, the guerrilla leader *par excellence* knew that, realistically, he was unlikely to raise an army capable of engaging, let alone defeating, Edward in the open field. Edward Bruce had forced him into a corner and he was apprehensive at the prospect of meeting Edward on his terms rather than his own. A defeat in 1314 could easily topple him from his still shaky throne. At least he was consoled by the fact that, in addition to Roxburgh and Edinburgh, Linlithgow Castle had fallen to his forces. Now only a handful of minor castles held out for England, the only formidable strongholds being Berwick and Dunbar; these would be vital to Edward on his march north in the summer of 1314, acting as provisioning bases for his supply ships.

Edward was jubilant, confident of victory. If, as is certain, he knew of Bruce's siege of Stirling Castle, at least he knew where to find the elusive Scottish army and smash it with his heavy cavalry, archers and foot soldiers, many of whom were veterans who had served under his father in Wales and France.

As the summer drew near Bruce intensified his preparations for a battle he was reluctant to fight. At least on this occasion, his peasant army possessed more than the crude farm implements many of the Scottish host army of John Comyn had to fight with against Edward I's army at Dunbar in 1296. Also, the hard-won victories – albeit minor – at Glen Trool and Loudon Hill had forged a new fighting spirit in his men; a combination of experience, better weapons and armour, intensive training and, above all, the choice of favourable ground, would stand the Scottish army in good stead on the days of the fight at the Bannock Burn in Stirlingshire.

By 27 May Edward II and his vast army had reached the small Northumberland village of Newminster. It was there that he learnt of the compact signed by Sir Philip de Mowbray and Edward Bruce for the relief of Stirling Castle. Mowbray, given a safe-conduct from Bruce, appeared in person before the English king to deliver the news. Edward was delighted; now he knew precisely where Bruce's army would be on 24 June, the day of the deadline for the relief of Stirling. At last he would be able to confront his elusive enemy and destroy him.

The sizes of the English and Scottish armies at Bannockburn have never been satisfactorily computed. English estimates are as low as 1,300 cavalry and 7,000 foot soldiers;[7] other accounts give 3,000 cavalry and 15,000 foot[8] and 2,000 cavalry with 15,000–20,000 foot.[9] The latter figures are modern estimates and are probably more accurate than those given by near contemporary accounts which range from 60,000 to 100,000.[10] A clearer estimate is given in the English Patent Rolls of the time[11] which record 6,000 cavalry and 21,540 infantry – more realistic figures. The English baggage train was certainly impressive in size, giving an indication of Edward's strength; the train was loaded with equipment, tents, weapons and provisions, some 160 wagons alone containing live poultry to feed his men.[12]

The Scottish figures at Bannockburn are equally in doubt; some estimates are ridiculous at worst and dubious at best. Barbour's *The Brus* gives 30,000,[13] others nearer our time give 20,000.[14] Modern estimates favour 500 light cavalry and 8,000 foot[15] or between 4,500 and 6,000 in all.[16] So, given the more realistic of both sets of figures, at Bannockburn Bruce was outnumbered by about three to one.

As mentioned earlier, Edward's army contained many veterans from earlier Anglo-Scottish conflicts as well as those his father had fought in the process of subduing Wales. Among his *prominentes* were Gilbert de Clare, Earl of Gloucester, Humphrey de Bohun, Earl of Hereford and hereditary High Constable of England, Henry de Beaumont, Earl of Buchan (a title given by Edward as Beaumont had married a sister of John Comyn of Buchan), Aymer de Valence who had fought and decisively beaten Bruce at Methven in 1306, Edmund de Mauley, steward of the royal household and, most importantly, the young Sir Henry de Bohun, Hereford's nephew and cousin of the Earl of Gloucester. Others present in Edward's army and veterans of encounters with Wallace and Bruce were Sir Robert de Umfraville, Earl of Angus, Sir Robert Clifford and Sir Thomas Gray of

Heton. Hereford, Beaumont, Clifford and Valence had all been present on the field of Falkirk against Wallace in 1298.

Sadly, there are few contemporary accounts of what took place at Bannockburn. For much of the information, we have to rely on fourteenth century accounts written several years after the battle. Both Scottish and English chronicles are brief, often vague, contradictory and misleading. The main sources from the Scottish perspective are found in John Barbour's *The Brus*, written about sixty years after the battle. (Barbour was only two years old when Bannockburn took place but he was fortunate to have met some of the veterans who were present on the field.) Barbour's account is romantic and dramatic and, it has to be said, untrustworthy in many respects, on a par with Blind Harry's account of William Wallace which is also full of romance and untruths. The English version of Bannockburn is recorded in *Vita Edwardi Secundi* (*Life of Edward the Second*) which was reputedly written by an anonymous author thought to be a secular clerk in Edward's household, given his lofty style. Another fairly accurate account can be found in the *Chronicle of Lanercost Priory* in northern England; its unknown author(s) cover the period 1201 to 1346. Yet another reliable account is *Scalacronica*, written by Sir Thomas Gray of Heton, whose father was taken prisoner at Bannockburn. Thomas Gray junior was taken prisoner by the Scots in 1355 at the battle of Nesbit Moor; during his years in captivity in Edinburgh Castle he whiled away the hours writing a history of England and Scotland from the Norman Conquest in 1066 to 1362.

As to the site of the battlefield, its precise location has never been satisfactorily identified. As the Bannock Burn from which the battle takes its name runs from west to east to the south of Saint Ninian's church near Stirling and its castle, it is more than likely that the second day of the battle on 24 June 1314 was fought on the north bank of the Bannock Burn, the Scots emerging from the Torwood woods in the west to confront Edward in the east. Bruce's position on the second day of the battle was ideal ground for his foot soldiers but bad news for the English horsed knights and men-at-arms on whom Edward II relied to deliver the knockout blow to Bruce. The English foot soldiers were held in reserve to carry out a mopping-up operation of the wounded and disorganized Scottish spearmen. That was the master plan. It went horribly wrong.

The acres of woodland in the Torwood served to mask the strength – or, rather, the weakness of the Scottish army. The Carse of Balquhiderock, a boggy flood plain of the river Forth would also reduce the impact of the English cavalry. The old Roman Road which joined the road to Stirling offered the only dry, firm approach to Bruce's position, which is why he had his men dig hundreds of metre-deep pits containing sharp stakes and

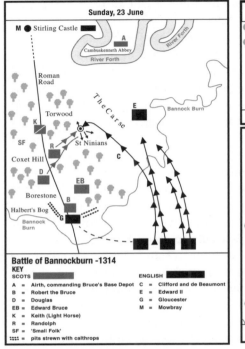

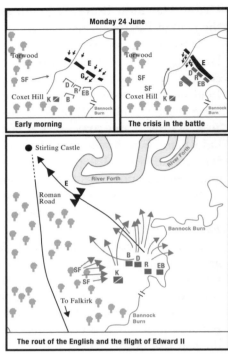

calthrops – four-spiked iron balls intended to maim horses – on either side of it and elsewhere on the field, similar to what he had used at Loudon Hill.

It is nothing short of surprising that Aymer de Valence, whom Bruce had defeated at Loudon, failed to alert Edward II of the possibility of these well-camouflaged obstacles being present at Bannockburn; perhaps he dismissed the idea, thinking that Bruce would not use the same tactics again. This was to prove a grave error which was discovered when it was too late. The English *destriers* or war-horses came to grief when they encountered the leg-snapping pits hidden by a light covering of loose twigs, grass and turfs.

Let us now consider the formations Bruce employed to meet Edward's army. He raised his standard at the Borestone, where he divided his force into three divisions, or battles. If we accept that the Scottish army numbered between 6,000 and 8,000, each battle organized in the *schiltron* formation would have contained between 2,000–2,500 spearmen, with a separate force of 500 light cavalry. On 23 June Thomas Randolph, Earl of Moray, commanded the vanguard, Edward Bruce the middle-guard with Bruce in charge of the rearguard, or reserve. The light cavalry was commanded by Robert Keith the Marischal (marshal) of Scotland and possibly Sir James Douglas. At the outset of hostilities, Randolph took up position with orders to guard the road which led to Saint Ninian's Church; it is not entirely clear whether this position was in or near the Torwood, south of the Roman Road, or immediately in front of the Church, but either is possible. It could be argued that, in the early stages of 23 June, Randolph was in fact positioned in the Torwood, then made a strategic withdrawal to the second position on the approach of the English cavalry. The drawback to both positions was that Randolph's *schiltrons* could be easily outflanked and isolated by the English coming up the road from Falkirk, one which branched off up the old Roman Road, a dry, hard surface ideal for heavy cavalry. Be that as it may, Bruce had set his trap skilfully; he had ordered his men to dig up the pathways through the woods and elsewhere, which would cause difficulties for cavalry and foot alike.

In the knowledge that Edward and his host did not cross the Border until 10 June, Bruce put the intervening weeks to good use, preparing his position and training his men to a peak of fitness. He also practised them in the art of fighting in *schiltron* formation which had served Wallace well at Stirling Brig and himself at Loudon Hill. The Roman Road was crucial in these operations, being firm and dry and leading to Stirling; Bruce accurately predicted that Edward would use the road to relieve the castle. Bruce's preparations were designed to limit the use of the 6,000-strong cavalry divisions and prevent an all-out massive charge on his army which would have destroyed it.

One can but speculate what was in the mind of Robert the Bruce on the night of 22/23 June 1314. Was he confident of victory? Did he sleep soundly? He knew in his heart he had chosen good ground for his men, ground that would protect them as much as was possible from the awesome English heavy cavalry. As the hours ticked away, no doubt he held a last council-of-war with his brother Edward, Randolph, Douglas and Keith. Edward Bruce was confident; Randolph was keen to prove his mettle, all thoughts of his earlier criticism of the way his uncle waged war forgotten – or conveniently put aside for the moment.

First Day: Sunday, 23 June, the Eve of the Vigil of St John the Baptist

Early that bright, warm summer morning, Bruce's camp was already astir. He sent the Black Douglas and Robert Keith to reconnoitre the approaching English army. What the two men saw on that soft June day must have turned their hearts to stone. Edward's army was an awesome sight to behold, exceeding the armies his father had led into Scotland in 1296 and 1298. In haste Douglas and Keith galloped back to the Scottish camp to report to Bruce. We have no way of knowing how Bruce reacted to their news but he must have been seriously troubled by what they told him. Despite the extremely favourable position he held, Bruce knew that if he withdrew, not only would Stirling be relieved but, more importantly, his authority and standing in Scotland would be lost, perhaps forever. He must have taken comfort from the fact that, during the night, there had been no desertions from his small army. That day would test Bruce to an extent as never before: if he withdrew from Bannockburn the Scots would damn him for being a weak and opportunist king; if he stood and fought, he might be defeated and lose everything. Bruce knew his army was no match for Edward's in terms of numbers but he placed his faith in the terrain he had chosen and the high morale of his troops. Also, he had four capable lieutenants in his brother Edward, Randolph, Douglas and Keith. And among his knights were David de Strathbogie, Earl of Atholl and Walter the High Steward of Scotland, his son-in-law.

As the hours ticked away the day became oppressively hot; the Scots lay in their concealed places, listening to the hooves of the enemy cavalry, the stamp of thousands of feet as the English army came into view. It must have been a terrifying sight. So many ... De Mowbray's garrison watching from the battlements of Stirling Castle must have felt relieved, knowing that, very soon, the Scottish siege would be lifted and Bruce's army annihilated. Almost a month had passed since Sir Philip de Mowbray had been given safe conduct to warn Edward of the deadline for the relief of Stirling.

The vanguard of the English army was led by Gilbert de Clare, Earl of Gloucester, and Humphrey de Bohun, Earl of Hereford; among their knights was Hereford's nephew Henry de Bohun who would play a brief but dramatic part in the prelude to Bannockburn that day. Stirling was ten miles distant, the Torwood half that. Where were the Scots? All Gloucester and Hereford could see was Sir Philip de Mowbray and his escort coming towards them; no doubt Bruce had granted de Mowbray safe conduct under the conventional rules of chivalry which allowed the commander of a beleaguered castle to parley with the commander of the relieving force. Thus far Bruce was playing by the rules; it would be the first and last time in the battle about to commence. Perhaps Bruce entertained a forlorn hope that were de Mowbray granted an audience with Edward II he might persuade the king not to attack the Scots as the size of Bruce's army was unknown. Mowbray was taken before Edward and informed him that the Scots were still in the vicinity, that they had destroyed the pathways through the woods and that Edward should advance with caution.[17]

Edward was unmoved by de Mowbray's pleas. He had not come all the way to Stirling to relieve a castle but to finally confront Robert the Bruce in a battle where he would defeat the Scottish king and regain control of the country. That day de Mowbray left Edward in jubilant mood, returning to the castle which he was certain would be relieved on 24 June. He was followed by the vanguard of Edward's army led by Gloucester and Hereford. The plan was simple. The English first division of cavalry, the vanguard, would approach Stirling through the Torwood; the second division of 300 knights and men-at-arms led by Sir Robert Clifford would guard Gloucester's right flank and proceed to Stirling Castle. With Clifford effectively to the rear of the main Scottish army, Bruce would be unable to withdraw in safety. The third division, led by Edward II himself, would remain in the rear as reserve, along with the thousands of foot soldiers who lagged behind the three cavalry divisions.

Gloucester and Hereford passed through the gloomy Torwood without incident, again relieved to emerge into the sunshine. Now the last obstacle was the woods beyond Torwood where Gloucester and Hereford rightly believed it was there they would confront Bruce and his army. The fact that the vanguard passed through Torwood without being attacked confirms that if Randolph had been positioned there he had withdrawn to the vicinity of Saint Ninian's Church.

Advancing with caution and still fearful of ambush, Gloucester ordered forward the contingent of Welsh foot soldiers attached to his division. The Welshmen were led by Henry de Bohun, Hereford's nephew who was keen to win acclaim in battle. The hot-blooded knight had boasted that he would either kill Bruce or take him prisoner.[18] De Bohun was foolhardy enough to press forward ahead of the Welsh foot, keen to strike the first blow; he cantered into the woods and was immediately lost from view in the dark interior. Then suddenly he saw Bruce, seated not on a war-horse but a palfrey, more suited to the wooded terrain. De Bohun recognized Bruce from the gold circlet or crown on his *basinet* or helmet; Bruce was armed only with a war axe as he busied himself organizing his division, the Scottish rearguard. De Bohun could not believe his luck.

It is not known who saw whom first. De Bohun lowered his visor and put spur to his war-horse. Probably the first Bruce knew of his assailant was the thunder of hooves coming towards him; realizing de Bohun was alone he stood his ground. De Bohun increased his canter to a charge and lowered his lance; the combined weight of horse and armoured rider was formidable and should have ensured a kill as de Bohun aimed the tip of his lance at Bruce's chest. Suddenly, at the last moment, the crucial moment, Bruce shifted his palfrey to the side so that the Englishman's lance could not strike home. Then, as de Bohun drew level with him, Bruce raised himself upwards and, standing in the stirrups of his palfrey, brought his axe down on de Bohun's head. The sickening impact not only cleaved de Bohun's *basinet* but his skull, killing him instantly. The blow was so fierce that the axe-head snapped from its wooden shaft, buried in the luckless knight's head. Bruce turned away to resume his positioning of the rearguard, shrugging off the rebukes from those Scottish lords who had witnessed the incident. They vociferously accused him of putting his life at risk. Bruce simply replied that he was sorry for the loss of his favourite axe.[19]

Although, in terms of the battle to come, this was a minor incident, it could have had serious consequences for the Scots; it was obvious that only one man would emerge unscathed from the encounter. To the English, de Bohun's violent death was a frightening spectacle; to the Scots, it was inspirational. Bruce's men poured out of the woods brandishing spears, axes and swords, smashing into Gloucester's and Hereford's division. After a brief fight the two sides withdrew, neither having been beaten. However, the Scots had won a psychological victory, the English suffered a loss of face, which was almost tantamount to a defeat.

Next to be challenged that day was Sir Robert Clifford's division which had slipped past Thomas Randolph's division, sent to protect the road to Stirling Castle. The very move that Bruce had predicted had happened; either Randolph was taken by surprise or he was preoccupied with other matters. Bruce chided Randolph for his lapse. (As many who were schoolchildren of this author's generation will remember, Bruce reputedly chided Randolph for his sin of omission by saying that 'a rose has fallen from your chaplet',[20] a chaplet being a heraldic device consisting of a garland of leaves bearing four flowers.) Whatever the truth of it, Randolph made haste to correct his error, compounding his dereliction of duty by disobeying Bruce's express orders not to engage the English on open ground. Perhaps courageous, Randolph's order to his *schiltron* to move against Clifford was also foolhardy and could have brought grief to a third of Bruce's army. Apart from the fact that the *schiltron* was the early equivalent of the British Army square used in the Napoleonic Wars, neither was intended to be a mobile formation; foot soldiers caught in open ground by cavalry stood little chance of surviving. The whole purpose of the *schiltron* was defensive but Randolph made an almost unthinkable decision; he ordered his *schiltron* to advance in formation towards Clifford and his associates, Sir Henry de Beaumont and Sir Thomas de Gray, with their 300 cavalry and Welsh foot soldiers in support.

The sudden appearance of the Scottish vanguard out of the woods unbalanced Clifford momentarily; he was thrown into indecision. There was a heated exchange between de Beaumont and de Gray as to how the English should respond to Randolph's challenge. Beaumont was for pulling back to draw the Scots farther away from their protective woods. Gray disagreed. Beaumont accused him of being afraid, a taunt which stung Gray who reputedly said he would not flee out of fear and proved his point by charging Randolph's *schiltron*, accompanied by a single English knight, William

Deyncourt, perhaps like Henry de Bohun, keen to win acclaim. In the ensuing charge Deyncourt was killed and Gray was taken prisoner.[21]

Shocked into action by this spectacle, Clifford and de Beaumont – both had engaged Wallace's *schiltrons* at Falkirk in 1298 – led their men forward, attacking Randolph on every side. Bruce was horrified when he arrived on the scene to ascertain how Randolph was resolving his earlier error. Sir James Douglas begged Bruce to allow him to assist Randolph; Bruce refused at first, then relented. At the sight of the Black Douglas, the English lost their grip of an opportune situation and began to disengage, falling back, then scattered. Most of Clifford's men sought refuge and safety in the main army.

At last the sun began to slip down behind the trees. It had been a long, gruelling and anxious day for both armies. For Bruce it had been one of unexpected success. He had achieved what he had set out to do – avoid having to commit his entire army against the might of Edward II in the open field. The Scots retired into the woods to a supper of bread and water, then a few hours of sound sleep. The English did not enjoy the same luxuries. All night they laboured in the boggy, waterlogged ground they occupied. During that short night a deserter from Edward's army crossed over the Bannock Burn; Sir Alexander Seton defected to Bruce, advising him that all was far from well in Edward II's camp and that if Bruce attacked the English the following day he would defeat Edward with ease.[22] The only disappointment Bruce suffered that night was the defection of David de Strathbogie, the Earl of Atholl, who harboured animosity towards Bruce's brother Edward.[23]

In the English camp men were tired, yet they could not sleep. The foot soldiers were weary after a thirty-mile march from Falkirk in oppressive heat. The cavalry were dispirited by the loss of Henry de Bohun and the capture of Sir Thomas de Gray. That night Edward's knights and men-at-arms did not lay off their armour and they kept their weapons close by, leaving their horses saddled and bridled.[24]

Edward's men were physically exhausted even before the bulk of his army had struck a blow against Bruce; they were also depressed and anxious, dispirited by the loss of two prominent knights. Only Edward II was ebullient, confident that on the morrow he would draw Bruce into the open and defeat him and his contemptible little army. Just one physical objective lay in his way – the Bannock Burn, a steep-sided, deep and marshy stream in 1314, unlike its modern descendant. Edward had to ford the stream before daybreak; he set his men the task of seeking all manner of wooden supports which would serve as walkways for his cavalry and infantrymen. Foraging parties scoured the vicinity of Stirling to obtain wooden doors, frames, roof beams from local cottages; even the thatch from these cottages was put to use to ensure a safe crossing of the Bannock Burn for Edward's men.

That stifling hot night of June, one of the shortest of the year, Bruce delivered a speech worthy of Winston Churchill in 1940. Bruce reminded those present of their suffering at the hands of the English; he spoke of those who had lost brothers, relatives and friends in combat as well as those who languished in English prisons, including his own wife and family. Of the English he said that their glory was in possessions, whereas for Scotsmen their glory was in the name of God and victory in battle. Heartened by the news he had received from Alexander Seton, Bruce spoke of the low morale in Edward's army, saying that if their hearts were cast down their bodies were worth nothing. He announced to his nobles and knights that the following day he intended to stand and fight but reassured those present that if they disagreed with his decision he would withdraw from the field. It was a clever speech which had the desired effect. With one voice his men said they were willing to stand and fight at his side. Bruce reminded the nobles that Edward had brought vast riches with him and that even the poorest among his army would enrich themselves with plunder in the event of victory. This was a skilful ploy, given the massive baggage train in full view of the Scottish army. Bruce ended his speech by reminding those present that they were not only fighting for their personal freedom and lives but also those of their wives, children and families as well as for their lands, not for the power Edward craved. That night the Scots slept well; their morale was high.

It was not so in the English camp on that shortest of nights. The reverses of that day hung heavily on the minds of some of the veteran leaders like Gloucester and Hereford. Both men knew that it was imperative that Edward's army must be as close as possible to the Scottish army, hidden in the depths of the woods. It was imperative that the English commanders should find ground firm enough to bear the weight of war-horses and their heavily armoured riders. The Bannock Burn proved a difficult obstacle so that it took most of the night for the heavy cavalry to splash across the burn and scramble up the Scottish side. Those that crossed over got little sleep; it was feared that the Scots might make a night attack, so they stood to in full armour. The men who had negotiated the burn were exhausted physically; now the strain began to take its toll mentally. Seeds of doubt had been sown that day, with the unexpected and bloody deaths of de Bohun and Deyncourt and the capture of Gray. It was rare for horsed knights to be killed in battle but the English had lost two of their most prominent warriors in a single afternoon, even before the main battle. Furthermore, the English vanguard had been repulsed ignominiously by foot soldiers. The conscript levies of English foot knew that all was not well in their army; the common soldiers looked up to the knights both as their betters and masters, men for whom they worked and to whom they owed their livelihoods. The success of their lords in battle had elevated them, an aristocracy of warriors who had proven their worth in countless battles. But as the foot soldiers slogged their way across the Bannock Burn murmurs of discontent drifted above the quiet, running waters of the burn. Only Edward himself seemed unmoved, determined to engage Bruce in a battle he had craved for years.

Second Day: Monday, 24 June, Feast of John the Baptist

As the first rays of morning sunshine began to insinuate among the trees of the Torwod the English army, drawn up on the north bank of the Bannock Burn, witnessed a sight they had not expected to see. The entire Scottish army began to emerge from the woods, in full view. Then, in the growing light of the summer sun, thousands of Scots suddenly fell on their knees to celebrate Mass led by the Abbott of Inchaffray who then delivered a speech urging the Scots to fight for their freedom. The sudden appearance of the Scots took the English completely by surprise. On seeing the entire Scottish host drop to its knees, Edward asked his companion, Sir Ingram de Umfraville, a traitor Scot, if the Scots intended to fight, then he joked that Bruce's men were begging for mercy. De Umfraville did not hesitate in his answer, saying that the Scots were not asking for mercy from Edward but from God for what they were about to do.[25]

The English knights hastily made the final preparations for a battle they had not expected to fight that early morning. At the head of the vanguard flew the banners of Gloucester and Hereford; the main division led by Edward hoisted the royal standard of the Plantagenet king with its device of three gold lions or leopards on a field of crimson. Opposite, a great mast bore the royal standard of Scotland, a red lion rampant with a red bordure on a field of gold. Bruce positioned his three divisions with Randolph's and Edward Bruce's abreast, the two forming a Scottish front line several ranks deep, about 6,000 spearmen. Bruce took up his position in the rear along with Sir Robert Keith's mobile unit of 500 light horse, ready to deploy wherever the English looked like outflanking Bruce's two main columns. Then Bruce ordered the Scots to advance at a measured pace towards the English vanguard.

There was considerable consternation in the English front lines of horsed knights and men-at-arms. Apart from the astonishing spectacle of finding the Scots still to their front after the previous day's skirmishing, some voiced their opinion that it was bad luck to fight on the day of the Feast of St John the Baptist and that the king should wait until the following day. Unsurprisingly, it was not the young, inexperienced knights who voiced this opinion but the veterans. Their plea for delay attracted scorn from the younger men who were anxious to gain honours for themselves. Chief among those countenancing caution was the Earl of Gloucester who made his disquiet known to Edward as to the state of mind in the army as well as arguing that Edward should respect the feast day. The English king was in no mood to entertain suggestions that he should delay the action. Edward even accused Gloucester of treachery and deceit when his leading commander begged him to wait until the next morning to attack Bruce. Gloucester responded by saying he was neither traitor nor liar, returning sullenly to the vanguard he commanded.[26] It was evident that there was unrest in the high command and that veterans like Gloucester were showing signs of breaking under pressure.

As the Scottish army slowly but steadily advanced, the knights and men-at-arms made their final preparations to engage Bruce's men. From their position, with the sun at their backs on that longest day – it is reckoned that Bannockburn was fought and won before 9am – the English cavalry could clearly see the thousands of Scottish foot soldiers, a solid mass bristling with spears. Curiously, despite the vital role the English archers had played in earlier battles such as Falkirk, they were hardly used in the battle, although some sources credit them with a role. Barbour's *The Brus* has the English bowmen driven from the field by Robert Keith's light cavalry but this is not confirmed by other accounts. If Edwards's archers were engaged at all, it was against the smaller formation of Scottish archers who had the benefit of striking home with their arrows more than the English bowmen, whose arrows were embedded in nothing more than the stout trees in the woods.

Leading the vanguard of the English heavy cavalry, Gloucester and Hereford ordered their knights and men-at-arms to advance at the trot, then a canter until the order to level lances was given, probably by the sound of a recognizable trumpet call. From the outset the ground Bruce had chosen to fight the battle discomfited the English heavy horse which could neither deploy nor avoid bunching up in a heaving mass of men and horses. The already crumbling unity of Edward's cavalry was compounded by the arrival of contingents of English foot soldiers. The Scottish *schiltrons* were packed so tight that they advanced like a thickset hedge which could not be breached.[27] Then, suddenly, the Scottish spearmen halted, readying themselves for Edward's by now charging cavalry, their lances levelled. The Earl of Gloucester was in the forefront; as he closed in on the Scottish vanguard he would have been close enough to see the grim, determined faces of the Scots in the front ranks, their spears bristling like a hedgehog. The English vanguard slammed into the solid phalanxes of Scots, a sickening, bone-crunching collision, with horses impaled on spears. Knights and men-at-arms were thrown to the ground, suffocating under the weight of their armour and the bodies of men and horses which began to pile up on them. Lances and spears that found their mark snapped in two, blood flew in the air, spraying both sides.

Gloucester had engaged Edward Bruce's division on the Scottish right wing. On the left Randolph braced himself for the coming impact, the English waves breaking on the rock that was Bruce's army. Moments after the English vanguard had smashed into the Scottish front line the main cavalry attack was launched, which rocked the Scottish spearmen. The foremost ranks began to show signs of crumbling, but Randolph rallied his men; the *schiltrons* all along the line held fast. Many English knights never struck a single blow that early June morning simply because in that close-packed, heaving mass of men and horses, they had no room even to draw sword. The grass grew slippery with blood, the waters of the Bannock Burn began to change colour ...

The battle was now raging out of control of both Bruce and Edward II. It had degenerated into a desperate, vicious hand-to-hand fracas, a frenzy of men indiscriminately hacking each other to pieces. In the melee Gloucester was somehow isolated and found himself alone; a body of Scots rushed forward, slaying his horse and dragging him to the ground where he lay helpless, unable to rise on account of the weight of his armour. The Scots offered no quarter; when Gloucester's body was retrieved later it bore a multitude of wounds.[28] At the height of their blood-lust the Scots were clearly not taking prisoners, not even men as rich in ransom money as Gloucester. The English onlookers must have been devastated by the sight of a prominent noble of England being slaughtered, the first time this had occurred for many years; added to this was the ignominy of the rank of Gloucester's slayers, mere common foot soldiers and countryfolk.

The constricted area of the field was now beginning to tell on Edward's army, restricting its ability to manoeuvre; weight of numbers was becoming a hindrance. Some three English cavalry divisions, numbering about 5,000, had attacked the Scottish lines but failed to shatter their ranks. Behind them the rear echelons of perhaps a further 1,000 knights and men-at-arms pressed forward in their eagerness to join the fight. Beyond them the massed infantry closed in behind. The narrowness of the field caused the cavalry to bunch up; thus disorganized and constricted, the knights and men-at-arms to the forefront were literally driven on to the spears of the Scottish *schiltrons*. With the weight of those pressing from behind, English casualties began to mount up dangerously. Another disaster came with the death of Robert Clifford, perhaps desperate to save face after his defeat by Randolph the previous day. In that cauldron of slaughter, the loss of one man was of little import; there was only brief mention made of his death.[29]

Trouble began to accumulate for Edward II; this time it came from the distant rear where thousands of troops as yet uncommitted to battle could hear but not see what was happening in the battle raging on the north bank of the Bannock Burn. Morale among the infantrymen was already low; they had learnt of the poor showing of the knights the previous day, nor was there any prospect of booty or renown for them even if Edward won the battle. It was at this point that an unplanned, unexpected but dramatic event took place on the Scottish side. Suddenly, a fresh army – or so it seemed to the disbelieving English – appeared from behind either the nearby Coxet or Gillies' Hills. It was the 'Small Folk' – those given the task of guarding the Scottish baggage train – who came streaming over the hill bearing 'banners' – common camp blankets nailed to poles, hoping to enrich themselves by plundering the English dead and Edward's huge baggage train. Some imaginative students of Scottish history interested in this aspect of Bannockburn have hazarded a theory that among the 'Small Folk' was a contingent of Knights Templars, the Military Order which had played a large part in European conflicts in the twelfth and thirteenth centuries, particularly during the Crusades. Although sworn to chastity, poverty and obedience, the Order had grown over-mighty and wealthy, which had aroused jealousy and ill-will, especially among the hierarchy of senior clergymen, including the Pope himself. Philip IV of France was resolved to enrich himself with their possessions and obtained the consent to proceed thus by Pope Clement V whom he had placed on the Papal Throne. The French Templars were arrested and subjected to extreme torture by which was extracted evidence of outrageous moral offences and grave heresies. The Order was suppressed by Clement V in England, France, Spain, Portugal, Germany and Italy but, for some reason, not Scotland. As Bruce was under excommunication for his murder of the Red Comyn in 1306, some believe that he condoned those Templars living in Scotland and even invited the excommunicated Templars in Europe to settle in Scotland. There is no evidence to support the theory that they were present on the field of Bannockburn at Bruce's side. If they had been, the appearance of even a small group of these medieval warriors in their distinctive white linen mantles with a red cross emblazoned on the left shoulder would have struck terror in the English army that day. The hard-nosed historian is unlikely to accept this theory, compelling though it is.

By now the crumbling English morale finally collapsed. Men began to drift away from the battle, crossing the Bannock Burn in droves. Crossing is too simple a word to describe the panic of the demoralized English; many fell into the waters of the deep ditch, drowning instantly, their bodies acting as a human bridge for those following and trampling them in their haste to gain the other steep side of the burn.

Despite the obvious fact that his battle was lost Edward II refused to concede victory to Bruce, nor quit the field. Aymer de Valence and a knight, Giles d'Argentan, entrusted with Edward's safety, urged the King to depart the field. Were the king to be killed or taken prisoner the ignominy was too appalling to contemplate. Edward was led forcibly from the field, his guardians holding the reins of his war-horse. The Scots were menacingly close and could have easily overtaken the three men. Once Edward was joined by his royal retinue and a body of 500 cavalry, d'Argentan considered he had fulfilled his duty to the king. Turning his horse to face the Scots, he galloped into their midst and was dragged from his mount, then unceremoniously hacked to pieces.[30]

Those English who managed to extricate themselves from this bloodiest of killing fields in the history of Scotland scrambled through marsh, plunging into stream and river, pursued by an uncontrollable horde of screaming Scottish spearmen intent on despatching as many as they could; they were determined that Bannockburn would finally finish the war and bring them freedom from English domination. Edward II ran with his demoralized troops, hoping to gain sanctuary in Stirling Castle. When he arrived at the gates he found them closed. The castle's constable, Philip de Mowbray, had a ringside seat at Bannockburn; from the battlements he watched the horrifying spectacle unfold. He knew that his king had lost not only a battle but, also, under the laws of chivalry, he must in all conscience surrender Stirling Castle to Edward Bruce. De Mowbray duly did so, leaving Edward with no other option but to make his way to safety in the south as best as he could.

On the battlefield the Scots rounded up the important prisoners who would be ransomed, or become hostages to allow Bruce to negotiate for the release of his queen and family who had remained in English custody since 1307. This occurred in due course. Among the first of Bruce's womenfolk to be released were his queen, Elizabeth de Burgh, his daughter Marjorie and his sister Christian. But that was in the future; Bruce was anxious to crown his spectacular victory with the ultimate prize – Edward II himself.

The terrified and frustrated king forced his way through the shattered remnants of his army with 500 horse, galloping to the one place he could expect refuge, the castle of Patrick, Earl of Dunbar. Edward was hotly pursued by the 'Good Sir James' (the Black Douglas), with only eighty light horse. Edward could have easily turned and stood against Douglas but he believed Sir James was only the vanguard of a much larger force of Scottish cavalry. Douglas pressed the fleeing English so relentlessly that they were unable to 'make water' i.e. attend to the call of nature.

With a greatly reduced escort – many of his men had deserted en route to Dunbar – Edward managed to reach the safety of Dunbar Castle, vanishing within its walls where Patrick Dunbar received him 'full gently'. However, shocked by and apprehensive about Edward's defeat, Dunbar could only offer the king a boat to take him to safety in Berwick. It is fruitless to speculate on the conversation which took place between Edward and Dunbar that day. *Scalacronica*, Sir Thomas de Gray's account of Bannockburn written forty-two years later, stated that those closest to Edward who escaped with him to Dunbar were saved but the rest came to grief. Patrick Dunbar received the king honourably and, under feudal law, offered Edward his castle, even removing his own family and household. This was no altruistic gesture on Dunbar's part; there was no doubt nor suspicion that Dunbar would do anything less than his 'devoir [duty], for at that time he was Edward's liegeman'.[31] From Dunbar, Edward sailed to Berwick, then south. Even after Edward's defeat the Earl of Dunbar briefly remained loyal to England; he would soon discover how lightly Edward valued his loyalty.

A contemporary account of Bannockburn stated that:

> Our costly belongings were ravished to the value of £20,000; so many fine noblemen and valiant youth ... all lost in one unfortunate day, one fleeting hour ... Assuredly the proud arrogance of our men made the Scots rejoice in their victory.[32]

The precise number of casualties on both sides at Bannockburn is difficult to quantify. One near contemporary account gives 30,000 English dead, a ridiculously over-inflated figure which has been challenged by historians closer to our own time.[33] A recent excellent account of Bannockburn by David Cornell lists forty-seven men of the rank of knight and above in an appendix to his book *Bannockburn: The Triumph of Robert the Bruce*; among these are Gilbert de Clare, Earl of Gloucester, Sir Giles d'Argentan, John Comyn, Lord of Badenoch, William Deyncourt, Sir Edmund de Mauley, Steward in Edward II's household, and Sir Henry de Bohun. Among the prominent captives were Humphrey de Bohun, Earl of Hereford, Robert de Umfraville, Earl of Angus, Ingram de Umfraville, Sir Thomas Gray of Heton, Marmaduke Twenge and Gibert de Bohun. In addition there were 700 minor nobles and several clergymen. (Most important of all the prisoners was the Earl of Hereford; he was exchanged for Bruce's ladies, as mentioned earlier, and the elderly Robert Wishart, bishop of Glasgow.) Scottish casualties of the rank of knight and above were light; the only nobles slain were Sir William de Vieuxpont (Vipont) and Sir Walter de Ross.[34] Cornell states that the number of casualties among the ranks of ordinary spearmen is impossible to estimate; he also points out that the majority of casualties suffered by the English were not in terms of those killed but taken prisoner although in his view an 'unprecedented number of English bannerets (men knighted on the field) and long-established knights were slain in the engagement' (page 234, *Bannockburn*). It would be a pointless exercise to attempt to quantify the number of dead on both sides; a conservative 'guesstimate' of ten per cent for both sides would produce fatal casualties of English at 2,500 and between 600 and 800 Scots. But this is pure conjecture on the part of the author. The bulk of the English casualties were lost not in battle but in the frenzied attempts of men to escape the field, many coming to grief in the waters of the Bannock Burn and the surrounding marshland.

Safe in England, Edward's response to the Earl of Dunbar's courtesy was swift and callous. Possibly persuaded by his court favourites that, in writing to the king in the autumn of 1313, Dunbar's letter begging Edward to come north to restore order was part of Bruce's strategy to lure Edward north and that Dunbar was in fact a traitor in English eyes. Edward was not noted for his political acumen and relied to an almost criminal degree on the advice of favourites such as Piers Gaveston, the Gascon adventurer who was murdered by Edward's nobles in 1312 for his overbearing attitude, his influence on Edward and that king's generosity to a man who was hated for his arrogance and undeserved wealth.

Edward II declared Patrick, 9th Earl of Dunbar a traitor to the English crown on 25 June – the day after his flight from Bannockburn. Dunbar's English lands were declared forfeit.[35] Dunbar was now reviled by both Scots and English; in desperation the luckless earl had no choice but to seek peace with Robert the Bruce. It says much for Bruce that he waived his own rule that the Scottish lands of every Scottish noble absent from the field of Bannockburn would be declared forfeited. For some reason we can only guess at, Dunbar was allowed to keep his titles and lands in East Lothian, Berwickshire and elsewhere; he was even made welcome at Bruce's court.

Robert Bruce's period of probation was now at an end. Even the English *Chronicle of Lanercost* described him as King of Scotland, which Edward II still refused to do. In November 1314, at Cambuskenneth Abbey, King Robert declared that those earls, barons and knights not present on the field of Bannockburn and whose fealty to England remained intact would lose their Scottish estates. These men became known as *The Disinherited*. That day, Bruce's words were uncompromising; all who

> had not come into his faith and peace ... are to be disinherited forever of lands and tenements and all other status in the Realm of Scotland. And they are to be held in future as foes of the king and the kingdom, debarred forever from all claims of hereditary right ... on behalf of themselves and their heirs.[36]

Bruce also extended his decree to include the English lands held by Scottish nobles from Edward II so that no Scottish male (or female) could thereafter be subject to dual allegiance to Scotland and England. (This is an important point which to a great extent challenges the view of many modern historians that ownership of English lands was never a major factor in the occasional lapses of loyalty in some Scottish nobles. It must be said that Bruce had scarcely a knight or noble in his army at Bannockburn who at one time or another had not sworn allegiance to England for possessions they held south of the Border.)

The English commentators on the reasons for the defeat at Bannockburn clutched at every straw borne on the wind they could imagine. It was the drunken Welsh foot soldiers, it was poor discipline, it was over-confidence, it was unchivalric quarrelling among Edward's commanders. The anonymous author of *Vita Edwardi Secundi* demanded to know why knights unconquered through the ages had run away from mere foot soldiers. The apologists did not – or would not – acknowledge the fact that it was Bruce's excellent choice of ground and his careful preparations which had won the day; Bannockburn was the prime example of Bruce's eye for ground favourable to him, a genius he shared with the Duke of Wellington. The terrain at Bannockburn was heavily wooded, offering cover from the English archers as well as boggy ground which reduced the effectiveness of the English heavy cavalry. Bruce was now acknowledged in Scotland as her true King.

As for Edward, he was fortunate to escape from Bannockburn, then Dunbar but this eleventh hour blessing was mixed. Departing from Dunbar by ship he was probably accompanied by Aymer de Valence and Henry de Beaumont, the future leader of Bruce's *Disinherited* who would cause much trouble for Scotland in the years to come. From Berwick the three men proceeded to York where they tried to come to terms with the calamity of Bannockburn, news of which quickly spread in England, then Europe, creating shockwaves that reverberated long after the defeat. Edward's only consolation was that his personal shield and privy seal, both lost at Bannockburn, were returned to him by the magnanimous Bruce.[37] In doing this Bruce was exercising his diplomatic skills; having beaten Edward in open conflict, he was intent on reaching a peaceful settlement with Edward and had no desire to further ruffle the English king's bedraggled feathers. Bruce knew that, despite his spectacular military and political success, he was in no position to dictate terms to Edward. England was still a formidable adversary and could easily raise another army against Scotland – providing Edward enjoyed the support of the English parliament which met in September 1314. That parliament was presided over by the powerful Earl of Lancaster who had not supported Edward's invasion of Scotland. The list of prominent names of those killed or 'missing in action' grew (as the records of the Great War of 1914–18 euphemistically described those killed without trace on the Western Front) those missing after Bannockburn were thankfully found to be Bruce's prisoners. At least that was a consolation to their families.

After Bannockburn, Edward II never again enjoyed the power he had inherited from his father Edward I, the Hammer of the Scots. After a lacklustre rule of another thirteen years, Edward II was horribly murdered by his French Queen Isabella and her lover, the Earl of Mortimer at Berkeley Castle in 1327.

Before that, Bruce now in his late forties suffered from ill health, mainly due to years of living rough and endless fighting. As yet he had produced no heir to succeed him so, to avert the chaos which followed the death of Alexander III in 1286, an assembly was convened at Ayr in April 1315 to settle the succession question. Should Bruce die without a male heir it was agreed that he would be succeeded by his brother Edward and his heirs male. As a contingency, in the event of a ruler in his minority, Thomas Randolph, Earl of Moray would be appointed regent to administer the country. In 1315 Bruce's daughter Marjorie by his first wife took as husband Walter, High Steward of Scotland. Pregnant in 1316, Marjorie died after a fall from her horse but her baby survived. Named Robert after his grandfather the King, the baby was declared heir presumptive to the throne of Scotland in 1318. The succession question was resolved in 1324 when Bruce's queen, Elizabeth, gave birth to their son David.

Bruce carried the war to England yet again hoping to bring Edward II to the negotiating table and acknowledge him as rightful king of a free and independent Scotland. At the same time the Irish in Ulster opened negotiations with Bruce to assist them in their struggle with England; this gave Bruce yet another opportunity to carry his war against another part of Edward II's empire. (It was announced that if Ireland fell to the Scots, Wales would be next.) In May 1315 Bruce's brother Edward landed at Carrickfergus with an army of 6,000; he had varying successes against the English there, although he was crowned King of Ireland in 1316. During that year and the next Robert Bruce was in Ireland supporting his brother.

Inverkeithing I

During Bruce's absence in Ireland conflict was never far away. In 1317 Edward II sent a fleet north to attempt a landing in Fife. The English ships landed an army, intent on establishing a bridgehead at Inverkeithing on the north side of the Forth estuary. Word reached Robert, Earl of Fife, one of Bruce's loyal followers, who hastened to Inverkeithing to confront the invaders. At first the English onslaught was successful, driving Fife and his men back. However, William Sinclair, Bishop of Dunkeld rallied the Scots who then forced the English back to their ships.

By the year 1317 Bruce controlled the whole of Scotland. King of a united country he now felt strong enough to challenge Pope John XXII who was meddling in Scottish affairs in the interests of England. The Pope had sent two cardinals to England to proclaim a truce between Scotland and England; if Bruce proved refractory, he was to be excommunicated again, along with any of his supporters who were troublesome. Messengers bearing letters for Bruce arrived; the letters did not address him as king, so Bruce informed the envoys that he could not possibly be the man they were addressed to! A second attempt to proclaim the papal truce in Scotland failed for the same reason. Bruce's second excommunication along with those of his supporters in general and the bishops of Scotland in particular did not weaken Scottish resolve. Bruce's next attempt to bring Edward II to the negotiating table and recognize him as king of an independent Scotland came in 1318 when he retook Berwick. The Black Douglas, Randolph and Patrick, Earl of Dunbar, were in the forefront of the siege; according to one account 'James de Douglas with the assistance of Patrick, Earl of March, captured Berwick from the English by means of treason by one of the town, Piers Spalding'.[38] The loss of Berwick was the severest blow to England since Bannockburn. However, that year was tinged with sadness for the Scottish king; his brother Edward Bruce bit off more than he could chew in Ireland by engaging an English army at the battle of Faughart, Dundalk, where he was defeated and killed. The succession to the Scottish throne was again at risk. However, Edward Bruce's campaign had not been in vain; he broke the power of the English in Ireland.

Edward II attempted to recapture Berwick in 1319 by laying siege to the garrison of Berwick Castle. Bruce responded by sending the Black Douglas and Thomas Randolph into Yorkshire with the somewhat farcical intention of seizing Isabella, Edward's queen, who was then living near York. Although this venture came to nothing, Randolph and Douglas routed a raggle-taggle 'army' cobbled together by the Archbishop of York at Myton-on-Swale. The motley band of clergy and countryfolk was no match for Randolph and Douglas. There were so many clergymen among the slain that the encounter was known by the Scots as the Chapter of Myton. This action threw the English besieging Berwick into confusion, Edward's nobles quarrelling and finally abandoning the siege.

And then on 6 April 1320, almost six years after Bannockburn, a battle which should have brought England's recognition of the sovereignty and independence of Scotland, the *Declaration of Arbroath* was drafted and sent to Pope John XXII. The *Declaration* ranks among the most significant documents in the Western world, let alone Scotland. The document is unique not only because it asserts a nation's right to independence, it proclaims that right to the international community of the day. It is also remarkable for its economy of words and therefore its clarity. The *Declaration of Arbroath* has been favourably compared with that other statement asserting personal freedom, the American *Declaration of Independence*, in that it affirms the protest of a small nation against the illegal and undemocratic aggression of a larger one. *Arbroath* is an eloquent declaration of Scottish independence as well as the presentation of Robert Bruce as Scotland's legitimate king. It is memorable for its unequivocal statement that

> for as long as a hundred of us are left alive, we will never be subject to the domination of England. It is not for glory, riches or honour that we fight, but for that liberty, which no good man will consent to lose but with his life.[39]

Even today these defiant words inspire us and rank alongside the stirring speeches of Winston Churchill when Britain was fighting for its very survival in 1940. What is striking about the document is that there is no mention of God, nor of the divine right of a king to rule. Propaganda and a surrogate Scottish constitution it may be; rhetorical it certainly is, but the text is free from judicial, legalistic and bureaucratic language, all of which would have detracted from the immediacy and directness of its message. If the *Marseillaise* comes closest to expressing the comradeship of ordinary citizens in arms against tyranny, the *Declaration of Arbroath* is the response of the soldier-nobles of Scotland who had sworn to defend the rights of the common man. Well, up to a point. Modern university degree students of Scotland's history would be penalized for ignoring the fact that both the Scottish Church and the magnates who ruled their tenants and workers were not acting solely out of altruism; both wished to preserve their standard of living at the expense of the common working men who stood shoulder to shoulder at Bannockburn, bleeding for Bruce and the nobility.

Sadly, the impact of the *Declaration of Arbroath* was lost on England; it did nothing to discourage Edward II's ambitions in Scotland. Neither did the document achieve its other purpose – that of persuading the Pope to remove the sentence of excommunication from Bruce, his chief supporters and the Scottish clergy. Nor did it persuade Edward II 'to think again' as the 'National Anthem' *Flower of Scotland* assures us today. However, some who counselled Edward II did indeed pause to think again which led to the signing of a thirteen-year truce at York on 30 May 1323. Bruce was thereby given a breathing space; he sent Thomas Randolph, Earl of Moray, to Rome to petition for papal recognition of his title and the removal of his excommunication and that imposed on his chief advisers, including the scions of the Scottish Church. Randolph was informed that excommunication would be rescinded only on the restoration of Berwick to the English crown. (Who was it that said that the Church of Rome is more preoccupied with politics than religious belief?) Bruce refused to give up Berwick and continued to suffer the Pope's displeasure.

The year 1327 was memorable in the constitutional history of Scotland. On 15 July the Scottish parliament convened at Cambuskenneth Abbey; it was distinguished by the appearance for the first time of the representatives of the burghs – royal, regal and barony – thus giving the merchant-trading classes a voice in the running of the country. From that day on Scottish parliaments would be comprised of the Three Estates – the Lords spiritual, temporal and secular members of the community of the realm. It was the first attempt to give the ordinary people of Scotland a vote.

By 1327 the troubled but triumphant reign of Robert Bruce was nearing its end. His stubborn enemy Edward II had been dethroned in 1326 by his disaffected Queen Isabella and her supporters, then murdered by her and her lover, Roger Mortimer, who governed England during the minority of Edward and Isabella's son, the future Edward III. The young king was only fifteen when he ascended the throne in 1327; from the outset his reign was beset by difficulties, not just those caused by Scotland but within his own kingdom. Edward III's advisers felt that, as far as Scotland was concerned, there was only one course open to him. In December 1327 Edward's counsellors opened negotiations with Bruce; these talks resulted in the Treaty of Northampton in May 1328 which brought Bruce his reward for years of struggle and deprivation to achieve the freedom of Scotland from English rule. The treaty recognized Scotland as an independent kingdom, her king as rightful sovereign. As a pledge of friendship it was agreed that Bruce's son David would marry Edward III's sister Joanne.

The end was nearing for Bruce, his health rapidly failing. On 7 June 1329 Bruce died at Cardross, Dunbartonshire, of a disease which is unrecorded but was possibly leprosy. His relatively short reign of twenty-three years was one of momentous importance to Scotland. He was undoubtedly the greatest King of Scotland. The word Bannockburn should have been carved on his headstone – if it had been raised. Bruce's remains were buried in Dunfermline Abbey, although his heart was removed for burial in the Holy Land; it never reached there as we shall see in the following chapter.

The deliverance of Scotland by Bruce from the ambitions of Edward I and Edward II would have gladdened the heart of William Wallace, a man Bruce admired but did little to help during the former's struggles between 1297–98. It would be comforting if the words spoken at the end of the film *Braveheart* by the actor playing Bruce at Bannockburn were fact: You have bled with Wallace. Now bleed with me.

Notes

1. *CDS*, vol.v, No.472.
2. *CDS*, vol.ii, No.1236.
3. *CDS*, vol.iii, No. 337 dated October/November 1313.
4. *Rot. Scot.*, vol.i, No.446.
5. Pugh, *Swords, Loaves and Fishes: A History of Dunbar,*p.98; Cornell, *Bannockburn*, p.106.
6. *CDS*, vol.ii, No.1923.
7. Cornell, op.cit., p.146.
8. Oliver, *A History of Scotland,* p.122.
9. Lynch, *A New History of Scotland,* p.124
10. Hume Brown, *History of Scotland,* vol.ii note to p,157 doubts 100,000; Brotchie, *The Battlefields of Scotland* also doubts this figure given in Barbour, *Bruce.*
11. *Calendar of Patent Rolls,* 1216 et seq.
12. Hume Brown, op.cit. p.408; *Vita*, pp52–3; *Chron. Lanercost*, p.206.
13. Quoted in Brotchie, op.cit., p.77.
14. Brotchie, op.cit. p.78.
15. Lynch, op.cit., p.124.
16. Cornell, op.cit., p.152.
17. *Scalacronica*, p.73.
18. *Vita*, op.cit., p.51.
19. Oliver, op.cit., p.123.
20. Barbour, op.cit., p.432; *Chron. Lanercost*, p207; *Scalacronica*, pp.73–5.
21. *Scalacronica*, p.75. This was written by his son, Sir Thomas Gray of Heton while in captivity after the battle of Nesbit Moor, 1335 (see Chapter 6).
22. Barbour, op.cit., p.506.
23. *Scalacronica*, p.75.
24. *Ibid.*
25. Barbour, op.cit., pp.470–2.
26. *Vita*, pp.51–2.
27. *Ibid.*, p.52.
28. *Ibid.*, p.52–3.
29. *Ibid.*, p.54.
30. *Scalacronica*, p.77; Barbour op.cit., pp.494–6.
31. *Scalacronica*, p.79. *Chron.*
32. *Walsingham (Historia Anglicana).*
33. Barbour, *Bruce* gives 30,000; this figure is disputed by Hume Brown op.cit., p.160 and Brotchie, op.cit., pp.85–6.
34. See note 33.
35. Dunbar's lands were in Beanley, Northumberland. About three years after Bannockburn, Edward II issued a writ in favour of his clerk, Stephen de Blount; the lordship of Dunbar was Edward's gift to Blount 'by rebellion of Patrick de Dunbar, a Scotsman'. (*CDS*, vol. iii No.536 dated 2 February 1317). Of course, Blount had little chance of realizing the income from his gift until Scotland was once more subjugated.
36. *APS*, vol. I, p.464.
37. *Chron. Walsingham*, pp.141–2.
38. *Scalacronica*; Pugh op.cit., p.100.
39. Quoted from Pugh, op.cit., p.100.

Chapter 6

The Wars of Independence: 1329–1371

Before the Treaty of Northampton was signed on 4 May 1328, Edward III declared in a written statement that:

> we will concede for us and all our heirs and successors ... that the kingdom of Scotland shall remain forever separate in all respects from the kingdom of England, in its entirety, free and in peace, without any kind of subjection, servitude, claim or demand, with its rightful boundaries as they were held and preserved in the times of Alexander [III] of good memory king of Scotland last deceased, to the magnificent prince, the lord Robert, by God's grace illustrious king of Scots, our ally and very dear friend, and to his heirs and successors.[1]

If only these words had been true. Within three years of Bruce's death, war was resumed.

Bruce's victory at Bannockburn had brought him recognition among his own people as their rightful king; the need to establish his authority once and for all had been the prime reason for fighting the battle. Once he consolidated his rule and convinced his detractors that his claim to the throne was legitimate the civil war in Scotland had come to an end at long last. Although he had made provision for his successor – his brother Edward in the event of his dying without a male heir – his son David born in 1324 succeeded him. (The birth of a son was fortuitous, as Edward Bruce had been killed fighting the English in Ireland in October 1318.) Apart from a half-hearted plot by Balliol's residual supporters in 1320 to unseat Bruce, the remainder of his reign was peaceful. The authority of Bruce as King of Scotland was established not by the Treaty of Northampton but by his victory in 1314. The treaty of 1328 simply gained Bruce the formal recognition of his legitimate right to be King of Scotland. For this reason Bannockburn was and remains the most iconic battle in the entire history of Scotland.

The body of Bruce was scarcely laid to rest in Dunfermline Abbey when Edward III found an excuse to denounce the Treaty of Northampton. Even so, the proposed marriage between Joanne or Joan, Edward's six-year-old sister and Bruce's four-year-old son David took place on 12 July 1328. Pope John XXII also let it be known that he recognized Bruce as King of Scotland and that the ban of excommunication had been lifted from him.

Before we examine the reigns of David II (1329–71) and Edward III (1327–77), there is a postscript to Bruce's death on 7 June 1329. His remains were laid to rest beneath a tomb of Parisian marble in Dunfermline Abbey; however, at his own request, Bruce's heart was removed, embalmed and placed in a locked casket and given into the custody of the 'Good Sir James' the Black Douglas. (The custodian of the key to the casket was an Ayrshire knight, Sir Simon of Lee, whose family later adopted the name of Lockhart for obvious reasons. Today Simon of Lee's descendants are known as the Lockharts of Lee.) Bruce wished that his heart be carried to the Holy Land for interment. Douglas, ever the dutiful and faithful servant, set off for Jerusalem in 1330 by way of Spain. That country was occupied in part by Moorish Saracens against whom King Alphonso XI of Castile was waging a war to oust them from his country. Douglas was invited to lead a division of the Castilian army – a Christian force containing both Scottish and English knights – which being the man he was, he could not resist. Douglas and his force were surprised by a Moorish army at Teba, Andalusia, on 25 August 1330. Douglas led his men into battle, reputedly throwing the casket containing Bruce's heart in front of him, rallying his Scottish comrades with the cry that Robert Bruce was once again leading them to victory. Nearly every knight in Douglas's command was slain; the casket was later retrieved and brought back to Scotland – possibly by Sir Simon of Lee – to be interred in the grounds of Melrose Abbey where it rests today.

The legacy Robert Bruce passed on to his young son David was a Scotland united behind the Bruce family. David II, aged seven, was crowned at Scone on 24 November 1331. As provided for in his father's will, Thomas Randolph, 1st Earl of Moray was appointed regent of Scotland. Under the Treaty of Northampton, those barons of Scotland described as the *Disinherited* by Bruce in an act of parliament on account of their absence from the field of Bannockburn were to have their lands restored. Randolph refused to implement that clause of the treaty. Certain of these barons enjoyed a special relationship with the English Crown which gave Edward III the excuse to interfere in the business of those who administered Scotland. With Bruce dead and his son a mere boy on the throne, Edward made no secret of his intentions; he was resolved to take advantage of the claims of the *Disinherited*, which would lead to further unrest in Scotland and would not cost his treasury a penny. Edward cultivated a special friendship with Edward Balliol, son of the deposed King John. Early in 1332 the confused and parlous state of Scotland was being used by England to justify a third war of independence. Edward III took it upon himself to encourage the ambitions of Edward Balliol to regain the Scottish crown on behalf of his disgraced father. In Edward III's mind, Edward Balliol would resolve his problem with Scotland if Balliol became king there; Balliol's takeover would cost Edward III little and he would have Balliol in his pocket. Balliol had promised Edward his allegiance and fealty were he to be crowned king of Scotland; he would also offer Edward vast tracts of land in Scotland, the inhabitants of which would be required to swear fealty to England.

After their alienation by Bruce the *Disinherited* had lived in exile in England, swearing fealty to Edward Balliol. The majority were Scotsmen but among them were English knights who had also lost their Scottish estates and were excluded from the terms of the Treaty of Northampton. These men were intent on recovering their lands; in return they would recognize Edward Balliol as rightful king of Scotland. For his part, Balliol easily convinced Edward III of the justness of his demands; Edward, an impetuous but politically astute monarch, disguised his political motives under the cloak of chivalry – as had his grandfather, Edward I, during the constitutional crisis known as the *Great Cause* of 1291. Not yet strong enough in his own kingdom to launch an all-out invasion of Scotland, Edward's support for Balliol and the *Disinherited* was a cheap option in perpetuating the war.

So Edward Balliol, with Edward III's clandestine agreement – the English king had made a public show of his opposition to Balliol's proposals but was happy to take advantage of it – began his invasion of Scotland in the summer of 1332. With a pitifully small force of between 1,500 and 2,000 he sailed into the Firth of Forth in August. Landing at Kinghorn, Fife, Balliol marched unopposed to Perth.[2] Chief among his lieutenants was David de Strathbogie, Earl of Atholl, who would later become Balliol's representative in Scotland.[3] The Good Regent, Thomas Randolph, Earl of Moray died in Musselburgh on 20 July and was succeeded by the less popular Donald, Earl of Mar. There is good reason to believe that Balliol anticipated covert assistance from Mar who was known to sympathize with the plight of some of the disinherited Scottish nobles.[4] War was about to break out.

Dupplin Moor

The Earl of Mar took up his position near the river Earn, on the heights of Dupplin Moor, south-west of Perth. On the night of 11 August the Scots were so confident of victory they began drinking heavily. At midnight one of Balliol's lieutenants,Sir Alexander de Mowbray, led a handpicked force over the Earn at a ford shown to him by Murray of Tulliebardine, a traitor in Mar's army.

The ensuing battle on 12 August was a total disaster. As the Scots advanced, Balliol's knights dismounted to form a solid line at the end of the narrow glen through which Mar's men would have to pass. Balliol's foot soldiers contained many archers whose relentless showers of arrows took their toll. Mar's men, also on foot, closed with Balliol's knights and men-at-arms in vicious close-quarter combat. The Scots pressed hard on Balliol's front line, the attack losing momentum as men bunched together, unable to manoeuvre. The main Scottish division or battle marched into this sprawling, heaving melee, falling in their hundreds and crushed underfoot by the lines of their own men following behind. Those who managed to extricate themselves from this undisciplined mess fled, pursued by a small force of Balliol's knights who remounted their war-horses. Of the five loyal Scottish earls who took part in the battle, three were killed and over 2,000 of their men lay dead in the glen. The English casualties were surprisingly light. Edward Balliol had won a spectacular victory against all the odds stacked against him. Mar's superiority in numbers proved his undoing, along with poor choice of terrain and leadership. His position, lacking the cover of woods, offered prime targets to Balliol's archers. Among the dead was a natural son of Robert the Bruce who had openly accused Mar of treachery, then spurred his horse to charge Balliol's men alone; he was killed instantly. Estimates of Scottish casualties range from between 2,000 to 13,000 to Balliol's thirty-five killed. It was said that the Scottish dead were piled as high as the length of a spear; among them were Donald, Earl of Mar and Hugh, 4th Earl of Ross whose daughter Euphemia married Robert the Steward, the future King Robert II. Dupplin Moor was the worst defeat of Scottish arms since Wallace's disaster at Falkirk in 1298.[5] The numerically superior Scottish army was beaten by confusion, abysmal leadership and drunkenness. Honesty, loyalty, determination and national pride were the real casualties at Dupplin Moor.

Despite his victory at Dupplin, Balliol's situation was precarious; he knew that escape or reinforcement lay in the Firth of Tay, where his fleet of ships was commanded by Henry de Beaumont, the effective commander of his forces. De Beaumont, a survivor of Bannockburn nearly twenty years earlier, was ready to repel any attempts on his small fleet by the Scots loyal to David II.

The crews commanded by de Beaumont were raised chiefly by those English lords who had lost lands granted to them by English kings before and since Bannockburn, along with those native Scottish lords Bruce had disinherited in 1314 on account of their absence from Bannockburn. The *Disinherited* army of 1332 hardly deserved the name, consisting of 500 mounted knights and men–at–arms and possibly 1,000 infantry. Balliol's chances of success in gaining the throne of Scotland did not look in the least promising. The fleet commanded by Henry de Beaumont lying off the Firth of Tay was Balliol's means of escape should he be defeated at or near Perth, which he intended to occupy after his victory at Dupplin Moor. De Beaumont's evacuation fleet was attacked by John Crabb, a Flemish sailor and engineer in the pay of David II; Crabb captured de Beaumont's flagship, only to be repulsed by the remainder of Balliol's ships, which destroyed Crabb's entire fleet and secured Balliol's escape route by sea.

The Scots abandoned Perth, from where Balliol proceeded to Scone and had himself crowned King of Scotland by the Earl of Fife and the Bishop of Dunkeld. Balliol marched his small force from Scone to Roxburgh, where on 23 November he formally recognized Edward III as his lord and feudal superior. During his brief period as pretender to the Scottish throne, Balliol issued charters which declared the country a vassal state of England. However, the nationalists loyal to David II had recovered from the confusion which followed Dupplin Moor. A force was gathered by John, second son of the late regent, Randolph, Sir Archibald Douglas and his kinsman William Douglas, the 'Knight of Liddesdale'; in December 1332, they surprised Balliol at Annan, killing his younger brother and cutting off his followers. 'King' Edward Balliol narrowly avoided capture, escaping over the Border partially clothed and riding an unbridled horse.

Matters deteriorated in 1333 when Edward III, taking counsel from his nobles, received unqualified support for an invasion of Scotland and the occupation of Berwick, a Scottish royal burgh since 1318. Edward ordered his nobles to assemble with their followers at Newcastle–upon–Tyne in May 1333; his army included Earls Percy and Neville of Northumberland and Lords Lucy and Mowbray.

In the spring of 1333, Edward III bypassed Berwick and entered southern Scotland, marching as far as Scone, taking Edinburgh Castle, then the castle of Dalkeith, home of the Earl of Douglas. By summer Edward had made his headquarters at Roxburgh to prepare for his siege of Berwick. Around this time the Scots suffered a double disaster; the regent Sir Andrew Murray and his kinsman William Douglas, the 'Knight of Liddesdale' were taken prisoner by the English in separate engagements. Balliol, still smarting from his ignominious flight from Annan the year before began the siege of Berwick in March. In May Edward III joined Balliol who had dug trenches, destroyed the conduits supplying the town's water and cut all communications with the Scots. The engineer John Crabb who had failed to destroy Balliol's fleet the year before near Dupplin had changed sides; Crabb knew the defence systems at Berwick intimately, having assisted Robert Bruce in his siege of Berwick in 1318.

The new regent, Sir Archibald Douglas, was faced with a dilemma all too familiar for the time – the terms under which Berwick would surrender if these were not met by 11 July. In the game of war, the conditions were typical of sieges during the Middle Ages. Edward III dictated that Berwick would have to be relieved by a Scottish army on the north side of the Tweed. Alternatively, a division or 'battle' of at least 200 Scottish knights would have to enter Berwick between sunrise and sunset with the loss of no more than thirty men. If these conditions were not met then Sir Alexander Seton, the commander of the town, would surrender it. The truce negotiated by Seton was due to expire on 11 July; in a show of goodwill Seton offered his son as a hostage to Edward III. The deadline arrived; Berwick should have surrendered but Seton held out, knowing that help was at hand with the arrival of Sir Archibald Douglas, Guardian of Scotland and a strong army.

To reduce the pressure on Berwick, Douglas led his force into Northumberland on 11 July, where he proceeded to destroy Tweedmouth in full view of Edward's army. Edward did not move. Then a small party led by Sir William Keith managed to force its way into Berwick which technically met Edward III's second condition. Douglas sent a message to Edward, demanding that the siege be lifted; Edward replied that in his eyes Berwick had not been relieved. Edward then began to execute Scottish hostages every day, one of whom was the third and last surviving son of Sir Alexander Seton. Seton watched his heir Thomas being hanged before the town wall. Atrocities such as these would only cease when Berwick was surrendered. Seton negotiated a second truce which stipulated that he would open the gates of Berwick on 20 July if the town was not relieved on that day. The loss of Berwick to the Scots in 1318 had become a matter of honour to Edward III; regaining it would restore his standing among the English nobility. Sir Archibald Douglas had little choice but to fight the English king on ground not of his own choice.

Halidon Hill

Edward III took up position on Halidon Hill, a 600–foot eminence two miles north-west of Berwick which offered him an excellent view of the town and the surrounding countryside. Douglas, still in Northumberland, re-crossed the Tweed to the west of Edward's position, making camp at Duns on 18 July. On the following day he approached Halidon Hill from the north-west, occupying a higher eminence, known as the Witches' Knowe from where he could study the size and position of the English army. The size of the respective armies is not entirely clear; some accounts give 13,000 Scots and 9,000 English; the former figure was probably nearer 18,000, the latter undoubtedly in excess of 9,000.

Edward was accompanied by Henry de Beaumont who had been with Edward Balliol at Dupplin Moor the year before; de Beaumont would have advised Edward about the tactics which had given Balliol his victory. Edward organised his army in three divisions or 'battles'; the left wing was commanded by Balliol, the right by Thomas Brotherton, Earl of Norfolk and Marshal of England, while Edward

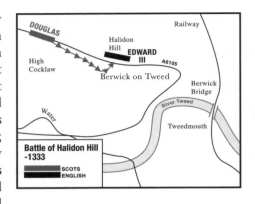

himself took the centre. Importantly, the flanks of each of the three battles were protected by troops of English and Welsh longbowmen; clearly, Edward had paid heed to de Beaumont's advice about Dupplin Moor. (He would use his bowmen to even greater effect at Crecy in 1346.)

Douglas drew up his forces in four battles of *schiltrons*; he commanded the left wing, Robert the Steward (the future Robert II) the centre and John Randolph, 3rd Earl of Moray on the right, with Hugh, Earl of Ross in reserve. Douglas had to descend from the Witches' Knowe into a boggy plain before he could attack the English – uphill. Douglas knew this would be no cavalry battle but one dominated by England's archers who had decimated Mar's army at Dupplin Moor.

As the Scots laboured across the marshy plain that lay before Halidon Hill, Edward ordered his packed wedges of archers to commence their deadly work. The arrows began to fall thick and fast, taking their toll of the Scottish spearmen in their unwieldy *schiltron* formations designed for stationary defence rather than as mobile formations. The *Chronicle of Lanercost* tells us that

> the Scots who marched in the front were so wounded in the face and blinded by the English arrows that they could not help themselves and soon began to turn their faces away from the blows of the arrows and fall …

Yet still the Scots came on. Moray's by now depleted battle closed with Balliol, with Robert the Steward attacking King Edward in the centre, followed closely by Douglas. Moray's *schiltron* began to disintegrate in the vicious hand-to-hand fighting with Balliol's troops; the Scots were exhausted after their struggle through the marshy terrain, then the uphill climb. Douglas and the Steward arrived too late to save Moray; his spearmen began to flee down the hill, showered by English arrows and pursued by Edward III's by now mounted knights. The Scottish centre was constricted; as at Dupplin they bunched up and then panic set in, the entire front line collapsing in confusion. In the headlong flight only the rearguard commanded by Hugh, Earl of Ross and his Highlanders stood firm until they were overwhelmed. Robert the Steward and Moray escaped; Douglas, with three Scottish earls, Ross, Carrick and Sutherland lay dead on the field along with thousands of Scots; the lowest estimate was 14,000.[6] Edward III's casualties were light. The following day, 20 July, Berwick surrendered.

In 1334, Robert the Bruce would have found much to disappoint him in Scotland. His son David II and the young boy's English Queen Joan were sent to France out of harm's way. Edward III was master of Scotland which would be ruled in his name by Edward Balliol. At an obsequious parliament held in Edinburgh on 10 February 1334, Balliol proclaimed Edward III as his Lord Paramount; then on 12 June, at Newcastle, Balliol ceded 2,000 *librates* (82,000 acres) nearly twenty-three per cent of prime agricultural land from the Solway Moss to the Firth of Forth to Edward III 'for ever'. Included in this shameful transaction were the important castles of Roxburgh, Berwick, Dunbar and Edinburgh.

In 1335, Edward came to Carlisle from where he mounted a robust campaign against Sir Andrew Murray of Bothwell, now leading the pro-Bruce faction in Scotland. Murray was the son of the Andrew Murray who had fought alongside Wallace at Stirling Bridge and had lost his life in that battle. In July Edward moved into south-west Scotland, plundering many towns including Roxburgh. At the same time Balliol advanced from Berwick up the east coast, followed by his cousin Guy de Namur and 2,000 Flemish mercenaries. Namur had arrived too late in Berwick to join Balliol's force; on his way to Edinburgh the Fleming was constantly harried by Douglas of Liddesdale, John Randolph, Earl of Moray and Patrick, Earl of Dunbar.

Burghmuir

On 30 July, Namur was attacked in strength on the Burghmuir of Edinburgh by Douglas, Randolph, Dunbar and Dunbar's ally, Alexander Ramsay, Earl of Dalhousie. A brief, running fight ensued and Namur lost several of his men.[7] Forced to disengage, the Fleming led what remained of his 2,000 men down Candlemaker Row in Edinburgh where he prepared to make a stand in what today is the esplanade of Edinburgh Castle, seeking refuge in that castle's ruins. The beleaguered Flemish slaughtered their mounts to form a barricade, determined to resist their attackers to the bitter end. However, Namur and his force, disheartened by their losses and lacking food and water, surrendered the following day.

Young John Randolph, who had inherited the Moray earldom after his brother's death at Dupplin Moor chivalrously agreed to escort Namur to the Scottish border. Accompanied by James and William Douglas, Randolph was ambushed by an English raiding party from Roxburgh Castle; James Douglas was killed, William escaped and Randolph was taken in chains to the Tower of London. He would remain in custody there until 1341, although he was brought to Dunbar in 1338 as a bargaining counter during the siege of Dunbar Castle, defended by his sister, the famous 'Black' Agnes Randolph, Countess of Dunbar.

Despite minor victories the nationalist cause began to founder in the second half of 1335; there was disaffection among the nobles and a mini-civil war flared up between Balliol's erstwhile supporters led by David de Strathbogie, Earl of Atholl. Strathbogie had been forced to transfer his allegiance from Balliol to David II but returned to the Balliol camp after the Peace of Perth in August 1335 where he re-affirmed his allegiance to Balliol in return for the restoration of his earldom of Atholl. In addition Strathbogie was appointed as Balliol's Constable of Scotland, a somewhat empty title, given the events which followed.

Culblean

In the autumn of 1335, Strathbogie raised an army of 3,000 and with some siege engines, set out to conquer the north-east of Scotland in Balliol's name. His plan was simple – to eject the Bruce following there and replace it with the *Disinherited* nobles or their heirs from that region. Being autumn, every knight-tenant, landowner and humble cottar (crofter) was engaged in bringing in the harvest. Strathbogie's campaign was marked by the smoke from burning hayricks, his men feasting off slaughtered livestock. Then Strathbogie laid siege to Kildrummy Castle, east of Aviemore, where David II's aunt Christian Bruce was sheltering. (Christian Bruce was the wife of the Guardian, Sir Andrew Murray.) Strathbogie extracted a promise from Sir John Craig, commander of Kildrummy that unless a relief force arrived by 30 November (St Andrew's Day), the castle would surrender to him.

Sir Andrew Murray was in Bathgate engaged in negotiations with Balliol's commissioners when the news of Kildrummy reached him. Murray immediately broke off the talks and marched north with 800 knights and gentry including the Earl of Dunbar, Douglas of Liddesdale and Sir Alexander Seton along with about 3,000 infantry.[8] Learning of the approach of the relief column, Strathbogie withdrew from Kildrummy and bivouacked in the Forest of Culblean, near Ballater on Deeside. Sir John Craig, Kildrummy Castle's commander and his 300-strong garrison shadowed

Strathbogie, linking with Sir Andrew Murray and his force on St Andrew's Day.

Early in the morning of 30 November, Murray split his force into two divisions, himself commanding one, Douglas of Liddesdale the other. A half-asleep sentry in Strathbogie's camp heard the sounds of the approaching army. In the growing light, Strathbogie readied his men for an attack he expected to come from the rear of his camp. On that grey autumn morning nearly 4,000 men from the Lothians, the Merse and elsewhere stood in ordered lines among the trees of the Forest of Culblean; perhaps that November morning there was a mist which offered some protection from Strathbogie's archers. Strathbogie attacked Douglas of Liddesdale in a headlong frontal assault, charging in force to disable the Scottish wing. As the two groups clashed, Murray pressed forward with his division. In the ensuing melee Murray's men chased Strathbogie deeper into the wood. The battle was soon over; attended by five of his knights Strathbogie placed his back against a tree, fighting bravely until he was cut down, his body pierced by several swords.

Culblean was no Bannockburn but it brought back shades of Bruce's victories, giving Sir Andrew Murray the courage to continue the struggle. In many ways Culblean was the turning point in this, the second war of independence. The struggle was no longer one of loyalty to David Bruce or Edward Balliol but to the realm of Scotland. Culblean, a minor battle in the north, was won by men from the Lothians and the Merse, Lowlanders who had long been accused of being in the pocket of three English Kings – Edward I, II and III. The Lowlanders' victory at Culblean restored their honour. Even the chronicles of later years would look back on Culblean as a deciding factor in the struggle for Scotland's independence.

As mentioned earlier, by 1337 Edward III had lost interest in Scotland, the year he arrogantly declared himself King of France, which began the conflict known to history as the Hundred Years' War. Thereafter, Edward limited his intervention in Scotland's affairs intermittently and half-heartedly. Although the war between England and Scotland continued, it was no longer prosecuted with the same impetus and enthusiasm and scale as it had been in the days of Edward I.

In a succession of skirmishes and sieges, the Scots gradually cleared the English out of most of Scotland, although the south-east still remained in their possession. By mid-1337, the disinherited nobles had been forced into a small corner of south-west Scotland. Edward III was increasingly absent from England on the Continent, eager to pursue his ambitions in France which offered better rewards than a Scotland impoverished by years of warfare. He paid Scotland little interest, knowing that Edward Balliol was now a spent force on whom he could no longer rely. But the English still occupied the

Merse and Roxburghshire, reaping rich rewards from the fertile agricultural lands and lording it over the rural population.

And then came a minor but significantly morale-boosting event in January 1338. After Edward III rebuilt Edinburgh Castle in 1337, he was content to rest on his laurels, losing interest in the subordinate or satellite castles in the south-east – Berwick, Roxburgh and Dunbar – as he considered Edinburgh the key to controlling the area and allowing his forces to continue their occupation of a rich agricultural region where his troops could subsist at little cost to the English Treasury. With Edinburgh Castle in English hands, Dunbar Castle assumed an importance for the Scots as it kept open lines of communication with France, Scotland's ally. To allow him to further his ambitions in France, Edward appointed Thomas de Beauchamp, Earl of Warwick as his lieutenant in Scotland.

John of Fordun's *Chronicle* tells us that in the summer of 1337, Lothian suffered wholesale destruction while Patrick, 9th Earl of Dunbar and March, was campaigning with Sir Andrew Murray in Fife and Lanarkshire, reducing every castle in those counties which still held out for Edward III or Balliol. In Lothian, the ineffective Earl of Warwick was replaced by Richard Fitzalan, Earl of Arundel and William Montague, Earl of Salisbury; Arundel and Salisbury were appointed joint commanders of south-east Scotland. Salisbury would become the dominant partner in the events which took place in the first half of 1338.

The centre of resistance in south-east Scotland was Dunbar, East Lothian, where its virtually impregnable castle was left in charge of Agnes Randolph, Patrick 9th Earl of Dunbar's Countess. Because of the unrest in the south-east, Salisbury and Arundel decided that Dunbar Castle must be taken as it posed a threat to stability in the remaining English-held territory. Their strategy was also aimed at relieving pressure on castles in the vicinity still occupied by English or pro-English garrisons. While the siege of Dunbar Castle was in no sense a set-piece battle which qualifies as a Scottish 'killing field', it deserves a brief mention in this account because its successful defence prevented the need for a pitched battle by the Scots to regain control of the south-east of Scotland.

The siege of Dunbar began on 13 January 1338;[3] it would last for twenty-two weeks. 'Black' Agnes successfully withstood every attempt made by Salisbury and Arundel to capture the castle, by both fair means or foul; Salisbury tried bribery and blackmail to no avail. (Agnes's sole surviving brother John was brought from the Tower of London and displayed before her, Salisbury threatening to execute him if she did not surrender. Agnes simply replied that were he to do so, she would inherit the earldom of Moray!) In June 1338, Agnes was relieved by Sir Alexander Ramsay of Dalhousie, much to the annoyance of Edward III.

The elation of the Scots occasioned by the successful outcome at Dunbar was marred by the death of the regent, Sir Andrew Murray of Bothwell; he was replaced by Robert the Steward. The town of Perth remained in the hands of the English, so the new regent concentrated his resources into recovering it. For some unknown reason, Edward III recalled Edward Balliol to England before Robert the Steward began the siege of Perth; perhaps the English king had lost any residual confidence in Balliol, or he wished to spare him the embarrassment of possible defeat. Perth had been placed in the charge of a Thomas Ughtred, who may have been a Northumbrian, given his surname; Ughtred was a common name in that region of northern England during the time of the Bernician Angles.

Perth was a strongly fortified and walled town; however, the Scots aided by some French auxiliaries experienced little difficulty in bringing the pro-English garrison to the negotiating table. In August 1339, Ughtred capitulated and was permitted to march out of Perth with his force intact and return to England. The subsequent re-capture of the castles of Stirling and Edinburgh meant that by 1341, it was deemed safe for David II and his Queen Joan to end their exile in France. David Bruce was hampered by two incompatible political ends when he began his reign in 1341 at the age of seventeen. Scotland's ties with France through the *Auld Alliance* remained an obstacle to possible peace with England. David II could not feel secure on the throne of Scotland until England's claims to overlordship of the country were rescinded, which Edward III would not abandon until Scotland's alliance with France was terminated.

In 1346, Philip VI of France called upon David to relieve the pressure on France by Edward III who in August 1346 had scored a spectacular victory against the French at Crécy. David responded by raising an army and invading England with a formidable army in the autumn of 1346. He engaged the forces of Edward III at Neville's Cross, near Durham, on 17 October; decisively beaten, David was taken prisoner along with four of his senior earls and the Bishop of St Andrews. In addition, fifty barons were taken into captivity. Among the fatal casualties was John Randolph, 4th Earl of Moray who had been unceremoniously dragged before his sister Agnes during the siege of Dunbar in 1338. David II would spend the next eleven years in English captivity; in his place, Scotland was ruled by the weak Robert the Steward. Ironically, it was the battle of Neville's Cross which brought hostilities between Scotland and England to an end.

Nesbit Moor I

In August 1355 the first of two battles at Nesbit Moor took place; the Scots were driven to conflict due to the breakdown of negotiations for the release of David II from English custody. A raid on the lands of Patrick, 9th Earl of Dunbar led by Sir Thomas Gray of Heton and Lord Dacre, Warden of the English East March brought retaliation from Dunbar and William, 1st Earl of Douglas. The Scottish force was small but included a contingent of sixty French knights anxious to prove themselves against the English. The Scots burnt Norham village on the English side of the river Tweed, hoping to draw Sir Thomas Gray out of Norham Castle. Retiring with their booty, the Scots were pursued by Gray and Dacre who fell into a trap set for them by Dunbar and Douglas at Nesbit Moor. Although the number of troops on both sides was small, the English suffered the greater casualties; Gray and Dacre were taken prisoner and later ransomed. While Dunbar was content with the outcome, southern Scotland would suffer for his affair of honour. After a successful assault by Dunbar on Berwick in November 1355, Edward III recovered the town in January 1356, then led an army into Berwickshire and East Lothian, burning villages and towns up to Haddington. Edward's winter campaign is known in Scottish history as the *Burnt Candlemas* (2 February 1356); it was during this campaign that the famous and historic church of Haddington, the Franciscan Minorites or Grey Friars' *Lamp of Lothian* was destroyed.[13] However, the months of January and February 1356 were stormy and Edward's supply ships were wrecked, forcing him to retreat across the Tweed. Later that year, after his crushing defeat of the French at Poitiers, Edward could afford to be magnanimous to France's ally Scotland and he granted a truce with the no doubt relieved Scottish nobles governing the country.

When David II returned to Scotland from England, his need for money forced him to lean more heavily on the royal burghs to secure his income, known as the *Great Customs*, the taxes due to the Crown on goods bought and sold in the king's burghs. (The taxes due to the royal burghs themselves were known as the *Petty Customs*, petty being a corruption of the French *petit*, or small.) In return for their increased tax burden, the royal burghs secured a right to send representatives to the Scottish parliament, becoming known as the 'Third Estate', the other two being the Lords spiritual and temporal.

The second half of David's reign was beset by squabbling between himself and the nobles. After remaining in English captivity since his defeat at Neville's Cross, in 1357 David returned to a kingdom racked by feuds and disease, notably the Black Death, the plague which had first arrived in Scotland in 1349, although that outbreak was less severe in Scotland than in England.

David II died suddenly on 22 February 1371. There is a great deal in David's character which is hard to admire; arrogant, self-absorbed, quarrelsome, he alienated his nobles by his petty behaviour. Given his father's achievements, he should have tried to live up to these but he was never the man his father had been. He died without a male heir and was succeeded by his nephew, Robert the Steward as Robert II, a man he detested. Although the third war of independence would flicker on until 1390, hostilities were limited to Border bickering for many years of Robert II's reign, although full-scale war would erupt in 1385, as we shall see.

Notes

1. The Scottish duplicate of this indenture and Edward's charters – both in French – are to be found in the National Archives of Scotland (quoted in Oliver, *A History of Scotland*, p.128.)
2. Balliol had English knights in his contingent, men such as Henry de Beaumont, Gilbert de Umfraville, Earls Talbot, Ferrers and de la Zouche, all of whom possessed lands in Scotland until Bannockburn (Pugh, *Swords, Loaves and Fishes: A History of Dunbar*, p.399.)
3. Pugh, op. cit., p.399.
4. Hume Brown, *History of Scotland*, vol. i, footnote to p.171.
5. Pugh, op. cit., p.101.
6. English chroniclers give seventy lords, 500 knights and 30,000–65,000 foot, the last figure being ridiculous. Fordun admits he gave up counting the dead as a pointless exercise. Equally ridiculous are the English casualties – one knight, one foot soldier and an unquantified body of reinforcements from Newcastle who arrived late in the action.
7. In 1867 a large quantity of human bones was uncovered about five feet below ground at the northern end of the Burghmuir. (Grant, *Cassells Old and New Edinburgh.*)
8. The figure of 800 is considered absurdly low by Dr W.D. Simpson in his account of Culblean; he considers this figure relates only to men of chivalry – knights etc., and that Murray's force numbered 4,000, Strathbogie's 3,000, the figure given for the siege of Kildrummy (*Proc. of the Soc. of Antiquaries of Scotland*, vol. 64, p.205.)
9. Hume Brown, op. cit., vol.. i p.177.

Chapter 7

The Stewart Dynasty: 1371–1541

It is not by mere chance that, having reached the mid-point of this account, it is appropriate that this chapter should begin with the reign of Robert II (1371–1390), the first monarch of the House of Stewart or Stuart which would govern Scotland for the next three hundred years or so, with a gap between 1688 and 1702 when, in the latter year, the last Stuart queen, Anne, ruled a united Britain until 1714. Thereafter, the German House of Hanover, in the person of George I, succeeded to the throne under the Act of Settlement of 1701.

To do full justice to individual Stewart monarchs would require a book for each reign; in this account, their histories are limited to the battles they fought on Scottish soil and the political events which brought about these conflicts. Many of the Stewart killing fields were occasioned not by war with England but by civil wars caused by pretenders to the throne, first of Scotland, then of England, Scotland and Ireland. English kings still led or ordered invasions of Scotland, particularly during the period known in Scotland's history as the *Rough Wooing* between 1545 and 1547, when England meddled in the affairs of Scotland and attempted to dictate the line of succession to the Scottish throne in the lead-up to the reign of Mary, Queen of Scots. The key events and conflicts of the *Rough Wooing* are examined in the following chapter. In this chapter we are concerned with the killing fields of Scotland leading up to the mid-sixteenth century.

A truce signed between Scotland and England in 1369 to last for fourteen years was hardly observed. In 1377, an equerry of George, 10th Earl of Dunbar and March was slain at Roxburgh Fair, Roxburgh being occupied by the English along with Berwick, parts of Teviotdale and the castles of Jedburgh, Annandale and Lochmaben. George Dunbar demanded redress for the murder of his retainer from Henry Percy, Earl of Northumberland, Warden of the English East March which included Roxburgh. When Percy refused, Dunbar took the law into his own hands. He set fire to the town of

Roxburgh and slaughtered every Englishman he encountered.[1] In response, Percy delivered a strong complaint to Robert II on 14 October 1377 which the Scottish King studiously ignored. This tit-for-tat situation resulted in a retaliatory raid by Percy on Dunbar's earldom. This fiasco was known as the *Warden's Raid*; when Percy and his knights were asleep in their camp near Duns, the ordinary folk loyal to Dunbar surrounded the camp under cover of darkness, scaring off the English horses with heavy wooden rattles used to drive away birds from the grain at harvest-time. Percy's largely mounted force were forced to walk back over the Border in full armour, carrying their heavy lances on their shoulders.

Melrose and Benrig

In 1378 Sir Archibald Douglas and William, 1st Earl of Douglas, defeated Sir Thomas de Musgrave, governor of Berwick, at Melrose. Then skirmishing in the Borders continued. In 1380 William, 1st Earl of Douglas invaded the West March of England, while George, 10th Earl of Dunbar engaged a small English force of 200 led by Ralph, 3rd Baron Greystoke of Cumberland who was taking provisions to the English garrison of Roxburgh Castle. On 25 June Dunbar engaged Greystoke at Benrig, near St Boswell's, where he defeated and captured the English knight. Dunbar took Greystoke to Dunbar Castle where, with supreme irony, he entertained the luckless knight with the food intended for Roxburgh. John of Gaunt, the Duke was then sent to Scotland with Richard II's offer of peace or war; a treaty was signed at Berwick in 1380 for a peace which would last until 1383.

About the middle of April 1384, the French King Charles VI sent an embassy to Edinburgh to negotiate the recent treaty made with Richard II of England which would include Scotland. Disposed as he was to keeping the peace, Robert II received the French ambassadors cordially. At the same time, a party of thirty French knights and their esquires arrived in Montrose, Angus; they made their way to Edinburgh, announcing to Robert II that they wished to prove their prowess against England, which Robert sensibly refused to entertain. In defiance of his wishes, some of his barons held a secret meeting in St Giles Cathedral in Edinburgh's High Street and decided that they would support and encourage the campaign proposed by the French. They made a foray into the territories of the Earls of Northumberland and Nottingham which brought them much booty. For his part, Robert II the peacemaker despatched a herald to the English court, admitting that the French raid had been engineered by his own nobles but prayed that Scotland might benefit from the truce between France and England. Richard II granted this request but as the Anglo-French truce only lasted until October 1384, there was no guarantee of permanent peace. In June 1384 the Earls of

Northumberland and Nottingham exacted their revenge – not on the French adventurers but on southern Scotland. The two earls led an army into Dumfries and the Lothians, which were devastated; Edinburgh suffered damage and Haddington was burnt to the ground.

The year 1385 might be termed the Year of the French in Scotland. The Anglo–French treaty, due to expire in October 1384, was extended to May 1385. Robert II decided he would throw in his lot with France, sending envoys to Charles VI and asking him to despatch a large force to Scotland to make war on their common enemy, England. Charles VI responded quickly; in the summer of 1385, he sent Sir John de Vienne, Admiral of France. De Vienne arrived in Leith with a force of 2,000 auxiliaries and 1,400 suits of armour. Money was also promised but not paid in 1385; that did not happen until a year later. In support of Vienne, a French fleet was ordered to attack southern England but this part of the strategy was never carried out.

The planned invasion of England took place but with limited success, much to the disgust of the French. Initially, de Vienne's force received a warm welcome from the nobles in charge of the Scottish towns where they were billeted – Dunfermline, Queensferry, Dalkeith, Dunbar and Kelso. But the common folk did not share their feudal superiors' enthusiasm for the French guests, knowing that their presence would mean retaliation from England. Many thought that their presence was as bad as being invaded by England; for their part, the French were increasingly dismayed by the coldness of their reception. Consequently they did nothing to ingratiate themselves with the local population, foraging for their food and taking whatever they pleased until, at one point, a hundred of the French 'guests' were slaughtered by the populace of individual towns.

From the outset, there was disaffection between the Scots and the French. The campaign that followed did little to improve Franco–Scottish relations. The truth of it was that Robert II neither wanted – nor could he afford – an all-out war with England. De Vienne and his knights anticipated brilliantly staged pitched battles; what they got was a mere Border raid. An army of 30,000 led by the Earls of Douglas and Moray invaded Northumberland, penetrating only halfway between Berwick and Newcastle. Learning of the approach of a counter invasion force numbering 67,000 under the Duke of Lancaster and the Earls of Northumberland and Nottingham, the Scots retreated; much to the disgust of de Vienne, the Scots laid waste to the countryside as they went.

Richard II had taken the union of the French and the Scots seriously, so much so that in addition to Lancaster's force, he invaded Scotland with a second army. Richard did not spare Lowland Scotland; supported by a provisioning fleet, he put Melrose Abbey to the torch, then went on to burn

Dundee, Perth and Edinburgh. To the amazement of the French, the Scots made no attempt to defend themselves; instead they avoided Richard and broke into Westmorland and Cumberland, securing much booty. The French had hoped to win battle honours; by the autumn, de Vienne had had enough of what he saw was not chivalrous conduct but common brigandage. To his credit de Vienne honoured a pledge to the Scottish King that he would pay for the expense of maintaining his force in Scotland himself or promise to make good the debt, which was met in 1386 by the French King. De Vienne then set sail for France. The sole gain for the Scots in 1385 was that peace with England was restored until 1388, although Border hostilities continued.

In 1390, the aged and ailing King Robert II died at the unusually ripe old age of seventy-five. He was succeeded by his third son, John, Earl of Carrick, who had been appointed regent in 1388. In that year John had been kicked by a horse and was badly lamed for the rest of his life. When he ascended the throne he decided to shed his name John, which was considered unlucky on account of John Balliol (1292–96) and was crowned at Scone on 14 August 1390 as Robert III. At least Robert II died consoled by a further treaty of peace between Scotland, England and France which would last until 1392. Even though the English still held Berwick and Roxburgh, it was hoped that the treaty might be the final chapter in what was known as the third war of independence, the Scottish equivalent of what became known as the Hundred Years' War between England and France (1337–1453).

Nesbit Moor II

Robert III's reign was fairly peaceful until 1402, when hostilities resumed with England, occasioned by what was in effect a spoiling raid by Patrick Hepburn of Hailes, a minor noble whose family occupied the strong castle of Hailes near East Linton, East Lothian. In 1402, Scottish nobles launched a co-ordinated invasion of northern England; some 12,000 troops crossed the Border into Cumberland, raiding and looting in the Carlisle area, returning north with their booty. This led to a further small-scale raid by Hepburn of Hailes, John Haliburton of Dirleton and Robert Lauder of Edrington in Northumberland. The small force of 400 was pursued by George Dunbar, son of George, 10th Earl of Dunbar and March. The 10th Earl had defected to England in 1400 due to a quarrel he had with Robert III. Dunbar's daughter Elizabeth had been betrothed to Robert III's son and heir David, Duke of Rothesay; obviously with an eye on the future, Dunbar had paid Robert a substantial dowry to ensure the marriage would proceed. At the eleventh hour, young Rothesay jilted Elizabeth Dunbar after enjoying her favours in a form of marriage which Robert III declared was illegal. Rothesay subsequently married Marjorie Douglas, the daughter of Dunbar's most powerful rival in

Scotland, Archibald, 3rd Earl of Douglas. The King refused to repay Dunbar's dowry and, in a fit of picque, Dunbar declared himself for Henry IV of England. Branded a traitor, Dunbar lost his earldom and his lands in south-east Scotland, some of which were given to Hepburn of Hailes. George Dunbar and his sons were resolved to wreak vengeance on Hepburn; the latter's raid gave them the excuse they needed. With his father's blessing, George Dunbar, the future 11th Earl led 200 men from the Berwick garrison to punish Hepburn. On 22 June 1402, young Dunbar overtook Hepburn at Nesbit Moor, heavily defeating him at a place still known as Slaughter Field, Kimmerghame, about three miles south-east of Duns. Hepburn's casualties were high; Hepburn himself was killed and three of his closest associates, Sir Walter Haliburton of Dirleton, his son Thomas Haliburton and Sir Robert Lauder of the Bass were taken prisoner.

A small but significant action, the second 'battle' of Nesbit Moor had far-reaching consequences. The Scots were incensed by Dunbar's arrogance; Archibald, 4th Earl of Douglas, led an army of 10,000 into Northumberland, intending to teach Dunbar a lesson. They were met by Henry Percy of Northumberland and George Dunbar on 14 September 1402 at Humbleton (Homildon) Hill, near Wooler. Dunbar knew the tactics used by the Scots and stayed the impetuous Percy's hand, advising him not to attack Douglas but to allow the English archers to wreak havoc among Douglas's troops. Homildon Hill was a decisive victory for Henry IV, one which ended any further hostilities between Scotland and England and allowed Henry to consolidate his hold on the English throne.

By 1406 Robert III was old and feeble, illness hastening his death. The government of Scotland was in the hands of his unpleasant, ambitious brother, Robert, 1st Duke of Albany. Towards the end of his life, Robert III's Queen Annabella asked her ailing husband what he would like inscribed as epitaph on his tombstone. The sick king reputedly replied thus: 'Here lies the worst of kings and the most wretched of men in the whole kingdom.'[2]

In the year of his death, Robert feared for the safety of his son and heir James at the mercy of Albany, so he sent the eleven-year-old prince to France. However, the ship carrying James was captured off Flamborough Head on 22 March 1406 by English pirates who handed him over to Henry IV, no doubt for a fee. When he received the news, Robert III could not bear the shock; he died on 29 March. James, heir to the Scottish throne, would spend the next eighteen years of his life as a prisoner of two English kings, the second of these being Henry V. When the news of James's capture was made known in Scotland, Robert, 1st Duke of Albany was proclaimed regent of Scotland; during his regency, Albany ruled Scotland in his own name, not as representative of his nephew, the future James I.

Although there were no major battles fought between England and Scotland during Albany's regency, the Scots attempted to recover Jedburgh, Fast and Roxburgh Castles and the town of Berwick. Jedburgh fell in 1409; Fast Castle in Berwickshire was taken by Patrick Dunbar, son of the 10th Earl, now re-instated in Scotland, pardoned by Albany, the following year. Yet civil war loomed in 1411 when Donald, Lord of the Isles was recognized as the champion of Celtic (Highland) Scotland. Donald was courted as an ally by Henry IV of England who saw in him a man of importance and one to be cultivated. In 1411 the earldom of Ross fell vacant and Donald demanded the title and lands from Albany; his claim was based on his marriage to a daughter of Robert II.

Harlaw

To reinforce his claim, Donald gathered an army of 10,000 at Morven and marched it to Inverness, then to Bennachie and the moor of Harlaw, about eighteen miles from Aberdeen. Donald intended to plunder Aberdeen and make himself master of all northern Scotland to the river Tay. However, he was met by a smaller but well equipped army of nobles and burghers from Aberdeen led by Alexander Stewart, Earl of Mar, a natural son of Alexander Stewart, known as the Wolf of Badenoch The encounter was one of the bloodiest battles in Scotland's history. Donald suffered casualties of 1,000 – thought to be on the low side – to Mar's losses of 500 – also considered low. The carnage was so terrible that the field was known thereafter as the Red Harlaw. Donald effected his escape to his own territory; the following summer, Albany led an expedition against Donald and forced him to make submission and supply hostages for his continuing good behaviour.

In the same year, Gawain, or Gavin, son of the 10th Earl of Dunbar attacked the English in Roxburgh, torching the town as his father had; he then went on to Berwick where he destroyed the wooden bridge over the river Tweed. In 1416 Albany gathered a large army to inflict damage on Henry V by attacking Berwick and Roxburgh; Albany led part of the army against Berwick and Archibald, 4th Earl of Douglas was directed towards Roxburgh. Nothing was achieved, however; the episode is known in Scotland's history as the *Foul Raid* as the English retaliated by pillaging and burning Teviotdale, Liddesdale and the towns of Selkirk, Jedburgh and Hawick. The only other hostilities that marked Albany's regency were the temporary possession of Wark Castle in Northumberland and the burning of Alnwick by the Earl of Douglas in 1420.

During his eighteen years in English captivity, Robert III's son and heir James fell in love with Joan, daughter of John Beaufort, 1st Duke of Somerset and half-brother to Henry IV; the young couple were married in February 1424 and were allowed to return to Scotland on payment of James's ransom money.

The young man came back to a Scotland where much had changed. He resented the fact that his uncle Robert, 1st Duke of Albany, had done nothing to secure his release; furthermore, his son Murdoch, 2nd Duke of Albany, who had succeeded as regent on the death of his father in 1420 had little to gain from James's return home. On 13 May 1424, a few days before his formal coronation, James arrested Murdoch's son, Sir Walter Stewart; also taken into custody was James's brother-in-law, Malcolm Fleming of Cumbernauld and Thomas Boyd of Kilmarnock, probably because the Boyds and the Flemings had supported the Albany regents. James I was crowned at Scone on 21 May 1424, Murdoch placing the crown on his head. It was said that on the first day of James's return to Scotland, an unidentified Scottish courtier had commented on the misgovernment of the realm since 1406, with crimes going unpunished, which was malicious gossip. James reputedly responded thus: 'God granting me life, I will make the key keep the castle and the bracken bush the cow.'[3] James lost no time in stamping his authority; all ranks of people from the high born to the low soon discovered that in their new king, they would find a man of different stamp from his predecessors, Robert II and Robert III. From the outset, James set about playing off one magnate against the other. In a snub to the Earl of Mar, an Albany Stewart, James gave the earldom of Ross to Alexander MacDonald, son of Donald MacDonald, Lord of the Isles; for Alexander MacDonald, it was sweet revenge for his defeat at the battle of Red Harlaw. In the same year as his coronation, James arrested Murdoch's aged father-in-law Duncan, Earl of Lennox and Sir Robert Graham of Kincardine; the latter would exact a terrible revenge in 1437. The following year, James arrested Murdoch and Murdoch's other son Alexander; in retaliation, Murdoch's third son unwisely gathered a small force and descended on Dumbarton, torching the town and slaughtering thirty-two people including the governor of Dumbarton Castle, Sir John Stewart of Dundonald. This ill-advised raid gave James the excuse he needed to draw the Albany Stewarts' teeth. When parliament met in May 1425, Murdoch, his sons Walter and Alexander and the Earl of Lennox were found guilty of charges which are not recorded. All four were executed at the Heading Hill in Stirling.[4]

Lochaber

James was not finished by a long chalk. Despite the defeat at Harlaw, the Hebrides and the Highlands were still in a state of unrest. As we saw in Chapter 3, when the Hebrides were ceded to Alexander III in 1266, Scotland was obliged to recompense the King of Norway with a lump sum down payment and an annual sum of 100 merks in perpetuity, money which had not been paid since the fourteenth century. James settled the arrears due to the contemporary Norwegian king in a gesture of friendship. Then, in the spring of 1427, he held a parliament at Inverness, summoning Alexander MacDonald, Earl of Ross and 3rd Lord of the Isles and other leading chiefs in the Highlands. Believing they had nothing to fear, Alexander and the others duly attended Inverness, where forty of them including Alexander were thrown into prison. A peace lasting two years followed until 1429, when Alexander MacDonald, now at liberty, collected a strong force and burnt Inverness, the scene of his humiliation. His triumph was short-lived. James hastily raised an army and totally defeated MacDonald at Lochaber, in the district of Fort William at the west end of the Great Glen; MacDonald was imprisoned in Tantallon Castle, East Lothian. James had dealt with the Albany Stewarts, now he was seeing off any residual challenge to his authority in the Highlands and Islands, a high-handed and despotic approach that would lead to his premature death.

Inverlochy I
In 1431, while Alexander MacDonald was languishing in Tantallon, his kinsmen Donald Balloch and Alasdair Carragh raised a force to confront the royal army camped near Inverlochy Castle at the head of the Great Glen. The Islemen sailed from the Hebrides in their *birlinns* (galleys), landing downriver from Inverlochy. Alexander Stewart, Earl of Mar commanded the King's army; Mar was the sworn enemy of the MacDonalds of the Isles after Red Harlaw. The Islemen took Mar by surprise; their bowmen stationed on high ground wrought havoc among Mar's panic-stricken foot soldiers, then the entire force charged downhill to complete their victory. In less than a few minutes 900 of Mar's men lay dead and he was forced to seek refuge in the mountains. Alexander MacDonald was promptly released from Tantallon, his titles and lands restored. James I accepted that it was as dangerous to imprison the Lord of the Isles as it was to allow him freedom; however, parliament refused to grant him any money to mount further campaigns in the north.

At least James kept the peace with England through a succession of treaties. However, with the expiry of the treaty between Scotland and England in 1433, both countries were free to indulge in hostilities.

Piperdean
In the autumn of 1435, a minor skirmish in Berwickshire sparked off hostilities. More of a raid than a battle, it was in part a retaliatory response for James's treatment of George, 11th Earl of Dunbar whose estates and titles were forfeited that same year due to his father's support for Henry IV and winning for him the battle of Homildon Hill. George Dunbar's son Patrick had formed an association with Sir Robert Ogle, governor of Berwick and Henry Percy of Northumberland. Patrick Dunbar received a safe conduct to

visit Henry VI on 12 July 1435, no doubt to inform the English king of his plans. Dunbar, Ogle and Percy broke into the East March of Scotland that summer, plundering the former Dunbar lands now in the possession of James I. On 26 September, James complained to the English Privy Council about Percy's and Ogle's foray, which he said was in support of the deposed George Dunbar's son whom he described as 'Paton of Dunbar, the king's rebel'. By this time Ogle and Dunbar had fought a skirmishing action on 10 September[5] with the Earl of Angus, Adam Hepburn of Hailes and Sir Alexander Ramsay of Dalhousie at Piperdean, near Cockburnspath, Berwickshire. About forty casualties were sustained by both sides.[6] Ogle was taken prisoner along with others of his force – mainly renegade Scots – while Patrick Dunbar managed to escape across the Border where he was forced to live in exile, declared a traitor by James I. As for his part, Henry VI did not think it financially worthwhile to support the lost cause of the Dunbars.

Piperdean was not in itself an important battle but it encouraged James I to mount his first and only attempt to recover Berwick and Roxburgh from England. At the head of a large and well-equipped army, James's fifteen-day siege of Roxburgh Castle came to nought. James's cannon did little more than deafen both besiegers and defenders. Receiving word of the approach of a large English army, James beat a hasty retreat. This latest adventure proved to James's nobles that not only was their king avaricious and a profligate spendthrift, he was also weak in military strategy.

James believed that he could rule all Scotland simply by the scrape of his pen. During his short reign he alienated many of his powerful nobles and insulted the families of others. Among the disaffected was Sir Robert Graham whom James had imprisoned in 1424. On 21 February 1437, James and his Queen Joan Beaufort were residing in Blackfriars Convent, outside the walls of Perth. Graham and his associates broke into the Convent and made their way to the royal bedchamber. The alarm was raised and James managed to prise up the floorboards of his bedroom and conceal himself in the sewer below. The conspirators soon found him; Graham delivered the fatal blow with his sword. When James's body was brought back into the bedchamber, it bore sixteen stab wounds. Queen Joan managed to effect her escape with the young Prince James to Edinburgh Castle.

The teenage Prince was crowned James II (1437–60) in Holyrood Abbey. Archibald, 5th Earl of Douglas, grandson of Robert II was appointed regent; he died in 1439 and was succeeded by his sixteen-year-old son William, 6th Earl of Douglas. William's appointment was also short-lived; on 24 November 1440, Sir William Crichton and Sir Alexander Livingston, respectively governors of Edinburgh and Stirling Castles arrested William Douglas and his younger brother David in front of the King dining at Edinburgh Castle. The boy King James II wept as he had grown fond of Willie Douglas. This incident is known to Scotland's history as the *Black Dinner*. A few days later, William and David Douglas along with their chief adviser Malcolm Fleming of Cumbernauld were executed on Edinburgh's Castle Hill on a charge of treason. It is thought that William Douglas, with his bold and haughty temperament, posed a threat to Livingston's custody of James II – meaning Livingston's control and manipulation of the young king. Livingston was supported by Crichton, Chancellor of Scotland, but both could have been easily eclipsed by the Douglas family.

Livingston and Crichton got away with what amounted to the assassination of two members of the most powerful family in Scotland. Why? James 'the Gross' Douglas, Earl of Avondale, great-uncle of the murdered William Douglas became head of the family. Not only did Avondale's failure to avenge his relative surprise the nobles, they were surprised that he acted in concert with Livingston and Crichton over the next few years. When James, 7th Earl of Douglas and Avondale died in 1443 his son William succeeded him; he would prove a different man than his father.

In 1448, a nine-year truce concluded between Scotland and England expired. The long years of inactivity on both sides of the Border had frustrated both Scots and English. Hostilities resumed with the burning in May of Dunbar by Sir Robert Ogle and Henry Percy, the future 3rd Earl of Northumberland. A month later the Earl of Salisbury burnt Dumfries. The Scots retaliated by burning Alnwick and Warkworth in June and July. The stage was set for a major confrontation between Scotland and England.

Sark

The battle of Sark, also known as the battle of Lochmaben Stone was fought in October 1448. In retaliation for the incursions in East Lothian and Dumfries, William, 8th Earl of Douglas supported by his brother Hugh Douglas, Earl of Ormond and the Earls of Angus and Orkney gathered an army to meet the expected invasion of Scotland after the destruction of Alnwick and Warkworth. When the Scots advanced into Cumberland, Henry VI ordered the Percies of Northumberland to retaliate.

Henry Percy, 2nd Earl of Northumberland at the head of 6,000 men crossed the Border into Dumfriesshire in October, making camp on the bank of the river Sark, near Gretna and the Kirtle Water, a tidal waterway. Hugh Douglas, Earl of Ormond, mustered a force of about 4,000 recruited from Annandale and Nithsdale to confront him. On 23 October, Ormond engaged a numerically superior English army on the Sark. Northumberland arranged his army in three divisions with archers to protect his flanks; Ormond mirrored Northumberland's formation. The Scottish spearmen drove the

English backwards where they came to grief in the incoming tide. The English suffered 1,500 killed in battle and a further 500 were drowned by the tide.[7] The Scottish casualties have been given at as low as twenty-six and as high as 600.

In 1449, James II married Mary of Gueldres, daughter of Arnold, Duke of Gueldres and niece of Philip 'the Good' of Burgundy. It is perhaps no coincidence that after this marriage on 3 July 1449, James felt encouraged to remove the reins of power from some of his overweening family factions – the Livingstons, Crichtons and Douglases. Matters came to a head in 1452 when during a somewhat hollow and short-lived reconciliation, James invited the head of the Douglas family, William, 8th Earl of Douglas to dinner at Stirling Castle on 21 February. The following day the pair supped together, when James challenged Douglas about his intriguing with the Earls of Crawford and Ross, two families who with Douglas could have endangered the stability of James's reign. James urged Douglas to break with the rebellious earls; Douglas refused. In a fit of passion reminiscent of Bruce's murder of the Red Comyn in 1306, James plunged his dagger into Douglas, the signal for his attendant courtiers to follow suit. The body of Douglas was said to have suffered twenty-six stab wounds.

Arkinholm

The murder of the head of the family could not go unpunished by the House of Douglas. Between 1452 and 1455, James was constantly bedevilled by plots and threats but he bided his time, waiting for an opportune moment to crush the Douglases for good. James, 9th Earl of Douglas sought the help of the English King Henry VI, formally renouncing his allegiance to James. Matters dragged on until March 1455, when James mounted a campaign against the House of Douglas and their supporters. He carried fire and sword into Douglasdale, Avondale and Ettrick Forest. The 9th Earl of Douglas enjoyed considerable power in Scotland; his three brothers, Hugh Douglas, Earl of Ormond, Archibald Douglas, Earl of Moray, and James Douglas of Balveny raised a strong force and made destructive raids in the neighbouring countryside. The King's army, led by George Douglas, 4th Earl of Angus, caught up with the Douglas brothers at Arkinholm, Langholm on 1 May 1455 and routed them. The Earl of Moray was killed, Ormond was taken into custody and executed for treason, while Balveny escaped to England, joining his brother James, 9th Earl of Douglas who had not been present on the field of Arkinholm. The victory at Arkinholm was crowned by the fall of Threave, the strongest of the Douglas castles.

James's triumph over the Black Douglases was complete. A parliament held in Edinburgh on 10 June attainted the Earls of Douglas and Moray and

Douglas of Balveny; a further parliament in August that year declared the Douglas lands forfeit to the Crown or to those nobles who had supported James against the last of the Black Douglas earls. The suppression of the Black Douglases in 1455 was perhaps the greatest achievement in James II's reign; of the remaining five years of it, little of importance occurred. It was with England that James encountered most of his problems. During his struggle with the House of Douglas, the Wars of the Roses began in England; James supported the Red Rose House of Lancaster in the person of Henry VI, while the 9th Earl of Douglas received encouragement from the White Rose House of York in a struggle for the English throne that would last until 1497. However, with England distracted by this civil war, James took the opportunity to attempt the recovery of Berwick and Roxburgh, a duty he felt he owed to his kingdom and subjects. James made an unsuccessful attack on Berwick in 1455. No help was forthcoming from France in either money or arms, King Charles VII refusing to support James in open warfare with England. A truce concluded between Scotland and England was negotiated that year; it would last until 1459.

Lochmaben

Despite the truce, in October 1458, a strong force of Yorkist troops entered Annandale, Douglas territory. James II responded with an army which utterly routed the Yorkists; 600 were slain and 1,500 taken prisoner.[8] However, the Yorkist cause was gaining supremacy in England. By 1460 the House of York had taken the Lancastrian Henry VI as prisoner. This drove James to attempt what would be his last campaign – the recovery of Roxburgh Castle. Towards the end of July, James led a large army supported by formidable ordnance which consisted of several *bombards* or mortars usually loaded with stone rather than iron cannonballs. On 3 August 1460, James was observing one of his cannon bombarding Roxburgh when the piece exploded and a splinter from it mortally wounded him. James II was only twenty-nine; his son and heir was aged nine. Once again Scotland would have a child as king.

James III (1460–88) was crowned at Kelso Abbey on 10 August. He inherited a kingdom which enjoyed a prosperity not known since the last years of Robert the Bruce. By the wholesale confiscation of lands from dissident nobles in the previous two Stewart reigns, the Scottish Crown had attained a prominence which no single noble could dream of challenging. However, the overthrow of the great Houses of Dunbar, Douglas and others remained strong in the memories of the nobles who had retained their titles and lands. James's mother, the formidable and intelligent Mary of Gueldres, was granted guardianship of her young son by parliament in 1461. This caused some ill-feeling among the excluded faction led by James Kennedy, Bishop of St

Andrews and George Douglas, 4th Earl of Angus, head of the Red Douglases. (These difficulties would only be resolved by Mary of Gueldres's death in 1463.)

James III's reign began well. Under their new King, the Scottish magnates resumed the siege of Roxburgh Castle which was captured and destroyed, leaving only Berwick in English hands. Then events in England during the conflicts between the Houses of York and Lancaster (the Wars of the Roses) brought about the return of Berwick to the Scots in 1461 by the Lancastrian Henry VI as a reward for offering him shelter from the Yorkists who had defeated him in two major battles. The return of Berwick was a source of national pride as it had been in English hands almost continuously since 1296. (It would be retaken by the English in 1482, during the quarrel between James III and his ambitious brother Alexander, 3rd Duke of Albany, who sought the crown for himself.)

At least relations with England remained on a friendly footing, apart from continuing Border bickering; some of James's nobles, particularly the Border reiver families who made a lucrative profit from cattle and sheep stealing, were displeased by James's ill-advised cultivation of low-born favourites. James revelled in the company of men like Thomas Cochrane, an architect by profession, William Roger, a musician, James Hommyle, the royal tailor, William Scheves, court physician, astrologer and Keeper of the Royal Wardrobe, and others. James's chief critics were his brothers Alexander, 3rd Duke of Albany and John, Earl of Mar, who along with several other nobles abhorred his association with the commoners on whom he depended for advice. James would be at loggerheads with Albany during most of his reign, the latter seeking help first from France, then England, to depose his brother.

It was in the year 1479 that James began to experience troubles within his own kingdom that would bedevil him until the end of his reign. The bad feelings he engendered in his brothers Albany and Mar developed into a deep-seated hatred; Alexander, 3rd Duke of Albany was aged twenty-five and John, Earl of Mar was aged twenty-two. The twenty-six-year-old James had a family feud on his hands, one which ended only with Albany's death in 1485. This apart, James alienated many of his nobles by favouring commoners in preference to his courtiers. Also his love of seclusion – considered an unnatural trait in the communal life of the Middle Ages, when noble families sat down to dinner with their entire household including the inenials – an indication that the person who wished to be alone was suffering from acute melancholia, or in modern terms, depression. James also had a dislike of the activities and accomplishments expected from a feudal king and knight, which not only alienated his nobles but also the common populace, who preferred their kings to exhibit their royal superiority by outward shows of pomp, circumstance and above all else, the martial arts.

What we know about the closing months of James's reign in 1488 is that a full-blown conspiracy to unseat the king was made by several disaffected nobles – the Earls of Angus and Argyll, Lords Gray, Hume, Hailes, Drummond and Lyle, the Bishops of Dunkeld and Glasgow and importantly, the heir to the throne James, Duke of Rothesay. Prince James had been placed in Stirling Castle for his safety under the charge of James Schaw of Sauchie who, either by threats or promises of rewards, handed over the heir to the throne to his father's enemies.

Blackness

In the north James III found a ready response to his call for support. With the the help of the Earls of Atholl, Caithness, Crawford, Errol, Huntly, Sutherland and many of the minor barons, James gathered a formidable army. He met the rebels at Blackness in 1488, on the south shore of the Firth of Forth. After an indecisive skirmish in which Alexander Cunningham, 1st Lord of Kilmaurs distinguished himself in James's service and was granted the additional title Earl of Glencairn; for his loyalty the Earl of Crawford was also honoured, becoming Duke of Montrose. However the treaty agreed at Blackness was only temporary and not worth the parchment on which it was written as the rebels still held the heir to the throne, which effectively nullified it. (It is interesting, however, that James conferred on his second son the title Duke of Ross, which tells us something about James's view of the conduct of the heir-apparent his first son, James, Duke of Rothesay.)

Sauchieburn, 11 June 1488, St Barnabas' Day

Before Blackness, James had been obliged to take refuge in the north where he had obtained the bulk of his following and support. During his absence the rebels seized Dunbar Castle which was well stocked with both artillery and gunpowder. In addition, the rebels took possession of most of James's baggage train at Leith.

Was it a stroke of irony or superstition that James chose the feast of Saint Barnabas – saint of consolation – to confront his enemies? Also, Sauchieburn was close to the field of Bannockburn which James perhaps thought would bring him good luck. For good measure James had also armed himself with a sword which had belonged to Robert the Bruce, trusting it would secure his victory.[9] But the Bruce luck was not with him that day.

The Sauchie Burn, or small stream, is about two miles south of Stirling. Some accounts, notably Nimmo's *History of Stirlingshire*,[10] put the opposing forces at 30,000 for James III and his loyal nobles, and 18,000, nominally led by the heir-apparent, James, Duke of Rothesay. Several accounts of the battle are colourful and unreliable, notably those of the chronicler Robert Lindsay of Pitscottie and the historian George Buchanan, both of whose accounts were written in the sixteenth century.[11] However, it is accepted that, whatever the respective strengths of the opposing armies, Sauchieburn was a Lowland/Highland battle. The rebel army, mainly comprised of cavalry, was led by Border nobles such as Lords Home and Hailes and Galloway men led by Lord Gray. The royal army had as its leaders the Earls of Menteith and Crawford and Lords Erskine, Graham, Ruthven and Maxwell. On the eve of the battle Sir David Lindsay of Byres made a gift of a spirited grey horse to James III, assuring the king that, on account of its agility and sure-footedness, it would carry him faster than any other horse to and from the battlefield

On 11 June the royal army was drawn up in three divisions led by Menteith and Crawford, Erskine, Graham, Maxwell, Ruthven and Sir David Lindsay, although we are not certain who led which. The rebel army was also drawn up in three divisions; the first, comprised men of East Lothian and the Merse (Berwickshire), was commanded by Lords Home and Hailes; the second contained the men of Galloway and the west Borders and was commanded by Lord Gray; the third was in the nominal command of Prince James but he was subject to the directions of his commanders.

The battle began with exchanges by the archers until both sides closed and fought hand-to-hand with the sword. The action at close quarters at first went in favour of the royal army; James III's front line gained advantage, driving back the rebel front line. However, the second rebel division not only stood its ground but pushed back the first line into the royal front line which fell back on the two supporting divisions. The Border levies of Home and Hailes were particularly successful and very soon their determined attack began to turn the tide of battle in the rebels' favour. At some point in the battle James was either thrown from his horse and killed or was despatched by rebel soldiers. The colourful accounts referred to above have James's spirited horse bolting from the field; James also lost Bruce's sword which was later retrieved from the battlefield. There are conflicting and suspiciously romantic versions of the way James met his death. Some accounts say he was carried from the field on his horse and was murdered by an unknown assailant in a miller's cottage at Milltown. Others contend that he reached the safety of a mill, intending to remain concealed until dusk, but the rebels discovered the king's horse, a sure sign the rider was not far off; they eventually found him and slew him where he lay.[12] Yet another account[13] has James unable to control his unruly horse but managing to cross the Bannock Burn; there he encountered a woman filling a pitcher with water, she being the wife of the miller of Beaton's Mill. She reputedly dropped the pitcher which frightened James's horse so much that it shied and threw him to the ground with such force that he was badly injured. The miller and his wife then carried him into their house where James reputedly told the miller 'I was your king this day at morn'.

In her excitement the miller's wife ran to get a priest to hear James's confession. A 'priest' was brought and asked if the king was mortally wounded. James reputedly replied that he might recover but asked to receive the sacraments. The 'priest' did not hesitate: 'That shall I do heartily'. Then he drew his dagger and stabbed the king in the heart.

The hard-nosed historian must raise an eyebrow at these fanciful accounts. In all probability, James III met his end on the battlefield; his troops fought on bravely but finally gave up when rumours of the King's death spread through the ranks. We have no details of casualties but among the royalist dead were Alexander Cunningham, Lord Kilmaurs (Earl of Glencairn after the skirmish at Blackness) and Lords Erskine and Ruthven. Fatalities on both sides must have been high as the battle lasted several hours. James's followers carried his body to Cambuskenneth Abbey, where his remains were interred in the now ruined cloister. For the rest of his life, his son James IV wore a heavy iron chain round his waist and next to his skin to remind him of the part he played in his father's death.

The following day the rebel lords proclaimed James, Duke of Rothesay, James IV, then they proceeded to Edinburgh, capturing its castle which was still in the hands of James III's supporters. As James IV was in his minority, the chief offices of State were filled from the ranks of the nobles who had supported him. The position of Chancellor was held by the Earl of Argyll; Patrick Hepburn, Lord Hailes was appointed Master of the Royal Household; Robert, Lord Lyle was made Justiciar (chief political and judicial officer) and Alexander, Master of Home was appointed as Chamberlain. The most important role of guardianship of the King was given to Archibald Douglas, 5th Earl of Angus.[14]

The reign of James III, troubled as it had been at least avoided the devastations of war and there were no serious breaches in Scotland's domestic affairs. During his reign James IV would see the beginnings of the modern Western world which followed the Middle Ages. James IV was crowned at Scone in June 1488. In July an embassy was sent to Henry VII assuring the goodwill of Scotland towards England; the truce agreed in 1486 was thus renewed. The transition from the reign of one Stewart monarch to the next was never smooth, chiefly because several of the dynasty ascended the throne as children or boys in their teens. Two of the insurgents loyal to James IV, Robert, Lord Lyle and the Earl of Lennox, Governor of Dumbarton Castle, were however dissatisfied with the distribution of the king's favours and openly rebelled against the government; they garrisoned the castles of

Dumbarton, Crookston, near Paisley and Duchal in the parish of Kilmacolm, Renfrewshire, refusing to open the gates on the King's summons. By the end of July Crookston and Duchal had surrendered, although Dumbarton still held out. Furthermore, a rising in the north by Lord Forbes in Aberdeenshire gave impetus to the rebellion of Lyle and Lennox; Forbes gathered a force of men which took as its standard or banner the bloody shirt of the late James III.

Aberfoyle
The Earl of Lennox, the prime mover in the short-lived rebellion, gathered a force of 2,000 in October 1488, marching north to gain new allies and increase support for the late James III. On the night of 11 October Lennox was surprised and defeated by the forces of James IV at a ford on the river Forth, in the parish of Aberfoyle.[15] Dumbarton Castle was recovered in the beginning of December and by the end of the year, peace was restored.

Henry VII made it known to James IV that he only desired peace; the English King suggested his daughter Margaret should be given in marriage to James to guarantee stability and peace between the two kingdoms. The wedding took place on 8 August 1503 at Holyrood Palace, Edinburgh, an event celebrated in the famous poem by William Dunbar, *The Thistle and the Rose*. Henry VII regarded the marriage as a 'Treaty of Perpetual Peace'. Perpetual was hardly a word with much currency in late Medieval Scotland and England; the treaty would last only for a decade.

Henry VII died in 1509 and was succeeded by his son, Henry VIII, aged eighteen; Henry VIII would prove to be a king of an entirely different stamp from his father. In the first two years of his reign Henry VIII's relations with Scotland were cordial in a sense not known for some time. That would change in the next two years when Henry turned against his brother-in-law James. Yet again, the object of their quarrel was Scotland's traditional ally, France and England's *bête noire*. In his ambitions in France, Henry VIII could not afford to alienate James IV, France's ally. To his credit, despite his alliance with France, James IV had no wish to antagonize England. He delayed any action against Henry VIII until 1512 when at the extremes of his patience James decided that only Scottish cannon and swords would decide the outcome of Henry VIII's quarrel with France.

In the first few months of 1513 James and Henry continued to exchange civilities. James's Queen, Margaret Tudor, took her husband's part, not just because she believed in him. Margaret nursed a personal grievance against her brother Henry, who had refused to give her certain jewels which were part of her inheritance. The final conciliatory letter from James to Henry was written on 24 May 1513. Henry ignored it. On 30 June he crossed the Channel to Calais to begin his invasion of France. On 26 July James sent the Lyon Herald to Henry with a message that was nothing short of a declaration of war. James then made preparations for his invasion of England; on 30 August he assembled an army of between 30,000 and 40,000 on the Burghmuir, Edinburgh.

James crossed the Border at Norham-on-Tweed and progressed to Twisel in Northumberland, where he took up position on 22 August on a hill called Flodden. At the battle of Flodden on 9 September the Flower of Scotland was decisively beaten by the Earl of Surrey, the same man who had brought James's wife to him. Among the thousands slain were James himself, along with thirteen earls – Crawford, Montrose, Huntly, Lennox, Argyll, Errol, Atholl, Morton, Cassilis, Bothwell, Rothes, Caithness and Glencairn, fifteen lords and Clan chiefs, the Archbishop of St Andrews, the Bishops of Caithness and the Isles, the Abbots of Kilwinning and Inchaffray and 10,000 foot soldiers. There was scarcely a family in all of Scotland who did not lose a member of their household. English losses were between 5,000 and 8,000, with only five men of rank.

Scotland was prostrated. The defeat at Flodden was commemorated in a poem *Lament for Flodden* written and published in 1756 by Jean Elliot (1727–1805) which captures the desolation and sadness in a constantly repeated line: 'The Flowers of the Forest are a' wede [wasted] away.'

Yet again a child wore the crown of Scotland; James V was only one year old when he ascended the throne. Although James IV had appointed his wife Margaret as regent in his will, with councillors James Beaton, Archbishop of Glasgow and the Earls of Huntly, Angus and Arran, a faction of nobles turned to a person who would suit their own ambitions to advantage – James V's cousin, John, 4th Duke of Albany living in France. But Albany was already acting on his own behalf. Louis XII of France sent two ambassadors to Scotland proposing that the *Auld Alliance* should continue and that Albany would come to Scotland with men and arms for the defence of Scotland against Henry VIII. (Albany's incompetence, coupled with the intrigues of Margaret Tudor, the Queen mother, would plunge Scotland into gross misgovernment and lawlessness during James V's minority.)

On 30 April 1314 Margaret Tudor gave birth to a posthumous son; then, on 6 August, she married the nineteen-year-old Archibald Douglas, 6th Earl of Angus. Against Margaret and Angus were ranged the powerful Lord Chamberlain Hume, the Earl of Arran, next in line of succession to Albany, and James Beaton, Archbishop of Glasgow and Chamberlain of the Realm. In July 1515 Albany arrived in Edinburgh and was proclaimed regent. As Margaret's marriage to Angus had invalidated her position as tutrix of the infant James V, Albany turned this to his advantage; he claimed the child. From that point on, Queen Margaret did her best to turn the affairs of

Scotland into a family tug-of-war. For the next nine years she and Albany would be at loggerheads until in 1524 Albany left Scotland for good, returning to France and a less stressful life. To his credit, during the years he governed Scotland, Albany had saved Scotland from England's aggressive policy which threatened the country's continuing independence.

With Albany gone, matters grew even worse. The Earl of Arran, next in line to the throne after Albany formed a confederation with Queen Margaret with a view to working towards his family's future in the succession. To this end he threw in his lot with Henry VIII. On 26 July 1524 Margaret and Arran retrieved the young James V from Stirling and brought him to Edinburgh where some of the leading nobles declared the twelve-year-old *de facto* king of Scotland. By 1524 Margaret had divorced her husband the Earl of Angus and was casting her eye on a third husband. Angus, one of the councillors appointed to rule Scotland along with Margaret had returned from a stay in France; what he found angered him. He immediately entered into a compact with the Earl of Lennox against Margaret and Arran; in the space of a few months, Angus was virtual leader of the country.

Linlithgow Bridge

Archibald Douglas, 6th Earl of Angus, head of the House of Red Douglas, had swiftly stamped his authority in Scotland; he took James V into custody in Edinburgh. The politics of this period are both confused and confusing; Angus and Lennox had acted in concert for a time but there was no love between the two families. Lennox was a special friend of the young King and he made it his mission to rescue James V from the clutches of the Red Douglases. At the beginning of September 1526 Lennox led a strong force from Stirling with the intention of rescuing James in Edinburgh; he was met at Linlithgow by the Hamiltons led by the Earl of Arran, head of the House of Hamilton. Lennox advanced from Stirling at the head of an army of about 12,000. At Linlithgow Bridge he was confronted by the Earl of Arran and 2,000 men who held the crossing at the river Avon. Knowing that more troops were coming from Edinburgh, Lennox decided to outflank Arran by fording the river. Arran, realizing Lennox's intention deployed his men to meet the threat; the Earl of Angus arrived with a further 2,000 troops from Edinburgh in time to place his men on Arran's left wing, launching an attack on Lennox's flank. The ensuing battle lasted two hours until Lennox's men broke. Lennox was captured, disarmed and probably murdered by Sir James Hamilton of Finnart, Arran's illegitimate son. The King would remain in the custody of the Red Douglases of Angus for another two years.[17]

In 1528 James managed to escape from Edinburgh and made his way to Stirling where he knew there were those hostile to the House of Douglas. Now free from the clutches of Angus, one of James's first acts was to issue a proclamation banishing the House of Douglas beyond the river Spey and forbidding any of the name Douglas to come within six miles of his person, such was his inveterate hatred of the family. In a packed meeting of the Convention of Estates (parliament in effect) in September 1528 a decree of forfeiture was placed on Angus; he and his brother, Sir George Douglas were forced to seek safety in England. James V now felt he was master of his own kingdom at last.

James V's reign (1513–42) effectively began around 1530 when he was faced with unrest in both the Borders and the Highlands and Islands. He subdued the unruly Armstrongs of Liddesdale and placed in ward several Border nobles including Lord Bothwell whom he suspected of encouraging the Border reivers. With the Borders subdued, James released all the Border chiefs save Bothwell, a decision he would have cause to regret in the future.

James next turned his attention to the Highlands and Islands where the chief cause of the disturbance, Archibald, 4th Earl of Argyll was defying James's writ. In 1531 James threw Argyll into prison, thus adding another noble to those such as Bothwell who conspired against him. The alienation of certain of his nobles, his close union with his clergy and his unrelieved antagonism towards Henry VIII would prove his undoing.

In 1537 James took as wife Madeleine, the third daughter of Francis I of France. Within two months of her arrival in Scotland, to James's great sorrow, Queen Madeleine died on 7 July. In 1538 a second wife was found for him in the person of Marie of Lorraine, daughter of Claud de Lorraine, Duke of Guise. Marie of Guise-Lorraine would prove one of the most talented, determined Scottish queens with an unremitting hatred of England. However, James's marriage did not sweeten his temper. In 1539 James deprived Lord Bothwell of the lordship of Liddesdale; then he alienated his natural brother, James Stewart, Earl of Moray by taking possession of Moray's lands and those of the Earl of Huntly. The list of alienated nobles was growing by the year.

In 1541 a terrible tragedy overtook the House of Stewart. Twin sons born to James's Queen Marie died within three days of each other, leaving the country without an heir. Despite this calamity James was hopeful of another heir and turned his attention to domestic matters. His chief adviser, Cardinal David Beaton, sworn enemy of England was hampering any possibility of friendly relations with England. Then, in October, the scheming Dowager Queen Margaret Tudor died at Methven, breaking the last surviving link with England. Open warfare was not far away, as we shall see in the following chapter.

Notes

1. *Chron. Pluscarden*: 'No single Englishman escaped his slaughter.'
2. Bower, *Scotichronicon*, vol. viii, p.45.
3. Hume Brown, *History of Scotland*, vol. i, p.211.
4. Hume Brown, op. cit., pp.212–213.
5. Pugh, *Swords, Loaves and Fishes: A History of Dunbar*, p.123.
6. Bower, *Scotichronicon*.
7. *Auchinleck Chron.*, pp.18–19.
8. Tytler, *History of Scotland*, vol. iv, p.145; Hume Brown op. cit., vol. i, pp.240–1.
9. Brotchie, *Battlefields of Scotland*, p.100.
10. Nimmo, *The History of Stirlingshire*, Chap.X1.
11. Pitscottie, *Historie and Chronicles of Scotland*; Buchanan, *A History of Scotland*.
12. Hume Brown, op. cit., vol. i, p.287.
13. Brotchie, op. cit., pp.101–2.
14. *Accounts of the Lord High Treasurer of Scotland*, p.lxix.
15. Hume Brown, op. cit., vol. i, p.298.
16. Brotchie, op. cit., pp.115–16.
17. Hume Brown, op. cit., vol. i, p.372.

Chapter 8

The Rough Wooing and Mary, Queen of Scots: 1542–1568

The year 1542 began with talk of a meeting between James V and Henry VIII in January; what might have emerged from this cannot be certain, although the main topic would have been France, the country mainly responsible for the ill feeling between Scotland and England. The antagonism between Francis I of France and Henry VIII had reached breaking point and James could hardly refuse Francis's request for help, being bound to France as his father had been. For his part, Henry resorted to desperate measures to physically remove James from Scotland and politically from French influence; he even contemplated kidnapping James and bringing him to England. Fortunately, Henry's council of advisers refused to agree to this proposal which would have contravened the laws of Western Europe, let alone England. Frustrated by this rebuffal, Henry took the first step towards open warfare.

Haddonrigg

Hostilities began – or rather were resumed – in August 1542 when Sir Robert Bowes, Deputy Warden of the English East March led a force of 3,000 into Teviotdale; Bowes was accompanied by the exiled Archibald, 6th Earl of Angus and his brother, Sir George Douglas. Bowes was intent on pillaging the Scottish east and middle Marches but was halted by the Earl of Huntly who had gathered a small band which was reinforced by the timely arrival of 400 Scottish lancers led by Lord Hume on 1 September, the very day of the battle. Huntly and Hume captured 600 of Bowes's men including Bowes himself; the English dead numbered seventy.

When Henry VIII learnt of this humiliation, he ordered a full-scale invasion of Scotland, the main objective of the campaign being to capture Edinburgh. The Duke of Norfolk, son of the Earl of Surrey, victor of Flodden, made preliminary arrangements for the invading army. However, Norfolk soon appreciated the logistical problems of provisioning Henry's army of 40,000. Norfolk's success did not realize Henry's expectations although he burnt Roxburgh, Kelso and about twenty villages. Poorly supplied and harried by the Earl of Huntly and Lords Hume and Seton, Norfolk was obliged to retreat in disorder to Berwick where he disbanded his army.

James V was keen to mount a retaliatory raid in northern England but was frustrated by his nobles' lack of enthusiasm for war. Although he managed to assemble an army of at least 10,000 backed by the great churchmen he favoured, James soon discovered how unpopular he had become among his nobles, the real fighting men. On 23 November James's army lodged at Langholm and Morton Kirk. Before daybreak on 24 November the two divisions crossed the river Esk, intent on raiding in the vicinity of Carlisle. However, Sir Thomas Wharton, Deputy Warden of the English West March had collected a force of 3,000 and sallied out of Carlisle to confront the invaders. The two armies came face to face near the river Esk, east of Gretna Green, Dumfriesshire. James was not present; he remained at Lochmaben to await the results of the battle.

Solway Moss

There was confusion in the Scottish army as to its leader. Sir Oliver Sinclair, a favourite of James V claimed he had been given the King's commission; this was disputed by Robert, Lord Maxwell, Warden of the Scottish West March. Sinclair persisted in his claim and the command structure collapsed even before a blow was struck. Although Maxwell's position was near Gretna, the battle of Solway Moss was fought on the English bank of the river Esk. James's army of 10,000 was confronted by Wharton's 3,000; it outnumbered the English by more than three to one and should have ensured a Scottish victory. Wharton planned his strategy with great care; he had to entice the Scots onto a tract of land where it would be difficult for them to deploy in full battle array. Wharton also deceived the Scots into thinking his force was larger than it was. Confusion in the Scottish command was blatantly advertised by Sir Oliver Sinclair who boasted to the English in the field that he, not Maxwell, was James V's commander in chief. Maxwell was dumbstruck by this egotistical show and his following refused to support Sinclair in the ensuing 'battle'. The English suffered seven casualties, the Scots twenty. In their panic, the Scottish spearmen were forced to escape by the only means available to them, a narrow ford across the Esk near the hill of Arthuret, beyond which was the Solway Moss, or marsh from which the battle takes its name. As they attempted their escape, many Scots were drowned. The prisoners taken at Solway Moss numbered 1,200, including two earls, five barons and more than 500 other gentry. James, lying prostrate in Lochmaben Castle suffering from a fever, joined in the retreat from Solway Moss. His life came to a close in Falkland Palace, Fife, where on 14 December 1542, he died more due to a lack of a will to live than illness. His legacy to Scotland was the birth of a one-week-old baby daughter, Marie. Before dying, James made a gloomy prediction about the dynasty of royal Stewarts: 'It cam wi' [came with] a lass and it will gang [go] wi' a lass.' James was, of course, referring to the way the Stewarts came to the throne through Marjorie, daughter of Robert the Bruce and her marriage to Walter, the High Steward of Scotland in 1315. His prediction did come true, but not until 1714; Stewart monarchs would rule Scotland, then Scotland, England and Ireland for the next 170 years, with a break of fourteen years between 1688 and 1702. (The last Stewart monarch of Britain, Anne, died childless in 1714, when the throne of Britain passed to the Hanoverian George I under the Act of Settlement of 1701.) James was only thirty when he died; his passing was marked more by the common folk, who had a genuine affection for their King, calling him the *Gaberlunzie* (beggar) *King,* the *Red Tod* (fox) and *King of the Commons*, the last on account of his habit of assuming disguises and mingling freely with his people with the purpose of discovering their needs.

Born on 8 December 1542 the baby Marie was crowned Queen of Scots in the Chapel Royal of Stirling Castle on 9 September 1543. The date chosen for her coronation was deliberate; it was the thirtieth anniversary of her grandfather James IV's defeat at Flodden. According to one modern historian[1] the baby sat on her mother Marie of Guise's knee; it was said that when the sceptre was near the baby, she reached out and clutched it with her tiny hand. Those witnessing the ceremony took this to be a favourable omen. Once again Scotland would be ruled by a French regent, Marie of Guise-Lorraine, this time for the next eighteen years. (From here on, her daughter Marie, the future Queen of Scots' is called Mary to distinguish her from her mother.)

News of James's death and Mary's birth must have sounded sweet political music to Henry VIII's ears. After Solway Moss Henry had harvested a rich catch of Scottish magnates – the Earls of Glencairn and Cassillis, Lords Maxwell, Fleming, Somerville, Oliphant and Gray being among the prominent nobles. Henry would put these hostages to good use in his determination to bring Scotland to her knees by a combination of political and diplomatic pressure. He also saw a way of ending the *Auld Alliance* between Scotland and France, thereby forcing Scotland to develop closer political and trading links with England. To this end he embarked on a policy to arrange the marriage of his son Edward VI to the infant Mary, Queen of Scots. However, Henry reckoned without the strength and determination of Marie of Guise-Lorraine, one of the most formidable queens in Scotland's history.

At the outset James, 3rd Lord Hamilton and 2nd Earl of Arran, next in line to the Scottish throne, was appointed regent. Henry VIII did all in his power to create instability in Scotland and he possessed a Trojan horse in the persons of Archibald Douglas, 6th Earl of Angus and his brother Sir George Douglas, exiled from Scotland since 1528 for opposing James V; both might return across the Border and exert their considerable influence and following in furthering Henry's ambitions. In January 1543 Angus and Douglas did in fact return to Scotland, shortly followed by the captives from Solway Moss; a kind of Fifth Column, each and every one of them was bound by a pledge – made secure by hostages for their release – to promote English interests. Henry VIII argued that it was Cardinal David Beaton of St Andrews who was the villain of the piece, fomenting unrest in Scotland by his opposition to the English Reformation taking place and seeking Catholic France's assistance at the expense of Scotland's stability. With the return of the Solway Moss prisoners – known as 'English Lords' and 'assured Scots', these men secured the arrest of Beaton who was then warded in the Earl of Morton's house in Dalkeith. A pro- English party thus formed, it seemed to be the prevailing political group. At a meeting of the Committee of Estates on 12 March, English interests gained yet another coup; three ambassadors were appointed to negotiate with Henry VIII regarding a marriage between the infant Queen Mary and Henry's son, the future Edward VI, then aged five years. Further power came the way of the pro-English party with the arrival in Dunbar of Sir Ralph Sadler, Henry's sagacious Secretary of State with orders to secure a marriage contract between Mary and Edward. It was soon apparent, however, that the nation was opposed to any form of alliance with England. On Beaton's side and favourable to France and the Catholic religion were powerful nobles – the Earls of Huntly, Moray, Bothwell and Argyll who were now demanding the release of Beaton. Then two important persons arrived from France – the Earl of Lennox and the regent Arran's illegitimate brother John Hamilton, Abbot of Paisley; both were staunch supporters of France and the Catholic faith. Abbot Hamilton was particularly influential, exerting considerable power over his weak brother, James, Earl of Arran and regent of Scotland. However, negotiations with England went ahead; on 1 July a treaty was signed at Greenwich between the two countries. The Treaty of Greenwich stipulated that Mary Stewart would marry Edward in her tenth year; further, there was to be an inviolable peace until a year after the death of one or other of the young couple. This was less than Henry VIII had hoped for; he had demanded that Mary be sent to England in 1543 and that the Scots break their alliance with France. The Scots would not give way; Mary would stay in Scotland until her wedding and France was to be included in the treaty of peace. For the moment Henry was content to leave things as they were, hoping in the future to exert further influence on the domestic affairs of Scotland.

Meanwhile, the pro-French party was gaining ground. The regent Arran was wavering in his attitude towards England; French gold was literally flowing into Scotland and it was thought that Marie of Guise's brother was poised to bring an army to the Scots' aid. At the end of June a French fleet was sighted off the coast which further strengthened the pro-French party led by Cardinal Beaton. On 21 July Beaton and the Earls of Huntly, Lennox, Argyll and Bothwell entered Linlithgow at the head of between 6,000 and 7,000 men, intent on seizing the young Queen. Despite the counsel of Sir Ralph Sadler, now residing in Scotland in order to keep Henry VIII informed of developments, the Earl of Arran entered into negotiations with Beaton; the result was that the Queen was to be taken into the custody of four persons, two to be named by Arran and two by Beaton. On 26 July the Queen was taken from Linlithgow Palace to Stirling Castle and was thus safe from any further English attempts to abduct her.

On 25 August Arran ratified the Treaty of Greenwich, although only those nobles favouring England attended the ceremony in the Abbey Church of Holyrood Palace, Edinburgh. Learning of Arran's volte face regarding the young Queen's custody, Henry VIII was consumed with rage. At first he had opposed Arran's appointment as regent, then he had not only supported him but provided him with money – bribes in effect. Then Henry offered his daughter Elizabeth by Anne Boleyn in marriage to Arran's son, promising to make Arran king of Scotland but only north of the Firth of Forth. Arran changed his mind in the face of the prevailing politic weather; one day he supported the alliance with France and the Catholic faith, the next he was pro-England and the introduction of the Reformation in Scotland. Finally, Arran exhausted what remained of Henry's patience by submitting to Cardinal Beaton on 8 September.[2] The following day, the infant Queen Mary was crowned at Stirling. Arran remained in nominal charge of the kingdom but was subject to the direction of a council, two of whose members were the Queen mother, Marie of Guise, and Cardinal Beaton. As a pledge of his loyalty, Arran placed all the strong castles in the hands of Beaton. An irascible Henry VIII virtually exploded at the news, despite the fact that he still controlled a significant group of powerful Scottish nobles – Earls Angus, Glencairn, Cassillis and Rothes and a large number of barons including Angus's brother, Sir George Douglas of Pittendreich.

No matter, French help came in late autumn, when seven French vessels arrived with money and munitions, encouraging the pro-French party to even bolder measures. Lords Somerville and Maxwell, two of Henry's 'assured Scots', were seized en route to England in November with treasonable documents on their person; Sir Ralph Sadler was obliged to seek refuge in Tantallon Castle, stronghold of the Angus Red Douglases. A further three of Henry's confederates, the Earl of Rothes, Lord Gray and Henry Balnaves, the last named being a close associate of the arch-architect of the Reformation in Scotland, John Knox were taken into custody. In the autumn of 1543 Henry VIII ordered Sir Ralph Sadler to buy Dunbar Castle as a secure place to house his 'tresour', the money to be used to bribe his Scottish adherents. Sadler replied there was no hope of that as the castle was held by 'a stout man who beareth none affection for Englonde'. That man was Robert Hamilton of the Briggs.[3] A Scottish parliament convened on 3 December 1543 decreed that the Treaty of Greenwich was null and void as it had been sanctioned by the regent Arran against the wishes of the nation. The alliance with France was renewed, stringent laws against heresy (the Reformation) were enacted and Cardinal Beaton was appointed Lord Chancellor of Scotland.

The defection of Arran to the pro-French party did not however discourage the pro-England party. In January 1544 Earls Angus, Lennox, Glencairn and Cassillis gathered a considerable following at Leith and attempted to draw Arran and Beaton out of Edinburgh and settle the argument by trial of arms. The proposed battle never took place and, by April, the pro-England party was discredited. Arran's defection and the collapse of the 'assured Scots' threw Henry VIII into a paroxysm of rage; at war with France, Henry knew that the Scots would prove a thorn in his side, so he was determined to chastise them by whatever means he could, rendering them incapable of offering any real support for France. On 4 May 1544 an English fleet commanded by the veteran Edward Seymour, Earl of Hertford, appeared off Newhaven in the Firth of Forth and landed troops at Leith. Arran and Beaton gathered together a force but, after a feeble attempt to engage Hertford, they fled to Linlithgow, leaving the English to plunder Leith and an area of five miles around Edinburgh Castle (which Hertford had been unable to capture) including the burning of the Palace of Holyrood. Having chastised the people of Edinburgh to his satisfaction – Hertford claimed that he had utterly destroyed Edinburgh which was untrue, although a number of townspeople lost their lives.[4] Hertford made his way back home by land, burning several towns and villages in East Lothian including Tranent, Haddington and Dunbar. At Dunbar, Hertford's army camped outside the town; on 25 May the townspeople went to bed expecting their houses to be torched the following morning. Hertford did not disappoint them. On the morning of 26 May many men, women and children were either burnt to death or suffocated by smoke.[5] Informing Henry VIII of his campaign, Hertford wrote thus:

> We have brent [burnt] the townes of Haddington and Dunbarre which we
> dare assure your majeste [sic] be well brent, with asmany [sic] other piles,
> gentlemens [sic] and others [sic] houses and villages [6]

There was at least one positive outcome from Hertford's invasion; it
reconciled for a time the leaders of the pro-French and pro-English parties,
although the Earls of Glencairn and Lennox continued to hold out against
Arran and Beaton. First Glencairn, then Lennox were respectively defeated
in what can only be described as skirmishes at Glasgow and Dumbarton;
Lennox was forced to seek refuge in England. The worst the Scots had to fear
came from English troops who now occupied a large part of the Border
country. In November 1544 Hertford destroyed Jedburgh and Kelso and took
Coldingham Priory which he converted into an armed camp for his Irish
levies. In retaliation, Arran collected an army of 8,000 and borrowing a large
cannon and several smaller guns from Dunbar Castle, arrived at Coldingham
on 29 November, battering away fruitlessly at its walls for a day and a night.
He then abandoned the siege, leaving the by now compliant Earl of Angus to
make his way back to Dunbar with the artillery train. As a finishing flourish
to his campaign, Hertford destroyed several hamlets in the Merse, burnt
Melrose Abbey and desecrated the tombs of the Black Douglas earls, family
ancestors of the Red Douglases of Angus.

Hertford's invasion was the opening campaign of what became known in
Scottish history as the *Rough Wooing*, Henry VIII's attempt to force Scotland
into an alliance with England. The year 1545 opened with a renewal of the
conflict from Coldingham and other places in English hands. The English
Border nobles seized every opportunity to wreak havoc on the Scottish East
March. Despite his pro-English sympathies and his antipathy towards the
regent Arran, Archibald, 6th Earl of Angus would not allow the insult to his
ancestors' tombs at Melrose to go unpunished.

Ancrum Moor

In February 1545 Sir Ralph Evers, Warden of the English Middle March
who had destroyed the Douglas tombs at Melrose was confident of further
success. Henry VIII had granted Evers all the land he could conquer in the
Merse and Teviotdale. The Earl of Angus learnt of this and reputedly
responded thus:

> If they [the English] come to take seisin [possession] in [sic] my lands, I
> shall bear them witness to it, and perhaps write them an instrument with
> sharp pens and red ink [meaning swords dipped in English blood.][7]

On 17 February he backed up his threat at Ancrum Moor, three miles from Jedburgh, Evers led a force of 5,200 into the Border country; his army was comprised of 3,000 German and Spanish mercenaries, 1,500 English Border reivers and 700 pro-English Scottish reivers. He marched into Jedburgh where he learnt that a Scottish army was lying near Melrose and proceeded there. Finding no enemy in the vicinity, he torched the town of Melrose, then made camp near Gersit Law, intending to march back to Jedburgh the following day.

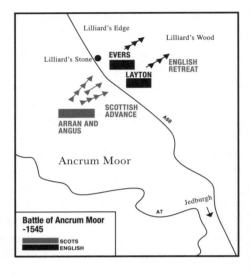

Angus had managed to muster a local force of 1,000 and he was joined by a similar number of troops led by George Leslie, 4th Earl of Rothes. Then the Earl of Arran arrived with a contingent of about 500 Fife levies and took command of the army which numbered about half of Evers' force. The following day, 17 February 1545, Evers broke camp and began his return to Jedburgh, when a small force led by Angus waylaid him, constantly harrowing his force then disappearing into the hills. Finally, Angus appeared before the invaders, probably taunting them, then retreated to the nearby Palace Hill. Evers gave chase; when he reached the summit of the hill he saw the entire Scottish army at the foot of the hill. Angus' raids had been designed to lure Evers into a full-scale battle on terms and ground favourable to the Scottish army drawn up in disciplined formation. The Scots had their backs to the setting sun which dazzled the advancing English who were also disadvantaged by the smoke drifting from the pistols and arquebuses discharged from the Scottish front line. However, it was the Scottish pikemen who won the day with their long spears. The pikemen charged a by now floundering Evers who was unable to re-deploy his men on the summit of the Palace Hill. The Scottish chronicler Robert Lindsay of Pitscottie tells us that

> the Scottismen's speares war [were] longer then [than] the Inglismen's be [by] ... an elne [possibly an *ell*, or forty-five inches.] quilk [which] when they joyned with the Inglismen had them all riven doune [torn down, or destroyed] befor evir [before ever] the Inglismen's spears might touch thame [them.][8]

Then the Scottish Border reivers among the English switched allegiance at the eleventh hour, turning on their former allies. The victory was complete. English casualties were 800 and included Evers, with 1,000 taken prisoner. Scottish losses were given as two which is an absurdly low figure. Whatever the precise casualties, Angus had won a resounding victory, avenging the despoiling of his ancestors' tombs. The defeat at Ancrum Moor, also known as Lilyard's Edge, was one of the worst ever inflicted on the English in the Scottish Borders. A monument was raised to commemorate the battle in the mid-eighteenth century; the memorial fell into disrepair so another version was erected in the following century, bearing the short poem which had been inscribed on the original monument. The poem was dedicated to a young woman called Lilliard whose sweetheart had been killed by the English and who took up arms against them at Ancrum Moor, where she was cut to pieces:

Fair maiden Lilliard
lies under this stane [stone],
little was her stature
but muckle [great] was her fame,
upon the English loons [lads]
she laid monie [many] thumps,
and when her legs were cuttit off
she fought upon her stumps.

The story of Lilliard is apocryphal, however, as the location of Ancrum Moor was known as Lillyat Cross in 1378. However, the monument is known as Lilliard's Stone.

The disaster at Ancrum was particularly discomfiting to Henry VIII who was facing a potential invasion of England in the spring of 1545, with French assistance on its way to Scotland. Henry tried diplomacy, making peace feelers to the Earl of Cassillis to the effect that if the Scots honoured the Treaty of Greenwich he would overlook their late 'offences' – meaning Ancrum Moor – and regard them as friends and allies. Nothing came of this approach. In May, Francis I sent a French fleet to Scotland with a strong force of 3,000 foot and 500 horse commanded by Lorges de Montgomery; the Scots raised an army which brought the total strength to 6,000. This force crossed the Border in August but, as had occurred before, nothing of note was achieved. The French returned home, the promised invasion of England having failed.

Henry bided his time to wreak his revenge on a recalcitrant Scotland. In September 1545 he was resolved to punish the country with added severity. Again, the task of bringing the country to heel was given to the merciless Earl of Hertford who crossed the Border with an army of English, Irish, Germans,

French, Spanish, Italians and Greeks. It was harvest-time and Hertford burned and pillaged his way through southern Scotland; the Scots themselves admitted that they had never before been 'so burned, scourged and punished'.[9] In the course of his expedition, five market towns, 243 villages and sixteen fortified places were destroyed. Hertford also partly demolished the Abbeys at Melrose, Dryburgh, Roxburgh and Coldingham Priory before he returned across the Border. The following year the pro-French Cardinal Beaton, Henry's arch-enemy in Scotland was murdered by Scottish Protestants seeking revenge for Beaton's execution of the Protestant reformer George Wishart. This was the sole consolation for the English king in 1546. Henry VIII died on 28 January 1547; he had scourged Scotland to a degree unsurpassed by any English king since the reign of Edward I. His young son Edward VI being in his minority, England was governed by Henry's intractable and ruthless agent, Edward Seymour, Earl of Hertford, now elevated as the Duke of Somerset and Lord Protector of England. Somerset continued the late King's policy towards Scotland; he attempted to negotiate with the Scottish leaders, warning them that if they did not abandon their alliance with France England would consider this an act of war. The sole alternative was alliance with England and the marriage of the infant Queen Mary and Edward VI. To reinforce his second proposal, Somerset invaded southern Scotland in the first week of September 1547, hoping to impress the Scots with a show of strength.

On this, his third invasion of Scotland, Somerset was determined to bring Scotland to the negotiating table with cannon rather than casuistry; his political credibility was at stake and he knew the voices of opposition to him in England would not long remain silent should he fail to bring the Scots to heel. With war imminent it was decided to send the five-year-old Queen Mary to safety in France on 29 July 1547. Somerset crossed the Border with an army of 18,000; his idea of reasonable force was marked yet again by a dreary succession of burnt religious houses, market towns, villages and fortalices. On reaching East Lothian he burnt Dunbar and Haddington for a second time. As for the regent Arran, he sent the fiery cross throughout the entire realm of Scotland, the fiery cross being the ancient symbol of war or rebellion hitherto used by the Highland clans. The summons was obeyed.

In that early autumn, Somerset established a base at Eyemouth, Berwickshire, for the troops he left behind as a rearguard screen; from Eyemouth he proceeded to Dunglass, destroying its fortalice and the castles of Innerwick and Thornton. Somerset was surprised that the regent Arran had not attempted to oppose him at the Paths of Pease, or Pease Glen, outside Cockburnspath, a sickeningly deep and dangerous ravine which was virtually impossible to cross save by a narrow wooden bridge. Although a few trenches had been dug in the vicinity, Arran made no serious attempt to confront the invader – perhaps deliberately so, following the time-honoured strategy of luring English armies away from their supply bases while pursuing a scorched earth policy to deny food to the invaders. On his campaign, Somerset was supplied by Admiral Lord Clinton's fleet sailing up the east coast and parallel to the land advance. Also, Somerset's invasion occurred before the harvest, so there was no time to gather in or burn the ripening crops. Once again the poor Merse and East Lothian tenant farmers were forced to watch their homes, possessions and the rewards of the agricultural year go up in smoke or be confiscated. The ferocity of Somerset's onslaught had one positive effect; it instilled courage and stiffened the resolve and determination of every Scot, particularly the Merse and East Lothian fighting men; they answered Arran's summons to war, flocking in their hundreds to Mussselburgh's market cross, the rallying point in the south-east.

Somerset passed within cannonshot of Dunbar Castle but the garrison did little more than discharge a few 'diverse shottes', as an English eyewitness commented.[10] No attack was mounted from the castle and Somerset easily brushed aside Arran's cavalry stationed near Dunbar. On 8 September Somerset reached Pinkie Cleugh on the outskirts of Musselburgh, six miles south of Edinburgh; his provisioning fleet commanded by Admiral Clinton had already dropped anchor off Fisherrow on the Musselburgh coast. The 4th Earl of Argyll, the 4th Earl of Huntly and the 6th Earl of Angus, all bitter enemies, nonetheless joined Arran.

Pinkie Cleugh

Somerset occupied the high ground of Falside (modern Fa'side), facing Musselburgh and the North Sea. Fa'side is more steep ridge than moor but it offered an excellent view of Arran's army on the plain of the river Esk below. Somerset's army numbered 10,800 infantry supported by 1,400 pioneers and German arquebusiers; a large artillery train was supplemented by the guns of Admiral Clinton's eighty warships moored off Fisherrow; the cavalry numbered 6,000 which included a contingent of mounted Italian arquebusiers. The cavalry was led by Lord Grey of Wilton, the infantry was commanded by John Dudley, Earl of Warwick and Duke of Northumberland, Lord Dacre of Gillesland and Somerset himself. The English infantry were armed with longbow, bill (halberd), sword and arquebus, the clumsy forerunner of the musket. Against Somerset's 18,200 were ranged Arran's infantry led by the Earls of Angus, Huntly and Arran himself; it consisted mainly of pikemen, Highland bowmen and some arquebusiers, a force totalling 22,000 supported by 2,000 light cavalry commanded by Lord Home. The Scots also possessed more than thirty artillery pieces of various calibres.

Arran drew up his army on the west bank of the river Esk, along Edmonton Edge; his left flank was situated near the sea, while his right flank was protected by the Shire Moss, boggy ground which offered protection over the numerically superior English cavalry. His cannon and arquebusiers were positioned behind makeshift fortifications – probably *gabions*, the large wicker baskets filled with stone and earth for protection against enemy shot. (Some of the Scottish artillery was pointed seaward to keep Clinton's warships at a distance.) Somerset's position on Fa'side Ridge was about three miles east of Arran's front line; it was fortified by trenches and gun emplacements. The battle of Pinkie Cleugh was fought over two days.

First day, Friday, 9 September
Hostilities commenced in late afternoon with Lord Home leading what might be justifiably termed a forlorn hope of 1,500 cavalry; taking up position at the west end of Fa'side Ridge, Home somewhat chivalrously but unrealistically challenged Lord Grey's horse. The attack had little chance of success, Home being outnumbered four to one. Even so, Somerset was reluctant to commit his cavalry at this stage, although he relented, ordering Lord Grey forward with 1,500 heavy and 500 light horse. Despite the fact that the English had the sun beginning to set over the Pentland Hills, near Edinburgh, in their faces, they charged the Scots, cutting them up so badly that Arran lost the bulk of his cavalry in a single action. Later in the day Somerset camped by the shore of Aitchison's Haven (modern Morrison's Haven), overlooking Arran's position. The two armies settled down for the night, each confident of victory the following day.

Second day, Saturday, 10 September
On the morning of the second day, a Saturday, Somerset brought his army off Fa'side to join his forward elements at Inveresk; it was then that he discovered Arran had moved his army across the Esk and was rapidly advancing on his position, reforming on the plain of Pinkie Cleugh. (Cleugh is an old Scots-Gaelic word for glen, or narrow valley.) The reason behind Arran's re-deployment remains unclear; his former position had several advantages which could have discomfited Somerset, particularly his cavalry. There was little room for manoeuvre on Arran's left flank, his right was protected by the Shire Moss and the fast-flowing river Esk to his front presented a difficult obstacle for the English cavalry and infantry alike. The only access across the river was a narrow wooden bridge, reputedly of Roman origin; Pinkie might have been another Stirling Brig, Wallace's resounding victory in 1297. But history is full of might-have-beens ...

The main battle opened with a cannonade from Clinton's fleet, anchored off Fisherrow, Musselburgh, killing the Master of Grahame and twenty-five men standing near him.[11] Despite this, the Scots came on in good order. Arran's army was arranged in three formations; his left wing was commanded by George, 4th Earl of Huntly, his right by Archibald Douglas, 6th Earl of Angus while Arran commanded the centre. Angus was faced by Lord Dacre and his division; Angus should have enjoyed the added protection of Home's cavalry on his flank but the remainder, badly bloodied the previous day, did nothing but stand motionless, hoping to take advantage of any break in the English lines to allow them to raid Somerset's baggage train. Facing Huntly on the Scottish left wing were the Earl of Warwick, with Sir Thomas D'Arcy's *hagbutters*, the English name for arquebusiers. Warwick was flanked by Lord Grey's formidable cavalry, flushed with the previous day's victory over Lord Home. In the centre Somerset faced Arran.

At the outset Somerset positioned the bulk of his cavalry opposite Arran's right but the Scottish pikemen drove them off, inflicting heavy casualties on the horse; Lord Grey was badly wounded by a pike thrust in his mouth and neck. At the height of the battle the Scots very nearly captured the English Royal or King's Standard; the staff bearing the flag snapped in two, the standard bearer managing to escape with the flag. But gradually the English horse began to take its toll of Arran's tightly packed pikemen; added to their onslaught were the continuing cannonade from Clinton's warships and the showers of arrows from the English archers. The pikemen of the Lothians, Lanark, Ayr, Renfrew and Stirling gave a good account of themselves against the English shire infantry but a renewed attack by the re-formed English horse drove them back, albeit in steady order. At this point the Highland bowmen in Huntly's division mistook the redeployment of Arran's force as a retreat and they broke ranks, possibly hoping to benefit from the looting of Somerset's baggage train. Dismay spread among the Lowland levies as they watched the Highlanders streaming away from the field. Pounded on three sides by naval bombardment and field artillery, hagbutters and the deadly English archers, Arran's formation began to disintegrate. In the ensuing melee Sir Pedro de Gamboa's mounted

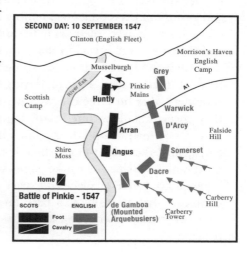

Italian arquebusiers galloped alongside the Scottish right wing, discharging their weapons into the packed mass of pikemen while the left wing was showered with arrows which could not fail to find a mark. The confusion in Arran's three formations degenerated into wholesale panic; Arran himself was among the first to ride from the field, followed by the bulk of his shattered army. Pursued by the English cavalry, many Scots were drowned in the fast-flowing river Esk while many more came to grief in the boggy wetlands of the Shire Moss.

Scottish casualties at Pinkie were given as 6,000[12] with between 1,500 and 2,000 taken prisoner, although few were of high rank; among the captives were Lord Hay of Yester, Colquhoun, Laird of Luss, and Robert Hamilton of the Briggs, captain of Dunbar Castle.[13] English losses were estimated at between 500 and 600. At the battle of Pinkie, the Scots were equipped with medieval weaponry – the spear or pike, sword, axe, longbow and a few arquebuses, the men protected by nothing more than iron helmets and padded leather jerkins or *jacks* and wooden targes; the Highland elements were even more poorly equipped. The English army fought with the halberd, longbow, crossbow, sword and arquebus. Modern historians agree that Pinkie was the first 'modern' battle fought on British soil, combining infantry, cavalry, artillery and a naval bombardment in support of the land forces. A medieval army had been beaten by a Renaissance army.

We have to thank William Patten, an officer in Somerset's army, for his eyewitness account which describes the Scots' arms and their mode of fighting:

> They cum [come] to the felde [field] well furnished all with jak [stout padded doublet or upper garment] and skull [cap], dagger, buckler [shield] and swords, of exceeding good temper and universally good to slice. Hereto everie man his pyke, their array towards joining with the enemy they cling and thrust so nere [near] in the front rank shoulder to shoulder together, with their pykes in both hands straight afore them and their followers so hard at their backs, layinge [laying] their pykes over their foregoers' shoulders, that no force can well withstand them ... Standing at defence they thrust shoulders nie [nigh] together, the fore ranks kneeling stoup lowe [stoop low] before, their fellows behynde holding their pykes, the one end against their right foote, the other against the enemye breast high, the third ranke crossing their pyke points with their forwarde, as thus each with other so nye [nigh] as place and space will suffer through the whole warde so thicke, that as easily as a bare finger perce [pierce] through the skyn [skin] of an angry hedgehog as ony [any] encounter to frunt [front] of their pykes.[14]

Pinkie Cleugh, known as Black Saturday, was the worst disaster in Scotland's history since Flodden. The day after the battle Leith was committed to the flames, then Broughty Castle, near the mouth of the Tay; the island strongholds of Inchcolm and Inchkeith were slighted in September, followed by the occupation of all of Annandale by the Earl of Wharton. Before these events, however, Somerset had been recalled to England on pressing political affairs. The main objective of Pinkie had not been achieved, however; the Scots had no thought of seeking peace with England by giving up their young Queen.

After his defeat Arran had little option other than to turn to France and renew the *Auld Alliance* which he negotiated in December 1547. As a condition, however, he was requested to hand over certain important castles including Dunbar, Eyemouth and Inchcolm; the French set about creating a defensive chain of forts along the east coast of Scotland which incorporated these strongholds. Then, in April 1548, Lord Grey of Wilton, Somerset's cavalry commander at Pinkie, occupied Haddington; Grey believed 'the keeping of Haddington to be the winning of Scotland' which, to modern eyes, seems something of a spin on his modest achievements in Scotland. No matter, Grey spent the next two months fortifying the market town; by the end of June he was surrounded by 14,000 French and Scottish troops commanded by Andre Montalembert, Sieur d'Esse. The Treaty of Haddington signed by France and Scotland on 6 July promised Mary, Queen of Scots to the Dauphin François, heir to the throne of France and only son of Henri II and Catherine de Medici.

The siege of Haddington would last from June 1548 to September 1549. For his part, Grey delegated the command at Haddington to Sir James Wilford so that he could direct operations from Berwick. On 7 July Grey was able to despatch 2,000 troops with powder and shot to Haddington but only 400 managed to get inside the town walls. Another relief column of 15,000 led by the Earl of Shrewsbury found that Haddington was in no danger of capitulating, so Shrewsbury returned to Berwick, torching Dunbar yet again. Before returning over the Border, Shrewsbury rebuilt and strengthened the fortalice of Dunglass and installed a garrison of 3,000 German mercenaries to defend the area, a forward thinking measure to cover the inevitable withdrawal of the English troops from Haddington in the autumn of 1549. In England a court coup toppled Somerset and the war virtually came to a close. Somerset was executed; the war he had so ruthlessly prosecuted against Scotland seemed to have achieved nothing save death, misery and poverty for the people of south-east Scotland.

In the spring of 1550 England and France signed the Treaty of Boulogne on 24 March which brought a welcome respite to the Scots; part of the treaty stipulated that England would relinquish any Scottish strongholds still in its possession. Further, the main castles would be garrisoned by French soldiers which did not sit well altogether with the Scots. It seemed to the Scots that they had exchanged one formidable enemy for another, albeit one kindly disposed to them – at least on the surface. Their young Queen was in French hands and would become the wife of the heir to the French throne; furthermore, the Queen Mother, Marie of Guise Lorraine, encouraged by her brother, the Duke of Guise, and the Cardinal of Lorraine had become extremely powerful, intending to make Scotland a French province. The Scots were also tiring of the presence of d'Esse and his large army; at one point, there was a fight between the citizens of Edinburgh and the strangers in which many lives were lost. Marie of Guise could not wholly dispense with her French soldiers in the running of the country but she sent home as many as she could, retaining only enough to garrison the most important castles in the kingdom. In the next four years Marie increasingly took hold of the reins of power from the weak Earl of Arran who had shown just how little power he excercised as regent. Backed by France, Mary of Guise made a bid for the regency of Scotland in 1550. As for Arran, he was a spent force; he had been opposed to the late alliance with France for purely family reasons, hoping that his son might be a suitable husband for Mary, Queen of Scots. The Treaty of Boulogne had effectively denied him that opportunity; to smooth his ruffled feathers, Arran was offered the Duchy of Chatelherault in France, a bribe he initially refused.

In September 1550 Marie of Guise, accompanied by several of the leading Scottish nobles, visited the French court, where they accepted French gold in exchange for their support of Marie's claim to the regency. A deputation was sent to Arran from France requesting him to demit the office of regent and again offered him the Duchy of Chatelherault by way of compensation. Against his will Arran agreed to both and in November 1551, Marie returned to Scotland. The bargain struck with Arran was that she would assume the regency when her daughter Mary, Queen of Scots reached the age of twelve. Pressure was brought to bear on Arran both from Scotland and France; on 12 April 1554, seven months before Mary's twelfth birthday, Marie of Guise was formally appointed regent of Scotland.

On 24 April 1558 Mary, Queen of Scots married François, Dauphin of France. The wedding ceremony took place in Notre Dame Cathedral, Paris; an unusual splendour attended the event which was perhaps an indication of the political importance attached to it. A public treaty signed five days before the wedding stipulated that if Mary died without heirs Scotland would be given to France, the crown of Scotland placed on the Dauphin's head. For obvious reasons, this aspect of the treaty was kept secret.

(*Left*) Aberlemno Stone depicting what is believed to be a scene from the Battle of Dún Nechtáin, 685. (*Right*) Close-up of Aberlemno Stone showing detail. (*Courtesy of the Rev. Brian Ramsay, Aberlemno Parish Church, near Forfar: Photograph by Mark Hoogiemstra*)

Possible site of the first Battle of Dunbar, 1296. (*Courtesy of John V. Harris*)

Athelstaneford Visitor Centre, commemorating the Battle of Athelstaneford, AD 832. (*Courtesy of John V. Harris*)

Wallace Monument, Abbeycraig, Stirling. (*Courtesy of Simon Lee*)

Detail of two statues of William Wallace. (*Courtesy of Simon Lee*)

t) Full stature of Robert the Bruce by C. d'O. Pilkington-Jackson. (*Right*) Close-up of Bruce
*e*lding his war axe. (*Courtesy of Simon Lee*)

*b*ert the Bruce. (*Courtesy of Simon Lee*)　　　　Oliver Cromwell. (*Author's collection*)

James Graham, 1st Marquis of Montrose.
Painting attributed to William van Hauthors
(*Courtesy of the National Galleries of Scotland*)

David Leslie. (*Author's collection*)

Monumental inscription commemorating the Battle of Dunbar, 1650. (*Author's collection*)

n, Lord Graham of Claverhouse,
Viscount Dundee. Painting by an unknown
st. (*Courtesy of the National Galleries of Scotland*)

Charles Edward Stuart, Bonnie Prince Charlie.
(*Author's collection*)

immossie Moor. (*Courtesy of Simon Lee*)

Monument to the raising of the Jacobite Standard at Glenfinnan. (*Courtesy of Simon Lee*)

...ne depicting the Battle of Culloden, 1746, from an engraving published in 1797. (*Courtesy of the ...onal Museum of Scotland*)

...lliam Augustus, 1st Duke of Cumberland. Painting ...after Sir Joshua Reynolds. *...rtesy of the National Galleries of Scotland)*

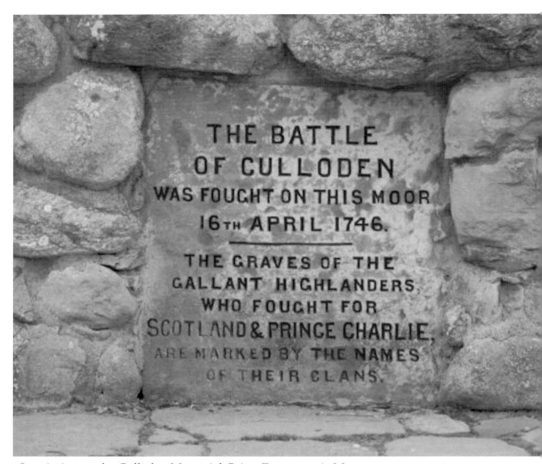

Inscription on the Culloden Memorial Cairn, Drummossie Moor. (*Courtesy of Simon Lee*)

Clan Mackintosh grave. (*Courtesy of Simon Lee*) Clan Fraser grave. (*Courtesy of Simon Lee*)

By 1559 the Reformation was gathering momentum. Several nobles including Lord James Stewart, illegitimate son of James V – and Mary's half-brother – Lord Erskine, Keith, the Earl Marischal, the Earl of Glencairn, Erskine of Dun, Lords Morton and Lorne had all sworn to embrace the new religion; they and many others signed covenants stating they would never rest until they had established Protestantism as the state religion of Scotland. These nobles styled themselves the Lords of the Congregation and declared they were determined to see the back of Marie of Guise and the French who were staunchly Catholic; their cause was strengthened when the Catholic Mary Tudor of England died in 1558 and was succeeded by the Protestant Elizabeth I of England, Henry VIII's daughter by Anne Boleyn. The Lords of the Congregation now felt they could rely on the support of a powerful England whose interests were bound up with those of Scotland. In the face of the growing Protestant rebellion, Marie of Guise had no other option but to abandon the negotiating table and resort to the sword.

On 24 May Marie raised levies of men from Clydeside, Stirling and the Lothians in support of her French troops, ordering them to attend upon her at Stirling. In response, the Protestant Lords strengthened the defences of the town of Perth, one of the earliest walled towns in Scotland. With a force of about 8,000 French and Scottish troops, D'Oysel, Marie's chief adviser, advanced to Auchterarder, some twelve miles from Perth. Marie treated with the insurgents for terms; their response was that Perth would be surrendered if she gave assurances that all who embraced the new religion would be afforded freedom and security of worship. To back their demands, the Protestant Earl of Glencairn at the head of 2,500 men recruited in Ayrshire marched on Perth. It was stalemate. Marie compromised; she agreed not to quarter any French troops in Perth and granted freedom of worship, whereupon the gates of Perth were opened to her. Marie observed the letter but not the spirit of this agreement; she occupied Perth, installing not French but Scottish troops in French pay. In addition, she treated the civilian inhabitants of Perth with harshness which led to further confrontation. It was clear that Marie was playing for time, determined to keep Scotland a satellite of France until her daughter Mary and her husband the Dauphin could take up the throne of Scotland as rightful sovereigns.

The rebels led by Lord James Stewart and the Earl of Argyll evacuated the town and summoned the Protestant gentlemen of Angus and the Mearns, Aberdeenshire to meet them at St Andrews on 3 June. While residing at Falkland Palace, Fife, Marie learnt of this move. With a force led by Henri D'Oysel and Arran, now Duke of Chatelherault she advanced on the rebels who with some 3,000 troops took up position on Cupar Muir or Moor. Battle was avoided, with Marie agreeing to a truce of eight days to allow her to draw up a new understanding. Both sides withdrew to consider their position. Marie's second offer was as hollow as the first. D'Oysel wrote to the French ambassador in London, informing him that only French troops could back up the regent Marie's authority; to this end, D'Oysel sought French reinforcements. During the brief truce, the rebels had not been idle; they opened negotiations with Elizabeth I of England which would ultimately lead to the establishment of Protestantism as the state religion in Scotland as well as uniting the destinies of the two countries.

The truce had no sooner expired than hostilities recommenced. The Protestant Lords relieved Perth and by 29 June Perth, St Andrews, Dundee, Stirling and Edinburgh were firmly in their hands. Marie had no option other than to retreat to her base of Dunbar Castle, where she built an additional outwork or fort to accommodate more of her troops. Dunbar was to be the landing place for the French reinforcements she expected.

All was not well in Edinburgh, however; after the Lords of the Congregation took the capital their 7,000 following had dwindled to a mere 1,500. Marie lost no time in exploiting the situation. She marched with D'Oysel and Arran to confront the rebels at Leith Links in July, again playing for time. The Lords of the Congregation were in no position to dictate terms; they agreed to evacuate Edinburgh, allowing the townspeople to choose their own religion. Then Marie received welcome news; on 10 July, Henri II of France had died of a wound received in a tournament and her daughter, Mary, was therefore Queen of France. This news encouraged Marie to further prosecute her ambitions in Scotland with increased fervour. The Lords of the Congregation had no option but to seek help from England, so John Knox was sent south to open negotiations. Knox got no further than Berwick from where he brought back a less than encouraging response from Elizabeth I's secretary Sir William Cecil to the requests of the Protestant Lords. Money would not be a problem but military support would; in 1559 about two-thirds of Elizabeth's subjects were Catholics and it would not sit well with them were she to enter into a war in support of Protestant rebels in Scotland. The arrival in August of 1,000 French soldiers with their wives and children at Leith left the rebels in no doubt that Marie was in Scotland to stay, despite the fact that the Protestant army now numbered 8,000 against the French 3,000. On 25 November the Lords of the Congregation suffered a reverse in a running street battle in Edinburgh and were forced to retreat to Stirling. Marie's staunch supporters, the Duke of Chatelherault (Arran), the Earl of Glencairn, and Lords Boyd and Ochiltree made their base in Glasgow. Chatelherault's son James, now titled Earl of Arran, had joined the Protestant Lords James Stewart, Ruthven and the Earl of Rothes with John Knox and made their base at St Andrews. The two factions agreed to meet again at Stirling on 16 December 1559.

Marie of Guise did not waste time on niceties; she occupied Edinburgh although she failed to persuade Lord Keith, the Earl Marischal, to surrender the castle. The arrival of further French troops gave Marie the advantage; on Christmas Day she despatched D'Oysel with a major force to drive the Lords of Congregation from Stirling which he did with ease. Then he set about gaining St Andrews which proved a more difficult task as he was beset at every turn by the Scots led by the Earl of Argyll and Lord James Stewart. Skirmishing took place over three weeks, with neither side achieving supremacy. Then, on 23 January 1560, a fleet of unidentified vessels appeared in the mouth of the Firth of Forth; D'Oysel thought it was the French fleet, expected for some weeks. He was shaken to learn that it was an advance squadron of a large English fleet sent by Elizabeth I to blockade any further attempts by the French to land reinforcements.

Then at Berwick-on-Tweed, Lords James Stewart, Ruthven and three other commissioners met the Duke of Norfolk and concluded a treaty on 27 February which promised English military aid to enforce the Protestant religion in Scotland. Marie of Guise was now in desperate straits. On 4 April the Scottish and English armies joined forces at Prestonpans; two days later they invested Leith. The large French fleet bearing fresh troops and armaments never materialized, having been driven back to France by storms. Marie was also suffering from a disease which would carry her off in about two months. Marie's army was now concentrated in Leith and she, at her own request, was received into Edinburgh Castle.

Leith

The Anglo–Scottish army advancing on Leith numbered 9,000 English and 10,000 Scots but, after a few weeks, desertions reduced the total of 19,000 by half. Lord Grey of Wilton besieged Leith which was defended by 4,000 French troops. On 14 April the French sallied out and slew 200 English soldiers; then, on 7 May, a combined Anglo–Scottish assault on Leith was brilliantly repulsed, leaving 800 dead and wounded English and Scots in the trenches. However, the death-knell of the French sounded on 10 June with the demise of Marie of Guise from dropsy. Less than a week later teams of commissioners from England and France convened at Leith on 16 June with powers to effect peace. From the outset the French contended that any treaty which might be concluded would be exclusively between France and England as François, or Francis II of France, regarded his Scottish subjects – he and Mary, Queen of Scots being joint sovereigns of Scotland – as nothing less than rebels. The Treaty of Leith was signed on 6 July; its terms were straightforward. All French subjects in Scotland were to return home, with only 120 soldiers, sixty at Inchcolme in the Forth and sixty at Dunbar Castle remaining to arrange safe conducts for the departing French. No pronouncement was made on religion, however; there could be little doubt in the minds of the Lords of the Congregation how this omission should be interpreted. Henceforth Scotland would be a Protestant country. The Treaty of Leith marks the modernization of Scotland and the adoption of the Protestant faith as the state religion.

In December 1560 Francis II of France died suddenly of an ear infection; Mary, Queen of Scots' reign as Queen consort of France thus came to an end. It was only a matter of time before she would return to her native Scotland and ascend the throne. Even before she set sail from France, Mary indicated the policy she would follow in her kingdom. In February 1561 she sent emissaries to the Scottish Council of Estates to urge the renewal of the *Auld Alliance* which the Estates resolutely refused to do. In response to her request the Protestant leaders urged upon Mary the necessity of leaving religion in Scotland as she found it.

On 19 August 1561 Mary stepped ashore at Leith, attended by a few French retainers and a handful of diplomats. Within five days of her arrival Mary and her household attended Mass in the private Chapel of Holyrood Palace. Her half-brother, Lord James Stewart, had to personally bar the door of the chapel against a group of angry Protestants led by John Knox. The following Sunday Knox preached a particularly violent sermon in St Giles Cathedral, Edinburgh, to the effect that one Catholic Mass was more fearful than 'if 10,000 armed men were landed in any part of the realm, of purpose to suppress the whole Protestant religion'.[15] He would later rant about the 'monstrous regiment of women', meaning not only the young Queen Mary but the frocked clergy of Rome. Knox and Mary remained irreconcilable enemies throughout her brief reign from 1561 to 1567.

On 6 September 1561 Mary chose her chief councillors; among these was her half-brother, Lord James Stewart, James Hamilton, the Duke of Chatelherault, his son, James, Earl of Arran, the Earls of Huntly, Argyll, Bothwell, Hay of Errol, Morton, Glencairn, Montrose, William Keith, 4th Earl Marischal and Lord Erskine. However, in the first four years of her reign, Mary would be guided by her chief Secretary of State, William Maitland of Lethington and Lord James Stewart who would later be elevated to the earldom of Moray. Of the pair, Maitland was more astute, being a diplomat rather than a politician. At least the two men were agreed on a common aim; the need for an eventual union of the crowns of Scotland and England and, as a means to this end, the recognition of Mary, Queen of Scots as immediate successor to Elizabeth I. (It is perhaps surprising that the two Queens never met, even during Mary's incarceration in England between 1568 and her execution in 1587.) The year 1562 produced little of advantage to the foreign and domestic policies of Mary and her advisers. The chief event was the defeat and death of the powerful Earl of Huntly in the autumn of that year.

Corrichie

The cause of the downfall of George Gordon, 4th Earl of Huntly is not entirely clear. In August 1562 Mary set out from Edinburgh on an itinerary of her northern provinces, something she had long considered due in order to acquaint herself with that part of her kingdom. Her northern visit was marred by the contumacy of Huntly's second son, Sir John Gordon of Findlater, who had broken his ward in Edinburgh Castle for some misdemeanour and refused to submit to Mary at Stirling, as she had ordered him to. The Earl of Huntly invited her to his castle at Strathbogie but in view of his son's behaviour, Mary wisely declined. At Inverness she was insulted by the garrison of the castle which, in the name of Lord Gordon, refused her admission. The inhabitants of the area rose in support of their queen and the castle was surrendered the following day, when its captain was hanged and some of the garrison sent to prison for life. Sir John Gordon of Findlater refused to give up his castles at Findlater and Auchindoune; his father, the Earl of Huntly also disregarded Mary's summons to her presence. On 17 October Huntly was declared an outlaw. This was possibly a grave error on Mary's part; Huntly was the head of the north-east clans and enjoyed a considerable following. It is believed that his rebellion against Mary was not aimed at her but her Protestant advisers. A devout Catholic, Huntly had urged Mary to reinstate the 'true' religion; already at odds with some of her nobles over her policy of religious tolerance, Mary was acutely embarrassed by Huntly's ultimatum. The bigoted Protestant nobles dismissed Huntly's claim that his opinion should carry more weight than any other noble as, in his view, he was the first in rank among the Scottish nobility, whatever their religious persuasion. The Protestant nobles called Huntly's bluff and an army led by Mary's half-brother, James Stewart, now Earl of Moray, was assembled; Moray, with the Earls of Atholl and Morton led 2,000 Lowlanders against Huntly. When Huntly received the news of the approaching army, it is said that he became indecisive and had to be persuaded by his wife to take the field.

Huntly commanded a force of only 700 or 800 clansmen on the day of Corrichie which was fought on 28 October 1562. Moray's 2,000-strong force had been recruited mainly from East Lothian and Fife. He drew up his force on rising ground at Meikle Tap (Big Top) near Aberdeen; Moray's army contained Lowlanders he knew he could trust and Highlanders whom he could not. For his part, Huntly was not dismayed by the superior force confronting him as he believed many in Moray's army were friends of his and would defect during the course of the battle.

Moray launched his attack with the dubious clansmen who made little impression on Huntly's front line, perhaps deliberately so; they broke and came running back to Moray's position, hotly pursued by Huntly's clansmen. Moray's main battalion of Lowland spearmen levelled their weapons to receive both pursued and pursuers, not caring who they slew. Huntly's Gordons charged in Highland fashion in disorderly lines with sword and targe; they were no match for Moray's spearmen. Huntly's men retreated, Huntly being thrown from his horse; he could not rise again, being corpulent and weighed down by his armour. Moray's dubious clansmen returned to the field to take part in the slaughter – and plunder – of Huntly's men, 120 of whom were slain. Among those taken prisoner were Huntly and his two sons, Adam and John. Huntly died that night, short of breath; some accounts give the cause of his death as apoplexy.[16] Huntly's son, Sir John Gordon of Findlater was executed for treason on 29 October. Huntly's eldest son and heir George was also charged with treason, even though he had not been present on the field of Corrichie. He was sent to prison in Dunbar Castle where he languished for the next three years.[17] Finally reinstated as the 5th Earl of Huntly by Mary in 1565, Gordon became one of her staunchest supporters.

Modern historians consider the somewhat farcical battle of Corrichie as a clan battle; this author disagrees with this view. Corrichie did indeed involve clansmen on both sides but it was a battle fought by Lowlanders against Highlanders, not by Clan Gordon against Clan Stewart or Stuart, as Mary began to style herself. The battlefield of Corrichie was commemorated by a memorial stone raised in 1951; the Gaelic inscription is translated as 'remember the day of Corrichie'. The battlefield is now largely obscured by woodlands.

The question we must ask is this: why did Mary, Queen of Scots acquiesce in the defeat and ruin of the Earl of Huntly, a Catholic and one of her most loyal supporters? The answer can only be Huntly's defiance of Mary's mother, Marie of Guise and punished by the latter for his treasonable contact with England during the term of Marie's regency. Mary was probably made aware of this. She would have had little confidence in a noble – Catholic though he undoubtedly was – who attended the sermons of John Knox, albeit as a somewhat intemperate listener; in the event of a renewed civil war it was likely that Huntly would have placed his sword in the service of whichever party was the more powerful. For all her faults Mary preferred an open foe to a devious friend.

Mary's relationship with Elizabeth I was never cordial; the English queen resolutely refused to acknowledge Mary as her successor, although, in the eyes of Catholic Europe, Mary was the rightful heir-apparent to the throne of

England, Elizabeth being considered illegitimate, despite her being Henry VIII's lawful daughter. Mary and her late husband Francis II had assumed the titles of King and Queen of France, Scotland and England; but England was Elizabeth's and would remain so until her death in 1603.

In 1563 Mary lost a formidable ally in France when her uncle the Duke of Guise was assassinated. Mary, a widow, was determined to marry whomsoever she chose, including a powerful Catholic king; even her closest advisers, Maitland of Lethington and James Stewart, Earl of Moray were not averse to the prospect in the hope that such a marriage would force Elizabeth to recognize Mary as her rightful successor. But Elizabeth, alarmed by the prospect, was not sufficiently cowed; she sent her agent Thomas Randolph to Scotland with a message to the effect that were Mary to follow this course of action she would regard it as a breach of friendship with England.

The following year the question of Mary's marriage absorbed both herself and her council of advisers; Elizabeth suggested her favourite Lord Robert Dudley whom she elevated to the Earl of Leicester to make him a more suitable husband. For her part, Mary agreed to the marriage on one condition – that with Dudley should come the recognition of her right to succeed Elizabeth. As Dudley was a Protestant he was not only acceptable to Maitland and James Stuart, Earl of Moray but also to John Knox, who eagerly welcomed the prospect of a Protestant king of Scotland. Dismissing Mary's condition out of hand (it is doubtful whether Elizabeth was ever remotely enthusiastic about Dudley's marriage to Mary), Elizabeth rejected the alliance and Mary was left to take responsibility herself for her matrimonial affairs. She made a disastrous choice in her second choice of husband, Lord Darnley.

Henry, Lord Darnley, was the son of Matthew, 4th Earl of Lennox, and Lady Margaret Douglas, daughter of James IV's widow Margaret Tudor and Archibald Douglas, 6th Earl of Angus. The seventeen-year-old Darnley was Mary's cousin and next in line to her in the succession to the throne of England. At Mary's request, Elizabeth I permitted the exiled Earl of Lennox to return to Scotland; it may be remembered that Lennox had supported the English during the *Rough Wooing*. Lennox, a Catholic, would be a welcome ally for various reasons, the main being that he would act as a counter-balance to the over-mighty Protestant Hamilton family as well as being a check to other powerful nobles. The prospect of Lennox's return was anathema to the Earl of Moray and Maitland of Lethington; they feared he would present an obstacle to their progress while others of the Protestant party found his return in September hateful; these fears were not lessened when, in December, Mary restored all Lennox's honours and lands.

Mary and Darnley were married in accordance with the rites of the Catholic Church in the Chapel Royal of Holyrood on 29 July 1565. As grandson of Margaret Tudor, Henry VIII's sister, Darnley's marriage to Mary strengthened their respective claims to the English throne. As for Mary, she had frightened Elizabeth I and she gave the great Catholic houses of Europe hope that the true religion might be re-established not only in Scotland but also England, where Elizabeth's still considerable number of Catholic subjects posed a threat to the Protestant religion. Many of Mary's nobles were angered by her marriage, seeing it a threat to the Reformation in Scotland. Mary's response was to crush those Protestant lords who had voiced their displeasure at her choice of husband. Mary was eager to engage the insurgents – the Duke of Chatelherault and Earls Moray, Rothes, Glencairn and Lord Boyd – in a battle which never materialized. While Mary rode about gathering support and stamping out pockets of rebellious subjects, the Duke of Chatelherault gathered a force of 1,200 horse and made his headquarters at Dumfries. By 8 October Mary had gathered sufficient support to engage the insurgents but they had vanished across the Border. Mary was now mistress of her kingdom for the first time in four years. This episode became known as the *Roundabout* or *Chaseabout Raid*, the highwater mark of Mary's brief reign.

From the outset Mary's matrimonial troubles with Darnley are extensively recorded. They quarrelled repeatedly because she withheld the Crown Matrimonial from Darnley, which meant he could never style himself King of Scotland. Darnley, immature, boastful, frequently drunk and cowardly, vented his wrath on his wife by indulging in extra-marital liaisons. When the renegade nobles of the *Chaseabout Raid* were pardoned and allowed to return to Scotland, the Earl of Moray persuaded Darnley to join a plot to murder Mary's Italian (Catholic) secretary and favourite, David Rizzio, whom Moray and his associates believed to be either an English spy or an agent of Rome. The assassination took place on the night of 9 March 1566 when a heavily pregnant Mary was enjoying a late night supper with Rizzio and a few friends. The plotters, led by the aged Patrick, Lord Ruthven, James, 4th Earl of Morton, Lord Lindsay and their associates, broke into the Queen's private chambers and dragged Rizzio into the corridor and messily knifed him to death, leaving Darnley's own dagger beside the corpse to implicate him. Fearing she would be the next victim, Mary and Darnley rode to her castle at Dunbar to seek sanctuary. There, supportive nobles such as George, 5th Earl of Huntly (whom Mary had pardoned after three years in captivity following the battle of Corrichie), the Earl of Atholl and James Hepburn, 4th Earl of Bothwell joined Mary at Dunbar. Gathering an army with Mary at its head, the force of about 4,000 re-entered Edinburgh on 18 March, the renegade nobles having fled to Linlithgow the day before. On 19 June Mary gave birth to a son who would become James VI of Scotland, then James I of England.

Relations between Mary and Darnley did not improve after the baby's birth. Alienated both from his wife and the renegade lords, Darnley consoled himself with extra-marital liaisons, thereby further distancing himself from the Queen. In desperation, Mary turned to James Hepburn, 4th Earl of Bothwell a noble who, for the three years prior to 1565 had spent his time either in prison or in exile in France. Mary showered gifts on Bothwell; on 7 June 1566 he was given the inheritance of Dunbar (excepting its castle) as well as other lands and honours, including the appointment of Admiral of Scotland and Warden of the Borders. With his castles of Hailes, near East Linton and Borthwick in Midlothian, Bothwell became over-mighty in a very short space of time.

In January 1567 Bothwell met up with the Earl of Morton and Secretary Maitland of Lethington at Whittingehame, East Lothian,[18] ostensibly to form an alliance; however, it is generally believed to have been a meeting to discuss ways of getting rid of Darnley. Darnley's subsequent murder at Kirk o'Field in Edinburgh on the night of 9 February 1567 inevitably led to accusations against Bothwell as prime suspect. It is widely accepted that Mary played no part in Darnley's murder; in fact, it is thought that Darnley intended to blow up Kirk o'Field with Mary inside but he reckoned without the counter-plot against him. Kirk o'Field was indeed destroyed by gunpowder thought to have been placed there by Darnley who was found dead in his nightshirt in the garden, with strangulation marks on his neck;[19] beside his body were a chair and a rope. However, it became clear that Darnley had been strangled by hand. It was a tragic and ironic coincidence – if that is what it was – that two separate plots conjoined on that fateful night. The identities of Darnley's murderers remain a mystery today, not helped by the crude bias of the state archives which point the finger of suspicion at Bothwell.

The Scottish crown now lay tantalizingly within Bothwell's reach; he was close to the Queen and her dissolute husband was now out of the way. Matters came quickly to a head. Accusations were made against both Mary and Bothwell regarding Darnley's murder; Bothwell swore that he was innocent of the crime but, for good measure, forced several leading Protestant and Catholic nobles to sign a document attesting to his innocence and indicating their willingness to accept Bothwell's declared intention to marry the Queen should she accept him. On 24 April he intercepted Mary on her way from Stirling after a visit to her infant son James and led her – some historians believe Bothwell actually kidnapped the Queen – to Dunbar Castle. There he reputedly and repeatedly raped her, then forced her to sign two marriage contracts, one written in Scots, one in French. On 7 May Bothwell's divorce from Lady Jean Gordon, sister of George, 5th Earl of Huntly was conveniently settled; then, on 15 May, Bothwell and Mary were married. (At that time, and possibly still today, May was considered an unlucky month for marriage.)[20]

The consequences of the marriage were immediate. It was one matter to offer support for Bothwell but quite another to suffer his overweening authority; several nobles, including those who had signed Bothwell's bond in April promising support, formed a coalition. Calling themselves the Confederate Lords, they attempted to arrest Bothwell at Borthwick Castle. He eluded capture, managed to reach Haddington, then Dunbar, where Mary joined him; in her haste to escape from Borthwick Castle, Mary could find only male clothing to wear.[21] The citizens of Edinburgh were now convinced that Bothwell and Mary had been instrumental in Darnley's murder and many responded to the Confederate Lords' call to arms against the queen.

Carberry Hill

Bothwell hastily scraped together a force of 2,000 from East Lothian and the Merse, recruited mainly by the few nobles remaining loyal to Mary – Lords Seton and Hay of Yester being the most resolute among the Catholic minority. The two armies met at Carberry Hill, close to the field of Pinkie, Musselburgh, on 15 June, a month to the day after Mary and Bothwell's wedding. Both sides were about equally matched in numbers although the Marian force had the advantage of seven or eight pieces of artillery from Dunbar Castle. Most of that sultry afternoon the two armies did little more than glower at each other, neither side willing to make the first move. Bothwell's artillery fired a few desultory shots at the rebel picquets but inflicted no casualties. Mary was eager to join battle; but did she know it, the Confederate Lords were by no means united, nor were they predominantly Protestant. At least two, the Earls of Borthwick and Semple were Catholic and the Earl of Cassillis had changed his religion no fewer than three times in the past seven years. A publicly proclaimed aim of the Confederate Lords was to rescue Mary and her infant son James from Bothwell; their true purpose will be revealed shortly.

Neither side desired to shed blood. The Confederate Lords believed that delay would bring them success. As the afternoon wore on Mary awaited reinforcements which never materialized. Her army dwindled rapidly as men deserted, ignoring her taunts of cowardice. Finally, Mary and Bothwell were left with only sixty men. A compromise was reached; if Mary crossed over to them the Confederate Lords would give safe-conduct to Bothwell to Dunbar. Mary was led to Edinburgh dressed in a short, red petticoat, the only female attire she could find at Dunbar that morning. The colour of the garment spoke volumes; not only was it a reminder of the detested scarlet of Rome, it was that of the common whore. In the streets of Edinburgh Mary was jeered by a hostile populace.

As for James Hepburn, 4th Earl of Bothwell, he escaped to Dunbar, garrisoned its castle with kinsmen and friends, then took ship for Orkney and Norway. It was there that his unsavoury past caught up with him. He was arrested by the Norwegian Viceroy, cousin of a Norwegian lady with whom he had had an affair and who lent him money; the lady sued him for the loan which Bothwell was unable to pay. Bothwell's end was pure Greek tragedy; sent to prison for the remainder of his life, he died insane in a Danish prison at Faarvejle, near Dragsholm Castle on the island of Zealand on 14 April 1578.[22] His death was unmourned by Mary, Queen of Scots.

On 17 June 1567 Mary was taken to Lochleven Castle where, on 24 July, she was forced to sign three documents under the terms of which she abdicated in favour of her son, James VI. Mary's half-brother James, Earl of Moray was appointed regent; he in turn nominated the Duke of Chatelherault, Earls Lennox, Argyll, Atholl, Morton, Glencairn and Mar as governors of Scotland. On 29 June James VI was crowned at Stirling, John Knox preaching the coronation sermon.[23] Everything seemed to point to peace and stability, save for Mary. The deposed Queen had one more shot left in her locker.

Langside

Mary languished in Lochleven Castle until 2 May 1568 from where she escaped with the help of a pageboy, Willie Douglas. Making her way to the town of Hamilton, Mary was welcomed by the Hamilton family – staunch enemies of Mary's half-brother James, Earl of Moray now regent of Scotland. In Hamilton Mary hastily gathered a formidable force which contained no fewer than nine earls, nine bishops, eighteen lords and a hundred barons who swore to defend her and restore her to the throne. The regent Moray was in Glasgow when he learnt of Mary's escape from Lochleven. He immediately raised an army to confront his half-sister in the vicinity. According to Sir James Melville's *Memoirs*, Mary, residing at Hamilton, was not minded to fight a battle; instead, she agreed with her advisers that she should make her headquarters in Dumbarton Castle, there to receive her loyal subjects and gain a political – and bloodless – advantage over her opponents and thereby regain her crown. When Moray received word that Mary was making her way from Hamilton to Dumbarton by the Dumbarton Road which led past Glasgow, he was resolved to confront her in battle. Moray marched his force to the village of Langside, south of Glasgow, hoping to intercept Mary there. Accounts of the sizes of Mary's and Moray's armies suggest that the Queen commanded 5,000 to the regent's 3,000[24] although the figures may have been higher by 1,000 on both sides.

The two armies met at Langside. Mary's forces partly occupied Clincart Hill; the right wing of Moray's troops rested on the ground where a monument to the battle now stands, his left on the farm of Pathhead, part of which is now incorporated into what is known today as the Queen's Park. Among Mary's supporters were the Earls of Argyll, Cassillis, Rothes and

Eglinton, along with the Lords Somerville, Yester, Livingston and Fleming. Moray's force, inferior in number but superior in its commanders and discipline contained the Earl of Lennox – for long an enemy of the Hamiltons – the Earl of Morton and the militarily capable William Kirkcaldy of the Grange.

Mary's commander, the lacklustre Archibald Campbell, 5th Earl of Argyll was hardly equal to the task, despite his numerical superiority. Moray sent the competent Kirkcaldy of the Grange to observe Mary's position. The Queen's army was positioned on the south bank of the Clyde, Moray's on the north bank. Kirkcaldy rightly anticipated Mary's – or rather, Argyll's – intention to occupy the high ground of Clincart Hill, so he sent a force of horse supported by arquebusiers riding behind every cavalry trooper to cross the Clyde at the old wooden Brig of Glasgow (demolished in 1850). Kirkcaldy placed his men in the hedges, cottages and gardens of Langside village It is believed that the battle of Langside on 13 May 1568 began at 9am. The vanguard of Argyll's force charged along a road in an undisciplined mass, encountering Moray's disciplined spearmen and arquebusiers who poured a steady fire into the ranks of the advancing enemy.

Mary's commander in chief Argyll appears to have had no battle plan other than to engage his enemy; he simply believed that superiority of numbers would bring him victory. His colleague, a Hamilton whose name is not recorded, tried to force his way through Langside Village only to be met by a steady, withering fire from Kirkcaldy of Grange's arquebusiers in their places of concealment. Many of Hamilton's men were killed or wounded but he pressed forward only to be confronted by Moray's left wing placed on rising ground. Moray fought a defensive action, his spearmen holding their own, while Morton's Border pikemen attacked Hamilton's vanguard. Both sides engaged in a desperate push-of-pike until Argyll's right wing began to give ground. Sensing victory, Kirkcaldy of Grange brought up reinforcements and broke through Argyll's ranks while Moray, having repulsed Mary's cavalry, drove forward against Argyll's centre. The Marian forces were disintegrated and swept down the slopes of Clincart Hill. Mary watched the spectacle from a spot about a mile away from Langside, knowing she had been defeated.

The battle of Langside lasted about forty-five minutes. Some 300 of Mary's troops were slain; Moray's losses were unquantified but were probably much fewer. The site of Langside is commemorated in an impressive fifty-eight-feet-high monument surmounted by a lion, with one of its front paws resting on a cannon ball. The Battlefield Monument was erected in Battlefield Road, Langside, now a suburb of modern Glasgow.

A dispirited Mary, Queen of Scots, turned her horse south by way of Dumfries to the shore of the Solway Firth. On 16 May 1568 Mary crossed the

Border to Workington, Cumberland. She would never see Scotland again. Mary spent the remaining eighteen years of her life in England, a prisoner of Elizabeth I; she occupied her years engaging in unrealistic plots against Elizabeth until that Queen's patience finally ran out in 1587. In February of that year, Mary, Queen of Scots was found guilty of treason against Elizabeth. On 8 February Mary was beheaded at Fotheringhay Castle. She met her death with great dignity. There was no outcry in Scotland for revenge.

Notes

1. Oliver, *A History of Scotland*, p.172.
2. *Hamilton Papers*, vol. ii, p.256.
3. *Hamilton Papers*, op. cit., p.108.
4. Pugh, *Swords, Loaves and Fishes: A History of Dunbar*, p.23.
5. Pugh, op. cit., p.23.
6. *Hamilton Papers*, op. cit., p.379.
7. Hume Brown, *History of Scotland*, vol. ii, p.16.
8. Pitscottie, *Chronicles of Scotland*, vol. ii, p.441.
9. Hume Brown, op. cit., p.18.
10. Patten, *Expedicioune into Scotland*.
11. Brotchie, *The Battlefields of Scotland*, p.131.
12. Pugh, op. cit., p23; Hume Brown, op. cit., p.31; Brotchie, op.cit., p.132.
13. Pugh, op. cit., p.23.
14. Patten, op. cit., quoted in Brotchie, op. cit., p.130.
15. Hume Brown, op. cit., p.83; Oliver, op. cit., p.188.
16. Pugh, op. cit., p.27.
17. There is an interesting story on George Gordon's captivity in Dunbar. During his incarceration, Mary had signed a death warrant – not authorized by her – which some enemy of Gordon had slipped into a sheaf of documents which Mary signed unread. (The culprit may have been her half-brother, Lord James Stewart.) Fortunately for Gordon, his jailer at Dunbar, Simon Preston of Craigmillar refused to carry out the execution without Mary's personal confirmation of the warrant. Mary cancelled the death sentence and Gordon became one of her most loyal supporters. (Pugh, op. cit., p.27.)
18. Pugh, op. cit., p.29.
19. *Diurnal of Occurrents*, pp.105–6.
20. Pugh, op. cit., p.31.
21. *CSP Scot.*, vol. ii, No.523.
22. For four centuries Bothwell's mummified body was on display for the cost of a few pence until, in the latter half of the twentieth century, Scottish tourists complained to the Danish authorities that the remains of a Scottish nobleman should be given a Christian burial. The Queen of Denmark finally ended the gruesome practice and arranged the burial of Bothwell's remains. (Pugh, op. cit., p.33 and note 99, p.392.)
23. Hume Brown, op. cit., p.113.
24. *Diurnal of Occurrents*, p.130; Tytler, *History of Scotland*, vol. vi, p.36.

Chapter 9

Civil Wars: 1594–1654

T
he reign of James VI and I (1578–1625) is probably the most important of all the reigns of the Stewart or Stuart dynasty between 1371 and 1625 in that it saw the union of Scotland and England under one monarch, when James succeeded Elizabeth I in 1603 and became James VI and I. During his time as King of Scotland, James's reign was similar to that of his mother, Mary, Queen of Scots, in two respects. The first was that both reigns were beset by religious conflicts; the second is that there were few pitched battles fought. Both Mary and James were fortunate to have been spared the battles which had been a feature of the wars of independence. James VI's minority (1567–78) was not dissimilar to those of several of his forebears; like other Stewart kings who ascended the throne as children, his was beset by lawlessness, division and disorder largely caused by feuding nobles.

Much of the unrest in Mary's and James's reigns can be attributed to the adoption of Presbyterianism as Scotland's state religion; rather than fighting in the name of Mary, then James, the conflict was between Catholic and Protestant, although not exclusively so, as Catholic fought Catholic, Protestant fought Protestant, often spuriously in the name of the reigning monarch. During James's minority, no fewer than three regents – the Earl of Moray, James's half-uncle, then the Earl of Mar and finally the Earl of Morton – ruled Scotland. In 1570 Moray was assassinated by George, 6th Earl of Huntly whose family had been a thorn in Moray's side for years; Mar died of disappointment in 1572, 'the maist cause' of his death being 'that he loved peace and could not have it'.[1] Morton resigned on account of his unpopularity in 1578, then was executed for treason in 1581. All three regents experienced difficulties with those Catholic nobles who remained loyal to the deposed Mary, Queen of Scots. Countless conflicts between the King's party (James) and the Marian party (Mary) brought destruction and death; these conflicts involved the besieging of castles, destruction of property, forfeiture of lands and titles, execution, exile and the spilling of (mostly) innocent blood. As if this was not enough, there was an ever-present danger during James's reign – the spectre of the return of Roman Catholicism, either from within Scotland herself or from the Continent, chiefly in the person of Philip II of Spain, champion of the Catholic faith. At least James, like his mother, could draw some consolation from the fact that he experienced only one battle – that of Glen Livet in 1594. Although Glen Livet was fought between Highland clans, it cannot be considered a clan battle, outwith the scope of this book; it was a conflict between Catholic and Protestant, the last attempt of the adherents of Rome to re-impose Catholicism as the state religion of Scotland. To understand how Glen Livet came about, we need to look at the political situation in Scotland between 1588, the year of the Spanish Armada and 1594. The unrest was brought about by certain Catholic Scottish nobles intent on restoring the 'True Faith' to Scotland with the help of Philip II of Spain.

After the defeat of the Spanish Armada in 1588 and Philip's attempts to topple Elizabeth I from the throne of England, letters came into the possession of the English Queen written by the Catholic Earls of Huntly and Errol and addressed to the Spanish King. Huntly and Errol expressed their regret that the Armada had failed and promised assistance from Scotland in any future attempts by Spain to invade England. Elizabeth sent the letters to James VI, no doubt expecting the Scottish King to deal with his rebel subjects. The letters were a source of embarrassment to James whose policy had been to maintain a balance between his Protestant and Catholic subjects as evenly as public opinion would suffer. However, the clamour from the Protestant clergy for him to take action against the Earls of Huntly and Errol was such that James was forced to take punitive action against the rebels; in all conscience he could hardly ignore what was, in effect, treason. Huntly and Errol were subjected to a form of court hearing and Huntly was imprisoned in Edinburgh Castle for a few days. In April Huntly, Errol and the Earls of Crawford, Montrose and Bothwell gathered a force of 3,000 to challenge James's authority. Huntly made a show of menacing the royal army at the Bridge of Dee, near Aberdeen, but, on learning that James himself was at the head of the army, Huntly and his confederates backed down, disbanding their forces. The conspirators were tried by the Privy Council in Edinburgh but received light sentences; James was continuing his policy of keeping a balance between those among his nobles who were adherents of both religions. Huntly, Crawford and Bothwell were imprisoned for a few months, then set free in September. For a time it seemed that peace had broken out; then the nation's attention was distracted (then as now) by the royal wedding between James and Anne of Denmark in 1589.

The intriguers did not abandon their cause. Huntly, Errol and others continued to defy the royal writ and maintain their contact with Spain. Matters came to a head in July 1594 when Huntly and his confederates were declared guilty of acts of open rebellion which could not go unpunished. Then a Spanish ship arrived in Aberdeen bearing an envoy from Pope Clement VIII with letters for James and a sum of money; the Papal envoy was attended by three English Catholic priests. The Aberdeen magistrates seized the Papal envoy and his companions, taking them into custody. When Huntly and his associates learnt of this, they threatened to put the town to the torch and the sword if the prisoners were not freed. The Aberdeen town fathers had little option but to comply. James was forced to act, embarking on what was, in effect, a civil war which he had resolutely striven to avoid. In September he summoned his loyal nobles to raise an army and confront the rebels. Progress was slow, too long for the Presbyterian clergy; frustrated by and indignant at the delay, the ministers of the Kirk persuaded the nineteen-year-old Archibald Campbell, 7th Earl of Argyll to take up arms against Huntly in the field.

Glen Livet

On 3 October 1594 Argyll confronted Huntly and Errol near Glen Livet, Banffshire. The subsequent battle was fought at Altnachoylachan, or Altchonlachan, about two miles east of Glen Livet. Argyll's army of 10,000 outnumbered Huntly's by five to one; however, the former's Highland levies were lightly armed and wore no protective clothing other than plaids and bonnets. Huntly's force of 2,000 included heavy cavalry armed with lances and protected by chain mail; Huntly also possessed several artillery pieces which he would put to effective use.

Argyll was inexperienced in warfare but, assisted by the Earl of Atholl, he was confident of victory. Argyll's scouts had ascertained the strength of the opposing force, so he felt that his army would gain victory by sheer weight of numbers. However, apprehensive about Huntly's cavalry which could counter-balance his numerical superiority, Argyll held a council of war on 2 October, the night before the battle; he was advised to await the arrival of James VI and his army or, conversely, to stay his hand until Clans Fraser and Mackenzie from the north, then the Irvines, Forbes and Leslies from the Lowlands arrived, bringing cavalry. The impetuous youth declined to follow this sensible advice, no doubt offered by Atholl.

On 3 October Argyll took up position on the declivity of a hill between Glen Livet and Glenrinnes. His right wing comprised men from Clans Maclean and Mackintosh commanded by Sir Lauchlan Maclean; the left wing contained Clans Grant, Macneil and Macgregor led by Grant of Gartinbec; the centre was held by Clan Campbell led by Campbell of Auchinbreck. This, the vanguard, numbered 4,000, Argyll commanding the reserve of 6,000 in the rear. Huntly's van consisted of a mere thirty horse commanded by the Earl of Errol. Huntly led the bulk of his force behind this thin line of steel. Before the battle commenced Huntly's men prepared themselves by celebrating Mass and communion, making their confessions to a priest, just as Bruce's soldiers had done at Bannockburn. Their weapons were then sprinkled with holy water and a cross was placed on their armour, signifying they fought in defence of Christ.

Despite his immaturity and inexperience, Argyll had chosen favourable ground for his fight. To neutralize Huntly's heavy cavalry, Argyll placed his men on the declivity of a hill with a boggy marsh at its foot; he also had pits dug to discomfit Huntly's horses. The battle commenced with Huntly and Errol advancing at a slow but steady pace up the hill. Then Huntly ordered his cannon to open fire, the target being Argyll's yellow standard. Many of Argyll's Highlanders had never experienced an artillery bombardment before; the cannon threw them into confusion which Huntly was not slow to exploit. Charging Argyll's force with their cavalry, Huntly and Errol added to the confusion among the terrified Highlanders. The ensuing battle lasted for two hours, both sides fighting bravely and vigorously until at length Argyll's centre and left wing were completely broken. Argyll's fatalities were 500, Huntly's a trifling fourteen, although there were many wounded. Glen Livet was a victory won by well trained, well equipped cavalry, infantry and artillery against irregular infantry.

As for James VI and his 'relief' army, it would appear that the King had no intention of joining Argyll; his army remained in Dundee, where he received news of Argyll's defeat. Only then did he march north to destroy Strathbogie Castle and the House of Slains, respectively the chief residences of Huntly and Errol. The rebels Huntly and Errol were permitted to go into voluntary exile in Flanders and Germany, where they would remain until 1597 when James considered it safe for their return to Scotland. In 1599 James, who had always had a high regard for the Earl of Huntly, elevated him to the rank of 1st Marquis of Huntly, a signal honour which was testimony to the extent of the royal favour.

The second half of James's reign was spent in England where he quickly stamped his authority when he ascended the English throne in 1603. During the years 1603 to his death in 1625, James showed that he had inherited the heady ambitions of his mother, Mary, Queen of Scots. At his coronation on 25 July 1603 James I of England sat on St Edward's Chair in Westminster Abbey, the same chair Edward I, 'Longshanks', had commissioned in 1301 and under which had been placed the Stone of Destiny taken from Scotland by Edward I in 1296. From the outset of his reign in England, James favoured the establishment of a Great Britain but neither the Scots nor the English shared his enthusiasm. The Scots thought it a betrayal of the independence for which they had bled for three centuries, a loss of their identity; the English did not relish being unequally yoked to a financially poor and what they saw as a backward nation; the latter was hardly true, as Scotland possessed no fewer than four universities at the time.

James returned to Scotland only once during the remainder of his life, in 1617. In London he surrounded himself with Scots, alienating his English courtiers and particularly those of the Catholic faith who showed their anger by attempting to rid themselves of the king in 1605; the Gunpowder Plot of 5 November that year was not intended to destroy parliament but James himself. (Even today, we retain an indelible, if somewhat picaresque image of Guido (Guy) Fawkes wearing a wide-brimmed hat, conspiratorial cloak, tight hose and folded down boot-tops, looking for all the world like the melodramatic villains so beloved of the Victorian vaudeville stage, his furtive, *whitterick* (Scots for weasel) eyes darting from side to side. Who, however, remembers King James so graphically?)

James VI and I was regarded as the wisest fool in Christendom because his critics said he never spoke a foolish word, nor ever committed himself to a wise act. In his native Scotland there was still unrest, chiefly in the Western Isles, where James attempted to civilize the chieftains by exhorting them to abandon the old ways and traditions; the local populace reacted vigorously, refusing to become 'Lowlanders'.

When James died in 1625 he was succeeded by his son Charles (1625–1649). Barely five foot tall, Charles I was pious, studious, aloof and distant, which made him seem abrupt and lacking in charm; in addition, he was afflicted by a stutter and was slightly lame. In one matter, he was resolute; like his father before him, Charles believed that he ruled by Divine Right, not subject to the whims and vagaries of the prevailing political climate. It was this and, to a lesser extent, his tinkering with and meddling in the form of religious worship in both England and Scotland that would bring him to grief. James had re-introduced episcopacy in Scotland, a policy his son would support. After 1603 any attack on the bishops would be considered as an attack on the king himself.

Charles I visited Scotland in 1633, some eight years after his coronation in Westminster Abbey. At his coronation in Holyrood Palace, Edinburgh, the crown of Scotland was placed on his head by a bishop wearing what John Knox had once called Papist rags – white *rochets* (surplice-like vestments worn by bishops and abbots), white sleeves and, horror of horrors, a crucifix to which the bishops present bowed as they filed past. Charles thus not only alienated his lowly subjects but his clergy and nobles as well; the latter were particularly incensed by the passing of Charles's Act of Revocation which annexed all church and Crown lands that had been alienated since the accession of Mary, Queen of Scots in 1542. Hardly a single Scottish noble escaped the loss of lands, teinds (taxes) and heritable rights. The political significance of this was to drive the nobility into a union with the Presbyterian clergy, thus restoring an alliance which, during the period of the Reformation, had been so disastrous for the Crown. The consequences of this would bring down Charles I, particularly on the field of battle.

In 1636 Charles issued his Code of Canons to bring the Scottish Kirk further into line with the Anglican Church; hot on its heels was Archbishop William Laud's *New Book of Common Prayer*, which would replace Knox's *Book of Common Order*. Laud's book was published in 1637 and was immediately branded Popish. On Sunday 23 July 1637 James Hannay, Dean of St Giles' Cathedral in Edinburgh, ascended the pulpit to read from the prayer book which resulted in a riot among the congregation. According to legend, one of the female worshippers heard a gentleman in the pew behind her utter 'Amen' to what Dean Hannay had been reading aloud. The elderly lady's name has come down to us as Jenny Geddes; she turned round angrily to confront the gentleman, reputedly shouting 'Traitor, dost thou say Mass at my lug [ear]?' and struck him on the face with her Bible. Then, for good measure, she reputedly hurled her *creepie* [a low stool or footstool used in church] at the head of the Dean himself. A large part of the congregation stormed out of St Giles' Cathedral to continue their protest in the High Street. (It is now thought that the entire episode was stage-managed beforehand, possibly including Jenny Geddes's dramatic outburst.) The ferment quickly spread through all of Scotland, leading to the signing of the National Covenant in Greyfriars Churchyard, Edinburgh on 28 February 1638. The country was on the brink of civil war.

The National Covenant was the reaffirmation of the Confession of Faith drawn up in 1581 by the Scottish reformers abjuring Popery in all its forms. The signatories to the 1638 Covenant were required to swear an oath to maintain religion in the same state as it was in 1580 and to reject all innovations introduced since that time. In time, it would be followed by the Solemn League and Covenant, a contract entered into by the General Assembly of the Church of Scotland and commissioners from the English parliament of 1643, having as its object a uniformity of doctrine, worship and discipline throughout Scotland, England and Ireland according to the word of God and the example of the best reformed Churches. Copies of the 1638 Covenant were sent to every parish in Scotland where some of the more ardent of its supporters signed the document in their own blood.

First Bishops' War

Early in 1639 Charles I intended to gather an army of 30,000 and invade Scotland; lacking the support of his English Protestant subjects who sympathized with the Scots, Charles could raise only 10,000 troops. The Scots responded by taking steps for the nation's defence; the forces against Charles were raised by Alexander Leslie who had fought in the army of Gustavus Adolphus of Sweden and held the Swedish rank of field marshal. The 'war' was bloodless save for a skirmish known as the *Trot of Turriff* where, in Aberdeenshire, the Earl of Huntly's supporters routed a few Covenanters. Leslie led an army numbering 18,000 infantry and 3,000 cavalry to Duns Law to confront Charles's expected invasion force. Neither side wished to resort to battle, so a compromise was reached; Charles and Leslie signed a peace treaty known as the Pacification of Berwick on 18 June 1639, Charles agreeing to restore the liberties the Covenanters demanded.

Second Bishops' War

The ink was hardly dry on the Berwick treaty when each party to it accused the other of breaching its terms. Charles complained that the Covenanters had not disbanded their army as promised; in turn the Covenanters accused Charles of not having evacuated Berwick and other places on the English side of the Tweed. Bickering continued until the spring of 1640 when Charles decided he would draw the teeth of the rebellious Scots once and for all. He summoned an English parliament and demanded that it subsidize an army to subdue the Covenanters; it soon became apparent that the English were unwilling to support Charles in the coercion of his Scottish subjects. On 17 April 1640 Alexander Leslie was appointed commander in chief of the Scottish army being raised by the Scottish parliament's War Committee; by July Leslie commanded a force of 20,000 well equipped and well provisioned soldiers. On 20 August Leslie crossed the Tweed and entered Newcastle where he drove away a force of Charles's supporters at Newburn-on-Tyne on 30 August. From the outset Leslie made it clear that his quarrel was not with the English nor had he come to northern England to plunder, let alone fight a battle. His quarrel was with Charles I, his intention being to defend the desire of both Scotland and England – to obtain a lasting settlement and peace on both sides of the Border. Leslie made the Scots' demands clear to Charles; nothing less than the abolition of episcopacy and recognition of the National Covenant would satisfy Scotland. Charles prevaricated, then consented to meet with the Scots in his own time and on his own terms. As part of the negotiations, the Scots insisted that he subsidize their army to the tune of £850 a day while it remained on English soil.

The English Long Parliament met on 3 November 1640 but was in no great hurry to conclude a treaty with Scotland, regarding Leslie's army as part of that of England; Leslie's continuing presence in the north gave the English parliamentarians exactly what they wanted – a firm hold on Charles and his madcap enterprises. Finally, a settlement was reached on 10 August 1641; the Scots demanded – and secured – the impeachment and execution of Thomas Wentworth, Earl of Strafford who had urged Charles to put down the rebellion with a firm hand. Another gain for the Scots was the fall of William Laud, Archbishop of Canterbury the hated author of *Laud's Liturgy* with its strong leanings towards Roman Catholicism. Laud was impeached and imprisoned in the Tower of London until 1645, when he was declared guilty of high treason and beheaded. At the close of the so-called Second Bishops' War, the Scots could rightly say that they had achieved all their demands. However, despite this success, the Covenanter party was in truth divided; Archibald Campbell, 8th Earl of Argyll demanded nothing less than the deposing of Charles, while James Graham, Earl of Montrose, one of the first to sign the National Covenant, had drawn closer to the King, plotting against Argyll. For this he was put in prison; Montrose would not forget this insult to his House easily. Montrose's head was Presbyterian but his heart was with the Royalist cause. In August 1641 Charles arrived in Edinburgh to address the Scottish parliament, anxious to convince its members that he was a man of peace. His efforts failed miserably. Charles had not come to Scotland as a peacemaker but to establish a following to support him in his planned dismissal of the Long Parliament. Argyll was now appointed leader of those opposed to Charles; for purely political reasons, Argyll was elevated to the rank of Marquis, while Alexander Leslie was created Earl of Leven.

In November Charles returned to England; he would never set foot in Scotland again. We need not dwell overlong on his quarrel with the English Long Parliament and his attempt to arrest five MPs, which brought about the English Civil War, although the remainder of this chapter is devoted to the effects of that bloody conflict in so far as it affected Scotland. In the third week of August 1642, Charles raised the Royal Standard at Nottingham. The main question the English parliamentarians sought answer to was this: on which side would Scotland fight? Whatever their grievances against Charles, the Scottish people preferred monarchy to any other form of government; after all, Charles was a Stuart and a Scot with an impressive pedigree and whose forebears had resisted England in the past. A considerable percentage of those zealots who had signed the National Covenant would take Charles's side in the conflict. And yet ... There were those in the Covenanter or Kirk party who dared to look into the crystal ball of the future, rightly deducing that if Charles triumphed over the English parliamentarians, Scotland would be his next victim. This was not a prospect universally accepted north of the Border; many men like James Graham, 1st Marquis of Montrose did not subscribe to this view but, in this aspect of his character, Montrose followed the dictates of his heart and his emotive beliefs; a brilliant military strategist and tactician, he fought in the name of the King, abandoning the Covenanters and repudiating his signature on the National Covenant he had signed only four years before. When Charles gained a slight advantage over the parliamentary army at Edgehill on 23 October 1642, it seemed he might again become master of England, then Scotland. It was obvious to most Scots on whose side they should fight. Both Royalist and Covenanter parties began to lay their plans. Montrose offered to raise an army for Charles on receipt of a royal commission to that effect; in the eyes of the English Royalists Montrose was seen as little more than an opportunist adventurer. On 2 August 1643 the General Assembly of the Church of Scotland – the leading *vox populi* mouthpiece which had virtually replaced the Scottish parliament – decreed that Scotland would be party to a bond of mutual defence and action with England, which had been mooted by the Convention of Estates appointed by parliament the previous month. Both Houses of the Scottish parliament endorsed the bond which became known as the Solemn League and Covenant; the General Assembly and the Convention offered the new Covenant as an alliance with the English parliament. It was not the kind of treaty the English would have preferred but with Charles's victory at Edgehill the previous autumn, they were hardly in a position to quibble over, let alone dictate, terms. There were conditions, however; the Solemn League and Covenant demanded no less than reformation of the religion of the entire British kingdom 'according to the word of God' as the purest form of worship – meaning, of course, uniformity of doctrine and polity according to the reformed Kirk of Scotland. The English read the words but had no intention of heeding them; on 25 September 1643 the English parliament formally accepted the new Covenant in the interests of furthering their war with Charles I. As mentioned above, it is outwith the scope of this book to discuss the several battles fought on English soil during the course of the English Civil War. The rest of this chapter will concentrate on those killing fields in Scotland which were occasioned by that war fought for Charles I by James Graham, Marquis of Montrose during his brilliant campaign of 1644–45, the 'Year of Miracles'.

On 1 February 1644 Montrose received Charles I's commission he had so ardently sought – appointment as the King's Lieutenant Governor of Scotland. Charles had been in correspondence with the Marquis of Antrim who had promised to raise an Irish army of 10,000 which would invade the west of Scotland and be commanded by Montrose. In the event only 1,600 arrived, led by a giant of a man, Alastair or Alasdair MacColla MacDonald whom Montrose and others would call Colkitto, a corruption of the Gaelic for one who is left-handed. (From now on, MacDonald will be referred to as MacColla.) MacColla was a fierce warrior rather than a soldier; he originated in Antrim and like the rest of the Clan MacDonald, harboured an intense hatred of the Clan Campbell whose chief was Archibald Campbell, 1st and only Marquis of Argyll, a fervent Covenanter who hated Charles I and all he stood for. MacColla arrived in Scotland with Irish mercenaries recruited from Antrim, Ulster, Dublin and Connaught, eager to engage the forces of Argyll rather than serve Charles I.

On 30 August 1644 Montrose raised the King's standard at Blair Atholl. It is perhaps appropriate here to comment on Montrose's eagerness to entertain an Irish (Catholic) force and lead it against his own countrymen, men who were little more than savages who would give and expect no quarter in the coming battles. Montrose embraced MacColla and his band, salving his conscience by insisting that he was obliged to do so under his sworn duty to Charles I; furthermore, it was Charles himself who was responsible for the recruitment of MacColla and his Irish mercenaries. Montrose was thus able to swallow his pride, believing that he should fight his campaign with the resources his sovereign King had provided. Montrose was a realist even if he was compelled to enter the service of Charles by the promptings of his heart; he knew that the Irish auxiliaries had no enthusiasm whatsoever in supporting Charles I; MacColla and his men came to Scotland for plunder and revenge on the hated Clan Campbell. MacColla's men were warriors rather than soldiers, possessed of great courage, endurance and determination, making them a formidable force in Montrose's army. In point of fact, the Irish *were* Montrose's army until he was able to recruit men from the northern clans to his cause. (Despite Montrose's spectacular victories in a single year, Charles, that unhappy King, suffered resounding defeats at Marston Moor and Naseby; in the latter battle, on 14 June 1645, Oliver Cromwell and his New Model Army decisively defeated the royal army.)

Meanwhile, the Covenanter party in Scotland did not rate Montrose as a military commander likely to succeed. In Montrose the Covenanter leaders saw a man capable of fighting a purely defensive campaign until he was defeated; they predicted that his barbaric Irish allies would desert him after a few victories, content to return to Ireland with the booty they won from their brigandage in north-east Scotland. Perhaps that was the reason why the Covenanter leaders and the Presbyterian clergy sent raw recruits against Montrose, forces led by successive incompetent generals. After all, the important campaign against Charles I was fought across the Border in battles won with the help of Alexander Leslie, Lord Leven and his nephew David

Leslie who helped Cromwell to achieve his spectacular victory at Marston Moor on 2 July 1644. However, the news of the Royalist defeat at Marston Moor only spurred Montrose on to greater efforts in Scotland. Montrose's King might have suffered a reverse in England but his commander in Scotland made it his mission to redress the balance in the north.

Tippermuir

In late summer 1644, Montrose opened his campaign, his main purpose being the capture of Perth. Montrose joined with MacColla and his Irish regiments and on 1 September, they advanced on Perth, only to be confronted by Lord Elcho's Covenanter army. Facing Montrose's 2,000 foot and 150 cavalry were Elcho's 7,000 infantry and between 700 and 800 cavalry. Although seriously outnumbered, the morale in Montrose's force was high and many of his soldiers were experienced veterans. Montrose occupied Methven Hill at Tippermuir, about three miles from Perth. The right wing of the Covenanter army was commanded by Lord Elcho, the centre by James Murray of Gask and the left wing by Sir James Scott of Rossie, the sole veteran commander in the Parliamentary army. That day, Montrose placed Lord Kilpoint on his left wing, with 400 archers and the men of Lochaber, with their famous axes, ideally suited for unhorsing cavalry. MacColla's three Irish regiments held the centre and Montrose commanded the right wing against the experienced Rossie. Montrose drew up his men in a three–line–deep formation which meant that his front line was longer than that of Elcho. It is obvious that Montrose wished to convince Elcho that the Royalist force was larger than it was.

At the outset of the battle the Covenanters shouted their battle cry of 'Jesus and no quarter'. Montrose addressed his men, his speech omitting any reference to religion; instead he spoke about the way his troops should conduct themselves that day. Reputedly, he exhorted those of his Highlanders who lacked weapons to fight the enemy with stones of which he said there was an abundance on Methven Hill; once despatched by a well aimed missile, the men were urged to avail themselves of their fallen opponents' swords!

Battle commenced on the morning of Sunday, 1 September. An early assault by Elcho's cavalry was driven off, then Montrose's Highlanders attacked Elcho's musketeers from the rear while MacColla's Irishmen assaulted the Parliamentary centre, exposing themselves to musketfire. The battle quickly developed into a rout; while the experienced Rossie tried to hold the left wing intact, Montrose led his Athollmen in a wild charge which slammed into Rossie's men, driving them back into the main body of Covenanters. The field became a bloodbath, Elcho suffering 2,000 casualties, with 1,000 taken prisoner; Montrose's losses were light. Many of the townspeople of Perth who had ventured out to watch the battle were slain in the general retreat during which most of Elcho's dead met their end fleeing along the roads and paths to Perth, pursued by the Irish and the clansmen. Tippermuir made a legend of Montrose, proving his genius as a military strategist and tactician; the battle was the first blow in Scotland in the war of the three kingdoms fought in Charles I's name.

After Tippermuir, most of Montrose's Highlanders went home with the booty they had plundered in Perth, leaving the Royalist army with only a few of MacColla's Irish levies. However, less than two weeks after Tippermuir, Montrose learnt that the Marquis of Argyll was advancing from Stirling with a large army. Montrose evacuated Perth on 4 September and marched up the north-east coast; on the way he attempted to take Dundee but the burgh was well defended and refused to surrender. However, Montrose's diminished force was increased by the arrival of MacColla's three Irish regiments totalling 1,500; in addition, Montrose had managed to recruit 100 MacDonalds and two invaluable troops of horse, the latter numbering forty-four in all (a horse troop usually consisted of sixty men). Arriving at Aberdeen on 13 September, Montrose demanded the town's surrender; the local burghers refused, so a Covenanter force led by Lord Balfour of Burleigh sallied out to confront Montrose. Montrose's army was deployed on a flat-topped ridge overlooking the How Burn valley, about half a mile south of Aberdeen. Burleigh's force numbered about 2,500 consisting of two regular regiments – his own and that of Lord Forbes – along with the Aberdeen militia and some local levies; Burleigh also commanded 500 cavalry, which contained three troops of regulars.

Aberdeen II
Montrose drew up his force on one side of the valley, the How Burn or stream separating the two armies. Montrose and MacColla held the centre of the Royalist line with MacColla's Irish regiments and about two dozen horse supported by musketeers. Sir William Rollo who had been present on the field of Tippermuir commanded the right flank, Colonel Hay the left. The battle began with Hay driving off a detachment of Covenanter musketeers from the protection of a few farm buildings at the west end of the valley. A counter-attack by Captain Keith's Covenanter horse was repulsed, although a force of Burleigh's musketeers advanced to recover the farm buildings Keith had lost. Then Sir William Forbes of Craigievar advanced with fifty horse to attack one of the Irish regiments positioned to the left of Montrose's centre. The Irish musketeers coolly opened their ranks to allow Forbes's men to pass through them, then they closed ranks and fired a volley into the cavalrymen's backs. Nathaniel Gordon's Royalist horse charged the routed and confused Covenanters, capturing Forbes and his second in command in the melee.

Then Lords Crichton and Fraser mounted several cavalry attacks against Sir Thomas Ogilvy's few Royalist horse; Crichton and Fraser made little progress against Ogilvy but they managed to pin down two of the three Irish regiments to prevent them reinforcing Montrose in the centre. However, Montrose and MacColla led the third Irish regiment to confront Burleigh's main position; after a brief firefight, the Irishmen threw away their muskets and charged the Covenanter centre with swords and dirks, scattering Burleigh's men like sheep. The Aberdeen militiamen collapsed in the face of this wild, frontal assault; Burleigh's entire force fled in panic to Aberdeen, where they were pursued and slaughtered in the town's streets by the wild Irishmen. Montrose's losses were light, Burleigh's numbered 160.

Aberdeen then suffered three days of rape, pillage and plunder which to his discredit Montrose made no attempt to stop; the atrocities committed in his name did great damage to his cause and reputation.[2] On learning of the approach of Archibald, 1st Marquis of Argyll's army of 4,000 foot and 900 horse, Montrose could not and did not expect support from his Royalist rival, the Marquis of Huntly who stood aloof, pursuing his usual game of courting both Royalist and Covenanter parties whenever one or the other could serve his interests.[3] At Aberdeen's market cross, Montrose read out the King's proclamation rejecting the Covenant, then he withdrew into the mountain fastness of Aberdeenshire, where his force was reduced by the departure of MacColla with 500 Irishmen, intent on recruiting more men in the west Highlands. Montrose attempted to raise men from the local clans, chiefly the Clan Gordon at Strathbogie (modern Huntly); he managed to recruit a few hundred clansmen but was unable to secure Gordon support due to the absence of their chief, the Marquis of Huntly, who distrusted and was jealous of Montrose; besides, Huntly's heir Lord Gordon had joined the Covenanters.

Fyvie

On 27 October Montrose was camped in the forests at Fyvie; he sent some of his now reduced force to capture the castles of Fyvie and Tollie Barclay with a view to seizing the provisions held there. The following day Argyll caught up with Montrose's weakened force which had taken up position on a rocky slope to the rear of Fyvie Castle. Argyll's first charge drove Montrose's men farther up the hill, where the Royalist commander rallied his men with a speech reminding them of the glory they had already won in the service of their King. Then he ordered a young Irish officer, Colonel O'Kean, to drive Argyll's men out of the ditches they occupied at the foot of the hill; O'Kean did so, despite being heavily outnumbered. Argyll then made a half-hearted attempt to retaliate with five troops of his cavalry (about 300 men) led by the

Earl of Lothian; Lothian's cavalry were confronted by Montrose's fifty horse, his entire cavalry force, but they were supported by musketeers whose withering fire drove off Lothian's troopers. The day ended in Montrose's favour. Argyll allowed Montrose to slip away to Blair Atholl where many of his supporters deserted him. Believing that the Royalist cause would wither on the bough in the coming winter, Argyll was content to retire to winter quarters in Edinburgh. Montrose, weak though he undoubtedly was, still had a few tricks up his sleeve.

In late November MacColla rejoined Montrose at Blair Atholl, having recruited 1,000 men from Clans MacDonald, Maclean and Cameron. MacColla, a MacDonald, was eager to strike at his traditional enemy, the Campbells, but Montrose was reluctant to involve himself in internecine clan warfare. However, MacColla was able to persuade him to make a daring raid on Inverary, the stronghold of the Campbell Marquis of Argyll. The weather was unusually mild for the time of year and Montrose and MacColla plundered the area of Argyleshire for several weeks between December 1644 and January 1645.[4] Although unable to take its castle, the town of Inverary fell and any Campbells found there were slaughtered without quarter.

Inverlochy II

By the end of January 1645 Montrose had marched north to Kilcumin (modern Fort Augustus) in Inverness-shire, where he learnt that the Covenanter leader Lord Seaforth blocked his way further north with a force of 5,000; to the south, the Marquis of Argyll with his Campbells and reinforcements from Lord Leven's army in England were advancing towards him with a force of 3,000. A lesser spirit than Montrose might have thrown in the towel at this point but he was a man of an entirely different stamp. Montrose, ever the genius of strategy, boldly decided to double back and attack Argyll; with MacColla, he marched his army of 1,500 in a flanking movement in the mountains. The Irishmen and the Highlanders completed a thirty-mile march through difficult terrain in less than two days. Montrose and MacColla descended on Argyll and his Campbells at the foot of Ben Nevis during the early hours of 2 February, Candlemas Day.

Montrose deployed his Highlanders in the centre of his line with the Irish on his flanks; Sir Thomas Ogilvy's troop of horse formed the reserve to the rear. Argyll, disabled by a dislocated shoulder, sought shelter in his galley moored in Loch Linnhe and left Sir Duncan Campbell of Auchinbreck in command. Auchinbreck deployed his men to the front of Inverlochy Castle near Fort William; his centre was composed of 1,000 Campbells and 500 men of Argyll's own regiment. Regulars from the Covenanter army were posted on the wings and commanded by Lieutenant Colonel Roughe from the Earl of

Tullibardine's Regiment and Lieutenant Colonel Cockburn leading the Earl of Moray's Regiment.

Montrose attacked at dawn to deny Auchinbreck the benefit of broad daylight which would have given him the opportunity to gauge the Royalist strength.[5] Despite a withering fire from the Covenanter musketeers on the flanks, the Irish advanced, holding their fire until within musket range – about fifty yards was the extent of the accuracy of a musket – when they fired a single volley into Auchinbreck's men, then they threw away their muskets and charged the Covenanters with sword and dirk as they had done at Aberdeen, scattering them. Then the Royalist clansmen, many of whom were traditional foes of the Campbells, charged Auchinbreck's centre, slaughtering hundreds, including Auchinbreck himself, whom MacColla personally beheaded with his sword. At Inverlochy, the power of the over-mighty Campbells was broken for many a long year; witnessing the destruction from the safety of his galley, Argyll sailed to Edinburgh. Montrose's casualties at Inverlochy were 250; Argyll lost 1,500.

In some ways, Inverlochy was the highwater mark of Montrose's campaign insofar as recruits flocked to the royal standard, including George, Lord Gordon, who defected from the Covenanters with his regiment of horse. Gordon's Horse, together with Ogilvy's troop, gave Montrose an effective cavalry force for the first time. The Marquis of Huntly, already alienated from Montrose, grew ever more jealous of his rival, especially after the defection of his son George and because Montrose, one of the first signatories of the National Covenant, had supported the Covenanters during the so-called Bishops' Wars.

Montrose went from strength to strength; by the end of March, his army numbered 3,000 and 250 cavalry; he was not only joined by Highlanders but also Lowlanders recruited from the Marquis of Huntly's lands in Aberdeenshire. Now the Irish regiments led by Alasdair MacColla comprised only a third of Montrose's strength whereas, before, they had formed the nucleus of his forces. With his now greatly increased and well equipped army, Montrose attacked Dundee on 4 April 1645, gaining access to the town through a breach in its crumbling town wall, routing the town militia and plundering the burgh. Alerted about the approach of a Covenanter army despatched from England by Lord Leven and under the command of Lieutenant General Baillie, Montrose beat a hasty retreat by way of Dundee's east port as Baillie was entering by its west port.

Baillie, with his 3,600 foot and 300 cavalry, was anxious to protect the routes to the south of Scotland and prevent Montrose from attacking Edinburgh; such was the sheer power and magnetism of Montrose's reputation. Baillie sent his second in command, Major General Hurry to the north-east with two regiments of foot and a detachment of horse on a campaign to neutralize the Royalist Gordon Clan. Montrose countered this move by marching north in support of the Gordons; Hurry then withdrew into Inverness-shire, gaining reinforcements as well as luring Montrose into hostile territory. For his part, Baillie marched the bulk of his army up the east coast, harrying Royalist territory as he went; his plan was to snare Montrose between himself and Hurry.

Auldearn

On 8 May 1645 Montrose had made his camp at the village of Auldearn, near Nairn. Auldearn itself was occupied by MacColla's Irishmen and William Gordon of Moneymore's newly raised regiment. The bulk of Montrose's force was scattered over a wide area to the east of Auldearn, seeking shelter from the driving rain of a typical Scottish spring day. Having been alerted to Montrose's whereabouts, Major General Hurry undertook a night march, hoping to catch Montrose in a surprise dawn attack on 9 May. By now Hurry had received further reinforcements from the Earl of Findlater, Campbell of Lawers and the Laird of Buchanan. Hurry's force of 3,000 infantry and 300 horse now equalled Montrose's army in strength. Arriving near Auldearn, Hurry's own musketeers ruined his opportunity for a surprise attack by firing off the damp powder in their muskets to clear them, thus alerting MacColla's sentries posted around Auldearn. MacColla mustered every soldier he could find and marched to the nearby Garlic Hill, about a mile south-west of Auldearn. From this vantage point he watched Hurry's men deploying; although heavily outnumbered, MacColla prepared to hold off Hurry while Montrose gathered the rest of his army.

In the opening stage of the battle on 9 May an intense firefight between Sir Mungo Campbell of Lawers's veteran regiment took its toll of MacColla's men, forcing them off Garlic Hill and back into Auldearn Village, where they took up positions in the buildings, cottages and gardens. Lawers pressed home his attack until his force encountered boggy ground at the foot of the sloping approach to the village. During this phase, Moneymore's regiment occupied Castle Hill at the north end of Auldearn and began to pour an enfilading fire into the advancing Covenanter left flank. As this flank began to flounder in confusion, MacColla led a charge from the village, forcing Lawers to retire to Garlic Hill, where he regrouped and drove MacColla back into Auldearn for the second time. A fierce hand-to-hand fight ensued as MacColla struggled to maintain his position. By now his situation was desperate; MacColla anxiously scanned the surrounding landscape for signs of Montrose.

Montrose had in fact arrived with the bulk of the Royalist army and was positioned behind Auldearn from where he directed his counter-attack on

Hurry, preoccupied with his fight with MacColla. Montrose divided his cavalry, sending in half under Lord Aboyne to the south of the village and Lord Gordon's to the north and Castle Hill. Aboyne led the first charge against the right flank of Hurry's force; he surprised a troop of Covenanters sent to guard the right flank. In the confusion the troop leader, Major Drummond ordered his men to wheel their horses in the wrong direction and they collided with their own infantry. As Aboyne's men slammed into Lawers's regiment, Lawers retreated to Garlic Hill; as he did so, Gordon's horse appeared in the north from behind Castle Hill and charged Lawers's left flank, completing the rout of Lawers's brigade of two regiments. The battle continued on Garlic Hill; the Royalist infantry surged forward, overwhelming the remnants of Lawers' brigade and charging up the hill. The battle became a rout; Hurry and the remains of his army fled across the river Nairn to the safety of Inverness. There are no details of Montrose's casualties but these were probably light; Hurry and Burleigh suffered the loss of 1,500 men, mostly infantry.

Having defeated one Covenanter force at Auldearn, Montrose turned to meet Baillie whom he knew he would have to defeat in order to break out of the Highlands and menace central Scotland. For the next few weeks Montrose and Baillie manoeuvered across Morayshire and Aberdeenshire, each seeking an advantageous spot to attack each other. During this lull MacColla again returned to the west Highlands on a recruitment drive.

Alford

Finally, the two armies met on 2 July at Alford, some twenty miles west of Aberdeen. Montrose occupied a strong position on Gallows Hill which overlooks a ford over the fast-flowing river Don. Approaching Montrose's position from the north, Baillie was unable to see Montrose's men who had occupied the reverse slope of Gallows Hill; Montrose left a small force on the summit of the hill, hoping this would encourage Baillie to attack him, which the Covenanter general obligingly did. Baillie thought the Royalist army was in retreat, so he ordered his cavalry across the ford to outflank Montrose. As he did so, Montrose formed his entire army on the crest of Gallows Hill. Unable to retreat to a safer position, Baillie was forced to deploy his infantry in a marshy area close to the river Don, which is where Montrose wanted him to be. Baillie ordered his men to take whatever cover they could in the hedgerows and wet ditches. Both armies formed up in the standard formation; infantry in the centre, cavalry on each flank.

Baillie's infantry of 2,000 and 500 or 600 cavalry had a slight numerical advantage over Montrose's 2,000 foot and 250–300 horse. Lord Gordon's cavalry were placed on the Royalist right wing, Lord Aboyne's on the left, both supported by a few companies of MacColla's Irish mercenaries. The centre was held by the Irish, Strathbogie's men from Huntly, Colonel Farquharson of Inverary and the MacDonalds. Baillie's army was composed of six regular infantry regiments – those of the Earls of Cassillis, Glencairn, Lanark and Lords Callander and Elcho. Lord Balcarres commanded the Covenanter horse on the left wing, Sir James Hackett on the right.

Lord George Gordon opened the battle by charging down Gallows Hill to engage Balcarres's cavalry, veterans who had fought in the Cromwellian battle at Marston Moor. This was the first decisive cavalry action between Montrose and the Covenanters in the civil wars in Scotland. Balcarres stood his ground and even looked like driving Gordon back until the latter was reinforced by the Irish mercenaries who threw away their pikes and muskets, resorting yet again to the sword and dirk to hamstring Balcarres's poor horses. This was too much for Balcarres's troopers who broke and fled. On the opposite wing Lord Aboyne was engaged in a messy contest with Hackett's horse, exchanging desultory carbine and pistol fire. Gordon rode his troopers round Baillie's rear and joined in the attack on Hackett. In the ensuing fight Lord George Gordon was killed by a stray musket ball thought to have been friendly fire. But, with the Covenanter wings broken, Baillie's infantry also broke and were put to flight. On this occasion, Montrose's casualties were reckoned as several hundred, Baillie losing 1,500. The Covenanter armies could afford such losses; Montrose could not.

After Alford, Baillie offered his resignation which parliament accepted, although he remained in command until his replacement, Major General Munro, serving in Ulster could take up his post as commander in chief of the entire parliamentary army. Meanwhile, Montrose was growing from strength to strength; MacColla rejoined him in July with 1,400 recruits, added to which were 200 Athollmen led by Patrick Graham of Inchblackie. Montrose now commanded the largest force he had ever had – 3,000 infantry and 500 horse, the latter commanded by Lord Aboyne, Colonel Nathaniel Gordon and Lord Airlie. After raiding the north-east for provisions, Montrose led his men into Perthshire, making his base at Dunkeld. The Scottish parliament, forced to leave Edinburgh due to an outbreak of plague, arrived in Perth, resolved to concentrate all the available manpower to defeat Montrose, who was intent on taking Edinburgh and thereby commanding the entire central Lowlands. A new Covenanter army was raised but, while it outnumbered Montrose, the recruits were untrained and poorly disciplined. Early in August, Montrose marched out of Dunkeld and crossed the Firth of Forth at Stirling, intending to menace Lowland Scotland. Again his adversary was the luckless Lieutenant Colonel William Baillie whose replacement had not yet arrived from Ireland.

Kilsyth

Ranged against Montrose were the four infantry regiments of the Marquis of Argyll, Lord Crawford-Lindsay, Colonel Robert Home and the Earl of Lauderdale as well as a regiment of survivors from Auldearn and Alford commanded by Colonel Kennedy; a further three regiments of raw recruits from Fife brought Baillie's strength up to 7,000, with two regiments of cavalry numbering 800 led by Lord Balcarres and Colonel Barclay. Montrose was aware that the Earl of Lanark was mustering a second army in Glasgow and the south-east, so he resolved to engage Baillie before the two armies could conjoin. On 15 August Montrose halted at the village of Kilsyth, between Glasgow and Stirling, on a high meadow overlooking the Glasgow road, intent on ambushing Baillie; however, on this occasion, Baillie out-manoeuvered him, attempting to occupy higher ground above Montrose's position. To achieve this end Baillie sent forward Major Haldane with a battalion of musketeers to secure the high ground before Montrose could dispute it. Haldane's men came to grief against a company of Clan Maclean skirmishers ensconced in some farm buildings; the Macleans were reinforced by MacColla and a contingent of MacDonalds. In frustration, Baillie ordered Colonel Home forward to secure the contested higher ground. However, Home either misunderstood his orders or felt compelled to disobey them to go to Haldane's assistance. In vain, Baillie struggled to re-deploy his forces as regiments in both armies were sucked into the skirmish around the contested farm buildings, a skirmish which soon developed into a full-scale battle on ground not of Baillie's chooosing.

Meanwhile, Lord Balcarres rode his cavalry regiment north of Montrose's position, intent on securing the ground Baillie desired; Balcarres's advance was briefly stalled by a troop of Royalist horse commanded by Captain Gordon. Gordon was soon in danger of annihilation until Lord Aboyne came to his rescue, galloping across the entire Covenanter front under heavy musket fire. Balcarres stood his ground and forced Aboyne to retreat. The Covenanter advance was only halted when Montrose ordered in the remainder of his cavalry under Nathaniel Gordon

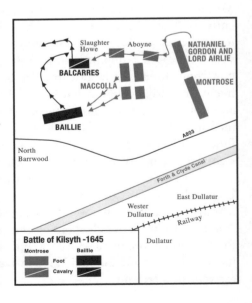

and Lord Airlie in a counter-attack. Exhausted and outnumbered, Balcarres's troopers were driven from the field. Now it was the turn of Montrose's infantry.

The flight of Balcarres's horse exposed the right flank of Baillie's army to the Royalist cavalry reinforced by MacColla in a full frontal attack; the Covenanter line began to crumble and give ground which induced panic among the raw Fifeshire levies who fled in disorder from the field. The battle was soon over. Perhaps Kilsyth was Montrose's crowning glory;[6] in the battle his casualties were light whereas Baillie's losses were in the region of a staggering 4,500, more than half his entire army. Montrose was now master of all Scotland, the Earl of Lanark having abandoned his newly-raised army; Lanark fled across the Border, joining the parliamentary Committee of Estates who had also journeyed south, unable to enter Edinburgh on account of the plague. Montrose occupied Glasgow where he issued a summons for the convening of a new Scottish parliament in the name of Charles I.

However, brilliant though Montrose's campaign undoubtedly was, it must be viewed in the broader context; the wars of the Covenanters in Scotland were dwarfed by the wars of the three kingdoms, the Scots fighting on all three fronts. Montrose had been ably supported by the warrior Alasdair MacColla but the latter was neither fighting against the Covenant nor for Charles I; a MacDonald, MacColla had fought against the Clan Campbell, venting his spleen on a traditional and hated enemy. Montrose attempted to convene a parliament in Scotland which he hoped would convince the nation that his victories had been fought in a just cause; further, Scotland should now intervene in the Royalist cause south of the Border against Cromwell and in aid of the rightful King. It was a forlorn hope. In June 1645 Charles was decisively beaten at Naseby. Apart from this final blow to Royalist hopes, Lowland Scotland regarded Montrose as nothing better than an instrument of the Devil; even powerful nobles such as the Earls Home, Roxburghe and Traquair faced the reality of the situation, no longer prepared to risk their lives, titles and estates in a lost cause. In any case Nemesis was just round the corner, waiting to claim Montrose.

Philiphaugh

With Scotland virtually in his pocket Montrose could now offer Charles assistance in England, despite the tragic defeat of the King at Naseby. His force was greatly reduced by the departure of Alasdair MacColla and his men; MacColla refused to cross the Border as that would mean his enemies, the Campbells, could menace Clan MacDonald in his absence. The two warriors parted company, Montrose riding south in the hope that he would recruit more men; his force now comprised only 500 or 600 Irish musketeers, 100 foot and a few horse, possibly about 100. The expected recruits failed to materialize.

Meanwhile, in England, news of Montrose's spectacular victory at Kilsyth had reached Alexander Leslie, Earl of Leven, commander in chief of the Scottish Covenanter army at Newark. Leven ordered his nephew, David Leslie, lieutenant general of the Scottish horse with 6,000 cavalry and dragoons and 1,000 foot to confront Montrose before he crossed the Border. Leslie switched his route to the east coast, possibly to deny Edinburgh to the Royalists and to cut off Montrose's supply of recruits from the Highlands. Then, learning that Montrose was camped near Selkirk, Leslie doubled back, believing he had Montrose in his grasp. The two forces met at Philiphaugh, near Selkirk, on 13 September 1645.

Montrose, quartered in Selkirk, had left elements of his small force on the south side of the Ettrick Water near Philiphaugh. A contemporary account described the Royalist position as being protected by:

> on one hand, an impassable ditch, and on the other, Dikes and Hedges, and where these were not strong enough, they [the Royalists] further fortified them by casting up ditches, and lined their Hedges with Musketeers.[7]

Leslie had arrived at Melrose on 12 September and advanced up the Tweed Valley, driving away the Royalist picquets on sentry duty; incredibly, Montrose's main force was not forewarned of Leslie's approach. The next morning, one shrouded by a thick mist, Leslie divided his force; one half would attack the Royalist position frontally, the other half executing a flanking manoeuvre round the nearby Howden Hill to attack Montrose in the rear. Montrose was not on the field that morning until gunfire alerted him to the presence of the Covenanter army; by the time he got there, he found his men in utter confusion, although they remained firm behind their strong defences. His musketeers had already repulsed two of Leslie's attacks. Then Leslie's flanking force arrived, ensuring Montrose's utter defeat in a short, sharp fight. Unrealistically, Montrose attempted to save the day by sending in his paltry 100 cavalry against 2,000 of Leslie's dragoons; this forlorn hope was a last ditch and pointless attempt. With thirty companions, Montrose escaped to Traquair; most of his Irish troops perished in the battle; a hundred were slaughtered when they sought quarter.[8] (A Presbyterian clergyman accompanying Leslie's army instructed the loyalist officers to commit this foul act.) The remaining prisoners were marched to Newark where, along with about 300 camp followers – mainly women and children – they were shot. Leslie's casualties at Philiphaugh were trifling; Montrose lost 500.

Montrose's force, now reduced to 250 Irishmen, a handful of cavalry and accompanied by the Earl of Crawford and Sir John Hurry who had changed

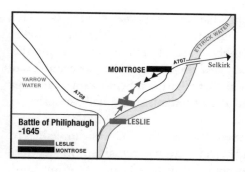

Battle of Philiphaugh -1645

MONTROSE

YARROW WATER

A708

A707

Selkirk

ETTRICK WATER

LESLIE

LESLIE
MONTROSE

sides after his humiliating defeat at Auldearn, carried on a guerrilla war in the north. Charles I, now a prisoner of the Covenanter army at Newark, ordered Montrose to lay down his arms in the spring of 1646; refused a pardon by the parliamentary Committee of Estates, the three men went into exile, Montrose to Norway on 3 September, where he would remain until 1650, encouraged to return by Charles II to win Scotland for him from the Covenanters he detested but who were vital to his hoped-for success. (In point of fact, Charles was forced to swallow his bile and make peace with the Covenanters, as we shall see.)

With Montrose out of harm's way, the Covenanter party in Scotland could breathe easily again; public peace was restored; by the end of 1645 the country was stable enough to allow Sir David Leslie to return to England. On 5 May 1646 Charles I surrendered himself to the Scottish army at Southwell, near Newark, Nottinghamshire; the Scots withdrew to Newcastle with their prize, safer ground from where they could negotiate with the English parliament. The Scots had drawn up the Solemn League and Covenant in 1643 which they had hoped England would embrace, re-fashioning the Elizabethan Protestant Church 'according to the word of God and the example of the best reformed churches' – meaning of course, Scottish Presbyterianism. The Scots put it to Charles that, were he to support the new Covenant and continue the war, they would do all in their power to reinstate him on the thrones of Scotland and England. Charles wanted the latter but not the former. The English parliament now wished to rid itself of both King and Scots. The Scottish army was owed £2 million in arrears as payment for its support of the Cromwellian forces; they had to content themselves with only £400,000, half of which would be paid before they re-crossed the Border into Scotland. As for their royal prisoner, the Scots were faced with three choices. They could set him free, allowing him to go abroad, but that might lead to further civil war; they could take him to Scotland which, for many, was unacceptable, given Charles's track record regarding the Scottish Kirk and the threat to all the advantages they had gained in their recent relationship with England; or they could turn him over to the English parliament. The third option offered the Scots little choice; the English parliament let it be known that if the Scots refused to deliver Charles into their hands, this would be regarded as an act of war. Realistically, there was no other option but the third; Charles was in fact abducted by a company of soldiers in Sir Thomas Fairfax's New Model Army. In June 1647 the Covenanter Scots huffed and puffed about this illegal act but opinion in Scotland was divided on what the response should be. The argument brought to the surface the conflicting opinions which, since 1645, had existed between the General Assembly of the Church of Scotland and the Covenanter regime as to what precisely *had* the Wars of the Covenant been fought for. What is even more ironic was that Charles, a Scot by birth, had no love for his Scottish subjects, detested Presbyterianism and had no desire to be 'rescued' by the Covenanter regime.

When the Scottish army re-crossed the Border, it was immediately disbanded although 6,000 foot and 1,200 cavalry remained in service, ostensibly to suppress the troublesome Royalist Clans Gordon and MacDonald, which Sir David Leslie achieved with little bloodshed. What was more important at this juncture was the division of the Covenanter party in two factions. In the knowledge that the English parliament had no intention of meeting the full arrears due to the Covenanter army which had played a crucial role in the English Civil War, nor the adoption of the Solemn League and Covenant south of the Border, the Covenanter regime was split down the middle. The radical Covenanters resolutely opposed Charles I and all he stood for were, in turn, opposed by those who continued to entertain hopes of finding a way to work with Charles. Beneath the superficial surface of stability, restless forces were gathering. An apprehensive Radical or Kirk party and a confident Engager party – so-called because, in December 1647, that moderate Covenanter faction signed a Treaty of Engagement with Charles – could no longer continue as full and equal partners in the government of Scotland. Charles signed the treaty on condition that he would introduce a three-year experimental period of a form of Scottish Presbyterianism in England, a condition which fell far short of the demands of the Kirk party, led by Archibald Campbell, 1st Marquis of Argyll. The Kirk party wanted to impose the Solemn League and Covenant in its fullest terms on England in perpetuity, anything less being seen as a betrayal of its fundamental principles which weakened the ideal of a religious union throughout Scotland and England. The Engagers appear to modern eyes as a somewhat naïve faction, given Charles's track record on the matter of Scotland's religious preferences. By 1648 the Engagers had become the predominant voice in the Scottish parliament and authorized an army led by James, Duke of Hamilton to march into England to enforce the agreement signed with Charles.

Mauchline Moor

In June 1648 the Kirk party met at Mauchline, Ayrshire to celebrate the Eucharist; following the ceremony, some 2,000 Kirk party supporters gathered on Mauchline Moor to declare their opposition to the Engagement. Into this gathering rode John, 1st Earl of Middleton with five troops of

Engager cavalry; after some discussion the Kirk party men were given an amnesty provided they surrendered. About two-thirds did; the remaining 850 or so prepared for battle. Middleton was reinforced by 800 foot and 1,000 cavalry and after a short sharp fight, some thirty or forty radicals were killed on the field, the Engagers winning a victory which would have its consequences two years later, at Dunbar. The defeat of the Engagers by Oliver Cromwell at Preston on 17 August 1648 put an end to their aspirations. The Engagers were not only driven from the field of Preston but also from political credibility and any hopes of retaining the upper hand in the future government of Scotland. Henceforth, those who had been Engagers were termed *Malignants* by the Covenanter Kirk faction, now the ruling party in Scotland supported by the General Assembly of the Church of Scotland.

After his victory at Preston Oliver Cromwell came to Scotland on 5 October 1648 when he enjoyed a convivial supper with the Marquis of Argyll who in the previous month had crushed the remnants of the Engager forces led by the Earl of Lanark, he who had fled from Scotland after Montrose's victory at Kilsyth. Cromwell earnestly believed that the rift between the Radical and Engager parties was caused by Charles I, with his stubborn, intractable refusal to bow to the will of his Scottish subjects. Cromwell was now openly describing Charles as 'the man of blood' who had caused the unnecessary deaths of countless English and Scottish men who had attempted to curb his powers in the interests of democracy and constitutional monarchy under which King and parliament would work together for the good of the nation. The purpose of Cromwell's brief visit to Edinburgh was to reach an agreement with the Radical Covenanter, anti-Engager party and the English Independent party in the English New Model Army to take action against any further attempts by the Engagers to upset the tranquillity of Scotland. Surprisingly, there was no mention of the arrears of subsidy due to the Scots for their assistance in the English Civil War, money that would never be paid.

The people of Scotland rejoiced in the defeat of the Engagers who had been influenced and led by the nobility – men like the Earl of Lanark and his brother the Earl of Hamilton. Those who governed the Radical Covenanters were drawn from the ranks of the common people – or more precisely, 'the middling sort', as the middle class was called at the time. The Marquis of Argyll had joined the middling sort, particularly espousing the cause of Archibald Johnston of Wariston, the Edinburgh lawyer who had drafted the original National Covenant in 1638. In England the Independents demanded that Cromwell bring Charles to trial, arguing that the King alone was responsible for the late Civil War and that he be tried for the crime of high treason. (One has to ask the question: how in all conscience could a king be put on trial for high treason against himself? The answer is simple; in the politics of the day, Charles was seen as a traitor by the people of England, if not Scotland.) Cromwell and his immediate associates wanted blood to wash away the tragedy of the Civil War and the blood could only be that of the King. On 30 January 1649 Charles I was beheaded outside the Banqueting House of Whitehall.

When news of Charles's execution reached Scotland on 5 February 1649 the general response was one of utter dismay and anger. Why? The Scots still believed that government – parliament in effect – required a king to head it, a harking back to the old feudal system, when a country without a king was leaderless and atrophied; one might argue that Scotland was the last medieval kingdom in the western world. Memories of the premature and tragic death of Alexander III in 1286 may have taxed the minds of contemporary historians and intellectuals both in the mid-seventeenth century but one must ask the question – why were the common people of Scotland transfixed by the execution of Charles? One can only assume the obvious: the English had killed one of their own, a Scotsman by birth and ancestry. The fact of the matter was that, in killing the King of England, the English had also killed the King of Scotland. Those in Scotland of the opinion that the nation needed a king were incensed by Charles's death; they conveniently put aside the fact that they desired a Covenanter king, which Charles had never and would never have been. The Scottish parliament proclaimed the late King's eldest son Charles II King of Great Britain, Ireland and France, the last title being a sop to the time of Mary, Queen of Scots nearly a century ago.

Scotland was in turmoil. The men responsible for the conduct of government – the Marquis of Argyll, Chancellor Earl of Loudon and Johnston of Wariston – were thrown into confusion. In Ireland the Marquis of Ormonde was at pains to rekindle the Royalist cause in Scotland, while on the Continent, James Graham, 1st Marquis of Montrose harboured hopes that he might reclaim Scotland for Charles II from Argyll and his Covenanter supporters by his sword. Publicly disowned by Charles but secretly encouraged by him, Montrose sailed from Sweden, making for Kirkwall, Orkney, in March 1650. He was carrying the commission of Charles and by April, had raised a force of 1,200 men; had he attempted his rising a year before he might have gained even more recruits before Sir David Leslie had crushed the Royalist Clans at Balveny, Banff in May 1649.

Carbisdale

Royalist hopes of assistance from Ireland were dashed by Cromwell's Irish campaign in 1649 which resulted in the fall of Drogheda on 3 September that year. (The date would assume a sinister significance in the life of Oliver

Cromwell; his victories at Drogheda, Dunbar and Worcester all occurred on the same date in September. Some said that Cromwell had made a pact with the Devil who promised him three victories in exchange for his soul on the anniversary of these triumphs. The propagandists had a field day on 3 September 1658, the day he died.)

Early in 1649 Charles II looked to Scotland for help; it was Charles' secret intention to use the threat of another campaign by Montrose in north Scotland to bring the Covenanters to heel. When talks between Charles and the Marquis of Argyll's commissioners broke down in the spring of 1649, Charles authorized Montrose to take whatever military action he could against the Covenanter party. Montrose responded by despatching the elderly Earl of Kinnoul with 200 Danish mercenaries as an advance guard to occupy Kirkwall, Orkney, in September. During the rest of 1649 and early 1650 Montrose on the Continent unsuccessfully attempted to raise funds for troops to serve in the Royalist cause.

On 23 March Montrose landed at Kirkwall with about 250 German mercenaries; he was accompanied by his former adversary Sir John Hurry whom it will be remembered changed sides after his defeat at Auldearn in 1645. About 1,000 Orcadians had been recruited by the aged Earl of Kinnoul but his sudden and untimely death had denied the raw recruits any form of training. On his arrival in Orkney Montrose received a letter from Charles, intimating that he would be rewarded by the Order of the Garter for his services. Charles also intimated that he would resume negotiations with the Covenanters at Breda in the Netherlands playing for time while Montrose raised the clans in the north.

On 9 April Montrose sent Major General Sir John Hurry across the Pentland Firth to secure a route to the south. Montrose followed with the main force on 12 April, declaring for Charles II at Thurso on 21 April. Dunbeath Castle in Caithness surrendered to him but he failed to take Dunrobin Castle in Sutherland; however, Montrose wisely installed small garrisons at various strongpoints to keep open his lines of communication with Orkney. Then he marched inland to Lairg in Sutherland, hoping to obtain recruits that never materialized. Many of the clansmen in the region had suffered at his hands during the campaign of 1644–45 so were unlikely to offer any support. Undaunted by this setback, Montrose marched his small force to Carbisdale, where he camped on the southern side of the Kyle of Sutherland. The area he chose was good ground on a flat stretch of land between the deep waters of the Kyle and the wooded hill of Creag a' Choineachen; at the southern end of his encampment the ground narrowed and Montrose ordered his men to prepare defensive earthworks.

In Edinburgh the Committee of Estates ordered Lieutenant General Sir David Leslie to march against Montrose from his base at Brechin, Angus. Leslie sent ahead Lieutenant Colonel Archibald Strachan with five troops of horse to Inverness where Strachan was reinforced by a company of musketeers from Mungo Campbell of Lawers's Regiment. On the road to Tain to link up with the Earl of Sutherland, Strachan was further reinforced by 400 Highlanders. On 27 April Strachan arrived at Carbisdale; his 230 horse, forty musketeers and 400 clansmen were heavily outnumbered by Montrose's 200 Danish and German mercenaries, 1,000 raw recruits from Orkney and forty horse. Strachan planned to draw Montrose out of his defensive position; he set an ambush for the Royalists, concealing four troops of his horse and forty musketeers in the thick broom. The 400 Highlanders recruited from Clans Munro and Ross were sent off on a wide flanking march over the nearby hills to protect the Covenanter left flank. When Strachan advanced with his single troop of horse Montrose believed this to be the total Covenanter strength, so he left his position, ordering in his cavalry commanded by Major Lisle to begin the attack. As soon as this happened Strachan sprang his ambush. The small Royalist cavalry troop was soon overwhelmed when all five Covenanter troops of horse advanced with their screen of musketeers. Major Lisle was killed and the surviving Royalist horse were thrown back amongst the raw Orcadians who promptly threw away their weapons and fled; 200 were drowned attempting to swim across the Kyle. All Montrose had left to confront Strachan with were his 200 mercenaries who took shelter in the nearby Scroggie Wood; the Danes and Germans fought well until the 400 Munro and Ross clansmen appeared over the hills to join in the attack, whereupon the mercenaries surrendered. Montrose's casualties were 450, with 450 prisoners taken, among them Sir John Hurry; Strachan's losses were a mere fifty. Montrose managed to escape on a horse given him by one of his officers; he reached Ardvreck, a few miles south of Ullapool where he was betrayed to the Covenanters by Neil Macleod of Assynt, an ally of the Earl of Sutherland. Montrose was taken to Edinburgh to stand trial for his life. In an ironic twist of fate, Charles II had written to Montrose ordering him to abandon his invasion as favourable negotiations were under way with the Covenanters in the Netherlands.

On 1 May 1650 Charles and the Covenanters signed the Treaty of Breda, the King disowning Montrose in order to secure an alliance. On 21 April Montrose was hanged at the market cross in Edinburgh's High Street; Hurry was similarly despatched later. Thus ended the last Royalist campaign in the north of Scotland; Montrose had become a legend in his own time, either worshipped or reviled. Montrose was denied the usual death by the axe reserved for the nobility; he was hanged, his body was dismembered, his limbs put on public display in Glasgow, Stirling, Perth and Aberdeen. With Montrose out of the way, Charles could now make the journey from the Netherlands; on 23 June he set foot on Scottish soil. Unfortunately for Charles that summer, so would Oliver Cromwell.

The Marquis of Argyll's government quickly realized exactly what Charles's arrival in Scotland meant. There was a distinct possibility of a Royalist uprising in support of Charles; also, the Covenanter or Kirk party was riven with division between those of incompatible and uncompromising views. These men were unwilling to forget their differences in the face of adversity in the form of the English parliament which regarded the Scots' alliance with Charles as a hostile act and a declaration of war. In July the Committee of Estates, acting in conjunction with the standing Commission of the Kirk, began to formulate plans for the nation's defence. Proclamations were issued for the levying of troops from every shire in Scotland to meet the expected invasion.[9]

By order of the English Commonwealth Oliver Cromwell and his capable Major General John Lambert and Colonel George Monck crossed the Scottish Border on 22 July with 16,000 troops comprised of ten infantry regiments, seven cavalry regiments and six companies of dragoons; the artillery train contained between eight and ten siege guns and twelve field pieces. Cromwell's army was supplied by ships sailing parallel to the coastline along the route of his advance. Cromwell hoped to avoid a battle as he had grown weary of war and had reluctantly assumed command of the parliamentary army after Sir Thomas Fairfax declined the appointment. Cromwell also had considerable respect for his adversary, Lieutenant General David Leslie, who had served with the parliamentarians against Charles I during the Civil War. As the Cromwellian army marched through the Merse they found the Berwickshire villages empty of young men. The Roundheads didn't rate the Scots as soldiers and found their womenfolk 'pitifully sorry creatures' who wailed about their husbands, brothers and sons being forced by 'the maisters tae gang tae the muster' [the masters to go to the muster] in Edinburgh, no doubt ordered there by the local baron Home of Wedderburn.[10] The English reached Dunbar on 26 July where badly needed supplies of biscuit and cheese were unloaded on the quay of the burgh's harbour (ever after known as the Cromwell Harbour).

From Dunbar Cromwell marched to Musselburgh, hoping to engage Leslie but the Scottish general kept retreating, the age-old strategy of the Scots to draw the English farther away from their supply base. However, about 1,300 English horse caught up with Leslie's rearguard *vedettes* at Fisherrow, Musselburgh, where a short, sharp fight took place. Cromwell made camp at Musselburgh while Leslie fell back on his defensive line of trenches dug between Arthur's Seat (Salisbury Crags, south of Edinburgh) and the port of Leith. The weather played a large part in Leslie's tactical success; the summer of 1650 was wetter and colder than usual. General George Monck's field guns shelled Edinburgh from Salisbury Crags while Cromwell's supply ships, unable to land their supplies, bombarded Leith. Attacks were mounted on Leslie's trench system; in one, 500 of Cromwell's troops were casualties and Major General Lambert was wounded, briefly taken prisoner, then rescued by his men.[11] Further manoeuvering by Leslie took the Roundhead army to the Braid Hills on the outskirts of Edinburgh, then Corstorphine Hill in August. The campaign was assuming all the characteristics of a Scottish country reel or dance. Cromwell's dispirited army withdrew to Musselburgh, then Haddington where, on 31 August, Cromwell offered Leslie battle on ground of Leslie's choice. Leslie refused; he knew that Cromwell's men were short of food and were falling sick with dysentery at an alarming rate. The troops even began to throw away their tents as useless encumbrances. All Leslie had to do was shadow the retreating English to Dunbar, where he expected Cromwell to evacuate his army by sea.

But all was far from well in the Covenanter army. During the summer recruitment campaign the parliamentary Committee of Estates had decreed that the Covenanter army raised by the shire committees appointed for the task be instructed not to accept any recruits with Royalist sympathies; further, those who had signed the Engagement with Charles I in 1646 were to be debarred. The Engagers, or Malignants as they were known, contained a number of professional, experienced officers and men, particularly NCOs; Sir Edward Walker, an English commentator, thought that the Scots had rejected some of their best men.[12] Before battle was joined at Dunbar on 3 September 1650, between 3,000 and 4,000 officers and men had been 'purged' from Leslie's army, an act to which Leslie made no secret of his opposition. One disgruntled reject ruefully commented that the Scottish army was being left 'to be run by Ministers' sons, clerks and other sanctified creatures who ever hardly saw or heard of any sword but that of the Spirit'.[13] Archibald Johnston of Wariston, the arch-architect of the National Covenant in 1638, that dour, implacable enemy of England and Royalists alike, noted in his diary on 16 August that:

Wee [we] spent al [all] day in going through al the regiments of Horse and Foote, and purging out and placing in of officers, wherein I [im] pressed upon their consciences ... the guilt and blood and mischief that many follow in haveing [having] Malignant, profane[e[scandalous persons and Ingagers [sic] in our airmy [army].[14]

The purging continued up to the very eve of the battle.

Dunbar II

On 1 September Leslie occupied a strong position on Doon Hill, about two miles south of Dunbar. His army consisted of about 15,000 foot and 6,500 horse.[15] Against him, Cromwell's army, depleted by sickness, numbered about 12,000, possibly even less.[16] On the eve of Dunbar Cromwell was outnumbered by at least two to one. From his strong position on Doon Hill, Leslie could have allowed the deteriorating weather, sickness in the English army and the lack of supplies to do his work for him without a shot being fired. However, he was beset by similar problems himself; it being harvest-time, he expected desertions from his army by men more preoccupied with bringing in the corn. Furthermore, the committee of Covenanter ministers sent to 'guide' him insisted that Leslie must follow the tactics revealed to them by the Lord of Hosts, meaning of course, God. The clergy proclaimed to the Scottish army that 'the Lord has given your enemies the Moabites into your hand'. (The Moabites had been masters of the Jews for many years but, by the time of king David of the Hebrews, they had become subservient to them. The Presbyterian clergy were of course quoting from Judges 3, verse 26 in the Old Testament.) Johnston of Wariston reputedly told Leslie that his orders and those of the clergy had the unqualified backing of the Scottish parliament's Committee of Estates, members of which were present on the summit of Doon Hill, expecting to witness Cromwell's defeat. Some historians maintain that the clergy ordered Leslie off Doon Hill but this is suspect; Leslie, an experienced military general, had to face the reality of the situation. He had neither sufficient food nor tents for his men on an exposed hilltop open to the four winds and atrocious rainstorms. To his credit, for the rest of his life Leslie insisted that he had ordered his army off Doon Hill and that he and he alone was responsible for the outcome at Dunbar.

On the Broxmouth plain below Doon Hill, an apprehensive Cromwell was preoccupied with the prospect of having to evacuate his army from Dunbar Harbour, as Leslie had sent a contingent of troops to Pease Glen, about seven miles south-east of Dunbar to block his escape by road. Before the battle Cromwell wrote to Sir Arthur Hesilrige, the governor of Newcastle:

> The enemy hath blocked up our way at the pass of Copperspath [Cockburnspath's Pease Glen]. He lieth so upon the hills that we know not how to come that way without great difficulty and our lying here daily consumeth our men, who fall sick beyond imagining.[17]

On Monday 2 September Cromwell was determined not to evacuate his men by sea and thus face a humiliating withdrawal; he made sure his men received a hot meal, then he and his staff retired to Broxmouth House, home of the

Duke of Roxburghe to observe the Scottish army through their telescopes, or as they were known then, perspective glasses. That afternoon Cromwell could not believe his eyes. The Scots had begun their descent from Doon Hill, a difficult move for horses and cannon; by 4pm Leslie's entire army was off the hill. An eyewitness in the English army recalled later that he had seen Cromwell bite his lip till the blood ran down his chin without his realizing it. Some of his staff officers nearby heard him reputedly mutter this to himself: 'God is delivering them into our hands, they are coming down to us.' The armies faced each other over the Brox Burn, a small stream now swollen by heavy autumnal rain.

Both armies spent a miserable night of high winds and freezing, driving rain; the other ranks had little shelter, many lying in the wet corn or grass. It is now thought that Leslie spent the late evening and early morning hours at Spott House, about a mile from the killing field of Dunbar, a view with which this author agrees. Most of his officers took shelter in the nearby farms and hamlets of Pinkerton, Oxwellmains and East Barns, the last nearly a mile from the battlefield. Sir James Holborn, commanding a brigade of troops from Stirlingshire and Clackmannanshire ordered his men to stand down and extinguish the saltpetre matches required to discharge their matchlock muskets a few hours before dawn in case the light from them gave away their positions. This measure, sensible though it was, denied the Scottish musketeers an advantage when battle commenced.

Leslie had held a war council, intimating that he would attack Cromwell at dawn on the morning of Tuesday, 3 September. Cromwell surprised him by attacking the Scottish front line at 4am in bright moonlight, the rain having stopped. Although the main phase of the battle came three hours later, when the sun rose, Leslie was wrong-footed from the outset. Major General Lambert's dragoons attacked the Scottish right wing stationed near Broxmouth House, Major General Sir John Browne's cavalry discomfiting Lambert's men with their long Spanish lances. For about an hour, Lambert and Browne, the latter aided by the Scottish cavalry commanded by Major General Sir Robert Montgomerie (who was absent for some reason), kept up a hot fight. Then Colonel George Monck led his foot brigade of three regiments across the Brox Burn which was in spate, attacking Lieutenant General Sir James Lumsden's brigade of three regiments in the Scottish centre. By keeping Lumsden pinned down by artillery fire, Cromwell prevented the Scottish regiments to Lumsden's left from coming to his aid. Then the English artillery began to fire into the rear ranks of the Scottish centre, doing its bloody work there as well as on the Scottish left wing which was crushed up at the base of Doon Hill, a position where their numerical superiority was more of a hindrance than help. On the extreme Scottish left wing, the infantry brigades commanded by Colonel John Innes, Major General Colin Pitscottie, Major General Sir James Holborn and the cavalry brigade of Colonel William Stewart faced a single infantry brigade of three regiments commanded by Colonel Robert Overton, along with the dragoon companies – the latter possibly fewer than 300 men – commanded by Colonel John Okey. Thus about 9,000 men on Leslie's left wing were ineffective, leaving the remaining 12,000 of 7,500 foot and 4,500 cavalry to face the 7,500 English foot and cavalry already engaged. (In addition, Cromwell had a strong reserve ready to exploit a break in the Scottish front line when the opportunity presented.)

In the centre Lumsden held his own against Monck's brigade; Lumsden greatly outnumbered Monck but his force comprised mainly raw recruits from the Highlands. Gradually, the experienced and disciplined English foot began to take their toll of Lumsden who, despite reinforcement by Sir James Campbell of Lawers's infantry brigade, began to give ground. Two of Lawers's infantry regiments – those commanded by Sir George Preston of Valleyfield and Sir John Haldane of Gleneagles – put up a stout resistance but were slaughtered to a man.

Cromwell, helmeted and gauntleted, bided his time until Lambert galloped up to his position near Oxwellmains hamlet and Broxmouth House, reporting that the Scots were about to break. The reserve which Cromwell had husbanded consisted of three regiments – his own foot regiment and those of Major General Lambert and Colonel Thomas Pride. Cromwell watched the

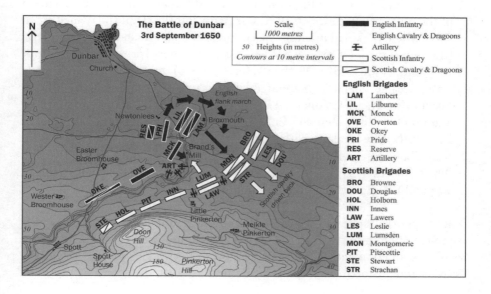

184 The Killing Fields of Scotland

musketeers and pikemen roll up the Scottish right and centre, the cavalry of Lambert and Colonel Robert Lilburne scattering the Scottish horse; many rode to Berwick to escape capture while others skirted the reverse slopes of Doon Hill to make their escape to Haddington and Edinburgh. The battle was over in three hours; the sun rose on that bloody field around 6am; the plain of Broxmouth rang with the hoarse cries of the English troops, proclaiming that the Lord of Hosts – the same invoked by the clergy in Leslie's army on 2 September – had given them victory.

The English account of the battle was reported to the English parliament as follows:

The night [of 3 September] proved bluftery [blustery] and wet, fo [so] that our Army fell not upon the Enemy at the hour appointed, till it was fomewhat [somewhat] later in the morning ... opposition was made by the Enemy with very great Refolution [resolution]; a very hot difpite [dispute] at Swords' point being between our Horfe [horse] and theirs. Five Companies of our Foot that were firft [first] commanded out, after they had difcharged [discharged] their duties, being over-poured [overpowered] by the Enemy, received fome repulfe [some repulse], [from] which they foon [soon] recovered; the Genral's [sic] regiment [i.e. Cromwell's own] timeofly [timeously] coming in ... at the pufh [push] of Pike, did break the ftouteft [stoutest] the Enemy had, and totally routing them, did full execution on them ... And now the beft [best] of the Enemies [sic] Horfe [horse] and Foot, who after the firft Repulfe [first repulse] were as stubble before them ... it became a total Rout, our men having the chafe [chase] and execution of them near eight miles; in all ... our Army loft [lost] not thirty men ... In this battle were killed upon the place and near about it, above four thoufand [thousand] men. Of private Soldiers taken prifoners [prisoners] above four thoufand [thousand]. Of their Horfe [horse] taken, killed and made unserviceable, about two thoufand [thousand]. Commission[ed] officers taken prifoners, as Colonels [,] Lieutenant Colonels ... about two hundred and ninety [which included Lord Libberton ?] and Sir James Lumsden of Innergelly, Fife [,] along with some of the Ministers. The foot Arms taken, were about fifteen thoufand. About two hundred Colours taken. Two and Thirty pieces of Ordnance [artillery] with the reft [rest] of their Artillery, Bag and Baggage, and all their ammunition taken.[18]

The supposed spot from where Cromwell launched his reserves was commemorated by a stone placed on the now disappeared Oxwellmains Farm road's conjunction with the former A1 road to Berwick. Thomas Carlyle, the essayist and historian, was present at the laying of the stone in the mid-nineteenth century to commemorate the Battle of Dunbar, also known as Tyseday's [Tuesday's] Chase and Dunbar Race. The memorial stone was inscribed as follows:

> 3 September 1650 Here took place the brunt of the essential agony of the Battle of Dunbar Thomas Carlyle. (The base of the stone bears the words The Covenant.)

Because of road improvements and the closure of the old A1, the stone was moved some half a mile or so from its original position to its present position on the slip road a few hundred yards past Broxburn Village and about a hundred yards from Broxmouth House; the hard-nosed historian will rightly contend that this makes a nonsense of the inscription. The only saving grace in the re-positioning of the memorial is that it can now be seen by tourists coming off the modern A1 by way of Broxmouth to visit Dunbar.

As a postscript to the battle Wellington probably spoke the wisest words when he said of Waterloo that next to a battle lost, there is nothing so dreadful as a battle won. Dunbar cost Leslie some 4,000 fatal casualties; Cromwell took 10,000 prisoners, releasing 6,000 as he could neither feed nor guard them; the remaining 4,000 fit or lightly wounded were force-marched to Durham where those 1,200 who survived the death march, though starved of food, were imprisoned in Durham Cathedral, the sick and dying placed in nearby Durham Castle. (In 2011, a resident of Dunbar, Mr George Wilson personally raised funds for the erection of a memorial plaque in Durham Cathedral to the Useless Mouths whom Cromwell could not feed. A moving ceremony conducted by the Dean of Durham Cathedral, the Very Reverend Michael Sadgrove took place on 30 November 2011 – St Andrew's Day – which the author was privileged to attend.)

After Oliver Cromwell's spectacular victory at Dunbar, David Leslie created a series of defensive strongpoints in central Scotland, basing the remnants of his army at Stirling. Cromwell, the experienced strategist, was quick to realize that the conquest of Fife and the capture of Perth were the keys to subduing all of Scotland; if he could hold Perth, he would deny Leslie supplies and recruits from the north.

Hamilton

After Dunbar, the New Model Army occupied various parts of Scotland, campaigning chiefly in the central belt, then in the Highlands. One area where the Covenanters were in strength was in south-west Scotland, so it was agreed that a Cromwellian presence was needed there. An English force commanded by Major General John Lambert, veteran of Dunbar, was garrisoned in

Lanarkshire at Hamilton, in the *Heiton* (high town) area of the town. Colonel Gilbert Ker, another Dunbar veteran, led a force of Covenanters in a surprise attack on Lambert's position on 1 December 1650. After some initial success, Ker's men were repulsed with heavy loss. The battle of Hamilton is also known as the battle of Heiton; it is commemorated by a metal plaque fixed to Cadzow Bridge, installed by the Hamilton Civic Society. Following the subjugation of Edinburgh, the Cromwellian army crossed the Forth in July 1651, ferried by specially constructed flat-bottomed boats at the Firth of Forth's narrowest point between South and North Queensferry. As North Queensferry stands on a narrow peninsula, it was rightly argued that it would provide a defensive bridgehead against any attempts by Leslie to contest an English landing in Fife. In July the local defences at the forts of Inchgarvie, Burntisland and Ferryhill sustained a systematic and prolonged bombardment. Under cover of darkness on the night of 16–17 July 1651, Colonel Robert Overton landed 2,000 assault troops in Inverkeithing Bay; Overton immediately began digging trenches while Major General Lambert organized the landing of a further 2,500 troops on 20 July. On learning of Lambert's crossing, David Leslie ordered Sir John Browne of Fordell to lead 4,000 infantry to Inverkeithing, supported by 1,000 cavalry commanded by James Holborn of Menstrie to pin down Lambert at his bridgehead. The Highland elements of Fordell's army were led by Sir Hector Maclean of Duart.

Inverkeithing II
The English occupied trenches on the Ferry Hills which rise about 240 feet above sea level; dominating these are Castland Hill and Meikle Hill which cover the coastal road to Rosyth and the road to Inverkeithing. Were the Scots to occupy these two eminences they would deny the English any movement forward but for some inexplicable reason Fordell chose to come off the hills to lower ground fronting the English trench system, from where shots were fired. Believing he was about to be attacked, Fordell ordered his men back to the higher ground. Lambert grasped this opportunity to send Colonel John Okey forward with his regiment of dragoons to attack the Scots' rear. Fordell drew up his main battle lines on the Whins, three eminences or outcrops of moorland rolling outwards from Castland and Meikle Hills towards Inverkeithing Bay. For his part, Lambert deployed his men with the bulk of his strength concentrated on the right wing as the ground on his left was rocky, difficult terrain unsuitable for his cavalry. Okey commanded the right wing; the infantry were placed in the centre and left and Colonel Robert Overton commanded the reserve infantry to the rear of Lambert's position.

It was at this point that Lambert learnt that Cromwell had fallen back on Linlithgow and that Fordell might receive reinforcements from Leslie at

Stirling. Lambert knew that this was his time to make a concerted attack on the Scots, so he ordered forward his infantry. Due to a bottleneck in the narrow peninsula the English formations had to bunch together dangerously, their left offering an easy target for the Scottish horse. The cavalry, with their long Spanish lances, swept through the English foot with ease. Lambert immediately despatched Overton's infantry reserve screened by a troop of horse to counter Fordell's attack. The combined force of musketeers and pikemen soon drove off the Scottish lancers and the fighting on the English left was quickly over. Lambert was now able to concentrate the bulk of his army on Fordell's position around the Whins. The crack, disciplined troops of the New Model Army soon put to flight the raw Scottish infantry; Fordell was left with only 200 horse and two infantry battalions to resist Lambert. Fordell was driven back to the level ground between Hillfield and Pitreavie. It was here, in the most heroic episode at Inverkeithing, that the Clan Maclean of Mull Regiment commanded by Sir Hector, 2nd Baronet Maclean of Duart, fought a fierce engagement to protect their chief. (Sir Hector's ancestor, Red Hector of the Battles, had fallen in the battle of Red Harlaw in 1411.) The clansmen shouted their Clan slogan 'Fear eil' airson Eachainn' (Another for Hector) until Maclean and 750 of his 800 clansmen lay dead on the field. Fordell's casualties were between 800 and 2,000 dead, with 1,400 taken prisoner; Lambert's losses were less than 200.

Although a battle on a much smaller scale than Dunbar the year before, the battle of Inverkeithing (also known as the battle of Ferry Hills) is considered of great importance and more decisive in Cromwell's Scottish campaign of 1650–51 as it gave him control of Fife and the north-east. Also, Cromwell deliberately loosened his hold on the south-east, convinced that Charles II and David Leslie would take the opportunity to invade England; Cromwell rightly believed that once out in open unfamiliar territory in England, the Covenanter army would become easy prey. His brilliant deduction succeeded; on 3 September 1651, a year to the day of Dunbar, Oliver Cromwell decisively defeated Charles and Leslie at Worcester. As for Inverkeithing, a small cairn erected in 2001 by the Clan Maclean Heritage Trust commemorates the battle of 1651.

When Cromwell left Scotland in the summer of 1651, he ordered his able commander General George Monck to subdue the rest of Scotland, which Monck did with only 6,000 troops, although these scant resources were stretched to the limit. Even so, in the six months between August 1651 and February 1652, Monck took the key towns of Dundee, Montrose, Aberdeen and Inverness. After the final disastrous defeat of Charles II at Worcester, by the end of 1651 Monck's forces in Scotland were doubled to 12,000.[19] By February 1652, Monck had not only subjugated Scotland but pacified her.

Monck's achievement was indeed impressive and bears testament not only to his military skill but also, more importantly, his adroitness as a diplomat, an attribute he would put to good use in 1660, as we shall see in the following chapter

In 1652 Monck was recalled to England to supervise the strengthening of the sea defences of Great Yarmouth during the Anglo–Dutch war; he would remain there until 1654 when he returned to Scotland. By that year there was open rebellion in northern Scotland by the Highland Clan chiefs chafing under the Cromwellian Commonwealth rule; there was even some unrest in Lowland Scotland. In 1653 the Clan chiefs had made it known to Charles II that they would rise for him, which prompted Charles to appoint Lieutenant Colonel John Middleton as his commander in chief. The Earl of Glencairn was made Middleton's deputy while the latter travelled on the Continent raising arms and money for the coming rebellion.

Middleton, a Covenanter who had fought in the English Civil War on the parliamentary side, had also been an Engager with Charles I in 1646; now he had taken up the cause of Charles II, probably out of bitterness at the treatment meted out to the Engagers by the fanatical Archibald Johnston of Wariston, the witchfinder general and persecutor of the Engagers in 1650. When Middleton returned to Scotland in February 1654, he was joined by several Clan chiefs, notably the Earl of Atholl, Lord Kenmure and the Earl of Argyll's heir, Lord Lorne. In April, Monck arrived to take command of the 15,000 strong Cromwellian forces, distributed throughout Scotland on garrison duties. Monck knew his objective of bringing order would have to be achieved quickly to discourage other Clan chiefs joining Middleton, Glencairn and Atholl. He organized his forces into five columns; his friend and colleague Lieutenant Colonel Thomas Morgan was given four of the columns, Monck himself commanding the fifth and largest. Monck began his campaign by torching hamlets and villages suspected of harbouring Royalist sympathizers, burning crops and driving off cattle. For the next three months, Middleton continued to elude both Monck and Morgan until the latter caught up with him in July.

Dalnaspidal[20]

Morgan had moved his columns eastwards from Braemar to Ruthven, marching south down the Spey Valley towards Dalwhinnie. At one point Monck and Middleton nearly joined battle but the former's men were exhausted from their marching and counter-marching in pursuit of an elusive enemy. Middleton commanded a force of between 1,200 and 3,000; his intention was to march north to Caithness where he expected ships to bring reinforcements, arms and ammunition. Middleton's route was by way of the western shore of Loch Garry and Dalnaspidal. However, on 19 July, Morgan surprised him at Dalnaspidal; he charged Middleton's 800 horse which had somehow become separated from the infantry. Many of the Royalist troopers were killed and several more – about 300 – were taken prisoner. Middleton was wounded but managed to escape to Caithness, where he was unable to recruit more than a few hundred men. Dispirited, he took ship for the Continent, re-joining Charles II at Cologne in September 1654. Dalnaspidal was hardly a battle; Morgan's losses were just four wounded. It was the last action in the Scottish civil war and brought the Royalist rising of 1651–54 to its close. By early 1655, most of the rebel leaders, including Glencairn, Middleton's deputy, had submitted to Monck who treated them fairly. Scotland was once more at peace. For the time being.

Notes

1. Hume Brown, *History of Scotland*, vol. ii, p.157.
2. Ibid, p.332.
3. Ibid.
4. Ibid.
5. Ibid, p.333; Oliver, *A History of Scotland*, p.223; Lynch, *Scotland: A New History*, p.274.
6. Hume Brown, op. cit., vol. ii, p333; Oliver, op. cit., p.224; Lynch, op. cit., p.274.
7. Campbell, A.: *A Despatch Announcing the Defeat of the Scottish Arms at Philiphaugh* (1645): quoted in the *Battlefield Trust* account.
8. Hume Brown, op. cit., vol. ii, p.335.
9. *APS,* vol. vi., pp.603 et seq.
10. Pugh, op cit., p.175.
11. Ibid, p.176.
12. Walker, Sir Edward, *Historical Discourses*, p.163.
13. Walker, Sir Edward, op. cit., p.623.
14. *Diary of Johnston of Wariston 1650–1654* (Scottish History Society, 2nd Series, vol. ii, p.18).
15. Walker, Sir Edward, op. cit. quotes Scottish sources as the source of his computation; see also Reese, *Cromwell's Masterstroke: Dunbar 1650*, p.39; also the *Harleian Manuscript*, a document compiled from interviews with Scottish prisoners after the battle from which E. M. Furgol, *A Regimental History of the Covenanting Armies 1639–51* computed Leslie's forces at 15,600; we know that Cromwell took 10,000 prisoners and 4,000 were slain on the field; Leslie escaped with about 5,000, mostly cavalry (see Reese, P. op. cit., p.40) which means he must have commanded at least 19,000 troops.
16. Reese, op. cit., p.40.
17. Cromwell's *Letters and Speeches.*
18. *APS,* vol. vi., part 2, p.808.
19. Reese, *The Life of General George Monck For King & Cromwell*, p.80.
20. An account of Dalnaspidal appears in Reese, op. cit. p.62.

Chapter 10

The Killing Time: 1666–1688

T he death of Oliver Cromwell, Lord Protector of the Commonwealth on 3 September 1658 left England leaderless; his successor, son and heir, Richard Cromwell, was a much lesser man than his father. Oliver was a big act to follow and it soon became clear that Richard was not up to the responsibilities he had inherited. As a result the army tightened its grip on the country to the point of ignoring parliament, itself dominated by militant republicans like Sir Arthur Hesilrige who with his filibustering coterie blocked every attempt by the legislature to enact laws. Eventually, Richard Cromwell decided to dispense with parliament which he dismissed on 22 April 1659. Thereafter, the army was in complete control, a situation that deeply dismayed General George Monck to the point of distrust and even abhorrence. Monck, now Governor of Scotland, made his base at Coldstream, the township in the Borders from which his own elite regiment of foot guards took its name.

Monck was determined to reinstate parliament and so he began his famous march south on 2 January 1660 with an army of 4,000; at least he enjoyed the support of his old and trusted friend, Major General Thomas Morgan, his subordinate during the Highland campaign of 1655. In taking this action, Monck had sought the approval of the Speaker of the House of Commons, William Lenthall, who informed him that the Rump parliament had returned to power[1] and that Monck would be welcome in London with his small army. It had become clear to Monck that the only alternative to the Cromwellian Republicans was the restoration of Charles II. To this end, he began to make preparations to smooth a path for the King's return. However, he first had to make England secure; his support for parliament earned him the appointment of Commander in Chief of the armed forces in England, Scotland and Ireland; Monck was also made a member of the Council of State, a General at sea, with the manor and Palace of Hampton Court settled on him and £20,000 for his public services.[2] On 22 March 1660, Monck declared for Charles II, to which parliament acceded; Monck personally greeted the King at Dover. The

Restoration of Charles II would turn out to be one of the most pitiful and dismal chapters in Scotland's history.

On Charles's return, exactly a century had passed since Scotland had rejected Roman Catholicism for Presbyterianism. During the period 1561 to 1649, two of the three Stuart monarchs who had challenged the new religious form of worship had not only lost their thrones but their lives – Mary, Queen of Scots and Charles I. However, Scottish people entertained hopes that lessons had been learned from these traumatic tragedies and welcomed the return of Charles in 1660. For his part, from the outset of his reign (1660–1685), Charles's attitude was unequivocal; he would make no compromise with the Covenanters on the matter of episcopacy. This policy was hardly reflected in his choice of appointments to the Privy Council, the executive arm of the Scottish parliament. Charles was acutely aware that many of the officers of state had been and continued to be unreconstructed supporters of the National Covenant. The Royalist William, 9th Earl of Glencairn who raised the Royal Standard for Charles during the Cromwellian Commonwealth period was appointed Chancellor of Scotland; John, 6th Earl of Rothes, who had been one of the leaders of the revolt against Charles I, was made President of the Privy Council, a position of considerable power; and John, 2nd Earl and Duke of Lauderdale, champion of the Covenant, was made Secretary to the Privy Council. Charles's intentions were obvious; it was his way of mollifying the strong Presbyterian following among the nobility, if not the common people. However, Charles intended to stamp his authority on Scotland one way or another through his instruments and representatives, the Episcopalian bishops. Charles acted precipitously, implementing his policy towards the hard line Covenanters in the most direct way.

On 8 July 1660, the Covenanter Archibald Campbell, 1st Marquis of Argyll who had travelled to London to seek an audience with the King was arrested and imprisoned in the Tower of London. At the same time, a Royal Warrant was issued for the apprehension of Archibald Johnston of Wariston, one of the co-authors of the National Covenant in 1638; Wariston was obliged to seek refuge in France where he remained in exile for the next three years. The Kirk of Scotland split into two factions. The majority party became known as the Resolutioners who somewhat unrealistically hoped that Charles, having sworn to uphold the National Covenant and the Solemn League and Covenant in 1650, would favour them. The minority party, known as the Protesters, had distrusted Charles from day one; the Protesters felt justified in their opposition when on 24 August 1660 on the instructions of the King, the Committee of Estates of the Scottish parliament (which had thus far not met in session) issued a proclamation banning 'all unlawful meetings ... without His Majesty's special authority'.[3]

This proclamation alarmed Resolutioners and Protesters alike until on 3 September the Resolutioners received a letter from the King which calmed some but made others uneasy: 'We do also resolve to protect and preserve the Covenant of the Church of Scotland, as it is settled by law, without violation.'[4] Of course what Charles failed to state was that the episcopacy introduced by his grandfather James VI and I the rule of the bishops would continue. Bishops were the King's representatives in Scotland; any disobedience shown to a bishop was considered insubordination to the monarch. The Resolutioners had to swallow their pride; the Protesters were even more determined to resist the King. On 1 January 1661, the Scottish parliament convened after an interval of nine years, Cromwell having dissolved it in 1652. The man chosen to represent Charles II was John Middleton, now elevated to Earl of Middleton, the former Covenanter who had supported Charles at Worcester in 1651 and again in the Highland Rising of 1654 when he had been defeated at Dalnaspidal by Thomas Morgan, Monck's able subordinate. Middleton's parliament passed no fewer than 393 legislative measures – acts which included the issue of copper coins for the benefit of the poor and stringent penalties on those who profaned the Sabbath by swearing and drinking excessively.[5] These were minor matters; what Middleton's obsequious parliament imposed on the people of Scotland was an affirmation of Charles II's right to appoint officers of State, the right to summon and dissolve parliaments at will and make war and peace as he saw fit. Charles was declared the supreme governor and sole arbiter over all persons and causes in Scotland. Charles was, in effect, made a dictator. Worse still, Middleton's parliament voted Charles an annual grant of £40,000 sterling (£480,000 Scots, a massive sum for a relatively poor nation) which was both unwelcome and unnecessary.[6]

That year, the over-mighty Marquis of Argyll, staunch supporter of the Covenant, while lacking the respect of both Resolutioners and Protesters, gained some esteem in the closing moments of his life. Sent from the Tower of London to Edinburgh's Tolbooth, Argyll was led out to face execution on 27 May 1661. That day, Argyll made some restitution for his lack of moral and physical courage. As he went to his beheading at the *Maiden* (an early form of the guillotine), his last words were reputedly thus:

'I could die as a Roman [Catholic] but choose to die as a Christian.'[7]

What was important about Charles's proclamation that the Church of Scotland would continue as it had been settled by law meant the continuation of the episcopacy imposed by his grandfather and confirmed by his father. The Scottish parliament of 1661 re-affirmed this law, although the Members quarrelled with each other, Middleton heading one faction, Lauderdale the other. Two acts sponsored by Middleton were aimed at discrediting Lauderdale. In one of the measures it was made compulsory for every person holding an office of State to declare that the two Covenants were unlawful, even seditious. Lauderdale continued his support for these, cynically announcing that he would sign a cartload of such oaths to that effect so long as he remained in office. The second of Middleton's measures backfired on its sponsor; his Bill of Indemnity proposed that twelve persons in the Privy Council should be declared incapable of holding office, the twelve to be determined by a ballot of parliament. Middleton had Lauderdale in mind, no doubt conducting a scurrilous campaign against him and cajoling parliament to include him. A clumsy manoeuvre, when Middleton's Bill of Indemnity reached Charles in London to receive the royal assent, Lauderdale had already informed the King of Middleton's absurdity and enormity; Charles agreed with Lauderdale and, in 1663, Middleton was dismissed from his position. Charles believed he was master of his northern kingdom – well almost; there were troublemakers in the wings, biding their time to challenge his authority. These men were diehard Covenanters.

As government intentions towards the Covenanters in the early years of the Restoration became increasingly clear, a substantial minority felt they had been cheated of the right to worship in the way Charles II had promised. To those men and women, the Marquis of Argyll and others were seen as martyrs to the cause. Matters grew worse when in 1663, bishops took up the offices they had abandoned in the previous decade in Scotland; this led to a mass exodus of Covenanter ministers who began to hold their services not in churches but in barns and the open air; these meetings were known as Conventicles and were declared illegal gatherings. In 1663 the scale of Conventicles had increased to such an extent that the government felt compelled to pass laws imposing fines on people who failed to attend worship in their parish churches. Under normal local arrangements these fines should have been levied and collected by the church heritors, the ennobled landowners, gentlemen farmers and property owners who contributed to the upkeep and running of churches; however, they too were subject to a rising scale of fines according to their means. Many landowners were sympathetic towards the nonconformists who applied a new name to these laws; they became known as the Bishops' Drag-Net.[8]

In 1638 practically the entire nation had supported the National Covenant but by 1663 only a minority of nobles and commoners subscribed to it, the majority of the landowning class opting to serve the King and thereby fatten their purses through royal pensions – a particularly lucrative source of income – as well as developing their commercial interests through royal patronage and increasing their political power. About two-thirds of the Scottish clergy had reneged on their support for the Covenant for much the same reasons. Another blow to the nonconformists came in 1663 with the blatant kidnapping of Archibald Johnston of Wariston in France by Charles's agents. Seen as a dangerous incendiary Wariston, now a sick man rapidly losing his faculties, was brought back to Scotland to stand a form of trial. An uncompromising opponent of Charles I and Charles II as well as his own people, Wariston hated the Engagers who had supported Charles I in 1646, as we saw in the previous chapter. The sick man was found guilty of treason, even if he was never formally charged with that offence; his continuing existence was seen as a threat to the principles enshrined in the Restoration, so he suffered the same fate as Argyll, the only difference being that Argyll, a noble, was beheaded, whereas Wariston faced the gallows, as befitted a commoner. It is not clear whether Wariston's passing was universally mourned but his death was seen as martyrdom by the nonconformists.

Although some of the disaffected clergy continued to hold services in their churches, the seat of unrest was at its hottest in south-west Scotland – Dumfries, Galloway and Kirkcudbright. By 1666 armed rebellion was not far away. Repressive measures by the Privy Council in Edinburgh against the nonconformist recusants increased which had the effect of building up a head of steam among the faithful. Among the military commanders who enforced the government's edicts was Sir James Turner; thrice between March and November 1666 Turner marched his forces into the south-west, levying fines as well as billeting his troops in the homes of the dissenters at their expense. During his third foray, Turner was lodging in Dumfries when a party of Galloway dissidents made him their prisoner on 15 November. The men were desperate although they had no wish to shed Turner's blood; certainly, they had no plans to mount a rebellion but having gone this far they could hardly turn back. On their return to Galloway, the dissidents apparently paused at the market cross of Dumfries to drink the King's health![9]

News of Turner's capture reached Charles in London and those nobles in Scotland who were loyal to him declared they would not allow this insult to the King to go unpunished. Among these was General Thomas 'Tam' Dalziel (Dalyell) of the Binns, scion of a West Lothian gentry family. Dalyell was a Royalist through and through; he had vowed never to trim his beard after the execution of Charles I, had fought for Charles II at Worcester in 1651, then served in the Polish wars of the Russian Tsar Alexei I, which earned him the title *The Muscovite Beast*. General Tam is also remembered for raising a cut-glass regiment, the Royal North British Dragoons in 1681, the first dragoon regiment in the British Army. The regiment was also known as the Scots Greys – not because they rode grey horses (which they did) but because they wore Russian field-grey greatcoats, a fact confirmed by Kathleen, Dowager Lady Dalyell of the Binns to the author in the 1970s.

The Turner incident – no more than a protest against military oppression – was seen by officialdom as nothing short of outright rebellion. On 21 November a proclamation denouncing the uprising was issued; it made no mention of clemency for any who might choose to surrender. The leaders of the 'rebellion' appealed for support from their brethren; the result was disappointingly poor although by 22 November the dissidents had managed to cobble together an army of sorts numbering 3,000. The motley band was commanded by an experienced soldier, Colonel James Wallace of Achens, near Troon, Ayrshire who had served in the foot guards in the parliamentary army during the English Civil War. At Lanark the poorly armed Covenanters took the desperate decision to march on Edinburgh to present their grievances to anyone who would listen to them.

Rullion Green

The prevailing conditions during the march from Lanark were appalling; it was the onset of winter with incessant freezing rain which made the dirt roads almost impassable. Not surprisingly, there were defections along the way, especially when James Wallace learnt that General Tam Dalyell was close on his heels. Vague promises were made; if the rebels laid down their arms, their lives would be spared. The Covenanter leaders had been led to believe that the townspeople of Edinburgh and the surrounding district were favourably disposed to their grievances which, sadly, was very far from the truth; the countryfolk on the outskirts of Edinburgh were at best sullen, at worst aggressive. Reaching Colinton Village about three miles west of Edinburgh, the dissidents conceded defeat; their only safe retreat to Ayrshire lay by way of the Pentland Hills, an area of bleak, inhospitable moors and boggy terrain. On 28 November they camped at Rullion Green; it was a frosty day and snow had fallen the night before. Wallace had intelligence that Dalyell was advancing from the west; messengers from the Duke of Hamilton arrived, pleading that Wallace and his men should surrender; Wallace responded, copying his reply to Dalyell saying that that he would surrender but only on condition that the Covenanters' grievances would be addressed. Nothing was agreed. By now Wallace commanded only 900 wet, hungry and dispirited men, many of them lacking proper weapons. He formed his force to withstand Dalyell's attack, expected at any minute; the horse were deployed on each wing, the right commanded by himself, the left by a Major Learmont. The largely unarmed infantry were placed in the centre. With this meagre force how could Wallace hope to defeat Dalyell's 3,000 well armed, well disciplined and well fed men? Then suddenly Dalyell appeared, forming his dragoons up for the attack.

Hunger and the appalling weather had already sapped the strength and morale of the dissident Covenanters. Wallace had placed his men on Bell's Hill, a favourable position to confront Dalyell's troops; Major Learmont managed to repulse the first cavalry charge on the left wing, then a second. Fresh troops were brought up and Dalyell advanced steadily, then he ordered simultaneous attacks on both wings which were successful, bringing his troopers face-to-face with Wallace's dispirited infantry. The outcome was never in any doubt; as that dreary November day drew to a close, the Covenanters broke and fled, leaving at least fifty dead on the field with about the same number taken prisoner. Dalyell's losses were negligible. Many of those who escaped death or capture never made it home; some perished in the treacherous Pentland Hills bogs, others were reputedly despatched by the local peasantry.[10] There is a single grave monument which might be said to refute the latter accusation. Near Cauldstane Slap, about twelve miles from Rullion Green, a solitary tombstone existed in 1913 bearing the following inscription:

Sacred To the memory of A Covenanter Who fought and was wounded at Rullion Green November 28, 1666 And who died at Oaken Bush the day after the battle And was buried here by Adam Sanderson of Blackhill.[11]

The site of Rullion Green is commemorated by a single small stone fashioned in the shape of a common and popular seventeenth century headstone; known as the Martyrs' Stone, it marks the last resting place of 'fifty true Covenanter Presbyterians'.

Dalyell led the sorry survivors of Rullion Green to Edinburgh where his troopers combed the streets for sympathizers; those who paused to watch the captives being led into the High Street Tolbooth no doubt did so in silence lest they might be implicated and taken into custody. The prisoners were subsequently brought before the High Court of Justiciary where they were interrogated by two formidable lawyers, Sir George Lockhart and Sir George Mackenzie (later known as 'Bluidy Mackenzie'). Mackenzie put a case for clemency on that occasion as the captives had been granted quarter at Rullion Green. Mackenzie argued that if clemency were denied, no one would ever again trust a promise of quarter. He was overruled on the grounds that the Rullion Green prisoners were not participants in a war, but guilty of an act of sedition. This manipulation of the facts was deliberate on the part of the prosecution which demanded nothing less than blood; the Pentland Rising, the alternative name for Rullion Green, had been proclaimed a rebellion, now it was reduced to a seditious act, punishable by imprisonment and even death. The argument was that the rules of war were inappropriate in this case. Ten of the prisoners were hanged on 7 December 1666; another five shared the same fate on 14 December. After execution the victims' right arms were cut off, these being the arms with which they had saluted the Covenant at Lanark; the severed limbs were sent to that town for public exhibition.[12] During the subsequent witch-hunt, another twenty-five men were hanged – four in Glasgow and a large number in Ayr.[13] A further fifty were transported in prison ships to Barbados. Rullion Green only served to stiffen resistance; the slaughter on a dismal November morning of men who had followed the dictates of their conscience would not be forgotten.

Even Charles II, the implacable enemy of Scottish Presbyterianism in general and the 'irreconcilable' Covenanters in particular, admitted that the Pentland Rising had been clumsily managed; the cruelty meted out only served to create martyrs. So the King made concessions to those who resided in the centre of anarchy in south-west Scotland; prayer meetings could be held as long as they were conducted indoors. Charles hoped that this concession would bring back the stray sheep to a church run by bishops subservient to himself. The hard-core radicals refused to comply. The open air Conventicles increased in number and size until they took on the appearance of military musters rather than prayer meetings. Charles was incensed by this flagrant disobedience; he was determined to bring the irreconcilables to heel with force. Between 1666 and 1673 several of the ringleaders, hellfire preachers like Alexander 'Prophet' Peden, minister of the parish of New Luce in Galloway, refused to sign Charles's Oath of Allegiance to the bishops and by extension the King himself. (The concept of 'loyal opposition' had not yet become accepted.) Of the 1,000 Presbyterian ministers preaching in Scotland, Peden and 260 others refused to comply. Peden was obliged to take to the heather, always one step ahead of his pursuers until he was captured in 1673 and thrown into the dank dungeon on the Bass Rock, off North Berwick, East Lothian. In time the Rock would become a prison for others of the same stamp, men like John Blacader, or Blackadder, who died on the Bass Rock for his principles.

At least one positive result from Rullion Green was the appointment of the Earl of Lauderdale as virtual governor of Scotland in 1667; Lauderdale replaced the bitter enemy of the Covenanters, James Sharp, Archbishop of St Andrews known as Judas Sharp to the irreconcilables. Lauderdale pursued a more conciliatory policy towards the irreconcilables and for the moment, peace was restored. However, in 1667, a propagandist book entitled *Naphtali* was published in support of the Covenanter cause. (Naphtali was the son of Jacob; in the Book of Genesis, he is described as 'a hound let loose; he giveth goodly words'.)[14] The book listed all the fines that the government's agent Sir James Turner had exacted from the dissidents; not surprisingly, Turner

198 The Killing Fields of Scotland

disputed the facts. Although the author of *Naphtali* was our old friend Anonymous, the book was written by two men – James Goodtrees, son of a former Edinburgh provost and James Stirling, a Paisley minister. The book was immediately banned and publicly burned.[15] Anyone caught in possession of a copy was subject to a fine of £10,000; it was described as 'a damned book that came to Scotland from beyond the sea'. *Naphtali* so incensed Andrew Honeyman, Bishop of Orkney, a prelate in the same mould as Archbishop Sharp that he was moved to publish a counter-blast. In 1668 Honeyman and Sharp were shot at in their coach in Edinburgh; Sharp escaped unscathed, Honeyman was wounded. Their would-be assassin, the Reverend James Mitchell, a minister who had taken part in the Pentland Rising walked away free; he would remain at large until 1678.

During the next three years, Lauderdale's lenient policy towards the recalcitrant Covenanters grew harsher. Open air Conventicles had become more numerous; what was worse, those who attended them had begun to carry weapons as well as their Bibles. This produced an understandable knee-jerk from Lauderdale; every year of his administration of Scotland from 1670 was marked by ever-increasing severity towards the irreconcilables. For this and other achievements, Lauderdale was elevated to the rank of Duke in 1672. No matter, Conventicles spread from the south-west to Fife, the coastal farmlands of Moray and Easter Ross as well as East Lothian and Berwickshire. In 1677 the Privy Council ordered a half-company (about thirty troopers) of the Earl of Linlithgow's Regiment to be quartered at Dunbar ready to act against Conventicles being held in the vicinity.[16]

In 1678 the would-be assassin of Archbishop Sharp, James Mitchell was brought to justice. Lauderdale would have spared Mitchell but Sharp insisted that Mitchell be despatched on the gallows in Edinburgh's Grassmarket, a demand which was duly carried out, making another martyr for the cause of the Covenanters. By way of revenge for Mitchell's execution Sharp was murdered on 3 May 1679 at Magus Muir, two miles from St Andrews. This episode brought a dismal close to Lauderdale's administration and caused yet another armed conflict between the government forces and the Covenanters.

Drumclog

On 29 May 1679, the nineteenth anniversary of Charles II's Restoration, a band of eighty armed dissidents converged on the village of Rutherglen, three miles to the east of Glasgow. They extinguished the bonfires lit in honour of the King; then, at the village market cross, they burned copies of all the acts passed by the government persecuting the Irreconcilable adherents of 'the true Kirk of Scotland'. This episode attracted more recruits to the cause; on 1 June a growing number of diehard Covenanters camped on Loudon Hill, near Strathaven, ostensibly to attend an open air Conventicle. Warned that government troops commanded by John Graham of Claverhouse were approaching, the insurgents agreed they would stand and fight. With a combined force of 1,500, some of whom were mounted, the Covenanters outnumbered Claverhouse's troopers. The Covenanters made for the advantageous position of Drumclog on Hairlawhill, beneath Loudon Hill, the scene of Robert the Bruce's victory over Aymer de Valance in 1307. (Perhaps the Covenanters chose the site with that in mind, trusting that history would repeat itself – if they thought in such terms. It is more likely that they chose the ground because it was boggy and unfavourable for Claverhouse's dragoons.) When informed that Claverhouse was not far away, the Reverend Thomas Douglas broke off his sermon with the words 'Ye have got the theory, now for the practice'.

On 1 June 1679, a peaceful Sunday morning, John Graham of Claverhouse was enjoying breakfast at an inn in Strathaven when he received word that a large Conventicle was being held at Drumclog. Claverhouse immediately called his troops to horse and rode furiously at the head of his men along the road to Darvel; on reaching the moor of High Drumclog, Claverhouse looked down on the motley crowd of farmers, shepherds, ploughmen and labourers commanded by Robert Hamilton, brother of the Laird of Preston, who resided near Prestonpans, East Lothian. Hamilton had chosen his ground well; it was boggy and treacherous for both horses and men. He had deployed his horsed men – they could hardly be called cavalry – and infantry in battle formation, mounted men on the wings, infantry in the centre. Some of Hamilton's men bore firearms and swords but the majority were armed with only home-made pikes, *cleeks* (hook-like devices used to prise vegetables out of frozen ground) pitchforks and other farm tools.[17] Facing them were Claverhouse's 150 well armed troopers; on Claverhouse's advance, Hamilton gave the order 'No quarter!' For a time the two sides exchanged a desultory musket fire; while Claverhouse was confident of victory, his cavalry were unable to engage the Covenanters in close combat as they had had to dismount on account of the boggy ground. Then William Cleland, one of Hamilton's commanders led a force round the side of Drumclog Moss and successfully attacked the dismounted troopers. In the ensuing short, sharp fight, Claverhouse was routed, forty-two of his men being left dead on the field; Hamilton lost six.[18] Drumclog was the first and last battle Claverhouse would lose in his relatively short life. In 1839 a monument was raised at Drumclog to commemorate the battle.

Although more of a skirmish than a battle, Drumclog had significant repercussions. The momentary success fired the imagination and morale of the Covenanters, attracting new recruits to the cause. But the victory would prove as brief as the flash of blue of a kingfisher darting across a river. However, encouraged by the volume of new recruits, Hamilton led his growing army to Glasgow, where he had many sympathizers. Be that as it may, Glasgow proved a difficult nut to crack, being heavily garrisoned by government troops. After a half-hearted assault on the town, Hamilton retreated to the town of Hamilton. When news of Drumclog reached London the

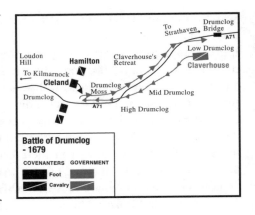

government considered that matters were serious enough to justify the raising of an army of 15,000 to put down what was seen as a full-scale rebellion. James Scott, Duke of Monmouth, Charles II's illegitimate son by his mistress Lucy Walters was appointed commander and sent north to confront the irreconcilables.

Bothwell Brig

On 22 June 1679 the two armies faced each other across the narrow bridge which spanned the river Clyde at the village of Bothwell, near Motherwell. The Covenanter army was placed on the south bank of the Clyde; Hamilton's force consisted of about 6,000, supported by a single cannon. The Royalist army commanded by James, 1st Duke of Monmouth, John Graham of Claverhouse and the Earl of Linlithgow numbered 5,000, supported by three field pieces. On that Sunday morning, Hamilton's picquets watched the Royalist musketeers blowing on their saltpetre matches for their matchlocks, preparing to storm the bridge.

Hamilton's commanders included David Hackston of Rathillet, John Balfour of Kinloch and William Cleland, the latter who had brought Hamilton success at Drumclog. Seven weeks earlier Hackston and Balfour had been among the men who murdered Archbishop Sharp on 3 May.[19] (Hackston would be apprehended and executed on 30 July 1680 for his crime.)[20] Hamilton and Monmouth both knew that success would be achieved by whoever held the narrow bridge across the Clyde, so the former entrusted David Hackston and 300 men from Galloway, Clydesdale and Stirling with its defence. The battle opened with the Royalist artillery firing on Hamilton's position but the fire was ineffectual, being too high; the single cannon Hamilton possessed returned a fire so effective that it silenced Monmouth's gunners. Monmouth could not use his field pieces against Hackston, knowing he needed to gain control of the bridge intact in order to attack the bulk of Hamilton's army on Hamilton Moss. For about an hour Hackston kept up a hot, masking fire, gallantly standing steady like the Roman hero Horatius who, with two companions, held the Sublician Bridge against the Etruscans in 507 BC. But Hackston was low on ammunition; calling for more, he was informed there was none to spare so he was forced to retreat. This shameful decision – there was a significant number of musketeers in the Covenanter army who could have given up their bullets, or relieved Hackston – cost Hamilton dearly. Monmouth could not believe his good fortune; he ordered his men to cross the bridge which they did in perfect formation.

The bulk of Hamilton's army was drawn up in good order on Hamilton Moss. However, on Monmouth's advance, Hamilton lost his nerve and fled the field, leaving his leaderless men to their fate. Claverhouse was first to attack, last to leave the field, accounting for most of the 600 casualties, 400 being fatal, with 1,200 taken prisoner. Some of the fugitive Covenanters sought sanctuary in Hamilton Parish Kirk, where they were butchered inside. Monmouth's losses were neglible; he treated his prisoners fairly, despite the urgings of Claverhouse to put them to the sword. (Ironically, Monmouth was censured by the government for his clemency, while Claverhouse earned himself the epithet 'Bluidy Clavers' after Bothwell Brig.) Victory at Bothwell Brig might have given the Covenanters a breathing space and possibly brought the government to the negotiating table. Sadly, it was not to be; the gallant country folk who stood in the front line that day were poorly led and inadequately provisioned. A monument to Bothwell Brig was erected in 1903, beside the modern bridge over the Clyde.[21]

Monmouth's prisoners were taken to Edinburgh and held in Greyfriars Churchyard – probably intentionally, it being the site where the National Covenant had been signed nearly forty years earlier. At least on this occasion there were no executions. Many of the prisoners resided there for several months, branded as rebels and traitors. In their open prison, half clad, ill fed and exposed to all weather, many were brought to submission; 400 swore an oath that they would never again take up arms. More than 250 diehards refused the terms offered by the government;[22] they were sentenced to transportation to the colonies in November 1679 but the prison ship carrying them to Barbados was

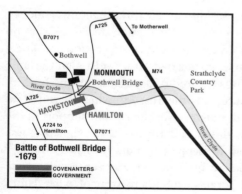

caught in a storm off Orkney, 200 of the prisoners perishing in the shipwreck. The Martyrs' Monument in Greyfriars Churchyard is an impressive memorial to the Killing Time.

Aird's Moss

The last armed conflict between the Covenanters and the government during the Killing Time took place on 20 July 1680 at Aird's Moss, near Sanquhar, Dumfriesshire, where the Reverend Richard Cameron and a party of Covenanters were attending a Conventicle. It was a morning of thick mist and Cameron and his people were taken by surprise by 120 troopers commanded by David Bruce of Earshall who had been tracking the group for several days. Some accounts [23] say the Covenanters numbered sixty-three, of whom only a pitiful few escaped by fighting their way through Bruce's troops, twenty-eight of whom were slain. Cameron and his brother were among the nine Covenanters who lost their lives; five others were wounded and taken prisoner, among them David Hackston of Rathillet who had fought gallantly at Bothwell Brig. Richard Cameron's head and right arm were cut off and taken to Edinburgh and shown to his father, imprisoned in the Tolbooth for nonconformity. A monument to the skirmish was later raised; beside it is the gravestone of Richard Cameron which bears his and eight other names. Annual commemorative Conventicles on the site began in 2002. Richard Cameron gave his name to the famous Cameronians (Scottish Rifles) regiment which was disbanded in 1968 after obtaining many battle honours over nearly three centuries.

Many of the Covenanter leaders who escaped from Bothwell Brig fled to Holland to join the English exiles opposed to Charles II at the time of the Restoration. They were subsequently joined by the Duke of Monmouth, exiled by his exasperated father Charles II on account of the former's involvement in the Rye House Plot to assassinate the King and his brother, James, Duke of York (later James VII and II).

In July 1681 James, Duke of York, was appointed Royal Commissioner of Scotland, passing two laws; one was the Act of Succession declaring 'that no difference in religion ... can alter or divert the right of succession and lineal descent of the Crown'.[24] This, of course, meant that James, a Roman Catholic and heir-presumptive to the throne was assured of accession on the death of his brother. The second of the measures was the Test Act which required all persons holding offices in Church and State to swear an oath in support of the Crown; a risible piece of legislation, this meant that whoever signed it was committed to being a Presbyterian, an Episcopalian and a Roman Catholic![25] Between 1681 and 1682, James's policy in Scotland was repressive; some historians consider that policy as a foretaste in microcosm of what James would have done in England after Charles II's death in 1685 if he had been given the chance. Judicial torture was still legal in Scotland but its use had to be authorized by the Privy Council, of which James was President; he personally witnessed several torture victims subjected to the 'boot', a particularly nasty instrument which was fitted to the victim's leg with wooden wedges hammered in to break the shinbones. Another cruel instrument was the 'thumbikins', attached to the thumb and screwed tightly until the joint was broken. While such atrocities mirrored those committed between 1640 and 1650 in the name of the Covenanter Church and its supporters against supposed witches, they discredited the government in Scotland and added to the martyrology of the Covenanters.

Bothwell Brig effectively brought an end to the aspirations of the Covenanters who had hoped to gain recognition through a feat of arms; to many of their supporters this had never seemed in any sense likely to succeed, nor to light the path to their desired goal – to worship in the manner enshrined in the National Covenant, not in any watered-down version. That unadulterated form of Scottish Presbyterianism expired on 22 June 1679. Even so, the remnants of the old-guard Covenanters continued to press for their religious rights, led by a young James Renwick, son of a weaver in Glencairn, Nithsdale. Renwick was ordained as a minister devoted to the Covenant. By 1685 Sir George Mackenzie, Lord Advocate of Scotland, had stamped his foot on the remnants. Bluidy [Bloody] Mackenzie had a long memory; he had abhorred the hysterical reaction of the General Assembly of the Church of Scotland to its belief that witchcraft and witches were on the increase during the 1640s, when several hundred, perhaps a thousand people – mainly women – had been executed for the supposed crime of witchcraft. Until Cromwell's invasion of 1650, the witch-hunt went on up to the very eve of Dunbar; on reaching Edinburgh in September 1650, Cromwell set free several people incarcerated in Edinburgh's Tolbooth awaiting trial for witchcraft. (After the Restoration the witch-hunt in Scotland reached its peak; between 1660 and 1663, several hundred people were executed – murdered in fact – by the Covenanter Kirk, hundreds more than Mackenzie sentenced to death during the Killing Time.)

Charles II died on 2 February 1685. Even as their King, his passing was hardly lamented by his Scottish subjects who had not seen his face for over three decades. Charles had been obsessed by two ambitions, one inherited from his father – a belief in the Divine Right of kings to rule their people – and the need to increase the contents of his purse. He had persecuted the Covenanters who had refused to submit to the form of religious worship he and his father before him had attempted to impose on them through bishops, the King's representatives. James Renwick, the minister and leader of the

Remnants, continued to oppose James VII and II until he was apprehended, tried and found guilty of treason. On 17 February 1688 Renwick was executed in Edinburgh's Grassmarket, another martyr to the cause. During his brief life, Renwick had ridiculed Prophet Alexander Peden who had been set free from his prison on the Bass Rock because, as Renwick said, he valued his own skin more than his religious principles, believing it was Peden's duty to become a martyr. Such was Renwick's own zeal that he was moved to produce a propaganda pamphlet *The Apologetical Declaration* – more a declaration of war on royal officialdom than a religious tract. The royal response was the Oath of Abjuration under which any man or woman could be stopped in the street and ordered to say 'God save the King', an admission which was anathema to the Remnants. Those who refused to say the four words were shot out of hand, without trial by jury. Perhaps the worst atrocity during the Killing Time occurred in May 1685, when two Wigtown women whose outspoken opposition to the King singled them out for a particularly horrible death. They were dragged to a beach and tied to stakes fixed below the highwater mark; as the tide came in and lapped at their chins, they were commanded to say the four words which could save them. Both refused, so the soldiers held their heads under the water until their struggling ended.[26]

While the Killing Time brought about few killing fields, it was not the lack of battles nor the relatively few casualties suffered in them that mattered. That period was tragic because dissident Covenanters leaders and their supporters needlessly sacrificed themselves for a form of faith and worship their consciences would not permit them to abandon, nor permit them to compromise with officialdom. The period 1666 to 1688 is one of the darker chapters in Scotland's history. Rullion Green was little short of a calculated, cynical and unnecessary massacre; Drumclog would have been better not fought at all as it led to the tragedy of Bothwell Brig. In turn, Bothwell Brig brought about a decade of betrayal, deceit, judicial torture, death and transportation to the colonies with their hostile climates and diseases which led to an early death. The Covenanters who lived their last days in Edinburgh's Tolbooth grew accustomed to the clink of jail keys, a chorus of doom in that dank, dark prison. For some it was the last sound they would hear on this earth. However, against the undoubted injustices perpetrated on these unfortunate souls, we must balance the atrocities committed by the Covenanter Kirk between 1640 and 1663 which executed some hundreds – possibly a thousand or more of those falsely accused of witchcraft. By way of contrast, during the period 1666–85, about 100 Covenanters were judicially murdered, 300 were transported and around 465 cut down in the field.[28] Was the Killing Time a form of poetic justice, or atonement, for the excesses of the Scottish witch-hunt between 1563 and 1685? This author is in no way a moral philosopher but one is tempted to revise the adage about the sword; those who live by the Bible often die by it … What is depressing about the Killing Time is that lives were lost needlessly fighting a government's repressive policy, one which simply did not work. In 1688 the Glorious Revolution brought the Protestant William and Mary to the throne; with them came the full and final recognition of Presbyterianism as the state religion of Scotland.

Notes

1. Reese, *The Life of General George Monck: For King and Cromwell*, p.130.
2. Ibid, p.141.
3. Hume Brown, *History of Scotland*, vol. ii, p.383.
4. Wodrow, R., *The History of the Sufferings of the Church of Scotland from the Restoration to the Revolution* ed. Revd R. Burns (Glasgow, 1829)
5. Hume Brown, op. cit. vol. ii, p.384.
6. Ibid, p.385.
7. Ibid, p.386.
8. Ibid, p.390; *APS*, vol. vii ,449, 455, 465, 480.
9. Ross, *The Killing Time: Fanaticism, Liberty and the Birth of Britain*, p.90.
10. Brotchie, *The Battlefields of Scotland*, p.172.
11. Ibid, p.172.
12. Ross, op. cit., p.93.
13. Hume Brown, op. cit., vol. ii, p.399.
14. Ross, op. cit., p.94.
15. Wodrow, op. cit., vol. ii, p.100.
16. Pugh, op cit., p.326.
17. Brotchie, op. cit. pp.173–80.
18. Ibid, p.182.
19. Hume Brown, op. cit. vol. ii, p.408.
20. Ross, op. cit. p.149.
21. Bothwell Bridge Battlefield, Groome, *Gazeteer of Scotland*; also Thomson, *The Martyr Graves of Scotland*.
22. Hume Brown, op. cit. vol. ii, pp.412–13.
23. Notably by the Revd Roderick Lawson, *The Covenanters of Ayrshire* (1904).
24. *APS*, vol.viii, 39.
25. *Ditto*; Hume Brown, op. cit. vol. ii, p.418.
26. Oliver, *A History of Scotland*, p.236.
27. The number of executions is by no means exhaustive, nor is the figure of 465 fatal casualties in battle. Some accounts such as Lynch, *Scotland: A New History* puts the field casualties at 'about eighty' (p.295); however, we know the dead at Rullion Green were fifty, Drumclog six, Bothwell Brig 400 (see Hume Brown, op. cit. vol. ii, p.412) and Aird's Moss nine, making a total of 465.

Chapter 11

Jacobites: 1689–1719

When the bloodless Glorious Revolution brought about the end of Catholic James VII and II's reign in December 1688, the spirit which had produced the National Covenant (1638), then the Solemn League and Covenant (1643) no longer prevailed in Scotland save for a minority of diehard Covenanters. It could be said that the Revolution Settlement which put William of Orange and Mary on the throne of Britain brought a welcome departure from an obsession with religion which had unduly influenced the policies and conduct of government in public affairs, particularly in Scotland. Secular rather than theological matters became uppermost; it was this rather than anything else which marked a turning point in the nation's history. Of course, episcopacy and Roman Catholicism continued to thrive in the Highlands and Islands but the majority of the Scottish population living in Lowland Scotland was now undisputedly Presbyterian. No longer were questions of religious creed, form of worship and Church government the determining factors and over-riding forces among the Scottish intelligentsia and the political rulers; expediency rather than unwelcome impositions and knee-jerk reactions would henceforth be the way successive governments dealt with ecclesiastical polity. After 1688, Scotland became preoccupied with new and progressive ideals and goals, chiefly in trade and manufactory, which directly or indirectly would benefit Scottish society in general and the middling sort – the merchant middle class – in particular. Economic considerations rather than theological argument preoccupied both government and people; material prosperity was seen by those who governed Scotland as the way to improvements in the standard of living, albeit in the name of the monarch.

Commerce between England and Scotland had always been patchy, the Scots traditionally trading with Europe, particularly the Low Countries. The chief sources of wealth derived from fishing and the export of cured and salted fish, the staple domestic and foreign diet during the winter months. Although Scotland's manufacturing industries were still in their infancy, the production and export of various kinds of cloth were on the increase; wool fells (fleeces) and animal hides had long been traditional exports for the production of wool and leather goods; salt, soap, cordage and gunpowder were also lucrative commodities both at home and abroad, woollen goods and linen yarn being particularly sought after. In 1688, Scotland was poised on the brink of an age of prosperity and peace not known since the time of Alexander III (1249–86). However, on the horizon were dark clouds that would cast a long shadow over Britain in general and Scotland in particular between 1688 and 1746. Those who threatened to upset the apple cart of peace and prosperity were called Jacobites, the followers of James VII and II and his descendants who took their name from the Latin *Jacobus* (James).

When James VII and II's wife, Mary of Modena, gave birth to a baby boy on 10 June 1688 they named him James Francis Edward Stuart; the arrival of the child offered a prospect of the continuation of a Catholic succession. For James's Protestant subjects on both sides of the Border and William of Orange in Holland, this was seen as nothing short of a calamity; concern was publicly voiced and James began to feel insecure on his throne when he learnt that William of Orange was gathering an army of 70,000 and preparing to invade Britain. William was the son of Charles II's eldest daughter Mary and was married to James VII and II's Protestant daughter Mary, making William an attractive Protestant alternative to the Catholic James. For his part, James was consoled by the knowledge that he had a strong ally and friend in John Graham of Claverhouse, known as 'Bloody Clavers' by his Covenanter enemies, 'Bonnie Dundee' by his supporters. In October 1688 Claverhouse had led an army of 13,000 in support of James whom he saw as the lawful King; for this and the suppression of the Covenanters, James elevated Graham to Lord Graham of Claverhouse, 1st Viscount Dundee. In return, Dundee swore to fight in the King's name from that day, which he would do until his untimely death the following year. Be that as it may, the Catholic King had his back to the wall, his hold on the throne growing ever more tenuous; an apprehensive James was desperate when William of Orange landed at Torbay, Devonshire, on 5 November 1688. Queen Mary of Modena and her infant son were sent to France for safety on 9 December, followed by James himself two weeks later. A dispirited Dundee returned to Scotland and dispersed his army, retiring to his country seat at Dudhope Castle, Dundee. Like the Marquis of Montrose before him, Dundee was unfortunate in the master to whom he offered his loyalty.

The Revolution was made glorious because it was bloodless. By February 1689 the English parliament had passed the Act of Succession which stipulated that no Catholic could occupy the throne. It was offered to and accepted by William and his wife Mary as joint rulers of England. On 13 February they were proclaimed King and Queen of England and Ireland but not Scotland. That was a matter which would have to be decided by the Scottish parliament. On 14 March 1689 a Convention of parliamentarians met in Edinburgh to vote on whether James or William and Mary should rule Scotland. In late-seventeenth century Scotland there were marked political and cultural divisions – Lowlander versus Highlander – and to a lesser extent, religious conflict. The majority of the Gaelic-speaking Clan chiefs were Episcopalians and Catholics who had supported the Stuart dynasty since the reign of Robert II in 1371; the English-speaking Presbyterians – the majority of the population – not surprisingly supported the Protestant William and Mary. John Graham, Viscount Dundee attended the March Convention; his voice was foremost among the dissenters who rejected the House of Orange in favour of the House of Stuart, the others being the Episcopalian and Catholic Clan chiefs. Dundee, a Lowland Presbyterian, strode out of the hall, intent on organizing another Convention at Stirling held in James VII and II's name. At Stirling Dundee's associates could not make up their minds, so he left the Stirling Convention in disgust, retiring to his home at Dudhope Castle, near Dundee. The Edinburgh Convention invited him to join the continuing debate or else – somewhat ominously – to 'lay down his arms'. Dundee replied that he was not under arms and that his wife was about to give birth; he requested leave of absence until a date which was convenient to him.

On 30 March the parliamentary Committee of Estates voted that, on account of his contumacy, Dundee would be declared a rebel and a fugitive from justice. On 4 April the Scottish parliament also declared that James had forfeited his Scottish crown and throne and offered the honours to William and Mary which they accepted. That same month, on hearing the news, Dundee raised James's standard on the Law Hill of Dundee and began recruiting an army. In the north several Clan chiefs had reason to support James who, when he was Royal Commissioner for Scotland between 1681 and 1682, had cultivated their friendship and rewarded them with lands belonging to the Marquis of Argyll when he was declared forfeit in 1681. However, Argyll's son, John, 2nd Duke of Argyll had declared for William and Mary and might soon attempt to recover his father's estates. Those Clan chiefs who had benefited from Argyll's misfortune were now fearful of losing their newly acquired property and increased prestige, so they readily answered Dundee's call for support. By now, Dundee had been appointed James's Lieutenant General in Scotland, although the documents confirming his appointment never reached him; the Irish messenger carrying the papers was intercepted, the incriminating documents being confiscated by government agents.[1] Among the Clan chiefs who joined Dundee were MacDonald of Clanranald, MacDonald of Sleat, MacDonald of Glengarry, MacDonald of Keppoch, MacDonald of Glencoe, Maclean of Duart, Stewart of Appin, Ewan Cameron of Lochiel and Macneil of Barra.

First Jacobite Rising, 1689–90

As we have seen, Dundee had been declared an outlaw; the task of bringing him into custody was given to Major General Hugh Mackay of Scourie, an experienced soldier who had led the Scots' Brigade in William of Orange's army against Louis XIV of France in the Wars of Alliance to keep the Netherlands free from French domination. William had not trusted many of his British officers but Mackay was an exception. Mackay was a soldier of whom Bishop Gilbert Burnett of Salisbury once said that he was 'the most pious man that I ever knew in a military way'.[2] With this in mind, William appointed Hugh Mackay as his commander in chief in Scotland.

Mackay immediately turned his mind to crushing Dundee and the rebel Clan chiefs who supported him. Dundee was no easy target; he out-manoeuvered Mackay on his march into the north; Dundee's objective was Glengarry, where he met the Clan chiefs with 1,800 recruits they had raised. It was Dundee's hope to confront Mackay on ground favourable to his Highland levies, weaker by far in numbers than Mackay's well armed, well equipped force of between 3,000 and 4,500.

Killiecrankie

Dundee considered that the soft underbelly of Scotland which would open the way to the Lowlands was Blair Castle owned by the Earl of Atholl. Learning of the approach of Dundee's army, Atholl made a lame excuse to absent himself from his castle, leaving it in the charge of his son and heir, Lord John Murray, a supporter of the Williamite forces. Dundee ordered Patrick Steuart [sic] of Ballechin, a relative of the Murrays, to hold Blair Castle for King James; the result was that Lord John Murray found himself in a strange situation – that of besieging his own castle. While the siege was in progress, Dundee learnt that Mackay was in Perth, intent on assisting Murray in the recapture of Blair Castle.

Dundee laid his plans carefully; he was determined to intercept Mackay at Blair Atholl at a point along the road through the hills. The clans had been

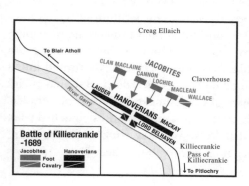

summoned but only Cameron of Lochiel had arrived with 240 Camerons; he had however sent his son and others to Morven, Sunart, Ardnamurchan and the surrounding districts to raise further recruits along the way to Blair Atholl. Ewan Cameron of Lochiel met up with Dundee before Blair Atholl, where they were joined by 300 Irish led by

Major General Cannon. By now Dundee's army numbered 2,400 and he resolved to march against Mackay, intending to confront the government forces in the Pass of Killiecrankie. There Dundee occupied a ridge above the Pass and when Mackay arrived he saw that the Jacobites occupied ground which was favourable to the clan mode of warfare – the Highland Charge. The two sides were unevenly matched; against Dundee's 2,400 were Mackay's 4,500 foot and four troops of horse.[3] Mackay's force consisted of the Earl of Leven's Regiment (his own regiment), Lord Kenmure's Regiment and the regiments commanded by Colonel Balfour, Lieutenant Colonel Hastings and Colonel Ramsay, Lieutenant Colonel Lauder's fusilier regiment, with James Hamilton, 2nd Lord Belhaven commanding the horse. Mackay's left wing was commanded by Lauder's fusiliers, then Balfour's Regiment, and the regiments of Ramsay, Kenmure, Belhaven and the cavalry and the Earl of Leven's Regiment holding the centre; the right wing was held by Mackay and Hastings. Dundee's right wing contained Clan Maclaine of Lochbuie, the Irish and the MacDonalds of Clanranald commanded by Colonel Alexander Cannon, a Lowlander, with Clans Macleod, Grant, the MacDonalds of Glengarry and Glencoe, Clan Morrison and forty horse commanded by Wallace of Craigie, then Cameron of Lochiel; the left wing was held by Clans Maclean of Duart, more MacDonalds and Clan Macneil of Barra. Dundee commanded the right wing. Among the Jacobite army was Rob Roy of Clan Macgregor, renowned for his skill with the broadsword.

The battle began with Mackay deploying his men in a line and ordering his fusiliers to fire on Dundee. Owing to the smaller number of men, the Jacobite line was much shorter than Mackay's so the Williamite army's firepower was concentrated and effective. The Jacobites were also disadvantaged by having the sun in their eyes, so they waited until sunset before attacking Mackay. At 7pm Dundee ordered the charge; the clansmen fired what muskets they possessed then threw them away, charging downhill with targe and broadsword. Mackay increased the rate of fire to counter the charge but a depression in the terrain shielded the advancing clansmen – Lochiel's men to the fore – who slammed into Mackay's centre. The Jacobite charge was so sudden and fast that the government troops did not have time to fix their plug bayonets into the muzzles of their muskets. Dundee's men swatted the unhappy government troops aside like flies. The battle quickly turned into a rout, Mackay fleeing the field, leaving 2,000 of his men dead. But victory did not come without a price; John Graham of Claverhouse, 1st Viscount Dundee, 'Dark John of the Battles', was fatally wounded. Cameron of Lochiel had tried to exact a promise from Dundee that he would stay back from the fight; Dundee would have none of it, begging to give 'one shear darg' [a day's harvest] to King James.[4] Dundee died along with between 600 and 900 of his Highlanders. As for the defeated Hugh Mackay, he would later return to the Continent to command the British Division in the Dutch-British-German army fighting for William of Orange (now William III); in 1692, Mackay was killed at the battle of Steenkirk, Holland.

Dunkeld

The Jacobites' morale was high after Killiecrankie. Dundee's inept successor, Colonel Alexander Cannon, appointed by James VII and II, led the the Jacobite army to the town of Dunkeld, Perthshire, on 21 August. Dunkeld was held by a single regiment of 1,200, the recently mustered Cameronians, Covenanter Lowlanders who who took their name from the Covenanter Reverend Richard Cameron (1648–80). The Cameronians were commanded by Lieutenant Colonel William Cleland who had given the Covenanters their victory over Claverhouse at Drumclog in 1679. Dunkeld not being a walled town, the Cameronians fought in the streets, a mode of fighting alien to the Jacobite Highlanders who were used to charging their foe with broadsword and targe after firing a single volley. Knowing they would not have to face a Highland Charge, the Cameronians had no intention of surrendering; they took up position behind the garden walls of Dunkeld Cathedral and the mansion house of the Duke of Atholl where they withstood a constant fire from the Jacobites ensconced in the nearby cottages. Sadly, in the first hour of the engagement, William Cleland, the hero of Drumclog and participant in Bothwell Brig was fatally wounded by two musket balls. Despite this setback the Cameronians kept up a hot masking fire until they ran out of ammunition when they stripped the lead from the Cathedral roof to make bullets. Then, with burning faggots attached to their pikes, they sallied out from their safe position, setting alight the houses occupied by the Jacobites and locking the doors. (It was said that in one house alone, sixteen Jacobites were burnt alive.) After four hours' fighting, the Jacobite survivors fled.

Cromdale

In May of the following year, Mackay, still in command of the Williamite forces in Scotland was determined to defeat the small Jacobite army commanded by Colonel Cannon. The remnant of the Highland element of the Jacobite force was led by Sir Ewan Cameron of Lochiel who, along with a few other Clan chiefs, wrote to James VII and II, complaining about his dwindling support for the rising. James sent clothing, arms, ammunition and provisions but no reinforcements other than a handful of Irish officers including Major General Buchan who assumed command of the Highland army. James was preoccupied with his invasion of Ireland, a disastrous venture which led to his defeat at the Battle of the Boyne on 1 July 1690* and the final destruction of the Jacobite campaign at Aughrim and Limerick the following year.

Buchan marched his force of 1,200 through Badenoch, hoping to attract more recruits from the Duke of Gordon's estates. The opposite occurred; during the march, 400 of his small force deserted but, undaunted, Buchan proceeded through Speyside, making his camp at Cromdale, east of Grantown-on-Spey on 30 April. There he was confronted by Sir Thomas Livingston, commander of the garrison of Inverness. As Livingston approached Buchan on the opposite bank of the Spey, the Jacobites began to retreat; Livingston's cavalry splashed across the river and attacked Buchan, who made a brief stand until a thick mist thankfully came down from the mountain Creagan a' Chaise; under cover of the fog, Buchan escaped but left 400 dead on the field. The following day about 100 survivors crossed the Spey seeking refuge wherever they might. Livingston caught up with the fugitives on the Moor of Granish, near Aviemore, killing a few and dispersing the rest. In many ways, Cromdale rang the death knell of the Covenant and its diehard supporters who had become an anachronism. The defeat at Cromdale ended the first Jacobite rebellion. The battle is commemorated by a plaque on the side of Cromdale Kirk.

With the death of Bonnie Dundee, the possibility of James VII and II regaining the throne had perished. The Glorious Revolution of 1688 was complete by 1690; that year Hugh Mackay erected a fort at Inverlochy which was named Fort William. Although warfare in the Highlands was now at an end, the disaffected Clan chiefs loyal to James were led to believe that a French fleet would land a force on the west coast of Scotland, a rumour which proved unfounded. As for William III, he cared little for Scotland and her people, regarding it solely as a source of recruits for his armies fighting Catholic France. William's Secretary of State for Scotland, John Dalrymple, the Master of Stair, convinced the King that the residual Clan chiefs could be brought to heel by making an example of one clan – that of Alasdair, the MacIain MacDonald of Glencoe. A proclamation was issued requiring the Clan chiefs to swear allegiance to William III on 1 January 1692.

The MacIain's clan were regarded as little more than cattle thieves, praying on their knees every Sunday and preying on their neighbours the other six days of the week. The clan was described as a thieving tribe, a damnable sept, the worst in all the Highlands. The MacIain went to Fort William to swear his oath but found that the officer in command, Colonel Hill was not empowered

---

* The battle took place on 1 July 1690 under the old or Julian calendar but under the new or Gregorian England calendar adopted in Scotland in 1600, the date became 12 July 1690. England did not adopt the new calendar until 1752, when eleven days were 'removed' in September 1752.

to accept his signature, so MacIain was sent to Inverary, where he duly signed the paper. He was five days' late. In the government's eyes MacIain was already a marked man, having fought in Bonnie Dundee's army at Killiecrankie, the over-riding factor in the Master of Stair's eyes for justifying the subsequent events of February 1692. In London, Dalrymple refused to accept the reason given by MacIain for his failure to submit on 1 January – bad weather – simply because he wanted to make an example that would convince the other Clan chiefs of their folly in supporting the Jacobite cause. He authorized two Campbells – the traditional enemies of the MacDonalds – Major Robert Duncanson and Captain Robert Campbell of Glenlyon to descend on Glencoe 'secret and sudden' to 'root out to purpose'.[5] William III was not informed of Dalrymple's plan; the slaughter of the entire MacDonald clan in Glencoe would serve as a lesson *pour encourager les autres*. On 1 February 1692 Glenlyon and 120 Campbells arrived in Glencoe, announcing his mission as that of tax collector; according to the traditions of Highland hospitality, Glenlyon and his men were wined and dined for the next twelve days. On 12 February Major Duncanson sent Glenlyon this message:

> To Captain Robert Campbell of Glenlyon ' for their Majesties service.' Sir, – You are hereby ordered to fall upon the rebels, the McDonald [sic] of Glencoe, and putt [sic] [all] to the sword under seventy. You are to have special care the old fox [the MacIain] and his sons doe [sic] upon no account escape your hands. You are to secure all the avenues, that no man escape. This you are to put into execution att [sic] five o' clock in the morning [of 13 February] precisely, and by that time, or or very shortly after it, I'll strive to be att [sic] you with a stronger party. If I do not come to you att [sic] five, you are not to tarry for me, but to fall on. This is by the king's special command, for the good and safety of the country, that these miscreants be cutt [sic] off root and branch. See that this is putt [sic] in execution without feud or favour, else you may be expected to be treated as not true to the king's government, not a man fitt [sic] to carry a commission in the king's service. Expecting you will not faill [sic] in the fulfilling hereof as you love yourself, I subscribe thee with my hand.
>
> Robert Duncanson

Ballacholis [Ballachulish], 12 February 1692.[6]

Glencoe

At precisely 5am the bloody work began. MacIain was shot out of hand as he was rising from his bed; his wife was brutally used – a euphemism for rape – and she died within a few hours. Although escape routes had been guarded, several of the MacDonalds managed to evade the Campbells in the snow-covered hills. In all, thirty-eight of the clan were butchered, including two children, two women and an old man of seventy years.[7] Of the massacre of Glencoe, William III wrote to Colonel Hill at Fort William thus:

> There is much talk of it here [London] that they [the MacDonalds] are murdered in their beds after they had taken the allegiance; for the last, I know nothing of it ... all I regret is that any of the sect got away.[8]

As for Dalrymple, he never wrote a word expressing remorse or regret for Glencoe; in his own eyes he had merely carried out his duty to the King.

After Glencoe there was peace in the Highlands, albeit a grudging acceptance of the Williamite monarchy. With a peaceful Scotland in the north and south, the Scottish parliament turned its mind to the expansion of manufactory, trade and commerce, not only with Europe but farther afield. National and international trading was the key, re-invigorating the economy as well as diverting peoples' minds from the scandal of Glencoe. In 1697 a Dumfriesshire financier, William Paterson, founder of the Bank of England, floated the idea of establishing a trading colony on the Isthmus of Darien, or Panama, to establish commerce with South America and Asia. It was a grandiose scheme; at first, English investment in the Darien Company formed in 1695 was robust until the Dutch East India Company put pressure on William III, with the result that English money was withdrawn. Indignant Scots subscribed £400,000, half the capital in the country. In 1698 five ships carrying stores and 1,200 colonists set off for Darien, in territory belonging to the King of Spain. The scheme was a disaster. Disease, fever-ridden swamps and attacks by hostile natives, then Spanish soldiers, took their toll of the colonists. 'New Caledonia' withered on the bough; within two years, the Company of Scotland had collapsed. The severe economic crisis of 1697 had worsened; matters grew worse in the first few years of the eighteenth century, when starvation stared many in the face.

It is perhaps appropriate here to discuss the origins of the Whig and Tory political parties, as these will occur in the text from now on. The terms were introduced into the language in the middle of the seventeenth century. The Whig or Whiggamore term is believed to derive from a command given by carters to their horses, urging them to move faster; the carters came from the south-west of Scotland. The word applied to the carters themselves and to the extremist Covenanters who, in 1648, marched from the south-west to Edinburgh in what was known as *The Whiggamore Raid*. From that time 'Whig' was a contemptuous term applied to extreme Presbyterians, then those who opposed Charles II and finally a cognomen ridiculing the Opposition party in parliament, those who denied the divine right of monarchs in the reign of William III, then Anne. The Whigs supported the Glorious Revolution , the Act of Settlement in 1701, the war with France and opposed a Stuart restoration. The Tory party took its name from Irishmen dispossessed of their lands and declared outlaws; the Whigs accused the Tories of relying on Irish Catholic support for the restoration of the Stuarts.

With the death of William III in 1702, his sister-in-law Anne, daughter of James VII and II succeeded him, the last of the Stuart dynasty to occupy the throne. William, never popular in Scotland and even less so after Glencoe and his blocking of the Darien Scheme, still harboured fears of a Stuart attempt to regain the throne. However, Anne was Protestant, as was her husband George, younger brother of Christian V of Denmark. In 1701 the English parliament had passed the Act of Settlement under which Sophie of Hanover, Charles II's cousin, would succeed Anne if she died childless, which she did; the intention was to deny the crown to a Catholic Stuart. William's fears were reflected in the English parliament, especially when in 1703, the Scottish parliament passed an act which declared that on Anne's death, Scotland would have the right to pursue an independent foreign policy. Many interpreted this as a tacit warning that the Scots could conceivably choose James Francis Edward Stuart as their king, a fear which was not without some foundation.

When the Treaty of Union uniting the two parliaments was signed in 1707 the mood in Scotland was one of both anger and frustration. The most vociferous of opponents, James Hamilton, 2nd Lord Belhaven and his colleague, Andrew Fletcher of Saltoun were in the minority; most of the nobles and gentry who voted for union had lost considerable fortunes in the failure of Darien and saw advantages in union England. In 1707 the majority of the people of Scotland did not want union; the nation's security was threatened by disturbances in the south-west, Ayrshire and the Highlands; in the last case, the Presbyterian Duke of Atholl made his views known throughout the north. In that year of 1707 the seeds of a second Jacobite rebellion were sown.

At the end of February 1708, alarming news reached London; France was preparing to invade England with James VII and II at the head of an army. At the time there were only 1,500 Royalist troops in Scotland, ill fed, ill equipped and unpaid. On 17 March the invasion force sailed from Dunkirk; the fleet consisted of five ships of the line, twenty-one frigates and two transports carrying 6,000 men. It was James's intention to land at Leith and capture Edinburgh, where only token resistance was expected. However, after some navigational problems, the French fleet did not drop anchor in the Firth of Forth until 23 March; the following day, before the landing could take place, the English fleet commanded by Admiral Sir George Byng appeared. Byng had been shadowing the French fleet commanded by Admiral Forbin since his departure from Dunkirk. Drawing his fleet up in battle formation, a procedure which took time and was dependent on favourable winds, Forbin slipped past Byng and made for the open sea. Thus *L'Enterprise d'Ecosse* came to a close; James, the Chevalier of St George to his friends, the Old Pretender to his enemies, had to slink back to France, having achieved nothing.[9]

When Queen Anne died in 1714 without heirs, George, Elector of Hanover became George I of Britain through his mother, Sophie of Hanover. The Whig party was jubilant, the Tory party despondent, as the majority of their supporters regarded the son of James VII and II the rightful heir to the throne. The proclamation of George I in Edinburgh on 5 August 1714 was, to say the least, disconcerting to the Jacobites. Unrest was growing, particularly in the Highlands; on 15 September 1714 a reward of £100,000 was offered for the apprehension of the Old Pretender should he set foot in any part of Britain.[10] A General Election took place in February 1715, the Scots returning an overwhelming Whig majority. The Jacobites were now openly challenging George I and his government, declaring it unlawful. A correspondent to John Forbes of Culloden, a wealthy landowner in Invernesshire wrote that:

'the vanity, insolence, arrogance and madness of the Jacobites is beyond all measure insupportable ...'

The writer proceeded to point out that Edinburgh was swarming 'with Papists and Jacobites' and that 'saddles were being manufactured in the capital for the use of dragoons in the Pretender's service'.[11] In March the same correspondent wrote that the Pretender was expected any day and that his supporters were ready.[12] During the next few months George I announced to parliament that the country faced grave danger and the reward of £100,000 for the apprehension of James was renewed. As a precaution the army and the Royal Navy were put on a war-footing; twenty-one new regiments were formed and the trained-bands (militia) were ordered to maintain a state of readiness. Sir George Warrender of Lochend, near Dunbar, Whig politician and lately Provost of Edinburgh – he had given up the latter appointment to take his seat in the House of Lords – wrote to the city fathers in Edinburgh, advising them how to keep control in Edinburgh. (An attempt by local Jacobites to take Edinburgh Castle in September prompted Sir George to urge Westminster to provide regular troops to be stationed in the capital during the emergency.)[13]

On 2 August John Erskine, 11th Earl of Mar* left London for the north, his intention being to send the Fiery Cross throughout the Highlands – the

---

* Mar was actually the 23rd Earl of Mar to hold the title, but the eleventh of the name Erskine.

traditional way of raising the clans – to gather in James Francis Edward Stuart's name. Mar had earned his soubriquet 'Bobbing John' on account of his predilection for changing sides when the mood and political climate suited him. He had been a Privy Councillor in William III's Scottish parliament, an adherent of James, 2nd Duke of Queensberry, who had been virtually alone in seeking the Treaty of Union as early as 1702 during Queen Anne's reign; Queensberry voted for union, Mar deserted him, then subsequently rejoined him. Mar was one of the principal movers in forming the Treaty of Union, then he changed his mind, confessing he regretted his actions. He had also been in correspondence with James Francis Edward Stuart for four years before Queen Anne's death in 1714. Next, Mar was fulsome in his praise and enthusiasm for the accession of the Hanoverian King George I. In an age when 'versatility' in politics was commonplace, Mar made a career of it; today, he is held in contempt by modern historians, not for his frequent changes of heart but because he courted first Anne, then George in the hope that these monarchs would fulfil his aims and ambitions in the power stakes, enriching himself along the way. However, George I had been fully briefed about Mar's deviousness; the King knew that Mar had been 'passed over', (to use a modern civil service term) for the important and lucrative post of Secretary of State for Scotland, a position that went to the Duke of Montrose. A further rebuff came when Mar was deprived of the custody of Stirling Castle which, as he took pains to inform Montrose, had been an hereditary Mar appointment for hundreds of years.[14] To whom else could Mar turn to seek redress of these real or imagined wrongs and insults but James Stuart, the Old Pretender?

Mar was soon in communication with every important Jacobite in Scotland. He summoned several Clan chiefs to Aboyne on 26 August where he outlined his plans for a campaign against the Hanoverian king and his government. Among those who responded were the Marquis of Huntly, eldest son of the Duke of Gordon, the Marquis of Tulliebardine, eldest son of the Duke of Atholl, George Keith, 10th Earl Marischal, James Carnegie, 5th Earl Southesk, James Maule, 4th Earl of Panmure, John Lyon, 5th Earl of Strathaven and Kinghorne, Earls Carnwath, Errol, Nithsdale, Traquair, William, 5th Earl of Seaforth and head of Clan Mackenzie, the Earl of Linlithgow and James Ogilvy, the future Earl of Airlie. (The sons of John Murray, 1st Duke of Atholl, a Hanoverian to the core, defied their father; Charles, George and William Murray declared for James.) Mar was possessed of a persuasive, silver tongue and soon won any remaining waverers over. After presenting his credentials from the Pretender, Mar agreed to raise the Royal Standard on 6 September at Castleton, Braemar where James Francis Edward Stuart was proclaimed King of Great Britain and Ireland.

Second Jacobite Rising, 1715

Like so many attempts to regain the throne for the Stuarts between 1688 and 1746, the 'Fifteen was beset by abysmal leadership. As James's commander in chief, Mar was notoriously unsteady; the extent of his incompetence will shortly become apparent. For its part, the Hanoverian government in London passed 'An Act for Encouraging Loyalty in Scotland' on 30 August, commonly known as the Clan Act. Under the terms of the measure, every Crown vassal found guilty of treasonable correspondence with the Pretender would forfeit his estates; furthermore, if the tenants of the guilty person remained loyal to the House of Hanover, they would live rent-free for two years. The effect of the Act was the opposite of what it set out to achieve; the hitherto wavering estate owners were driven to join Mar. The clans who answered Mar's call to arms included the Lochiel Camerons, the Campbells of Breadalbane and Glenlyon, the MacDonalds of Clanranald, the Mackenzies, Macleans, Macleods, Frasers and Gordons.

Mar had but sixty supporters at Braemar on 6 September; however, by the middle of the month, he was strong enough to capture Inverness – or rather, his associate Lachlan Mackintosh of Borlum did with 500 of his clansmen. The towns of Aberdeen, Dundee and Brechin favoured the Pretender and proclaimed their loyalty, enabling Mar to march south, reinforced by 4,000 Murray of Atholl and Campbell of Breadalbane clansmen. On 28 September Mar occupied the important town of Perth, which became the headquarters of the Rising. By this move Mar was able to prevent the forces loyal to the House of Hanover in the north and south from joining. On the surface all was progressing favourably; however, a shadow had appeared on the horizon on 1 September with the death of Louis XIV of France, the Pretender's staunchest Continental ally. The regent Duke of Orleans who governed France during Louis XV's minority made peaceable overtures to England with the result that the French ships equipped with men and arms, ammunition and gunpowder were de-commissioned. During the entire period of the 'Fifteen, not a single French musket reached Scotland.

The townships south of the Firth of Forth remained unswervingly loyal to George I and associations of volunteers were formed in the towns and the country districts. General Wretham was appointed commander in chief of the forces loyal to the Hanoverian king in Scotland; he made his headquarters in Stirling which gave him control of the main passages across the river Forth. However, a more distinguished and influential commander than Wretham was needed to rally the Hanoverian supporters in Scotland. That man was John Campbell, 2nd Duke of Argyll, a staunch supporter and mover of the Treaty of Union in 1707. Argyll had also distinguished himself in Flanders in the Williamite war against France, serving under the famous John Churchill,

Duke of Marlborough. Those Scottish magnates who supported the House of Hanover – the Duke of Roxburghe, the Marquises of Tweeddale and Annandale, the Earls of Selkirk, Loudon, Rothes, Haddington and Forfar – were ostensibly loyal but due to their animosity towards the Campbell clan, many refused to co-operate with Argyll. Argyll reached Stirling on 17 September where he reviewed his small force of 1,800 which was subsequently reinforced by 2,000 troops and volunteers from Glasgow and other towns. The Glasgow Volunteers under the command of Colonel John Blackadder were set to guard the old bridge of Stirling, remaining as rearguard when Argyll marched out of Stirling to confront Mar. (It will be remembered that Colonel Blackadder's father, the Reverend John Blackadder, the celebrated Covenanter minister and Martyr died in prison on the Bass Rock and was buried in the Church of St Andrew, North Berwick.)[15, 16] Then the Earl of Sutherland, loyal to George I mustered an army in the north which Mar later gave as his reason for declining to invade southern Scotland.

By October Mar's army numbered 12,000. On the day he had entered Perth, he had received a formal commission from the Pretender appointing him commander in chief of the Jacobite forces in Scotland. In many ways, this was the proverbial poisoned chalice, given the uncertainty of the resolve of his largely Highland force; one of the Jacobite officers made it known that the Highlanders would desert for three reasons – (1) if they were not committed to battle soon; (2) if they gained booty from a victory and; (3) if Mar was defeated. Mar kept his men interested by paying them regularly, the money coming from levying a charge on communities from Fife to the Moray Firth; he justified this unpopular measure by informing the town fathers that his treasure chest had not been enriched by any contributions from the Pretender, which must have led some to doubt the wisdom of their support.

Apart from minor skirmishing and raids there was no major confrontation between Mar and Argyll until November, when Mar emerged from Perth intending to cross the Forth and attack Argyll in Stirling. On 10 November Argyll received word of Mar's movements; two days later he marched out of Stirling by way of Dunblane, intending to confront Mar at Sheriffmuir, which he reached on the evening of 12 November. Mar proceeded to Auchterarder, then to the old Roman camp at Ardoch, making his camp at Kinbuck, about two miles from Sheriffmuir. The following morning Mar deployed his forces in battle formation before Argyll's position.

Sheriffmuir
On 13 November, a Sunday, Mar's army of 12,000 advanced towards Argyll's lesser force of about 6,000 which overlooked the road over which Mar was advancing. Argyll's left wing was commanded by General Wightman, the centre

by General Wretham; the entire
Hanoverian line was shorter than
Mar's on account of their smaller
numbers. Battle commenced with
Argyll's right wing, commanded by
himself, subjected to a murderous
fire. Undaunted, Argyll sent a
detachment under Colonel Cathcart
to attack Mar's left flank which had
the desired effect; Argyll's right wing
kept up a withering fire until the
entire left wing of the Jacobite army

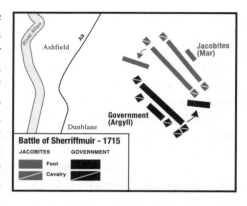

collapsed. The survivors greatly outnumbered those of Cathcart's men who
pursued them; they attempted several times to rally but without success,
dispersing after three hours of flight. Meanwhile, Mar's right wing vigorously
attacked General Wightman on Argyll's left wing; the wing collapsed in the face
of a Highland charge by Clans MacDonald, Maclean and the Breadalbane
Campbells which drove both Royalist foot and horse back in confusion. Mar's
victorious right wing took up position on the Stony Hill of Kippendavie where,
incredulously, they remained inactive while Argyll's right wing pursued the
other half of Mar's army. Argyll then joined forces with General Wightman but,
with only between 1,000 and 2,000 troops, he felt unable to attack Mar's 4,000
men on the rocky eminence. Neither side was willing to resume the battle, so
Argyll retired to Dunblane to re-group his by now scattered forces. By the
following morning Mar and his army had disappeared. Losses sustained by Mar
were 663 killed (including Alan, 13th Chief of the MacDonalds of Clanranald),
wounded, missing and captured, among the last being the Earl of Panmure.
(Panmure was executed in February 1716 for high treason.) Argyll's losses were
232 killed, wounded and captured.

Sheriffmuir was an inconclusive battle, both sides claiming victory,
although the result was conclusive insofar as Argyll's tactical success. The
Royalist press, notably the recently-established *Glasgow Courant*, trumpeted
on 14 November that 'His Grace the Duke of Argyll obtain'd an Intire
Victory over the Rebels in Sheriff Moor, a mile north of Dumblain.'[17] A
Royalist officer wrote to Colonel Blackadder in Stirling on 16 November, as
follows:

By a Royalist to Colonel Blackater [sic]: on the field near Dunblane our
right wing beat their left and their right wing our left. Their army was
reckoned 9 or 10000 men. Ours was not above 3400. Fifteen hundred of our
right wing chased 5000 of their left two or three miles. We have the marks

of victory. We have taken 14 colours and Standards, 4 of their cannon and about 100 prisoners.[18]

Mar's official despatch to Colonel Balfour, Governor of Perth states the following: 'We attacked the enemy on the end of the Sheriff Muir, carried the day entirely, pursued them down to a little hill on the south of Dunblane.'[19] In strategic terms, the day had been Argyll's as he had effectively blocked Mar's progress into the Lowlands, Mar being forced to retreat to Perth. A grateful government awarded those Royalist regiments containing the word 'King's' in their battalion designation a badge in the form of a white horse, the insignia of the House of Hanover. Discouraged by the loss of territory to the pro-government clans of Sutherland, Ross, Munro and Forbes and the deaths of Jacobite leaders such as John Lyon, 5th Earl of Strathaven and Kinghorne, Alan MacDonald of Clanranald and the capture of the Earl of Panmure, the dispirited Jacobite army melted away rapidly At Sheriffmuir, Mar had committed a grave error – that of allowing Argyll's army to march away intact, being afraid to risk his command.

On 23 December James Stuart landed at Peterhead even though the 'Fifteen was all but lost. He met Mar at Perth but was unable to convince him to undertake further campaigns, nor inspire his by now much reduced army. What was left of Mar's command retreated via Montrose and Ruthven, where the clansmen disbanded. Mar received a further blow when he learnt that Argyll's army had been reinforced by 6,000 Dutch troops; Mar made an approach to Argyll seeking terms but Argyll was unable to accommodate him; nothing short of unconditional surrender would satisfy George I. Sheriffmuir effectively put on hold the Jacobite cause for the next four years. As for 'Bobbing John', Earl of Mar, his estates were forfeited and he was forced into exile. Sheriffmuir gave rise to a popular ballad:

> There's some say that we wan [won], and some say that they wan,
> and some say that nane [none] wan at 'a man,
> but ane [one] thing I'm sure, that at Sheriffmuir,
> a battle there was that I saw, man,
> and we ran and they ran, and they ran and we ran
> and we ran as they ran awa' [away], man.[20]

A cairn monument to the Clan Macrae who fought on the left wing of Mar's army was erected on the site of the battle in 1915 with a plaque added later by the 1745 Association.

The spectre of Jacobitism in Scotland refused to go away even if by 1719 the cause had become something of a sideshow overshadowed by events in

Europe. The signing of the Treaty of Utrecht in 1712–13 brought to a close the War of the Spanish Succession which gave the crown of Spain to Philip of Anjou, grandson of Louis XIV. The various belligerent powers including England received territories by way of compensation for expenses incurred by the war; England received Gibraltar and Minorca from Spain, Nova Scotia, Newfoundland and Hudson's Bay in Canada and St Kitts in the West Indies from France. France also recognized the Hanoverian succession in Britain and undertook not to unite the crowns of France and Spain. However, Philip of Anjou, now Philip V of Spain, was determined to regain Spain's standing in Europe by invading Sardinia and Sicily in 1717–18. The British government responded by declaring these actions a violation of the Peace of Utrecht and despatched the Royal Navy to confront a Spanish fleet off Syracuse, Sicily, where Philip's navy was destroyed. Philip then declared war on Britain; his chief adviser, Cardinal Guilio Alberoni took the initiative by stirring up rebellion in Britain to forestall an attack on mainland Spain. Alberoni's plan was to exploit the matter of succession to the British throne by encouraging and supporting the Jacobites Highland Clan chiefs, claiming that James Francis Edward Stuart, James VIII and III (James's father James VII and II had died in 1701) and not George I was the rightful King of Britain. In doing so, Alberoni intended not only to destabilize the British throne but also to install a compliant king and parliament favourable to Spanish interests.

Third Jacobite Rising, 1719
In December 1718 James Butler, 2nd Duke of Ormonde, the most important of the exiled Jacobites was invited to join Alberoni in Madrid where plans were laid. Alberoni's strategy was two-pronged; he proposed that George Keith, 10th Earl Marischal would land in Scotland with 300 Spanish marines to raise the Highland clans in the west; at the same time, a fleet of twenty-seven ships and 7,000 troops commanded by Ormonde would invade either south England or Wales where there were Jacobite sympathizers of significant number. Unfortunately, Ormonde's fleet was badly damaged and dispersed in a storm off Cape Finisterre, most of the Spanish ships having to take refuge in various Spanish ports. As for France, Scotland's traditional ally, the regent Duke of Orleans still ruled the country and found it suited his foreign policy to remain friends with England, so the Jacobites could not expect any aid from that quarter.

Keith, Earl Marischal, one of the principal leaders in the 'Fifteen left Spain on 8 March; he landed on the Isle of Lewis early in April where he was joined by the exiled Earl of Seaforth, William Mackenzie, 5th Chief of that clan and the Marquess of Tulliebardine, both of whom had set sail from le Havre. As usual, the leadership squabbles which plagued all four Jacobite rebellions erupted almost immediately; Tulliebardine argued that he, not Keith, should command the Jacobite forces, which Keith conceded. Then there was further disagreement about strategy; Tulliebardine advocated delay, Keith argued for immediate action on the mainland. Because of their squabbling, a landing was not effected until 13 April, on an islet at the mouth of Loch Duich, Ross-shire. Keith had brought 2,000 muskets, ammunition and gunpowder for distribution to the Clan chiefs who unfortunately did not provide the anticipated number of recruits; no doubt the debacle of the 'Fifteen affected their decision, prompting the Clan chiefs to hedge their bets on the success of Ormonde's invasion in the south of England which, of course, had been aborted. News of this setback convinced the waverers that it would be imprudent to become involved in the rebellion and put at risk their lands and titles to no purpose. The 'Nineteen was doomed from the start.

Tulliebardine and Keith established their headquarters at Eilean Donan Castle, Loch Duich. Among those who came to Eilean Donan were John Cameron of Lochiel and Lord George Murray, second son of the pro-Hanoverian Duke of Atholl, along with a few Irish officers. Over the next few days, Tulliebardine and Keith were joined by a few hundred Highlanders from Clans Macrae and Macgregor, Rob Roy Macgregor, one of the most celebrated freebooters in Scotland's history, being among the latter. Heartened by the growing army, Tulliebardine – still reluctant to take action – and Keith marched from Eilean Donan Castle to recruit more clansmen with a view to capturing Inverness. The two Jacobite leaders agreed that they should leave a small garrison at Eilean Donan to guard the stores of gunpowder and ammunition. The garrison comprised between forty and fifty Spanish marines; occupying the castle as a base was a prudent move but storing the bulk of the ammunition and gunpowder there would prove to be a major tactical error.

By now the government had received news of the Jacobite landing in the area of Skye and Lochalsh and despatched five Royal Navy frigates to patrol the seas there in the first week of May. On 10 May, three of the warships anchored off Eilean Donan Castle; learning that the rebels were ensconced there, the ships' captains attempted to negotiate with the garrison which promptly fired on the small ships' boat carrying the negotiators, forcing them to withdraw. The captains of the frigates HMS *Worcester*, HMS *Flamborough* and HMS *Enterprise* returned the fire, bombarding the castle for about an hour. The following evening, under cover of a heavy cannonade, sailors and marines stormed ashore in the ships' small boats, taking the garrison prisoner, along with about 400 barrels of gunpowder and ammunition. The frigates spent the next two days reducing Eilean Donan Castle to ruins. HMS *Flamborough* took on board the Spanish prisoners and set sail for Leith.[21]

Cut off from escape by sea – even if they had possessed ships – the Jacobite army failed to recruit more than about 1,000 clansmen; hardly a few miles away from Eilean Donan, Tulliebardine and Keith were still intent on capturing Inverness, despite the news of Ormonde's aborted invasion in south England. On 5 June a government army led by General Joseph Wightman who had been present on the field of Sheriffmuir advanced south from Inverness to confront Tulliebardine and Keith; Wightman's force numbered 850 foot, 150 dragoons, 130 clansmen and six coehorn mortars. Wightman faced Tulliebardine and Keith at Glenshiel, a lonely spot a few miles south of Loch Duich, near the Five Sisters Hills.

Glenshiel

The valley of Glenshiel was good terrain, favourable to the Jacobite Highlanders who, if they could not execute the famous Highland Charge, were adept in sniping at their enemies from concealed positions behind boulders, birch trees and bushes. The Glen had a drovers' road which crossed the river Shiel by the contemporary single-arched stone bridge, an example of which is so beloved of modern tourists visiting the Highlands. At that point, the shoulder of a hill projects into the glen, causing it to narrow to a gorge. The shoulder was covered with heather, bracken and birch trees, offering ideal protection for musketeers. The Jacobites also strengthened their position by digging entrenchments on the contours of the hill to the north of the Shiel river; they also erected a stout barricade across the drove road that ran the length of the glen between the river and the entrenched hill. On high ground south of the river, the right flank of the Jacobite position was held by Lord George Murray, a boy of only fourteen years in command of elements of Clan Murray. To Murray's left, the centre was held by 250 Spanish marine regulars commanded by Colonel Don Nicolas Bolano. To Bolano's left were positioned Cameron of Lochiel's men, supported by Rob Roy Macgregor and forty of his clan. The line continued with Clan Mackenzie, commanded by Sir John Mackenzie of Coul, the Campbells of Ormdale and the Mackintoshes. On the extreme left flank, William Mackenzie, Earl of Seaforth was stationed on a steep incline. Facing the Jacobites was General Wightman's force of English and Scottish troops. Wightman's right wing was commanded by Colonel Jasper Clayton with his force of grenadiers, two battalions of foot, a Dutch regiment and companies from Clans Fraser, Sutherland and Mackay. The flank of Wightman's right wing rested on the road and the river Sheil held by his 150 dismounted dragoons. The weaker left wing was held by Colonel Clayton's own regiment commanded by Colonel Reading with eighty men of Captain George Munro of Culcairn's clansmen and the six coehorn mortars.

The engagement began between 5pm and 6pm, when Wightman's mortars lobbed shells into Murray's men on the right wing of the Jacobite army. Clayton's regiment supported by the men of Clan Munro attacked Murray but were repulsed until Murray's position was compromised by steady fire from Clayton's men, compelling him to withdraw to an exposed position which he had to abandon. Lacking sufficient men to attack the Hanoverian left wing, the Jacobite right wing was now vulnerable to attack. Murray's unsupported 150 men were forced to retreat. Now Wightman ordered his right wing forward against Seaforth on the Jacobite left; Seaforth's men occupied a strong position sheltered by rocks, but they gave way before they could be reinforced. All the while, Wightman's mortars had pounded the Jacobite front line, pinning down the Spanish marines in the Jacobite centre. The 250 or so Spaniards held their own until they saw their Highland allies deserting in droves; they had no other option but to surrender at 9pm. Wightman's losses at Glenshiel were negligible, with twenty-one dead and 100 wounded. On the Jacobite side, casualties were 100 dead, many wounded and most of the Spaniards taken prisoner. Three of the Jacobite commanders were seriously wounded – Lord George Murray, the Earl of Seaforth and Rob Roy Macgregor, although all three survived to fight another day. Cameron of Lochiel went into exile in France, the Earl Marischal to Prussia; the latter never returned to Scotland. The Spanish prisoners were taken to Edinburgh to be re-united with their compatriots from Eilean Donan Castle; all 274 were repatriated to Spain in October 1719.[22] Glenshiel was fought on the thirty- first birthday of James Francis Edward Stuart, recognized as James VIII and III of Britain by both France and Spain. On 1 September, James married Clementina Sobieska of Poland; a year later, she presented him with a son, Charles Edward Louis John Casimir Sylvester Maria – a mouthful for any registrar of births' book – better known in Scotland's history as Bonnie Prince Charlie, the Young Pretender.

Here, it must be said that the political history of Scotland between 1715 and 1719 was a period of government unacceptable to her people. Many unpopular measures were introduced by the Hanoverian parliament, beginning in 1715 when the government passed the Disarming Act forbidding the carrying of weapons in public but not banning their possession. The year 1716 began with the execution of the Earl of Panmure in February for his part in the 'Fifteen. Equally unpopular was the transfer on 3 September of thirty-nine Jacobite prisoners incarcerated in Edinburgh Castle to Carlisle where they were tried under English law. This incident was deplored by Scottish Whigs and Tories alike, as well as the majority of the population. A further bone of contention was the composition of the Commission set up to deal with the sale of estates forfeited by landowners who had taken part in or sympathized with the Jacobite rebellion in 1715. Four of the six Commissioners were Englishmen and members of the House of Commons, not the House of Lords. Sir John Dalrymple the Lord Advocate was against the punitive Commission; he advised the government that the proprietors should be pardoned but fined.

The government rejected Dalrymple's advice as being a clear indication that Jacobitism was still rife in Scotland. The Commission laboured under Scots law to meet its obligations; their efforts brought the government little by way of profit. The sale of the forfeited estates totalled £84,043; offset against that sum were the expenses of the Commissioners which totalled £82,956, leaving a meagre profit of £1,087. Perhaps the government might have gained more had they heeded Dalrymple's advice.

During the three Jacobite rebellions, the government failed to appreciate that it was not fighting solely against Jacobite sympathizers but the old complaint before and since the Union: the Scots resented English meddling in their domestic affairs. In 1725, the Anglo-Irish soldier General George Wade was placed in command of Scotland's security; between 1725 and 1737, Wade built over 250 miles of military roads and forty bridges in the central and western Highlands, not for the benefit of the local populace but the government. Should the Jacobite threat ever raise its ugly head again, the government would be able to quickly suppress any rising. Only time would tell whether this was a wise development.

Notes

1. Ross, *The Killing Time*, p243.
2. Holmes, Richard, *Marlborough*, p172.
3. Hill, *Celtic Warfare* 1595-1763.
4. Drummond, *Memoirs of Sir Ewen Cameron of Lochiel*, p276 (Abbotsford Club, Edinburgh 1842).
5. *Papers Illustrative of the Condition of the Highlands of Scotland*, pp67 and 71 (Maitland Club, 1845).
6. Douglas, *The Scots Book*, p318
7. Hume Brown, *History of Scotland*, vol. iii, p20.
8. Quoted in Mackay, A J, *A Memoir of Sir James Dalrymple, 1st Viscount Stair* (Edinburgh, 1873).
9. According to G Burnett, *History of His Own Time* (Oxford, 1823-33).
10. Hume Brown, op. cit., vol. iii, p157.
11. *Culloden Papers* (1625-1748), pp34 and 37 (London, 1815).
12. Ibid., p42.
13. Pugh, *Swords, Loaves and Fishes: A History of Dunbar*, p327; *Warrender Letters*, The Correspondence of Sir George Warrender of Lochend, Dunbar, Lord Provost of Edinburgh, 1715.
14. Hume Brown, op. cit., vol. iii, p160.
15. Brotchie, *The Battlefields of Scotland*, p206 footnote.
16. Pugh, op. cit., p73.
17. Brotchie, op. cit., p207 footnote.
18. Ibid. p208 footnote.
19. Ibid.
20. Quoted in Brotchie, op. cit., p209.
21. Dickson, *The Jacobite Attempt in 1719*.
22. Hume Brown, op. cit., vol. iii, p198.

Chapter 12

Jacobites: 1745–1746

Between 1719 and 1745 the political scene in Scotland was dominated by two factions. One was known as the *Squadrone Volante* (The Flying Squad), led by the Marquis of Tweeddale and the Duke of Roxburghe; the adherents of this party described themselves as independent patriots, Tories and Jacobites. Opposing them was the the faction which looked to John Campbell, 2nd Duke of Argyll ('Red John of the Battles' on account of his participation in several of the battles of the War of the Spanish Succession and the battle of Sherrifmuir). Argyll's party was known as the *Argathelians*, Argathelia being Latin for Argyll; the Argathelian faction was predominantly Whig and supported the House of Hanover. Argyll had supported the accession of George I. Along with his brother, Archibald Campbell, Lord Islay, Lord Chief Justice of Scotland, Argyll virtually ruled Scotland; Islay founded the Royal Bank of Scotland in 1727.[1]

In the General Election of 1722, the Whig party gained a large majority in the House of Commons. Argyll and Sir Robert Walpole worked together in the administration of Scotland although their different temperaments made them dislike each other intensely. Walpole, regarded as Britain's first prime minister, was a staunch Whig and what Dr Samuel Johnston would have described as a 'clubbable man'; possessed of a coarse wit and cheerful disposition, Walpole was loose in his morals and inelegant in his general manner. Argyll was a man of entirely different stamp, aristocratic, cultured, well-read, haughty, impetuous, selfish with an almost feudal sense of his superiority over the common man, although he treated his own household servants with respect. The writer Jonathan Swift described him as a petty intriguer, a greedy courtier and a factious patriot.

It became government policy to play the rival Squadrone Volante and Argathelian factions against each other, employing the age-old principle of divide and rule. From the accession of George I in 1714, the Tory Squadrone faction considered itself the most likely to enjoy royal favour and for a few years this was the case. However, in Scotland, it soon became obvious that the Argathelian Whig faction enjoyed the support of the majority of the nation; Argyll went from strength to strength, particularly after Sheriffmuir. In 1719, Argyll was appointed High Steward of the [Royal] Household, then he was elevated to Duke of Greenwich in 1720. When Walpole became Chancellor of the Exchequer and *ex officio* Prime Minister, the Argathelian faction exercised an authority in England which it had not hitherto enjoyed. However, it was not long before Argyll and Walpole clashed over the latter's fiscal policy in relation to Scotland. For example, in June 1725 Walpole levied a tax on every barrel of ale brewed in Scotland, a measure which Walpole believed would be more acceptable to the Scots than the hated Malt Tax they had resisted in 1713. The new tax was seen as a devious English imposition, an attempt to rob the poor man of his daily ale. Riots occurred, notably in Glasgow, a town which had proved the most loyal of the Scottish burghs to the Hanoverian government; the Edinburgh brewers took a more sanguine approach by refusing to brew ale until the obnoxious tax was repealed. The Squadrone's foremost adherents, the Duke of Roxburghe, Secretary of State for Scotland and Henry Dundas, the Lord Advocate also protested against the tax. Walpole resolved this problem by first removing Dundas from office, then Roxburghe and abolishing the post of Secretary of State for Scotland in 1725. Henceforth, Scotland would be administered by an English Secretary of State. (The post of Scottish Secretary would be reinstated a few years later, then abolished again in 1746 until 1885.) The new Lord Advocate, Duncan Forbes of Culloden received the news of Roxburghe's dismissal with ill-concealed delight. In principle, responsibility for Scottish affairs was given to an English minister; in practice, Scotland was administered by Archibald Campbell, Lord Islay, Argyll's brother, known as 'the King of Scotland'.

As for northern Scotland, measures were introduced in 1725 to ensure peace would be maintained in the Highlands, still regarded as a hotbed of Jacobitism. Lord Advocate Forbes introduced an Act for Disarming the Highlands as the previous act of 1715 had been largely ignored. Forbes's measure was based on a report by General George Wade who had surveyed the Highlands in 1725. Wade was appointed commander in chief of the army in Scotland; his mission was to keep the unruly north pacified which Wade believed would be achieved by the creation of several forts linked by good military roads.

When George II ascended the throne in 1727 on the death of his father, he retained his father's ministers, the Argathelians remaining the predominant faction; even so, Argyll and his brother Islay had become unpopular on account of their autocratic, overbearing hold in Scotland. Their unpopular policies drove many to join the Squadrone faction which began to attract Tory and Jacobite peers and commoners. By 1733, the Squadrone faction had grown strong enough to challenge the Opposition, entertaining hopes of a majority in the General Election of 1734. Although neither faction achieved their desired majority, the Argathelians continued to enjoy the support of Walpole despite their unpopularity in Scotland. In 1741, another General Election brought the Squadrone faction to power; the Duke of Argyll defected to the rival faction, chiefly on account of the animosity between himself and Walpole. As for Walpole, he resigned from the House of Commons; on his departure, the Marquis of Tweeddale was appointed to the revived office of Secretary of State for Scotland. Argyll had lost his former authority, power and credibility in Scotland; when he criticized Tweeddale's administration of Scotland, the English Secretary of State, Baron John Carteret, bluntly informed Argyll that Scotland would now be governed differently. Argyll's ego was bruised; his haughty temperament could not bear the humiliation and in March 1741 he resigned from the House of Lords. Argyll had dominated Scottish politics for seventeen years; in that time he had been criticized by his enemies for putting his own interests and those of his party first and favouring English interests at the expense of Scotland. On 27 May 1742, Argyll delivered his farewell speech in the Lords, retiring to his birthplace in Sudbrooke, Surrey where he died on 4 October 1743.[2]

In the period 1707 to 1744, Scotland's disaffection with England and the London government was not only political but geographical; the Scots felt that Westminster was too far removed from Edinburgh which they rightly believed meant that they were being overlooked and dismissed by their supposed partner; for its part, England regarded Scotland as a nation which from the thirteenth century had been the cause of so many wars in the past and more recently the Jacobite uprisings. Since 1707, to many Englishmen, Scotland had become little more than a colony, her political voice irrelevant, her people backward, particularly in the Highlands which were considered bordering on the barbaric, a region disposed to rebellion, discreetly and openly seeking the return of the Stuart dynasty. The Jacobites believed that the return of James VIII and III would restore Scotland's prestige and greatness; the events of 1745 would certainly confirm the views of the English regarding the exiled Pretender to the throne.

The main agent for the Jacobite cause in Scotland was George Lockhart who had been approached by the Old Pretender in 1718 to keep him appraised of developments in Scotland. Lockhart remained in constant correspondence with the Jacobite court in Versailles and St Germain-en-Laye until 1727. By then Lockhart had come to the conclusion that the Jacobite cause was dead in the water and so he retired from public life. There had always been the hope that events in Europe might raise enemies against England who would re-kindle the Stuart cause; by 1727 there seemed virtually no prospect of this occurring and Lockhart, together with many supporters of the exiled House of Stuart, had lost any surviving confidence in James Francis Edward Stuart's ability to regain his throne. Under Walpole's guidance, England continued to remain free from policies which might lead to war with Europe. However, a key moment arrived in 1739 with the outbreak of the War of the Austrian Succession which offered hopes of a Jacobite revival in the same way that the War of the Spanish Succession had provided an opportunity for the Jacobite disruption of 1708.

It all began with the affair known as the *War of Jenkins's Ear*, an incident which would not have been out of place in Jonathan Swift's *Gulliver's Travels*. In 1731, Captain Richard Jenkins, master of a brig out of Glasgow had been involved in trade with Spain's Caribbean colonies since the Treaty of Utrecht had settled the War of the Spanish Succession. But Spain had grown tired of the foreign traders and in 1731 Spanish coastguards boarded Jenkins's vessel; during an argument, they cut off Captain Jenkins' ear with a sword. When Jenkins reported the incident to parliament in 1739 – why did he take so long? – there was uproar in an England demanding redress against the outrage. On 19 October 1739 Walpole, the man of peace, reluctantly declared war on Spain, the incident of *Jenkins's Ear* melding with the War of the Austrian Succession. Apart from some British naval successes, little of note occurred until Frederick the Great of Prussia invaded Austria in 1740 to dispute the accession of Empress Maria Theresa which had been settled in 1713 by the Treaty of Utrecht. France and Spain supported Frederick; what had begun with a mutilated ear exploded into a major international incident. Jacobite sympathizers in Scotland welcomed the news, France and Spain both being longstanding supporters of the House of Stuart and enemies of the House of Hanover. Although Britain did not formally declare war on France, support for Austria was a tacit admission of hostility; both Britain and France took part in battles but described themselves as 'auxiliaries'. Matters came to a head on 27 June 1743, when George II at the head of a combined Hanoverian and English army defeated Louis XV of France at the battle of Dettingen. War between France and England had always presented the surest guarantee of a Jacobite resurgence; the most direct and effective way of threatening the security of Britain was to strike at England through Scotland, with support from the exiled House of Stuart. Louis XV needed a diversion to distract Britain, so he approached James Francis Edward Stuart, the Old Pretender, offering military aid and money for another Jacobite rising. But, by 1743, James was old and had lost interest in any hope of regaining the British throne, so he delegated the task to his twenty-three-year-old son Charles

Edward Stuart, a young man who had never set foot in Scotland nor led an army into battle. The appointment of the Young Pretender as he became known would prove disastrous.

A French invasion fleet on a scale much in excess of that of William of Orange in 1688 was planned for the year 1744; the fleet, commanded by Admiral de Roqueville set sail from Brest in February. It consisted of twenty-two warships carrying 4,000 troops, augmented by an army of 15,000 commanded by Marshal Maurice de Saxe to be conveyed in transports from the port of Dunkirk. Yet again, Britain was saved by the elements, February being a particularly stormy month. To make matters worse, Roqueville was challenged in the Channel by a superior British fleet commanded by Admiral Sir Charles Norris; the Frenchman was reluctant to risk his command and decided to make for home when another storm erupted. While the storm saved the warships, it destroyed de Saxe's troop transports and the invasion was aborted. That should have been an end to the matter but fate took an unfortunate turn in the person of the young Prince Charles Edward Stuart. The Prince alienated the people of Britain by his association with France, the enemy of England, if not the entire British nation; it was an association he would learn to regret for a variety of reasons, not least France's failure to support him when the moment arrived.

Fourth Jacobite Rising, 1745–46

On two occasions France had committed formidable fleets for the restoration of the Stuarts and twice the enterprises had ended in disaster. Never again would the French offer assistance on such a scale, although Louis XV would continue to make a public show – in France's interests – of creating mischief for the House of Hanover while failing to commit significant resources to the Jacobite cause in Scotland. Understandably, Louis was more concerned with the survival of his own throne and country. Although there was little love between the Prince and his father, it soon became apparent to the young man that he and he alone would have to draw his sword and liberate the people of Britain from the unhappy domination of the House of Hanover. That was what he believed. He also naively assumed that the entire populations of Scotland and England would rise in his support, providing armies which he would personally lead to victory, restoring his and his father's rights and honours. These were the dreams of an idealistic, stubborn young man who would cause not only bloodshed in Scotland but also bring about the end of a way of life in the Highlands which had existed for centuries.

The headstrong, romantic, determined, unrealistic and – it has to be said – jealous, vindictive, petty-minded and frequently inebriated Charles Edward Stuart (hereinafter simply referred to as the Prince) was a disaster waiting to happen in Scotland. When Louis XV informed the Prince that he required all his troops in his struggle with George II, the young man took the bull by the horns; he would achieve his ambition alone, flattering himself that his handsome face and his charismatic appeal would bring the Clan chiefs and their following to the standard of the House of Stuart, the White Rose and oppose the White Horse, the standard of Hanover. The Prince possessed all the symptoms often found in narcissistic egotists who indulge in self-delusion and are unable to face reality when their supposed abilities are found wanting. He relied overmuch on the advice of fawning favourites and romantics like himself rather than men who possessed the military skills and judge of character he woefully lacked.

During the wilderness years between 1719 and 1745, the Jacobite flame had been kept alight by the House of Stuart's generosity to certain Highland Clan chiefs who received honours, titles, money and other gifts. The foremost recipients were Donald Cameron of Lochiel, Simon Fraser, Lord Lovat, and James Drummond, Duke of Perth; these three men were part of an Association of Highland Gentlemen prepared to govern Scotland for the Prince. Through Jacobite agents such as William Macgregor (Drummond of Balhaldy) and John Murray of Broughton – a man who would prove a traitor to the Jacobite Cause – the Association kept in touch with the Old Pretender and the Prince. The Scottish Jacobites, usually at loggerheads with each other in their jockeying for position, were at least united in one aim which they believed would bring success to a rebellion – military assistance from France. Negotiations between Drummond of Balhaldy, Murray of Broughton and the French ministers came to nought; a lesser spirit than the Prince might have accepted the outcome but the failed talks only added fuel to the fire of the Prince's determination. The stalemate was broken on 11 May 1745 when the cream of the British troops fighting France was cut off at Fontenoy in France, where Marshal de Saxe defeated the British, Austrian and Dutch allied army commanded by the Duke of Cumberland, son of George II. Taking advantage of the confusion which gripped London, the Prince grasped the initiative; seeing a window of opportunity he impetuously borrowed 180,000 *livres* from a firm of bankers, persuading his father to pawn the family jewels but failing to inform him how he would use the money.[3] With this capital sum the Prince armed and equipped two ships – the *Elizabeth*, a frigate of sixty-eight guns and the smaller *Du Teillay* (sometimes called the *Doutelle*), a brig of eighteen guns. The *Elizabeth* carried the bulk of the weapons – broadswords, gunpowder, muskets and bullets; on 22 June the Prince boarded the *Du Teillay* and embarked from Nantes for Belle Isle; on 5 July he was joined by the *Elizabeth*. On board the *Du Teillay* the Prince was accompanied by the titular (nominal) Duke of Atholl (Marquis of Tullibardine), Sir John MacDonald,

Aeneas (Angus) MacDonald and the Irish Colonel Francis Strickland, Sir Thomas Sheridan, Colonel William O'Sullivan and George Kelly. These men became known as the Seven Men of Moidart.

Off the Lizard, Cornwall, the two vessels came in view of HMS *Lion*, a sixty-eight-gun British man o'war, whose Captain Brett immediately engaged the *Elizabeth*; for six hours the two warships fought it out, both being severely disabled. Finally, they disengaged, *Elizabeth* with the store of arms and ammunition having to limp back to France; *Lion* was too badly damaged to pursue her. It was hardly an auspicious start. The Prince was undeterred; under cover of a thick mist, the *Du Teillay* managed to evade two British men o'war; she eventually dropped anchor off the island of Eriskay in the Outer Hebrides on 23 July. It was a day of mist, rain and bitter wind. The Prince was disguised, wearing the soutane of an abbe, hatless, his long fair hair resting on his shoulders. The Prince had set foot on Scottish soil for the first time in his twenty-three years; in his heart, he believed he had come home.

The small party was led to Angus MacDonald's 'black house,' a makeshift dwelling of rough stones knitted together with a turf roof and no chimney; the smoke from the fire simply escaped through a hole in the thatch. Highland hospitality was meagre but nourishing; the Prince and his companions dined on freshly-caught flounders smoked over the peat fire.[4] A message was sent to Alexander MacDonald of Boisdale, South Uist, inviting him to attend on the Prince; he arrived the following morning. Boisdale's advice to the Prince was blunt and to the point; the Clan chief told him that, as he had brought neither troops nor weapons, he should go back to France. Boisdale brought other bitter news; Clan chiefs MacDonald of Sleate and Macleod of Skye shared his view. They too advised that the Prince should return to France as there was nothing for him in Scotland. A message also arrived from John Murray of Broughton in Edinburgh stating that without at least 6,000 troops the Rising stood no chance of success. It was heartbreaking news indeed.

The Prince returned to the *Du Teillay* that afternoon, setting sail after dark to avoid the British men o'war patrolling in the Sound of Barra. The following morning, the brig dropped anchor in the sea loch between Arisaig and Moidart, the country of MacDonald of Kinlochmoidart, Aeneas MacDonald's brother. In due course, MacDonald of Boisdale's brother, Donald MacDonald of Clanranald, Alexander MacDonald of Glenaladale and Aeneas MacDonald of Dalily arrived; after some discussion below deck, the company went on deck where a tent had been erected. They were joined by a tall young man to whom the anguished Prince turned, asking if he would help him.

The young man reputedly replied thus: 'I will, by God. Though not another Highlander should draw sword for you, I will.' The young man was Ranald MacDonald of Clanranald, one of the key figures and heroes of the

'Forty-Five and later Chief of his clan; henceforth throughout this chapter he is referred to as Young Clanranald.

Donald MacDonald of Kinlochmoidart was the first Clan chief to declare for the Prince, albeit reluctantly, along with his son and heir, Ranald MacDonald. At least it was a start. However, the Prince knew he had need of the most powerful Jacobite Clan chief of all, Donald Cameron of Lochiel. Along with the MacDonald chiefs, 'Gentle' Lochiel could turn the wavering Clan chiefs to the Prince's cause. When Lochiel met the Prince, his advice was blunt – go back to France. Then he changed his mind on condition that if the Rising failed, the Prince and his father would indemnify him against the loss of his estates as he had a bounden duty to look after his people. As a *quid pro quo*, Lochiel also asked that should the Rising succeed, his immediate family and clan would benefit from the estates of those Clan chiefs who did not join the Cause. (In this, Lochiel had an eye on the rich and fertile lands of the Duke of Argyll, chief of the Clan Campbell.) [5] The Prince agreed to Lochiel's conditions and intimated that he would raise his standard at Glenfinnan, which he did on 19 August 1745. (The standard consisted of a scarlet field with a white centre, the White Rose of the House of Stuart.)

On 19 August the Prince invited the gouty William Murray, Marquis of Tullibardine to read aloud his proclamation on that hot summer's day. Tullibardine proclaimed James of the House of Stuart 'King James the Eighth of Scotland and Third of England' and asserted his just rights to claim the three kingdoms of Scotland, England and Ireland. Also, his son, the Chevalier Charles Edward Stuart, would act as regent and what he did would be done in his father's name. By all accounts the proclamation was delivered in English and many present that day spoke only Gaelic; no matter, the message was soon understood, the brandy flowing freely. That fateful day, the Prince was flushed both by words and liquor.

Hostilities had actually begun five days earlier. The ageing John Gordon of Glenbucket had struck the first blow by taking into custody Captain Swettenham, a military engineer from Ruthven Barracks who had been ordered to reinforce Fort William. Swettenham was brought before the Prince who set him free after receiving his parole that he would not take up arms against him for a year and a day. The Prince knew – or was advised – that Swettenham would head straight for General Sir John Cope and inform him of the Jacobite army's whereabouts, which he duly did. Cope had begun his march from Edinburgh at the head of about 2,000 troops, intent on engaging the Jacobites before they could leave the Highlands and menace Lowland Scotland. Two days later, MacDonald of Keppoch and a party of Glengarry MacDonalds ambushed two companies of Royal Scots (about eighty men) under the command of a Captain Scott on his way from Fort Augustus to Fort

William. Four or five soldiers were killed and about a dozen wounded. The soldiers were taken prisoner without the loss of a single MacDonald; they were given the option of joining the Prince but they refused to a man.

Meanwhile in London, all was not well. After Walpole's resignation in 1742, Lord Tweeddale had been appointed to the revived office of Secretary of State for Scotland, while Lord Islay, now 3rd Duke of Argyll was still regarded as virtual ruler of the country. Tweeddale's policies were largely aimed at thwarting his rival Argyll rather than the good of Scotland; this explains why the government in Westminster had made no contingency plans to respond to an emergency which had been expected for some months. When Lord Marchmont proposed that he and several other nobles be given commissions to raise armed levies in Scotland, Tweeddale informed him there was no need as the irregular rebel levies of the Prince would be no match for well equipped, well trained and well fed government troops. One grave error on Tweeddale's part was the failure to provide arms and ammunition for local people to defend their townships against the rebels.[6] Also, the clans loyal to the Hanoverian government had surrendered their serviceable weapons under Duncan Forbes of Culloden's Disarming Act of 1725 whereas the disaffected Jacobite clans had kept theirs. Tweeddale refused to provide the loyal clans with weapons, arguing that he might be arming potential enemies.

General Sir John Cope commanding the government army in Scotland had his hands tied from the outset; Tweeddale informed him that he must make no important movements without first clearing them with Lord Advocate Craigie and Lord Milton, the Lord Chief Justice-Clerk, both being staunch allies of his and, by extension, opponents of Argyll, Tweeddale's rival. This was another grave error; through his divided counsel Tweeddale had offered the Prince an opportunity which would otherwise have been denied him. Incompetence and petty rivalry in government circles was more advantageous to the Prince than a French army and possible Jacobite recruits.

Despite Tweeddale's exhortations and bureaucratic red tape, Cope laid his plans carefully; he marched out of Edinburgh, intending to make for Fort Augustus, where he hoped to nip the White Rose in the bud before it could blossom. Had this occurred in August instead of September, in all probability, there would have been no 'Forty-Five. Cope's army numbered less than 1,500; of the 3,000 government troops in Scotland, most of the remaining 1,500 were raw levies dispersed among the strongpoints and garrisons throughout the north. However, Cope expected to recruit from the loyal clans along the route to Fort Augustus. In the event, not a single clansman joined him. At Dalnacardoch in the Forest of Atholl, Cope met Captain Swettenham whose news disquietened him. According to that officer, the Prince's army numbered 3,000 and was marching to the Pass of Corrieyairick to block Cope's road to

Fort Augustus. It seemed that battle would be drawn on ground favourable to the Highland mode of fighting, except for one detail unknown to Swettenham and Cope; the Jacobites possessed little shot and powder for a major engagement. In his camp at Glengarry, the Prince was informed that the incompetent Colonel O'Sullivan had buried most of the black powder, ammunition and the eighteen small cannon taken off the *Du Teillay* before she set sail for France. The vital ordnance had been concealed on the shore of Loch Eil as there were insufficient horses to transport it and the clansmen refused to be treated as pack animals. (The vital stores and field pieces were in fact dug up by the garrison of Fort William, from where spies had observed O'Sullivan burying them.)

No matter, the Prince declared that he would make up the loss of arms and munitions by defeating Cope. On 4 September, the Jacobite army reached Perth; the Prince confessed that he had but a single guinea (£1.05) in his purse, although he hoped to relieve the town treasury of the money collected by local taxes. At Perth the Prince was joined by several notable recruits – James Drummond, titular 3rd Duke of Perth,[7] Lord George Murray, Lord Nairne, Laurence, 10th Lord Oliphant of Gask, Lord Strathallan and James, Chevalier de Johnstone whose father was an Edinburgh merchant. The proceedings over the next few days took on the characteristics of a Highland reel. On learning of the Jacobites' position at Corrieyairick, a deep glen with steep, rock-strewn sides which could be easily defended by a small force, Cope altered his route to Fort Augustus, taking the right fork of the road at Spean Bridge and marching via Ruthven Barracks to evade the Prince. After some discussion on strategy in the Jacobite camp, it was agreed not to pursue Cope – much to the disgust of many clansmen hoping to gain booty – but to make for Edinburgh, leaving Cope to cool his heels in the north. This would prove a sensible tactic. The Prince crossed the river Forth at the Fords of Frew, arriving at the outskirts of Edinburgh on 16 September. At Colt Bridge, three miles west of Edinburgh, the Jacobite army encountered two dragoon regiments led by Colonel James Gardiner and Colonel Hamilton; the dragoons were in poor shape, they and their horses suffering from malnutrition. When they saw the rebel army, the two colonels ordered their men to disperse into the surrounding countryside as they did not consider them fit to take on the Highland army. This incident became known as the *Canter of Coltbrig*.

The Prince sent a polite summons to the Provost of Edinburgh, Archibald Stewart and the town magistrates requesting that he be allowed to enter the town; at first the town fathers refused and attempted to negotiate terms. The Prince would not accept anything less than unconditional surrender. On the night of 16 September, a body of Highlanders led by Cameron of Lochiel rushed the wicket gate at the Nether Bow, gaining entry without discharging a shot. The Prince was now master of all Scotland. The following day, he made a splendid entrance into Edinburgh; at the High Street's market cross, a proclamation was read out, declaring James VIII and III King of Scotland and the Prince his regent.

In the north, Cope received news of the Jacobite occupation of Edinburgh. Hoping for the arrival of promised reinforcements from the Duke of Cumberland's army in Flanders, Cope, now in Aberdeen, ordered transports to ferry his army from there to either Berwick or Dunbar. The Hanoverian army landed at Dunbar between 17 and 18 September; Cope's hoped-for Dutch reinforcements had not arrived in Berwick but he was resolved to march on the Prince while he remained in Edinburgh. Cope was anxious to defeat the Prince as he was fearful the Highland army would be reinforced by France and the as yet uncommitted clans. Time was of the essence.

Cope led his army from Dunbar on 19 September, reaching Haddington that afternoon. In Edinburgh, the Prince held a hasty council of war and it was agreed to confront Cope well away from the capital; on 20 September, the Jacobite army reached Carberry Hill overlooking Musselburgh, the selfsame spot where the Prince's ancestor Mary, Queen of Scots had surrendered to the Protestant Lords of the Congregation in 1567. Now reinforced by men from Clans Maclachlan, Glenmoriston and Atholl, the Prince's army numbered 2,400; facing him was Cope's slightly smaller army of about 2,100, although the Hanoverian army contained two regiments of dragoons – mainly comprised of the lacklustre Irishmen who had run away at Colt Bridge on 16 September – and six light field pieces and four mortars.

Prestonpans

Over the next twenty-four hours, Cope took up his position at Prestonpans, East Lothian, changing it no fewer than four times as he was unsure from which direction the Prince would attack. His final position faced east; his rear was protected by the high garden walls of Preston House, his right flank resting on a near impassable marsh known locally as the Riggonhead Defile. Cope's left wing was commanded by Colonel Murray and flanked by Colonel Hamilton's dragoon regiment; the regiments of Lascelles and Guise held the centre, with Lee's regiment on the right, flanked by Colonel Gardiner's dragoons. For some inexplicable reason, the artillery commanded by Lieutenant Colonel Whitefoord was stationed on the extreme right rather than the centre. During the night of 20/21 September, the Prince's war council were undecided whether the attack should be mounted from the east or the west; an advance from the east would be advantageous to the Highland army as the rising sun would be in the eyes of the Hanoverians.

The problem of an eastern attack was that the Prince's army would have to negotiate the difficult marshy ground without being observed or heard by the enemy picquets. Fortuitously, a local resident, Robert Anderson of Whitburgh, was brought before the Prince. Anderson was bold enough to suggest the Jacobites should indeed attack Cope from the east, where the ground was hard and dry. Then he volunteered to lead the Jacobite army through the marsh by way of a footpath he knew from his duck-shooting expeditions. This was a stroke of good fortune, boosting the morale of the Prince's commanders, Lord George Murray and James Drummond.[8] Before retiring for a few hours' sleep, Murray and Drummond discussed the formation of their battalions. There was some ill-natured bickering about the placing of the clans, mainly from the MacDonalds who insisted their traditional position in past conflicts was on the right wing, an honour they claimed was bestowed on them by King Robert Bruce at Bannockburn. Alistair MacDonald of Glengarry (son of the Clan chief who had not declared for the Prince) argued that they and not the Camerons under Lochiel should fight on the right. Furthermore, Glengarry reminded Murray and Drummond that only two weeks earlier in Perth, the Prince himself had said he would respect such traditions; Lochiel argued that young Glengarry was not the Clan chief and that his views were therefore irrelevant. Glengarry refused to give way and threatened to withhold his men from the fight, confirming that the MacDonalds of Clanranald, Keppoch and Glencoe agreed with him and they too would not participate in the battle. Lochiel gave way, reputedly declaring that he would not have it said that a Cameron had brought misfortune to the field.[9] Honour thus satisfied, the Prince's battle formation was agreed. The front-line right wing commanded by James Drummond, Duke of Perth comprised the four MacDonald clans and the Grants of Glenmoriston; the left wing was led by Lord George Murray and consisted of Lochiel and his Camerons, the Stewarts of Appin, the Atholl Brigade and Clan Macgregor commanded by Major James Macgregor, Rob Roy Macgregor's son. The second line was in the Prince's charge, with Clans Robertson, Maclachlan, Lord Nairne's own regiment and Clan Menzies.[10]

At about 4am, the Highlanders began their stealthy negotiation of the marsh. The column snaked through the Riggonhead Defile led by the Duke of Perth and his MacDonalds, with Lord George Murray and the Prince bringing up the rear; at one point, leaping over one of the many deep ditches, the Prince fell on his knees and had to be hauled to his feet.[11] As daylight began to break through the early morning mist at 5am, in the half-light Cope's Redcoats mistook the Highlanders swathed in their voluminous plaids for stunted bushes.[12] Then, as the sun broke through the mist, the Jacobites could see the light reflected by the Hanoverian army's metal trappings; many of the clansmen later admitted that on seeing the artillery and the dragoons, they did not expect to survive the action. No matter, the clansmen advanced steadily, Murray's left wing having been given the task of despatching the artillery guard and the cannoneers as soon as they came within musket range. When Murray's men opened fire, a veteran cannoneer panicked and fled, taking his powder flask with him; he was quickly followed by the rest of the gunners and the ordnance guard.[13] Lieutenant Colonel Whitefoord was left alone to discharge the loaded cannon. Single-handedly, Whitefoord managed to fire five of the six field pieces into Murray's men, inflicting several casualties including Major James Macgregor. When they saw their officer fall wounded, the enraged Macgregors broke into a wild Highland Charge. Colonel Gardiner's dragoons fired a single volley from their carbines then fled, most taking the road to Gardiner's private dwelling at Bankton, Tranent. Gardiner and a few of his more dependable men made a last stand around some old thorn trees; they were slain to a man. Gardiner was felled by a Lochaber axe, dying later of his wounds.[14]

Meanwhile in the centre, the Highlanders fired a single volley then threw away their muskets and discarded their cumbersome plaids to allow free use of their favourite weapons – broadsword, axe and dirk. The Redcoats fired a ragged volley prematurely then broke in disorder and panic, some failing to loose off a single shot. The clansmen executed savage work with their bladed weapons; heads were split to the shoulder, arms and legs hacked off; Hamilton's dragoons fared no better than Gardiner's men, the clansmen using scythes, swords and axes to hack at the horses' underbellies and legs, despatching the fallen riders without ceremony. For the foot soldiers there were only two escape routes from the carnage – by way of Preston House whose walls had been breached the day before and the track to Bankton House. Those who sought refuge via Preston House found the breaches too high for them to clamber through; precious few managed to make their escape that way. The clansmen gave no quarter, slaughtering the unfortunate men without mercy; soon the bases of the walls were piled high with the dead and wounded.[15]

Cope and a few of his officers attempted to rally the shattered command but the panic-stricken Redcoats could think only of flight. The Earl of Home managed to scrape together some 400–450 foot and dragoons to make a stand but 'as soon as a small body of Rebels appeared the dragoons could not be brought to move against them'.[16]

Some of Cope's officers ran away in a cowardly manner to seek safety wherever they could. The Prince had taken no part in the action; he was appalled by the blood-letting and galloped over the field of Prestonpans, pleading that the clansmen stop the massacre as Cope's men were his father's subjects and that he did not wish their deaths on his conscience. Some

Highlanders had shown quarter to their victims; the Camerons took many prisoners, as did Lord George Murray who stopped further slaughter by ordering his men to accept the surrender of several terrified Redcoats. At last the bloodshed ceased.

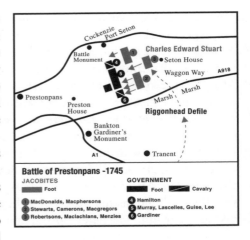

Battle of Prestonpans -1745

The battle of Prestonpans was over in less than fifteen minutes. Estimates of the Jacobite casualties vary; in his account the Chevalier de Johnstone, aide-de-camp (ADC) to the Prince gives between thirty and forty dead, with many more wounded. On the Hanoverian side accounts vary, the lowest estimate of Redcoat dead being between 150 and 500, the highest given as 1,300.[17] The government's official report gave 500 dead, 900 wounded and 1,400 taken prisoner. The six light field pieces, four mortars and around £4,000 in Cope's war-chest fell into the Jacobites' hands.[18]

Prestonpans was a spectacular victory for the Prince, won for him by the brilliant Lord George Murray, his haughty, hot-tempered commander, a man the Prince never trusted and detested for his outstanding military strategic and tactical skills.

The battle of Prestonpans, also known as the battle of Gladsmuir in fulfilment of an old Jacobite prophecy is commemorated by the famous ballad *Hey Johnnie Cope* with its endearing refrain or chorus:

> Hey Johnnie Cope are ye waukin' [awake] yet?
> Or are ye sleepin I would wit [guess]
> O haste ye get up for the drums do beat
> O fye Cope rise in the morning.'[19]

Another version goes thus:

> Hey Johnnie Cope are ye waukin' yet?
> Or are your drums a-beating yet?
> If ye are waukin' I would wait
> Tae gang [to go] to the coals in the morning.'[20]

(Going to the coals in the morning was a local phrase, deriving from the coalfields in the vicinity of Prestonpans and Tranent.)

Although Prestonpans was the highwater mark of the 'Forty-Five and instilled the Prince and his raggle-taggle Highland army with Jacobite hope and ambition at last realized, the morale-boosting glory which the Jacobites needed for the invasion of England, we must in all conscience place the victory in perspective. In so many ways, Prestonpans was a fluke, a lucky event which would lead to the ultimate conclusion; the untrained, undisciplined, ill equipped, frequently unpaid and often starving warriors – the clansmen were hardly soldiers – who followed the White Rose standard had little chance of ultimate success over the well trained, well fed, well equipped soldiers in the pay of George II, King of Britain. It is often the case that the outcome of the first major action in a military campaign will determine the pattern of what will follow; this appeared to be true after the delusory triumph of Prestonpans but sadly the outcome was never in any doubt. As for Cope, his soldiers were of poor quality, the second-rate sweepings of the Hanoverian army, the best troops being in Flanders. However, for the moment, the Prince and his Jacobites were in jubilant mood; they believed they could defeat anything that the London government could send against them.

Despite the victory, it is perhaps appropriate at this juncture to examine the deep divisions in the Jacobite high command which had existed almost from the outset of the 'Forty-Five, divisions which would bedevil the campaign up to the very eve of Culloden. The Prince was fired with enthusiasm and over-confidence; his personal charm won over the hearts and minds of the clansmen and their Chiefs. The truth of it was less attractive; he was a vindictive young man, jealous of the prowess and military skills of better men than those he favoured – Irish officers such as the grossly inept Colonel William O'Sullivan – most being incompetent and even reckless as unlike the Clan chiefs, they had nothing to lose in the event of defeat. The Prince could switch on his undoubted charm when it suited his purpose; he also paid grudging respect to Lord George Murray, the real leader of the Jacobite army. From the beginning, the Prince harboured a deep and ingrained distrust of Murray with, it has to be said, some justification. Despite having taken part in the 'Fifteen and 'Nineteen rebellions, Murray had made his peace with the Hanoverian government. Besides, his father John Murray, 2nd Marquis and 2nd Duke of Atholl was staunchly pro-Hanoverian, as was Murray's brother John, the future Duke of Atholl. (It was also said of Lord George Murray that he had initially disapproved of the 'Forty-Five and that he had made friendly overtures towards Sir John Cope before he joined the Prince.)[21] The Prince was aware of a rumour spread by a MacDonald woman that Murray intended to raise the men of Atholl, then lead them into service in the Hanoverian army. This was reported to the Prince by a Sir John MacDonald, a man jealous of Murray's military skills. From his later dealings with Murray the Prince apparently believed – and wanted to believe – this rumour which affected his subsequent treatment of Murray.

As for Murray, he was jealous of James Drummond, 3rd Duke of Perth, a Catholic in whom the Prince confided and often excluded Murray from his plans; Perth had never commanded a regiment nor fought in any major battle before Prestonpans. Perth was, however, a zealous supporter of the Jacobite cause, loyal to the Prince and his father; sadly, he lacked the ability to command men in the field. The Prince placed his trust in Perth simply because of his devotion to the House of Stuart. Murray's jealousy of Perth increased when the Prince appointed Perth and Murray as joint Lieutenant Generals of the Highland army, serving on alternative days as commanders in chief. If ever there was one, Murray and Perth were an ill-assorted pair. The animosity between the two men, one Protestant, the other Catholic, was one of several causes which would contribute to the failure of the 'Forty-Five.

After Prestonpans, the Jacobite army spent the next month in Edinburgh, enjoying good food and convivial company. During that time the Prince exercised the powers of a sovereignty he did not possess; he issued proclamations, commandeered supplies and the best horses from the outlying districts of Edinburgh to form the cavalry he lacked and which he would need in his proposed invasion of England. He also attempted to form a Scottish parliament which he promised would impose a ban on the 'Pretended parliament' of the Elector of Hanover (George II) when that parliament convened in London on 17 October. Wherever his authority was secure, the Prince appropriated public money from towns such as Glasgow, money he used to pay, feed and arm his men. The Prince promised the people of Edinburgh that he would abolish the union with England, the National Debt would be managed by a legal Scottish parliament and everyone in the kingdom would be allowed to worship in whatever manner and form they chose. It was all pie in the sky. Lowland Scotland was underwhelmed by the young Prince's promises and there was no movement among the staunch burghers of the towns to join the Jacobite cause. One bone of contention was the presence of the Prince's Irish (Catholic) officers in the army, men who had been favoured above the largely Protestant and Episcopalian clans in the north. These Irish adventurers had nothing to lose by supporting the Prince unlike the Clan chiefs who were risking all they possessed for the Jacobite cause. A further hindrance to the unity in the high command was the mutual dislike of and rivalry between Lord George Murray and John Murray of Broughton, the capable if devious secretary who influenced the Prince's decisions on many occasions. (Murray of Broughton would prove a traitor to the cause even before Culloden, later turning King's Evidence to secure his freedom.)

It was during his sojourn in Edinburgh that the Prince announced he would invade England, a proposal which did not sit well with the Clan chiefs; many had joined the Cause to restore the Old Pretender to the throne of Scotland, not caring about England where there had been no indication of a Jacobite rising. Wiser counsel suggested that the Highland army remain in Edinburgh until the French arrived in strength with money, arms, ammunition and provisions, as had been promised by the Treaty of Fontainebleau signed on 24 October, a month after news of the Jacobite victory at Prestonpans reached Paris. (The Treaty formally established a military alliance between Louis XV and the Prince as regent of Scotland; it was little more than gesture, a cynical promise made by a French King publicly declaring his support for the Prince; the real reason was that the Prince's 'adventure' would relieve pressure on the French army with the recall to England of the Duke of Cumberland's troops fighting Louis.) The French commitment to the 'Forty-Five was paltry; Louis XV knew that his navy would have to face the mighty Royal Navy as well as the notoriously capricious North Sea weather which had frustrated earlier French attempts to invade mainland Scotland. However, the French began to ship support for Scotland, albeit in penny packets; four French vessels reached the east coast of Scotland between 9 and 19 October carrying small arms, artillery, ammunition and specialist military advisers. Significantly, there were no French troops on board.

By the first week in November, the Prince commanded an army of at least 4,500 foot, 400 cavalry and twenty field pieces, largely supplied by French ships which had docked at Stonehaven and Montrose along with the six cannon and four mortars captured from Cope at Prestonpans.[22] The Jacobite army crossed the Border on 8 November, intent on taking Carlisle for use as a base on the march to London. Carlisle capitulated on 10 November.

London might have been as far away as the moon. On 30 November, the march on the capital began. The Jacobite army reached Derby on 4 December, by which month the Duke of Cumberland, recalled from Flanders with a superior army, had reached Lichfield, Staffordshire, less than thirty miles from Derby. The expected Jacobite recruits in England amounted to a paltry 300 raised in Manchester, along with three gentlemen from Wales and 'some few common people' from Preston who were incorporated into what became known as the Manchester Regiment.[23]

Despite the lack of English recruits, the Prince was inflamed with a false hope that all England would rise in his support, believing as he did that a French landing was imminent. It was a forlorn hope. Closing on the Jacobite army were two English armies, the Duke of Cumberland's 8,000 and Marshal George Wade's 10,000. A war council convened on 5 December decided that it would be unrealistic to continue the advance on London; a retreat north was the only logical option. The Prince alone protested against this decision but he was over-ruled. Between 6 and 20 December, the Jacobites marched back the way they had come, leaving the Manchester Regiment and a few clansmen in Carlisle; the town surrendered to Cumberland on 30 December; the garrison were taken prisoner, with many shot later on a charge of treason.

Inverurie II

The long, dreary retreat from Derby ended on 20 December, the Prince's twenty-fifth birthday, the day his dispirited army forded the river Esk at Longtown. From there the Jacobites marched to Glasgow, an openly hostile city. Despite about 500 desertions, the Prince's spirits were somewhat raised when news arrived that his forces in the north of Scotland had won a small but morale-boosting action on 23 December 1745 at Inverurie, about sixteen miles south-west of Aberdeen.

King George's commander in chief in the north, John Campbell, 4th Earl of Loudon despatched a Hanoverian force of 500 commanded by Laird Macleod of Macleod from Inverness to confront a Jacobite force commanded by Lord Lewis Gordon. Macleod was joined by the Laird of Grant and 500 clansmen, then George Munro of Culcairn and 200 Munro clansmen. This brought the government force up to 1,200. Facing Macleod were Lord Gordon's two battalions, one commanded by Lieutenant General James Moir of Stoneywood and Gordon of Abbachy, with five field pieces. Lord Gordon was joined by Lord John Drummond's contingent of French troops who had recently landed at Montrose. Gordon was further reinforced by Francis Farquharson, Laird of Monoltrie and 300 Farquharsons, bringing his force up to 1,200. The sides were thus evenly matched.

When word arrived in Macleod's camp that Gordon was in the vicinity, the Laird of Grant withdrew with his 500 clansmen, fearing his lands would be ravaged. George Munro of Culcairn and his 200 Munro clansmen were detached to occupy nearby Old Meldrum, leaving Macleod with only 500 men. Macleod, now outnumbered more than two to one foolishly decided to occupy the town of Inverurie. When Lord Gordon learnt of this incautious movement, he was determined to confront Macleod; to do so, he split his force, sending 300 French troops and clansmen to attack Macleod from the south-west while leading 800 clansmen to engage Macleod east of the town. Gordon took Macleod completely by surprise; despite a spirited defence by the Macleods who opened fire from ditches and behind walls, Macleod suffered many casualties, fifty of his clansmen being taken prisoner. Gordon's losses are not recorded. Inverurie was a minor action but a welcome Christmas gift for the Prince

By mid-January, the Prince received further recruits; some accounts number the Jacobite army at between 5,000 and 7,000, particularly if that of Colonel William O'Sullivan is to be believed. The account by James, Chevalier de Johnstone gives 8,000, including some French troops.[24] If these accounts are accurate, desertions reduced the strength of the Jacobite army, possibly by 1,000 by the time the Prince arrived at Stirling. There, the hapless young man insisted on a forlorn attempt to take Stirling's formidable castle, the gateway to the Highlands. The Jacobite army camped at Bannockburn; perhaps the clansmen hoped that some of the Bruce luck would rub off. The Prince wasted two days besieging Stirling Castle until news arrived that General John Hawley with 8,000 troops was camped at Callender House, Falkirk, the home of Lord Kilmarnock who had 'come out' for the Prince. After a fruitless and time-consuming attempt to take Stirling Castle, the Prince grudgingly agreed with Lord George Murray's proposal to attack Hawley. By 16 January, the Jacobite army occupied Falkirk Muir, a hundred-foot-high plateau overlooking Hawley's position. When Hawley was informed that the Prince was marching against him, he dismissed the idea out of hand, believing that the Jacobites were in no condition to mount an offensive.

Falkirk II

At 4pm on 17 January, the wind blew fiercely on Falkirk Muir; Hawley finally accepted the fact that some 5,000 Jacobites were about to attack him. Hawley had commanded a dragoon regiment at Sheriffmuir [25] and was hated by his men on account of his strict disciplinarian regime; before leaving Edinburgh, Hawley had constructed gallows in the town, boasting that he would hang many Jacobites there after he defeated the Prince. That cold winter day in January, freezing rain fell on the Highlanders' backs; Hawley's men took the full blast of the tempestuous weather in their faces. Having heard many stories of the Highlanders' dread of horses – no longer true – Hawley ordered his 700 or 800 dragoons to attack the right wing of the Jacobite army commanded by Lord George Murray; in the centre were the MacDonald Clans of Glengarry, Clanranald, Keppoch and Glencoe, with the Prince to the rear with some Irish picquets. As darkness began to fall, Hawley's horse drove into Murray's men who, as at Prestonpans, lay down in the grass and stuck bayonets and dirks into the horses' bellies, then dragged their riders down to finish them off with pistols as there was no room to swing a broadsword.[26] Murray's men pursued the fleeing cavalry, his men running as fast as the horses and dragging their riders to the ground, slaughtering them in full view of Hawley's foot soldiers. Those dragoons who managed to escape their determined pursuers cleaved a way through the shocked and dumbstruck foot; the front line delivered a desultory volley, the second line ran away without firing a single shot. The battle was over in twenty minutes. Hawley would later report to the Duke of Cumberland that his men were guilty of scandalous cowardice. (The gallows in Edinburgh were used to punish Hawley's own men; thirty-one of Colonel Hamilton's dragoons – the man who had fled the field of Prestonpans – were hanged for desertion and about the same number of foot were shot for cowardice.)[27] Falkirk cost Hawley more than 400 casualties to the Prince's loss of forty.[28] The Highlanders spent the night of 17 January robbing and stripping the dead Redcoats of their personal belongings and equipment.[29] The Jacobites gained a useful haul of tents, mortars, seven field pieces, a few hundred muskets and some barrels of powder as well as hampers of much-needed food, wines and liquors.[30]

After Falkirk, desertions from the Prince's army continued. Although precise figures are difficult to assess, it is thought that about 2,000 clansmen left the Jacobite army in the days that followed, although it is thought these desertions were temporary. Some Clan chiefs wanted to pursue Hawley's army to Edinburgh, thus consolidating the victory at Falkirk. The Prince would not hear of this somewhat ridiculous suggestion, given that that the Duke of Cumberland was marching north to reinforce Hawley. However, this sensible course was negated by the Prince's equally ridiculous insistence on returning to Stirling to subdue the castle, which was being 'besieged' (surely a euphemism for 'watched') by the Duke of Perth and 1,000 men. For months now it had become abundantly clear to men like Lord George Murray that the Prince was stubborn, delusive and vindictive towards any who offered sensible military advice which conflicted with his own grandiose and unrealistic strategies. He despised those who challenged his judgement him and was vindictive when they were proved right. The Prince's unrealistic plan to take Stirling, the government forts in the north, then march back into England with his outnumbered army beggars belief; it is hard to avoid the conclusion that he was either permanently drunk or had lost touch with reality. Further bad news arrived from France; the Prince was informed that there were no troops available for the invasion of England; Cumberland's departure with the best of the Hanoverian army to counter the Jacobite threat should have been an opportune moment for Louis XV to mount an invasion of England. Instead, he did nothing. The Prince had either lied to the Clan chiefs about the promised French invasion – or did he believe the nonsense he had been fed by the French king? Whatever the truth of it, he persisted with the siege of Stirling, a venture for which he was woefully ill-equipped, possessing neither siege guns nor specialist siege engineers; that apart, the clansmen refused to participate in a method of waging war unfamiliar to them. Desertions continued and many men fell sick.[31] Finally, Lord George Murray and the Clan chiefs put the situation bluntly to the Prince; retreat was the only option left, advice which the Prince reluctantly accepted, voicing his bitterness and aiming his bile at Murray: 'Good God, have I lived to see this?' Then he struck his head against a wall with such force that the blow made him stagger.[32]

The retreat north from Stirling began on 1 February; it was not a day too soon, as Cumberland occupied the town the following day. The Highland army divided, part going to Perth, the rest marching to Crieff where it was agreed that the army should wage a guerrilla-type war, which the Clan chiefs had suggested at Stirling. Then the army was re-organized in three commands; one headed by Lord George Murray and James Drummond, Duke of Perth proceeded by way of Montrose and Aberdeen; one led by Lord Ogilvy marched via Cupar-Angus and the third commanded by the Prince who was intent on taking the key Blair Castle. The ultimate aim was to capture Inverness.

On 10 February, the Jacobites took Ruthven Barracks, burning it to the ground; on learning this, Lord Loudon the government commander at Inverness led a force of 1,500 out of the town on 16 February, hoping to surprise the Prince whom he knew was staying at Moy Hall, less than ten miles from Inverness. The Prince was the guest of Lady Anne Farquharson-Mackintosh. Lady Anne had raised Clan Mackintosh for the Prince and was known as 'Colonel Anne'. Her husband, Clan chief Angus Mackintosh had served the Hanoverian government as a captain in the Black Watch, the regiment raised by General Wade to keep peace in the Highlands; Angus Mackintosh's support for King George was rather lukewarm. When Lady Anne received word of Loudon's approach, she gathered together a few of her servants to create a diversion; these retainers ambushed Loudon, repeatedly firing their muskets to give the impression that a larger force was attacking him. Loudon was panic-stricken, believing the entire Jacobite army was attacking him, so he fled back to Inverness. This incident became known as the *Rout of Moy*; it made a heroine of Colonel Anne. (In 1746, she was arrested for supporting the Prince, by way of punishment, she was placed in the custody of her mother-in-law; Colonel Anne died in 1787, remembered by the Prince as *La Belle Rebelle*, or Beautiful Rebel.) Two days after the Moy incident, the Prince took Inverness without loss, Lord Loudon and Lord President Duncan Forbes of Culloden having evacuated the town earlier the same day. At least the Prince, reinforced by a considerable force from the Moy Hall tenants and workers regained some of his hope for better fortunes in the weeks ahead; his morale was further boosted when Lord George Murray and the Duke of Perth reached Inverness with the rest of the army. The planned capture of the government forts was successful; Fort George capitulated on 20 February, followed by Fort Augustus on 5 March, leaving Fort William as the sole government strongpoint.

By now, Lord George Murray had complete charge of the army; had he been given sole command from the outset the 'Forty-Five might have been more successful or perhaps less bloody. It was even said that had Prince slept through the whole campaign and left Murray in charge, the result would have been different. In Perthshire, Murray had taken several small forts but he was unsuccessful in capturing Blair Castle due to the approach of Cumberland's army. This deepened the cloud of suspicion which had hung over Murray from the beginning; a paranoid Prince grew ever more doubtful of Murray's loyalty. Did Murray deliberately abandon his siege of Blair Castle because he was secretly in contact with Cumberland? This may have been a fantasy in the addled mind of the Prince, looking for a scapegoat for Culloden in the years to come. Be that as it may, Jacobite morale was raised when Lord John Drummond, the Duke of Perth's brother took the entire garrison of Keith, Aberdeenshire prisoner.

Cumberland continued his advance slowly, perhaps deliberately so as he knew it was seed-time, when the clansmen traditionally deserted for the spring planting, as they did at harvest-time. He marched his army from Stirling to Keith, then Aberdeen by way of Montrose. On 8 April, Cumberland evacuated Aberdeen, brushing aside the weak forces of the Duke of Perth and Lord John Drummond. Cumberland camped at Nairn, only eight miles from Inverness and the Jacobite camp at Culloden. On 14 April, the Highland army was fragmented; many were absent on various enterprises, chiefly foraging for food. The clansmen were starving. Murray of Broughton, who was responsible for the commissary fell sick; his duties were assumed by John Hay of Restalrig, an incompetent and unscrupulous quartermaster, possibly a thief into the bargain, diverting funds from the dwindling Jacobite war-chest into his own pocket. Apart from not having been paid for a month, the clansmen were staring starvation in the face; on the day before Culloden, many were fortunate to receive a single biscuit made from flour and water. Hay of Restalrig had promised tumbrels of food from Inverness; they never arrived. The men were in no condition to fight a major battle.

At Nairn, William Augustus, Duke of Cumberland was in buoyant mood on 15 April, the eve of his twenty-fifth birthday. Four months younger than his cousin Prince Charles Edward Stuart, Cumberland was liked and respected by his men, even if he was a strict disciplinarian and something of a bully. Cumberland was noted for his cool head in battle and his study of the art of contemporary warfare which he put into practice during the months of campaigning in Flanders against the French. He took the trouble to interrogate those who had run away from the fields of Prestonpans and

Falkirk; in doing so, he followed the example of intelligent generals such as John Churchill, Duke of Marlborough who listened to his sergeants' opinions and views before and after his several victories gained in the service of Queen Anne. During his many interviews with the survivors of Prestonpans and Falkirk, Cumberland found that it had been the ferocious Highland Charge which had caused the panic-stricken soldiers to quit their posts, so he began drilling his soldiers in a new tactic which he rightly believed would counter the shock of the Highland Charge. The solution was simple; it was based on the use of the bayonet and the technique Cumberland devised was eminently successful on the field of Culloden. When a clansman raised both arms, the left bearing the targe or shield for protection, the right wielding the broadsword to deliver a blow to the skull of his opponent, the Redcoat to the immediate right of the man attacking his neighbour would plunge his bayonet into the clansman's left armpit and his heart. Every Redcoat up and down the front line would be protected by the man on his right.

On 15 April, Cumberland's troops celebrated their general's birthday in fine style, feasting on the cattle they had brought from the south, beasts which had been abandoned by the Jacobite army in the retreat from Derby. The Redcoats enjoyed meat, bread, cheese and locally brewed ale. Contrast this with the Prince's household at Culloden House, home of Lord President Forbes, which the Jacobites had commandeered with its well-stocked cellar of claret and fine wines. A dinner of roast lamb had been prepared for the Prince's table but he pushed the plate away, saying that he could not eat such fine fare while his army was starving. The command structure began to disintegrate that fateful April evening.

The Prince made matters worse by excluding Lord George Murray from his plans, favouring his Irish officers, including the hapless Assistant General or Colonel O'Sullivan who mesmerized the Prince with his wild, fanciful and illogical ideas on strategy. It was O'Sullivan who chose Drummossie Moor for the coming battle, beyond the braeside south of Culloden House; he could not have picked a more advantageous spot for Cumberland's battle. The moor is a flat, open expanse of heathland which offers no cover, nor was it suitable for the formidable and effective Highland Charge. When Cumberland inspected the position, he could not believe his eyes, nor his luck; the ground afforded ample room for the government troops and artillery to pour a merciless fire into the Highlanders before they could even begin their attack, thus effectively negating the possibility of close combat hand-to-hand fighting in which the clansmen excelled. Lord George Murray immediately spotted the disadvantages of Drummossie; supported by a few officers he implored the Prince to allow him to seek out an alternative position which would give the clansmen a fighting chance. Murray favoured a stretch of uneven ground near

Dalcross Castle which offered the clansmen some protection from the murderous artillery fire as well as a safe retreat to Inverness should the day go badly. Murray's choice of ground might have reduced casualties and even offered a chance of success. He duly reported his findings to the Prince who dismissed his proposal out of hand, refusing to deviate from O'Sullivan's choice.[33] Then he announced that he would personally take command of the field with O'Sullivan as his second-in-command. The Prince was determined that Murray would receive no credit for the victory he anticipated. He alone would succeed that day. Culloden was the first and only battle he would ever command.

The author has walked the ground of Drummossie Moor on several occasions; it could not have been more advantageous terrain for Cumberland's foot, artillery and cavalry. Drummossie is flat moorland over which grey clouds always seem to hover; it is a sombre, eerie place suffused with the lingering sadness of that tragic day in April 1746. The silence is broken only by the raucous cries of foraging ravens, long believed to be the harbingers of death; the thick bracken and heather are broken only by the green patches marking the communal graves of the clans who took part, the names inscribed on simple, rough grey boulders that serve as tombstones. With a dry-stone wall on the right wing of the Prince's army side providing excellent cover for enfilading fire, the moor was a disastrous choice for the last stand of the Jacobites; in the words of an American Civil War commentator on the battle of the Crater during the siege of Petersburgh in 1864, when hundreds of Union soldiers were slaughtered in the massive hole created by their own mining of the Confederate position, Culloden must have been like shooting fish in a barrel.

On 15 April, what was left of the Jacobite army took up position on Drummossie Moor to the sound of cannon fire, which roused them to arms; the cannonade was not directed at the outlying Jacobite picquets but to celebrate the Duke of Cumberland's birthday. Arguments about clan positions in the front line arose; Murray and his Atholl Brigade were stationed on the right, the position claimed by the MacDonalds, but as many Glengarry men had deserted after the accidental shooting of one of their clan by a Keppoch MacDonald (see note 31), the point was not laboured.

No battle took place that day as Cumberland's troops were celebrating his birthday. At a meeting of officers that afternoon, the Prince agreed with Lord George Murray's suggestion that the Jacobite army should launch a surprise attack on Cumberland that very night, when the Redcoats would be soused; the plan was no more irrational than the choice of Drummossie Moor for the coming engagement. A desperate gamble, it might have borne fruit. There was a fly in the ointment, however; about a third of the Jacobite army was missing, foraging for food, perhaps even deserting. The events which followed are confusing, no two contemporary accounts being compatible on what took place. The army which the Prince commanded had shrunk to about 5,000 starving, weary clansmen, with a further 2,000 scattered in the area in search of food. Nonetheless, the Prince went ahead with the plan to attack Cumberland in Nairn, some eight miles distant. The army split into two columns led by Mackintosh guides, men familiar with the district. Then Lord George Murray discovered there was a gap about half a mile long in the army; men had simply disappeared or had literally dropped dead from hunger. Murray sent word back to the Prince that the rest of the army must close up so that every available man could participate in the attack. The Prince refused, ordering Murray to attack without further delay; Murray and his officers were taken aback. There simply weren't enough men; furthermore, if Murray waited for the arrival of the Prince, dawn was not far off and the element of surprise would be lost. Murray made the only decision possible – he ordered a retreat to Culloden. When the Prince learnt of this from Hay of Restalrig, he lost his temper, riding out to meet Murray, Lochiel, the Duke of Perth and Perth's brother, Lord John Drummond. He demanded to know what the devil they were about; he ranted and raved about his orders being disobeyed and that he had been betrayed, calling everyone around him traitors. He shouted that he and he alone commanded the army. The truth was that the Prince had lost command of himself.

Culloden

The Jacobite army returned to Culloden at about 6am on that fateful Wednesday morning of 16 April. A few hours of sleep failed to restore the hungry, weary men; they were awakened by the sound of cannon fire around 11am. This time, the gunfire was real. Colonel O'Sullivan rode out to view the Hanoverian army arranged in perfect parade-ground order. All told, Cumberland's army numbered between 10,000 and 14,000, although he committed less than half of his troops to the battle. His men had been falsely informed that the Highlanders would give no quarter, so no quarter should be offered them.

The Prince's army probably numbered 7,000 and was drawn up in three lines. On the right wing were the three regiments of the Atholl Brigade, with the men of Clans Robertson, Menzies, Rattray and Mercer under Lord Nairne, then the Camerons under Lochiel, the Stewarts of Appin, Clans Maclaren and Murray, then Lord Lovat's Frasers. In the centre were 'Colonel Anne's' Mackintoshes led by Colonel MacGillivray of Dunmaglas, the Macleans of Drimmin, the Macleods of Raasay, the Farquharsons led by Francis Farquharson, John Roy Stewart of Ardshiel commanding the

Edinburgh Regiment, then Clan Chisholm. The Duke of Perth commanded the left wing which comprised the MacDonalds of Clanranald, Keppoch and Glengarry with a few Mackenzies of Seaforth and Grants of Glen Urquhart and Glenmoriston. The weaker second line from left to right comprised the Irish picquets (foot soldiers in the French army) commanded by Brigadier Stapleton, the French Royal Scots (*Ecossaise Royale*) and the Duke of Perth's regiment. Next was what remained of Gordon of Glenbucket's regiment, the bulk of which had been left behind at Carlisle and taken prisoner by the Duke of Cumberland on 30 December 1745. The extreme right was held by Lords Lewis Gordon and Ogilvy. The third line from left to right contained Lord Kilmarnock's foot guards, then the cavalry of Lords Strathallan, Pitsligo, Balmerino and Elcho. On the extreme right, Fitzjames's Horse provided the Prince's escort. Once again, the MacDonalds complained they had been denied their traditional honour of fighting on the right wing; on this occasion their complaint was dismissed without further argument. Perhaps sense prevailed, given the extremely vulnerable right wing position occupied by Lord George Murray.

Facing the Jacobite army was the Hanoverian front line; from left to right were the regiments of Wolfe (8th Foot), Barrell (4th Foot), Munro (37th Foot), Campbell's Royal Scots Fusiliers (21st Foot), Price (14th Foot), Cholmondeley (34th Foot), St Clair's Royal Scots (1st Foot), Pulteney (13th Foot), Kingston (Light Dragoons) and Kerr (11th Dragoons). The front line was commanded by the Earl of Albemarle. The artillery commanded by Colonel Belfort was placed in the centre. The Hanoverian second line from left to right commanded by Major General Huske comprised Cobham (10th Dragoons), Sempill (25th Foot), Bligh (20th Foot), Ligonier (48th Foot), Fleming (36th Foot) Howard's Old Buffs (3rd Foot) and Battereau (62nd Foot), with Blakeney (27th Foot) behind Bligh's Regiment forming the reserve commanded by Brigadier Mordaunt.[34]* Cumberland's army contained three Scottish regiments; they were not necessarily fighting for him and England but for Scotland.

The Highland army numbered between 5,000 and 7,000. Facing the Jacobites was an army of between 10,000 and 14,000 although Cumberland committed only about 7,000 troops to the battle. When the hapless Colonel O'Sullivan viewed the entire Hanoverian army drawn up at Drummossie, he rode white-faced to report to the Prince. At one point O'Sullivan stated that the Prince had appointed him commander of the Jacobite army; when he was challenged on this claim by Lord George Murray, the Irishman backed down.

* The numbering of British Army regiments was not adopted until 1751 but is used here for ease of identification.

Again, the Prince was gripped by a terrible temper, drunk on whisky, ranting about the Scots who had betrayed him, declaring they were a treacherous race.[35]

Clan chiefs Lochiel and Keppoch begged the Prince not to fight on that day of wind, rain and sleet. Lord George Murray was undecided whether to fight; his position on the right wing was vulnerable to enfilading fire from the dry-stone wall which enclosed the pasture of Leanach, a wall that denied him any opportunity to manoeuvre. Murray asked the Prince to allow him to find more favourable ground but his request was again refused; the Prince made it abundantly clear that he was in command and O'Sullivan was his deputy commander. Although it cannot be stated with certainty, it is thought that the Prince rode from the field before the battle reached its climax; he certainly did not witness the carnage and debacle of Culloden. His absence from the field would explain why there was no order issued for the clansmen to begin their attack.

The battle commenced at 1pm with an exchange of artillery fire; the Jacobite guns opened up first but did little damage. Cumberland's artillery responded with a deadly cannonade; the professional artillerymen found their targets not in the front line but the rear where the Prince was stationed. This may have been deliberate, although some accounts consider the Hanoverian guns were firing too high, while others describe the cannonballs landing in the boggy ground, failing to find their mark. Be that as it may, clansmen began to fall like scythed grass in long orderly lines. When they saw their comrades being slaughtered, many Clan officers demanded the order be given for the attack. No such order came, possibly because the Prince had left the field with his small escort of Fitzjames's Horse. It is believed that after twenty minutes of incessant grapeshot, canister and ball, Lord George Murray ordered the attack. On the left wing the Duke of Perth urged the MacDonalds forward but they refused to face the hail of cannonballs; some threw themselves to the ground while others fled the field. The left wing began to buckle, it having lost many officers; those remaining MacDonalds became engaged in a firefight which they could not hope to win. Only the clans in the centre went forward, led by the heroic Colonel MacGillivray of Dunmaglas. Dunmaglas's charge veered to the right, crowding Murray's Atholl Brigade, already hampered in their movements by the stone wall of the Leanach pasture. On the other side of the wall, Murray's worst fears were realized; it gave shelter to the 8th Foot commanded by Major James Wolfe who would distinguish himself at Quebec in 1759 against the French General Montcalm. Wolfe's men poured a steady fire into the Athollmen. The Camerons and the Atholl Brigade – between 500 and 800 – charged Barrell's regiment and the Munros who had fled the field of Falkirk; Cumberland's men had been ordered to withhold fire until the clansmen were within thirty yards which they did, firing a deadly volley that decimated the charging Highlanders. Those left standing engaged in hand-to-hand combat, falling foul of the new bayonet technique introduced by Cumberland. Nonetheless, Barrell's Regiment split in two, allowing the clansmen to mingle with the Redcoats. One of Cumberland's officers, Lord Robert Kerr bayoneted the first Cameron he faced, only to be cut down by Gillies MacBean of the Mackintosh regiment, Kerr's head being split from crown to collarbone by the clansman's broadsword. Lieutenant Colonel Robert Rich commanding Barrell's Regiment lost his left arm at the wrist, then his right arm at the elbow.[36] Barrell's and Munro's Regiments then engaged in close-quarter combat while the Regiments of Sempill, Conway, Wolfe and Bligh moved in to form a three-sided enclosure, shaped like a horseshoe, trapping the clansmen inside and executing bloody work on them. Those who had no weapons reputedly resorted to throwing stones at their opponents.

The Jacobite second line was hardly committed, being fewer in number than the front line. Then the Argyll Campbells broke down the Leanach stone wall, opening the way for Cumberland's dragoons commanded by General Hawley who had a score to settle after the ignominy of Falkirk. The Hanoverian dragoons on both flanks attacked the disorganized clansmen. Now the flight began. Barely any of the 500 clansmen who had penetrated Cumberland's front line escaped with their lives. On the left, O'Sullivan with the Duke of Perth admitted to Captain O'Shea of Fitzjames's Horse (which had returned to the field) that the battle was lost. In his account written later, O'Shea claimed that he urged the Prince to leave the field or else he would be taken prisoner by the English dragoons. O'Sullivan's account flattered the Prince, glossed over his foul temper and insisted that he never heard the Prince utter a harsh word against Lord George Murray. (Too many other surviving accounts dispute O'Sullivan's narrative, chiefly those of Lord

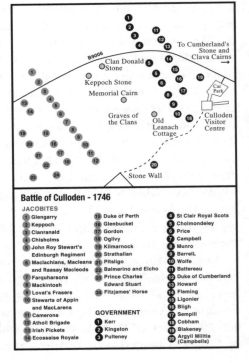

Battle of Culloden - 1746

JACOBITES

1. Glengarry
2. Keppoch
3. Clanranald
4. Chisholms
5. John Roy Stewart's Edinburgh Regiment
6. Maclachlans, Macleans and Raasay Macleods
7. Farquharsons
8. Mackintosh
9. Lovat's Frasers
10. Stewarts of Appin and MacLarens
11. Camerons
12. Atholl Brigade
13. Irish Pickets
14. Ecossaise Royale
15. Duke of Perth
16. Glenbucket
17. Gordon
18. Ogilvy
19. Kilmarnock
20. Strathallan
21. Pitsligo
22. Balmerino and Elcho
23. Prince Charles Edward Stuart
24. Fitzjames' Horse

GOVERNMENT

1. Kerr
2. Kingston
3. Pulteney
4. St Clair Royal Scots
5. Cholmondeley
6. Price
7. Campbell
8. Munro
9. Barrell
10. Wolfe
11. Battereau
12. Duke of Cumberland
13. Howard
14. Fleming
15. Ligonier
16. Bligh
17. Sempill
18. Cobham
19. Blakeney
20. Argyll Militia (Campbells)

Elcho and James, Chevalier de Johnstone, the Prince's ADC.) Another damning description of O'Sullivan's ineptitude came from the pen of Lord George Murray who in a letter to the Prince dated 17 April 1746 lays the blame for the disaster of Culloden on O'Sullivan as well as other blunders he was guilty of during the 'Forty-Five.[37] These began with the capture of the guns and stores from the *Du Teillay*, then the argument with Murray about the best position from which to attack Cope at Prestonpans and most damning of all, the disastrous choice of ground at Culloden. It should be obvious that after the 'Forty-Five, O'Sullivan, an unemployed, penniless Irish officer wrote his obsequious account for James VIII and III in the hope of obtaining a royal pension for his 'loyalty'.

Miraculously, Lord George Murray escaped unscathed, as did Lord Nairne and John Roy Stewart of Ardshiel; Cameron of Lochiel was carried away, both ankles broken by grapeshot, his brother Archibald being among the wounded. Fitzjames's Horse covered the retreat of some of the men intent on reaching the safety of Inverness; these survivors were relentlessly pursued by the Hanoverian dragoons and many were slaughtered along the road, the bloodshed continuing up to the very walls of the town. The battle of Culloden had lasted a single hour.

Aftermath

Estimates vary as to the casualties on both sides. The government's official account of Culloden gives only four officers and forty-six men killed and 259 wounded, including eighteen officers. Jacobite losses were about 1,200, possibly slightly less;[38] some accounts give 2,000 killed and wounded, half being killed. Cumberland took only 154 clansmen prisoners in addition to Lord John Drummond's 222 French of the *Ecossaise Royale*. Among the dead were Dumnaslas's standard bearer who had been among the first to fall in the Highland charge; Lord Nairne's brother, Robert Mercer of Aldie and his son – a mere child – lost their lives although their bodies were never found, possibly as they were burnt alive (see below); other fatal casualties included Gillies MacBean, Alistair MacDonald of Keppoch and his brother Donald as well as many MacDonald officers who braved the field when their clansmen refused to advance. Maclean of Drimmin was murdered when he went back to Drummossie Moor to look for his sons. Officers of Clans Fraser, Chisholm and Maclachlan who sought refuge in a barn were deliberately burnt alive.[39]

Those who escaped included Lieutenant General Lord George Murray who died in Holland in 1760; Lieutenant General James Drummond, 3rd Duke of Perth who died of wounds during his passage to France on the French frigate *La Bellona*. Perth's brother, Colonel John Drummond (later 4th Duke of Perth) also managed to escape along with Colonel John William

O'Sullivan, private secretary Sir Thomas Sheridan, Commissary John Hay of Restalrig, Donald Cameron of Lochiel who died in France in 1748, Young Clanranald and John Roy Stewart of Ardshiel. Sent to prison were William Murray, Duke of Atholl and Rannoch (the Marquis of Tullibardine) who died in 1746; old John Gordon of Glenbucket taken at Carlisle on 30 December 1745 died of dropsy before his trial. Another victim was the sickly Francis Strickland, one of the Seven Men of Moidart; Strickland was also captured at Carlisle and died of dropsy three days later. John Murray of Broughton turned King's Evidence and was discharged.[40] A further eighty men were executed, excluded from an Act of Indemnity passed in June 1747.[41]

Lord Balmerino, Colonel of the Horse Life Guards was beheaded on 18 August 1746 on Tower Hill, London as was Lord Kilmarnock on the same day. The eighty-two-year-old Simon Fraser, Lord Lovat, who although not present at Culloden had supported the Prince was also imprisoned in the Tower of London. Like Balmerino and Kilmarnock, Lovat was found guilty of treason. On his way to the scaffold, an old hag screeched at him, 'They're going to hang ye, ye old Scotch dog'. Lovat responded thus, 'I believe they will, ye old English bitch'.[42] Donald MacDonald of Kinlochmoidart, the first Clan chief to join the Prince, was hanged at Carlisle in October 1746.[43]

The site of Culloden is marked by a tall circular cairn which was erected in 1881 by Duncan Forbes; the memorial cairn stands about halfway between the opposing battle lines. The clan gravestones, rough boulders bearing the names of the clans are scattered about the field; later additions were the memorial to the Irish–French (1963) and the French Memorial (1994) commemorating the *Ecossaise Royale*. The battlefield is now under the management of the National Trust for Scotland.

Only a generation had elapsed since Mar's rebellion in 1715; despite the government's measures to pacify the Highlands – Wade's roads, the construction of forts, the creation of the Black Watch government regiment – yet another rebellion had occurred, one much more serious than Mar's and which had come close to success. Understandably, the government was even more concerned about the security in Highland Scotland which might support another Rising and threaten to topple the Hanoverian king. Accordingly, the Duke of Cumberland took measures to ensure there would be no such rebellion in the future. The severity of these measures made his name a byword for cruelty; in England, he was known as Sweet William; in Scotland he was called Butcher Cumberland and Stinking Billy. Even those who had little or no sympathy with the cause of the House of Stuart deplored Cumberland's excessive atrocities. One of Cumberland's chief supporters in England, Lord Chesterfield did not mince his words; he wrote that as Scotland had been the nursery of rebellion he hoped it would become its grave. Chesterfield proposed an act of parliament for transporting to the West Indies every man involved in the 'Forty-Five, arguing that this would be preferable to hanging a mere few and letting others go free to begin a new rebellion.

Cumberland remained in Scotland until 18 July, exacting retribution from the clans with torch, sword and musket. A disarming act much more severe than that of 1725 was passed; the penalties imposed for the possession of weapons ranged from a heavy fine, six months' imprisonment and exile to the colonies for a first offence, seven years' transportation for a second offence.[44] The wearing of Highland dress was proscribed, with penalties similar to those who transgressed the new legislation.[45] By these and other measures, the 'Forty-Five brought about the last vestiges of the feudal system; the people of Scotland had long since rejected feudalism and the clan system was a relic of feudalism. The common people, having seen the 'Protestant winds' destroy the French invasion fleets of 1708, 1715, 1719 and 1744 were convinced that God – and a Protestant god at that – was on their side.

The 'Forty-Five has often been called a civil war which is only partly the case. The Presbyterian clergy, the lawyers and Lowland burghs were all united in their hostility towards Jacobitism, the feeling most intense in the King's or royal burghs, with their special relationship to the reigning monarch.

As for Charles Edward Stuart, Bonnie Prince Charlie, there was little that was bonnie about him after his victory at Prestonpans. It is unnecessary here to revisit his flight in the heather and his association with Flora MacDonald other than to make the point that during his five-month period on the run, no Highlander ever claimed the £30,000 reward put on his head – so much for the Prince's accusations of betrayal by the clansmen. After his escape on 18 September 1746 by way of Skye and other parts of the west Highlands on the French frigate *L'Heureux*, all of Scotland must have breathed a sigh of relief. The Prince would never again set foot in Scotland which, but a year or so ago, he had called 'home'. In Rome, James Francis Edward Stuart the Old Pretender was pre-occupied not with the failure of the 'Forty-Five but how his arrogant, impetuous, hotheaded son would conduct himself in his future dealings with the French court. After all, the French had let both father and son down badly.

On his return to France, the Prince began to show signs of megalomania; deliberately avoiding words like 'defeat' and 'failure', he insisted that with a little help from France, he would soon be master of Scotland and England.[46] He assured Louis XV he would need only a 'handful' of men to achieve this; the handful became 18,000–20,000 soldiers, arms, ammunition and money. Louis XV, fighting a losing war in Flanders must have thought his cousin Charles was deranged. The Prince lied about his campaign, saying he had in fact reached London and that had he commanded a few thousand more soldiers at Culloden, he could have beaten Cumberland. The Prince was indeed deranged, unable to distinguish between fact and fiction, truth and lies.

On 1 January 1766, James Francis Edward Stuart, styling himself James III of Great Britain passed away; technically, his death meant that his elder son was now Charles III. By 1766, the Prince was a physical wreck, a stooping figure whose face was bloated and red with the effects of alcohol; with his dead eyes and a drooping, dribbling mouth, his fatty jaws merged with his neck which spilled over his cravat. He hobbled about unsteadily on legs that were weeping with ulcers;[47] he had become a disgusting, smelly old drunk at the age of forty-five. In 1772, despite his rapidly declining health, he married Princess Louise Stolberg-Gedern, daughter of Gustave Adolphe, Prince of Stolberg-Gedern who had been killed fighting for Empress Maria Theresa during the War of the Austrian Succession when Louise was only five years old. Before his marriage, the Prince had had two mistresses, Clementina Walkinshaw (by whom he had a daughter, Charlotte) and Madame Talmont, formerly Princess Marie-Louise Jablonowski. It has to be said that his marriage to Princess Louise was not intended to produce an heir; the Prince was only interested in companionship and the prospect of a French pension, as he was penniless. For a time he curbed his excessive drinking, then resumed his old ways. On 30 January 1788, Charles Edward Stuart, the Young Chevalier, the Young Pretender Bonnie Prince Charlie died aged sixty-five; his brother Henry was the last of the Stuart dynasty which ended with the latter's death in 1807.

Postscript

Culloden was the culmination of an ancient royal dynasty which reached back into the fourteenth century; it also heralded the end of a way of life in northern Scotland. The clan system was broken and with it the last vestiges of the anachronistic feudal conservatism which had propped it up for centuries. However, the Hanoverian government of 1746 learnt a valuable lesson; the brave clansmen could and would be transformed from warriors into disciplined soldiers. Scottish regiments were raised to fight in the American War of Independence, then against Napoleon Bonaparte, Czar Nicholas I in the Crimean War, Queen Victoria's 'Little Wars' against Dervish and Zulu, the two Boer wars and the two world wars of the twentieth century.

In the Highlands of Scotland, Charles Edward Stuart is still regarded today with ambivalence; in certain circles, his name is reviled, not only on account of his absurdly romantic adventure but also because he directly brought an end to a way of life which had existed for centuries. The clansmen in the north were not noted for their appreciation of literature nor the arts but they were possessed of a strong sense of place and their role in it. Of course, they loved oratory and music; they loved to dance, enjoyed family gatherings, bonfires, singing – and whisky. Most had little or no education and knew no trade or profession; those who could read rarely strayed beyond the Bible. But they were a strong, independent people, practical and reliable, loyal to their chiefs. They were basically farmers who doubled as warriors rather than soldiers. Many were forced to leave Scotland after the 'Forty-Five, like those of previous Jacobite Risings; many more were evicted during the Highland Clearances to make way for the more profitable sheep. Many ended up in the USA and Canada, dying there and laid to rest in scattered, remote graves in the wildernesses they struggled to tame. They were born fighting. They are remembered in poem and song, their sacrifice in a lost cause almost a distant memory. Almost. As the Nobel laureate American novelist William Faulkner famously wrote of the Deep South after the American Civil War:

The past is not dead; it isn't even past.

It is often said that history is not the study of the lives of individuals but entire nations and communities; this is true in part. In the context of warfare however, it is individual leaders or generals who create history – men like William Wallace, Robert the Bruce, John Graham of Claverhouse, James, Marquis of Montrose and others who played crucial roles in the history of the nation of Scotland. This is why biographies of such men have grown in popularity over the past century. Individuals do influence the course of history, for good or for ill. Hopefully, this account of the killing fields of Scotland has gone some way to illustrating the point.

Notes

1. The old Bank of Scotland founded in 1695 was suspected of Jacobite sympathies, so a new bank was chartered in 1727 as the Royal Bank of Scotland, Islay being appointed as its first governor. Rivalry between the two banks was intense.
2. Hume Brown, *History of Scotland*, vol. iii, p.228.
3. Ibid, p.274.
4. Pugh, *The White Rose and the Thorn Tree*, p.14; Kybett, *Bonnie Prince Charlie: A Biography*, p.119.
5. Pugh, op. cit. p.22.
6. In point of fact, burghs like Dunbar which had requisitioned a stand of arms during the emergency of 1708 were deprived of the weapons by Cope in 1745 on the eve of Prestonpans (Pugh, *Swords, Loaves and Fishes: A History of Dunbar*, p.328).
7. The title Duke of Perth was given to the earldom of Drummond by James VII and II at St Germain in 1695, confirmed by Louis XIV in 1701. Perth's eldest son James, titular 2nd Duke of Perth, was attainted for his part in the 'Fifteen. His son James Drummond, titular 3rd Duke of Perth (1713–1746), assumed the title in 1731 (*Burke's Peerage*).
8. Brotchie, *The Battlefields of Scotland*, p.220; Hume Brown op. cit. vol.iii., p.298
9. Pugh, *The White Rose and the Thorn Tree*, p.195.
10. Kybett, op. cit., p.150.

11. Duffy, Dr C., *Victory at Prestonpans*, p.8 (booklet prepared for Trustees of the Battle of Prestonpans (1745) Trust, Prestoungrange University Press).
12. Ibid, p.8.
13. Kybett, op. cit., p.150.
14. Gardiner's remains lie in the west end of Tranent Old Kirk graveyard (Brotchie, op. cit., p.221 footnote).
15. Kybett, op. cit., p.151.
16. Brotchie, op. cit., p.222 footnote (*Historical Papers, Jacobite Period,* Spalding Club vol. i, pp.279–82).
17. Duffy, op. cit., p.10 (150–300); Kybett, op. cit., p.153, cites a government army headquarters report listing 500 killed and 1,400 taken prisoner, of which 900 were wounded; Murray of Broughton's *Memoirs* gives eight Redcoat officers and 300 privates were killed, 400 to 500 wounded and 'almost all' taken prisoner. The official Jacobite report on losses states that four officers and thirty soldiers killed, with seventy or eighty wounded, almost tallying with Maxwell of Kirkconnell's account *Narrative of Charles, Prince of Wales' Expedition to Scotland in the Year 1745* (Maitland Club, 1841).
18. Brotchie, op. cit., p.223.
19. Robert Burns; Kybett, op. cit., p.155.
20. Brotchie, op. cit. p223 and footnote.
21. Hume Brown, op. cit., vol.iii, p.290.
22. Ibid, p.302.
23. Ibid, p.306.
24. Kybett, op. cit., p.187.
25. Hume Brown, op. cit., vol.iii, p.313.
26. Kybett, op. cit., p.189.
27. Ibid, p.189.
28. Hume Brown, op. cit., vol.iii, p.315.
29. Ibid, pp.315–16.
30. Kybett, op. cit., p.190.
31. Especially the entire Clan MacDonald of Glengarry, after Alastair MacDonald's young brother Aeneas or Angus was accidentally shot by a MacDonald of Keppoch while cleaning his musket (Kybett, op. cit., p.190; Hume Brown, op. cit., vol.iii, p.316).
32. Kybett, op. cit., p.193; Hume Brown, op. cit., vol. iii, p.316.
33. Kybett, op. cit., p.197.
34. Brotchie, op. cit., pp.232–4, footnotes give different battle formations for both armies.
35. Kybett, op. cit., p.205.
36. Ibid, p.208.
37. Quoted in Ibid, pp.212–13.
38. Brotchie, op. cit., p.235 footnote.
39. Kybett op. cit., p.209.
40. Ibid, pp.196–7.
41. Hume Brown, op. cit., vol.iii, p.327.
42. Johnson, Paul, *Heroes from Alexander the Great to Mae West*, p.172.
43. Kybett, op. cit., p.120.
44. Hume Brown, op. cit., vol.iii, p.328.
45. Ibid, p.329.
46. Kybett, op. cit., p.255.
47. Ibid, pp.275–6.

Appendix

Battlefield sites covered in this account. Those marked with a single asterisk are the sites currently (at May 2012) included on the *Inventory of Historic Battlefields* or proposed for inclusion by Historic Scotland. Those marked with a double asterisk are sites which Historic Scotland have investigated for inclusion but which have not met one or more of the selection criteria at the time of writing, although they may be added in future if new evidence and information comes to light. The sites are listed alphabetically under the counties where the actions occurred.

Aberdeenshire
Aberdeen I (1571)[1]
* Aberdeen II (1644)
* Alford (1645)
* Barra, also known as Inverurie I (1308)
Corrichie (1562)
Culblean (1335)
Cullen Fields (961)
* Fyvie (1644)
* Harlaw (1411)
Inverurie II (1745)
Lumphanan (1057)
Mortlach or Mortlake (1005)

Argyleshire
Glencoe (1692)[2]
Pass of Brander (1308/09)

Ayrshire
** Largs (1263)
* Loudon Hill (1307)
Mauchline Moor (1648)

Banffshire
* Glen Livet (1594)

Borders
Melrose (1378)
* Ancrum Moor (1545)
Arkinholm (1455)
Benrig (1380)
Haddonrigg (1542)
Halidon Hill (1333)
* Melrose (Skirmish Hill) (1526)[3]
Nesbit Moor I (1355)
Nesbit Moor II (1402)
* Philiphaugh (1645)
Piperdean (1435)
Solway Moss (1542)

Clackmannanshire
Dollar (877)

Dumfries and Galloway
Aird's Moss (1680)
* Glen Trool (1307)
Lochmaben (1458)
Sark (1448)

East Lothian
** Athelstaneford (832)
** Carberry Hill (1567)
* Dunbar I (1296)
* Dunbar II (1650)
* Pinkie Cleugh (1547)
* Prestonpans (1745)

Fife
** Bordie (1038)
Inverduvat (877)
Inverkeithing I (1371)
* Inverkeithing II (1651)

Forfarshire (Angus)
Stracathro (1130)

Highlands
Lochaber (1929)
* Auldearn (1645)
* Blar–na–Leine (1544)[4]
* Carbisdale (1650)
* Carrieblair (date uncertain)
* Cromdale (1690)
* Culloden (1746)
Dalnaspidel (1654)
* Glenshiel (1719)
* Inverlochy I (1431)
* Inverlochy II (1645)
* Mulroy (1688)[5]
Torfness (c.1034 or 1035)

Lanarkshire
* Bothwell Brig (1679)
* Drumclog (1679)
Hamilton (1650)
* Kilsyth (1645)
* Langside (1568)

Midlothian
Burghmuir (Edinburgh) (1335)
Leith (1560)
* Roslin
* Rullion Green (1666)

Berwickshire/Northumberland
Carham–on–Tweed (1018)[7]

Peeblesshire
Happrew (1304)

Perth and Kinross
Aberfoyle (1488)
* Dunkeld (1689)
* Dupplin Moor (1332)
* Killiecrankie (1689)
Luncarty (986)
**Methven (1306)
* Tippermuir (1644)

Renfrewshire
Renfrew (1164)

Stirlingshire
* Bannockburn (1314)
Falkirk I (1298)
* Falkirk II (1746)
* Sauchieburn (1488)
* Sheriffmuir (1715)
* Stirling Bridge (1297)

West Lothian
Blackness (1488)
* Linlithgow Bridge (1526)

Location Unknown
** Dún Nechtáin/Nechtansmere (685)
** Mons Graupius (83)

Notes
1. Not included in this account as it was a clan battle (see Foreword).
2. Glencoe was not a battle, but any account of Scotland's killing fields would be censured if the 'massacre' were excluded.
3. Not included in this account as it was a family or clan battle.
4. Not included in this account as it was a clan battle.
5. Not included in this account as it was a clan battle.
6. Included because, although fought just over the border at Longtown, Cumberland, it led to nearly two decades of English attempts to subjugate Scotland during this period, known as *The Rough Wooing* and subsequently the establishment of the protestant religion in Scotland, the cause of many subsequent battles.
7. Carham-on-Tweed is included because, although fought on the south (English) bank of the river Tweed, it decided the border between Scotland and England.

Select Bibliography

Primary Sources (state papers, acts of parliament and other official documents relating to the government of Scotland).

Accounts of the Lord High Treasurer of Scotland, 1475–1574, vols. i–xi, ed. T. Dickson *et al* (Edinburgh, 1877–1973).

Acts of the Lords in Council in Public Affairs, 1501–1554 ed. R.K. Hannay (Edinburgh, 1932).

Acts of the Parliaments of Scotland, 1124–1707, vols. i–xii, ed T. Thomson and C. Innes (Edinburgh, 1814–1875.

Calendar of Documents Relating to Scotland 1104–1576, Vols I–V & Addenda, ed. J. Bain (Edinburgh, 1881–1888) and G.C. Simpson and J. Galbraith (Edinburgh, 1986).

Calendar of State Papers Relating to Scotland 1509–1603 Vols I–II, ed. M.J. Thorpe (London, 1858).

Exchequer Rolls of Scotland, 1264–1600, vols. i–xxiii, ed. J Stuart *et al* (Edinburgh, 1878–1908).

Hamilton Papers, vols. i– ii, ed. J Bain (Edinburgh, 1890–1892).

Historic Documents of Scotland 1296–1706, ed. J. Stephenson (Edinburgh, 1870).

Scottish Correspondence of Mary of Lorraine 1543–1560, ed. A. I. Cameron (Scottish History Society, 1927).

Source Book of Scottish History, A, vols. i–ii, ed. Croft Dickinson, W., Donaldson, G. and Milne, I. A. (Edinburgh, 1956–1958).

Secondary Sources

Abercromby, P., *The Martial Achievements of the Scottish Nation* (2 vols) (R. Fairbairn, Edinburgh, 1711 and 1715).

Anderson, A. O. and Croft, W. (Ed), *Chronicles of Melrose Abbey* (Bannatyne Club, 1935).

Andrews, P., *Culloden Moor and the story of the battle* (1867; reprinted W.M. Mackay and Son, Inverness, 1920).

Auchinleck Chronicle, The, Ane Schort Memoriale of Scotis Cornikillis for Addicioun ed. T. Thomson (Edinburgh, 1819–1877).

Barbour, J., *The Bruce* ed. and trans. by A. J. M. Duncan (Edinburgh, 1999).

Barrow, G. W. S., *The Anglo-Norman Era in Scottish History* (Clarendon Press, Oxford, 1980).

Beaugue, Jean de, *Histoire de la Guerre d'Ecosse pendant les campaignes de 1545 et 1549* (Maitland Club, 1862).

Boece, H., *Scotorum Historiae a prima gentis origine* (History of Scotland) 2nd edition, Paris 1574.

Bower, W., *Scotichronicon* (The Chronicle of Inchcolm 1440–1445 vols. i–viii; a continuation of the Chronicle of John of Fordun) ed. S. Taylor, D. E. R. Watt, with B. Scott (Aberdeen University Press, 1991–1996).

Brotchie, T.C.F., *The Battlefields of Scotland* (T. C. and E. C. Jack, Edinburgh and London, 1913).

Brown, Dr Chris, *William Wallace* (The History Press, Stroud, 2005).
Buchanan, G., *Rerum Scoticarum Historiae* (A History of Scotland, 1583) vols. i–iv, ed. and trans. by J. Aikman (Glasgow and Edinburgh 1827–1829).

Chronicle of Lanercost Priory (Chronicon de Lanercost) 1272–1346 ed. J. Stevenson (Maitland Club, 1839); ed. and trans. by H. Maxwell (Glasgow, 1913).

Chronicle of Pluscarden (Liber Pluscardenis) vols. i–ii, ed. F. J. H. Skene and M. Buchanan (W. Paterson, 1880, rep. Biblio Life, 2005).

Chronicle of Walsingham (Chronica Maiora of Thomas Walsingham1376–1422 trans. Priest, D., Clark, J. G., (Clarendon Press, 2003).

Cornell, D., *Bannockburn: The Triumph of Robert the Bruce* (Yale University Press, USA, 2009).

Crammond, W., *The Annals of Cullen 961–1904* (Buckie, 1904).

Crichton, P., *Woodhouselee Manuscripts*: A Narrative of events in Edinburgh and district during the Jacobite occupation, September to November 1745 (Edinburgh, 1907).

Dickson, W. H., *The Jacobite Attempt of 1719* (Edinburgh, 1895).

Diurnal of Occurents in Scotland 1513–1575, ed. T. Thomson (Bannatyne Club, 1883).

Douglas, R. M., *The Scots Book* (R. Maclehose & Co. Ltd, Glasgow, 1935).

Fordun, John of: *Chronica Gentis Scotorum* (Chronicle of the Scottish Nation) trans. F. J. H. Skene ed. W.F. Skene (Edinburgh, 1871-1872).

Fraser, G. McD., *The Steel Bonnets* (Harper Collins, 1971).

Froissart, Jean, The Chronicles of Froissart trans. John Burchier, Lord Berners, ed. Macauley, G. C. M. (MacMillan and Co. Ltd, London, 1913).

Gardiner, S. R., *History of the Great Civil War* (London, 1889).

Gray, Sir Thomas of Heton, *Scalacronica 1272–1368*, ed. Stevenson,

J. (Maitland Club, 1836) trans. Maxwell, W. (Glasgow, 1907).

Groome, F., *Ordnance Gazetter of Scotland: A Survey of Scottish Topography, Statistical, Biographical and Historcial* (T. C. Jack, Grange Publishing Works, Edinburgh, 1882–1885).

Guisborough, W., *The Chronicle of Walter Guisborough*, ed. Rothwell, H., (Camden Society, London, 1957).

Hill, J. M., *Celtic Warfare 1595–1763* (J. Donald, Edinburgh, 1986).

Hume Brown, P., *History of Scotland*, Cambridge Historical Series, vols. i–iii (Cambridge University Press, 1902–1909).

Jackson, K. H., *The Gododdin: The Oldest Scottish Poem* (Edinburgh University Press, 1969).

Johnson, P., *National Trust Book of Castles* (London, 1978). Johnstone, Chevalier de, *Memoirs of the Rebellion in 1745 and 1746* (London, 1821, also D. Wyllie and Son, Aberdeen, 1870–1871).

Kybett, Susan M., *Bonnie Prince Charlie: A Biography* (Unwin Hyman, London, 1988).

Lockhart, G., of Carnwath, *Memoirs Concerning the Affairs of Scotland, Commentaries etc.* (Association for Scottish Literary Studies, 1995).

Lynch, M., *Scotland: A New History* (Pimlico, London, 1991).

Marran., P., *Grampian Battlefields* (Mercat Press, Edinburgh, 1990).

Marshall, R. K., *Scottish Queens* (Tuckwell Press, East Lothian, 2003).

Matthews, R., *England Versus Scotland: Great British Battles* (Pen & Sword Books Ltd, South Yorkshire, 2002).

Melville, Sir James of Hallhill, *Memoirs of His Own Life 1535–1567*, ed. Stewart, A. F., (London, 1929).

Miller, James, *The History of Dunbar* (William Miller, Dunbar, 1830, rep. 1859).

Moysie, D., *Memoirs of the Affairs of Scotland* (Bannatyne Club, 1830).

Murray, John of Broughton, *Memorials* ed, Bell, R. F. (Scottish History Society, 1898).

Nimmo, W. and Gillespie, R., *A History of Stirlingshire* (Hamilton, Adams and Co., 1880).

Oliver, Neil, *A History of Scotland* (Weidenfield and Nicolson, 2009).

Patten, W., *Expedicioune into Scotland ... of Edward, Duke of Somerset 1547.* An eye-witness account of the Battle of Pinkie (London, 1548).

Pitscottie, Robert Lindsay of: *Historie and Cronicles of Scotland*, vols. i–iii, ed. Mackay, A. J. G. (Scottish Text Society, 1899-1911).

Pratt, J. B., *Buchan* (Aberdeen, 1858; rep. Smith, Aberdeen and Blackwood, 1981).

Prebble, J., *Glencoe*: The Story of the Massacre (Penguin UK, 1973).

—— *Culloden* (Penguin Books, 2nd revised edition, 1996).

Pugh, R. J. M., *Swords, Loaves and Fishes: A History of Dunbar* (Harlaw Heritage, Balerno, 2003).

—— *The White Rose and the Thorn Tree* (Cuthill Press for the Prestoungrange University Press, Prestonpans, 2008).

Reese, P., *Cromwell's Masterstroke: Dunbar 1650* (Pen & Sword Books Ltd, Barnsley, 2006).

—— *The Life of General Monck: For King and Cromwell* (Pen & Sword Books Ltd, Barnsley, 2008).

Ridpath, J., *Border History of England and Scotland*, ed.

Ridpath, P. (Berwick, 1848).

Roy, General William, *The Great Map: the Military Survey of Scotland 1747–1755* (Birlinn, Edinburgh, 2007).

Royle, Trevor, *Civil War: The Wars of the Three Kingdoms 1638–1660* (Palgrave Macmillan, London, 2004, reprinted Abacus, 2005).

Shaw, L., *A History of the Province of Moray* (Glasgow and London, 1882).

Skene, W. F., *Celtic Scotland*, vols. i–iii (Edinburgh, 1886–1890).

Stephen, W., *The History of Inverkeithing and Rosyth* (G. & W. Fraser,1921).

Stevenson, D., *Revolution and Counter-Revolution in Scotland 1644–1651* (Newton Abbot, 1977).

Tacitus, Gaius Cornelius, *De Vita et Moribus Julii Agricolae* AD 93 (The Life and Death of Julius Agricola) trans. Bewley, A. (Oxford University Press, 1999).

Tytler, P. F., *History of Scotland 1249–1606*, 9 vols. (W. Tait, Edinburgh, 1840–1850 and W.P. Nimmo, Edinburgh, 1864).

Vita Edwardi Secundi (The Life of Edward the Second) by the so-called Monk of Malmsbury ed. Denholm Young, N. (London and Edinburgh, 1957; reprinted Oxford University Press, 2005).

Walsingham, Thomas, Chronicle of, 1376–1422: also known as *Historica Anglicana*, ed. Riley, H. T. (Rolls Series 1863-1864); ed, Amours, F. J. (Scottish Text Society 1903–1914) and English Historical Review, 2006.

Warrender Letters: The Correspondence of Sir George Warrender of Lochend, Dunbar, Lord Provost of Edinburgh, 1715 ed. Dickinson, W. C. (Scottish History Society, 1935).

Woolf, Alex, *Dún Nechtáin, Fortriu and the Geography of the Picts*, The Scottish Historical Review, vol. LXXXV, 2: No. 220 pp182-201 (October 2006)

Wyntoun, Andrew: *Oryginale Cronykil of Scotland* ed. Amours, F. J. (Scottish Text Society, 1903–1914).

Index

Tracing Your Family History?

Read Your Family HISTORY

ESSENTIAL ADVICE FROM THE EXPERTS

FREE COPY!

Your Family History is the only magazine that is put together by expert genealogists. Our editorial team, led by Dr Nick Barratt, is passionate about family history, and our networks of specialists are here to give essential advice, helping readers to find their ancestors and solve those difficult questions.

In each issue we feature a **Beginner's Guide** covering the basics for those just getting started, a **How To** … section to help you to dig deeper into your family tree and the opportunity to **Ask The Experts** about your tricky research problems. We also include a **Spotlight** on a different county each month and a **What's On** guide to the best family history courses and events, plus much more.

Receive a free copy of *Your Family History* magazine and gain essential advice and all the latest news. To request a free copy of a recent back issue, simply e-mail your name and address to marketing@your-familyhistory.com or call **01226 734302***.

Your Family History is in all good newsagents and also available on subscription for six or twelve issues. For more details on how to take out a subscription, call **01778 392013** or visit **www.your-familyhistory.co.uk**.

Alternatively read issue 31 online completely free using this QR code

*Free copy is restricted to one per household and available while stocks last.

www.your-familyhistory.com